17.95
13.80

MEDIA PERSONNEL IN EDUCATION

A Competency Approach

Margaret E. Chisholm
University of Washington

Donald P. Ely
Syracuse University

Prentice-Hall, Inc., *Englewood Cliffs, New Jersey*

Library of Congress Cataloging in Publication Data

CHISHOLM, MARGARET E
    Media personnel in education.

    Includes bibliographies and index.
    1. Instructional materials personnel.   I. Ely,
Donald P., joint author.   II. Title.
LB3044.C45   371.3'078   75-33054
ISBN   0-13-572461-9

© 1976 by Prentice-Hall, Inc., Englewood Cliffs, N.J.

Photographs used throughout this book were taken by STEVEN H.
DENNISON

Printed in the United States of America

10   9   8   7   6   5   4   3   2   1

Prentice-Hall International, Inc., *London*
Prentice-Hall of Australia, Pty. Ltd., *Sydney*
Prentice-Hall of Canada, Ltd., *Toronto*
Prentice-Hall of India Private Limited, *New Delhi*
Prentice-Hall of Japan, Inc., *Tokyo*
Prentice-Hall of Southwest Asia Pte. Ltd., *Singapore*

Contents

iii

Preface

The purpose of this book is to provide a broad perspective of the responsibilities of the media professional whether new to the field or already employed.

There are several contemporary trends in education which affect the role of the media professional. Among the most germane are: (1) greater access to information in a variety of formats; (2) a greater concern for the individual learner; (3) the introduction of new technologies into the process of teaching and learning; (4) the emergence of new types of schools; and (5) changing goals for education.

We have attempted to recognize these trends and the changing professional responsibilities accompanying them by outlining the competencies which contemporary media professionals are expected to possess. The competencies have been derived from special projects concerned with the professional education of media professionals conducted by the two major national associations in the field; the American Association of School Librarians and the Association for Educational Communications and Technology.

The concept of competency-based learning is becoming a major concern in all areas of education. Advocates of this approach argue that specific knowledge or skills which each individual must acquire can be stated. Further, the means for assessing each skill and judging the degree to which each competency can be accomplished has been learned. This book attempts to identify the competencies in the media field and to classify them into categories called *functions*. The competencies are listed according to function and guidance is given for attaining each competency. Mastery items are also included as checkpoints for each reader.

By using these functions and competencies as guidelines each reader should find it possible to chart a map for professional career development.

Acknowledgments

Very few books are written by one person. Direct and indirect contributions are made by colleagues and other authors who speak to the content of a new publication. It is doubtful that many new ideas are first presented in textbooks. However, new insights may come from novel configurations of existing information.

Many of the basic ideas for the competency statements used in this book come from the writings and personal contributions of Robert Case, Dale Hamreus, Anna Mary Lowrey, Kenneth Silber and C. James Wallington.

Discussions of the functions began in the Curriculum Development Institute held at Syracuse University during 1971–72 sponsored by the U.S. Office of Education. Credit for many ideas must be given to the participants in that year-long dialogue to: Keith Bernard, Al Bielby, Paul Elliott, Dennis Gooler, Marion Henry, John Johnson, Bob Knapp, Craig Locatis, Pamela Miller, Francis Murphy, Curtis Mustiful, Dennis Myers (especially for the material in Chapter 9), Mary Catherine Ware and Roosevelt Wright, Jr.

The ideas on educational futures in Chapter 17 were first developed by Dr. Geoffrey Squires and were adapted by the authors. For secretarial supervision and assistance beyond the call of duty, Helen Frostbutter receives our deepest gratitude. For special help in typing, our appreciation is extended to Patricia MacVittie and Patricia Crow.

MARGARET E. CHISHOLM
DONALD P. ELY

A Note
on Format

This is not an ordinary textbook. It is a reference textbook based on functions performed by media professionals. Each function is composed of competencies, many of which need to be acquired by the media professional. Since the reader may not necessarily go through the book according to the sequence of the chapters, it would be helpful to note the nature of the format so that the pattern can be understood no matter which chapter is being read. Each function and its related competencies are described in a single chapter beginning with Chapter 7. The format applies to the chapters on organization management, personnel management, design, information retrieval, logistics, production, instruction, evaluation and research. The synthesis—utilization— follows a different format.

Each chapter begins with a comprehensive description of the function. This overview includes the definition and types of activities which are performed as part of the function. Each competency within that function is then stated and discussed according to the following order:

First, there is a statement of each competency. *Second,* a *further description* of the competency is given with examples of its application. *Third, resources* for gaining the competency are provided. *Fourth,* a *mastery item* is provided to assess the understanding of the competency. The mastery item is usually only one part of the competency. It is, in the language of the behavioral psychologist, an en route objective. It is an attempt to assess only part of the competency—not all possible components of each competency. *Fifth,* is the *response* to the mastery item. It is one possible response to the mastery item and offers a check on your response. In many cases there are several possible responses.

THE COMPETENCY STATEMENT

This phrase indicates exactly what the media professional (or a member of the media staff) should be able to do. It is closely related to a behavioral objective [1] in that the individual who will demonstrate the competency is the subject of the statement. For example, the media professional "compiles and organizes orders for materials and equipment." In some cases the behavior should be demonstrated by a member of the media center staff but the media professional should be able to teach a staff member how to perform the competency and later, to supervise its operation.

The behavior itself is the activity which must get done. It should be stated in observable terms. There should be no doubt in the mind of the observer that an individual is performing the competency.

The competency statement is unlike a behavioral objective in that the *conditions* under which the behavior will be performed are not specified nor is the *degree* of acceptable performance given. Since it is difficult to specify the conditions under which the competency should be performed in only the most general terms, it is left to the individual student, professor, or job supervisor to state the conditions of performance (e.g.,,where it will be demonstrated— on a written examination, before a qualified jury, or in a field work location). The degree of acceptable performance is another variable which must be locally defined. This statement is usually quantitative. For example, the performance will be acceptable 90 percent of the time; or 95 percent accuracy is required in filling out the form; or no errors are permitted. These caveats are more appropriately assigned locally.

The reader should be able to read each competency and assess his own ability in relation to that statement. In some cases it would be quite appropriate to say, "I can already do that." If so, it might be helpful to have someone check you on that competency. Or, if you are sufficiently confident that you do possess that competency, you can move on to the next. These statements are intended to be performance guideposts. The competency statements are derived from actual observation of professionals and media staffs in the field. If you pass them by, you may find that your preparation is lacking when you are actually confronted with these or similar responsibilities later in your professional career. Confidence now will insure quality professional performance later in your professional assignment.

---

[1] A behavioral objective is a statement of instructional intent which usually includes the audience (who will display the behavior), the behavior (the action which can be observed), the conditions under which the behavior will occur and the degree of acceptable performance.

RESOURCES FOR GAINING COMPETENCY

Once the competency has been stated, the next step is to acquire the competency (if the individual does not already possess it). Competencies can be gained through a variety of means. Highly motivated individuals who have access to resources can learn some competencies on their own. Some people enroll in formal courses which appear to prepare for specific competencies. Still others use on-the-job experiences to gain new skills. And, of course, combinations of these approaches are also followed.

The specific materials used may be publications, films, videotapes, and multi-media learning modules. People such as teachers and practitioners also serve as resources. Learners are sometimes involved in simulations, games, programmed instruction, and role playing in an attempt to acquire proficiency.

Within the chapters that follow you will find a section in each chapter that is devoted to the resources available for acquiring competencies. These resources can be used by individuals or for class presentations by instructors. Most of the resources are published materials since these are the most accessible items. Certain on-the-job experiences are also suggested as additional resources which may be available to some people through employment or field experiences within an academic program. In some cases the desirable aptitudes and prerequisite skills are also given. Audiovisual resources for each competency are listed at the end of each chapter.

There are many excellent books already written about the organization and administration of media programs. These references are basic to gaining the competencies stated in Chapters 7–15. Rather than write still another book with the same content, the authors have recommended segments from the basic textbooks related to each competency.

For professors using this book for courses, the authors strongly recommend that the books listed at the end of this chapter be purchased in multiple copies, placed on reserve in the library, and be used as indicated in the text. Without these references much of the substantive base for each competency is missing. Other publications are cited, but this list constitutes those titles which are referred to in several chapters and therefore serve as a *core collection.*

There is no one best way for all individuals to gain a particular competency. For this reason, a variety of alternative means are suggested. The resources listed are very specific and have been selected because (1) the content is relevant; (2) the materials are accessible; and (3) the use of the resource is feasible. Providing alternative options to learning is consistent with the contemporary educational philosophy which holds that individuals can learn best when resources that match individual learning styles are available. The annotated learning resources listed here provide for multiple options for achieving competencies.

It is expected that teachers of professional courses will arrange to have the recommended resources available for students. It is reasonable to expect that most of the publications will be available in a good academic library and that the audiovisual media can be obtained through the media service organization in a higher education institution. The specific source for each item is given in case materials have to be ordered directly.

There is so much information needed to assist an individual in gaining most competencies that no one source would be likely to provide it. Therefore, it was decided to list resources where the best information is available. Some sources may have been overlooked but a thorough search was made to come up with the best current resources.

MASTERY ITEM

How does one know that the competency has been achieved? There must be a procedure or set of procedures that will assess the attainment of each competency. The ultimate test is performance on the job. Since this assessment is generally impossible, alternative approaches have to be followed. Observation of individuals in field settings or performance in simulated situations provides a sense of reality which approximates the actual situation.

The use of individual or group judgment of an individual's performance whether it is written, spoken, or demonstrated is often used. In these cases it is assumed that the person or persons doing the evaluating are competent themselves and are judging with consistent criteria.

But the real problem is how the individual can assess his own ability prior to or instead of someone else's evaluation. The use of self-administered tests is probably one of the most practical ways to make these judgments. The authors have chosen this method for helping the reader to evaluate some aspects of the competency being sought. It is assumed that each competency can be only *partially* tested within the scope of this book. Therefore, one *mastery item* is provided at the end of each competency section. Completing this item and checking the results in the response section which follows each mastery item will help the individual reader to determine how well he is doing in relation to one particular skill. However, the individual should be warned that a complete and accurate response to the mastery item does not mean complete and accurate attainment of the competency. Success on the mastery item is an indicator that you are on the right track and increases the probability of on-the-job success in this area.

The mastery item is a brief short answer quiz. It highlights one aspect of the competency. It might be helpful to look at the mastery item before going through the resources. You may be able to do it already, but remember that this is only one part of the total competency and accurate performance on one representative item does not guarantee success for all parts.

FOR BEST RESULTS

1. Read the competency statement. (Do you understand what you should be able to do? Can you do it?)
2. Survey the list of resources to determine which items you would like to use and check availability.
3. Read or view the materials or perform the tasks.
4. Test yourself by completing the mastery item and checking your answer in the response section.
5. Return to Step 3 if you have not mastered the item.

REFERENCES

BOWMAR, CORA PAUL. *Guide to the Development of Educational Media Selection Centers*. Chicago: American Library Association, 1973.

BROWN, JAMES W., NORBERG, KENNETH D., SRYGLEY, SARA K. *Administering Educational Media*. New York: McGraw-Hill Book Co., 1972.

DAVIES, RUTH ANN. *The School Library Media Center: A Force For Excellence* (2nd ed.) New York: R. R. Bowker Co., 1974.

ERICKSON, CARLETON W. H. *Administering Instructional Media Programs*. New York: Macmillan, 1968.

GILLESPIE, JOHN T. and DIANA L. SPIRT, *Creating a School Media Program*. New York: R. R. Bowker Co., 1973.

Media Programs: District and School. Chicago: American Library Association and Washington: Association for Educational Communications and Technology, 1975.

PROSTANO, EMANUEL T. and JOYCE S. PROSTANO. *The School Library Media Center*. Littleton, Colorado: Libraries Unlimited, 1971.

1 The School of Tomorrow— Today!

The context of any school media program is the school, the district, and the community. Using a middle school as an example, this context is spelled out as it relates to the educational goals of the school; the community in which the school is located; the students, administration, teachers and support staff; and the building itself. The fundamental role of the school as an information center means that users must have access to information located inside and outside of the school. The media professional must be dedicated to providing access to this information and to helping in its use.

There is no typical school in America today. To classify a school as "traditional" or "modern" would require a continuum placing "traditional" at one end and "modern" at the other. Individual schools could be placed at various points along the line depending on their unique characteristics. Any school is a composite of many factors—all of which contribute to the general character of that school. The style of its administration, the personality and competencies of the teaching staff, the characteristics of the student body, the facility itself, the expectations of parents and the community, and the quality and quantity of the resources available—all are a part of the whole and each contributes to the personality of that school.

For the purpose of this introductory chapter, let us focus on a school which can be placed on the "modern" end of the continuum. In doing so, we assume that schools are moving in this direction and that this is a desirable direction. Some schools may deliberately decide to remain traditional as an expression of their educational philosophy. But an overwhelming majority of schools are adopting innovative practices in organization, curriculum, and teaching methods. Many schools which do not yet fall into the "modern" category are moving that way. The school described here represents an actual or anticipated status for most schools in America today.

East Hills Middle School has not always been the dynamic, innovative school that it now is. It is difficult to identify the turning point. Some teachers feel it happened when the junior high school (grades 7, 8 and 9) was changed to a middle school (grades 6, 7 and 8). The president of the school board feels it was when the new principal was appointed. The students who started in the middle school and are now in the high school speak happily of the middle school's renovated building with its open spaces and free access to resources which the present high school does not permit. The media professionals attribute the turning point to the availability of federal funds to add materials and equipment to the media center's collection. And the parents feel the significant change came with the team approach to teaching and counseling. All of them are probably right. Almost any school is a complex organization with many simultaneously operating systems involving many people. Because of this complexity, it is difficult to consider the media program apart from the context of which it is a part. The purpose of this book is to consider those competencies which media professionals ought to possess. But these competencies are only useful as they relate to the goals and objectives of a school with its various publics: the teachers, the students, the administrators, the board of education, the parents, and the larger community.

Before we explore the media program personnel in general, let's consider East Hills Middle School as a specific example of a contemporary school in America—tomorrow's school—today!

EAST HILLS MIDDLE SCHOOL

Goals

During the six months when the East Hills building was being renovated from an elementary school to a middle school, the new principal was recruiting faculty members to begin in September. As individuals were hired, they joined an ongoing and growing committee which was working on the school's goals. They felt that the goals were essential points of departure for curriculum development.

The focus of nearly all the goal statements is on the individual learner. The faculty realized that there had been much talk about individual differences in their education courses, but that this concern had been largely forgotten in practice. Now they had an opportunity in a new school to design instruction for individuals and not for groups. The options available through a variety of media meant that alternative means for reaching objectives could be offered. So one goal statement emphasized the concern for the individual student.

Stemming from the concern for the individual is the need for growth in cognitive and affective areas. The cognitive area helps each student to gain the facts, knowledge, and skills which will provide verbal and quantitative literacy. The tools thus gained will help in problem solving. The affective area is concerned with emotions, feelings, and values. The goals committee indicated that development in this area was as important as the other. A well-balanced curriculum offers opportunities for cognitive and affective growth.

From the broad areas of cognitive and affective learning, certain other aspects were highlighted because of the special concerns of the school. One group from the goals committee met with parents from time to time and gained new insights. Some factual learning is useful for only a limited time and becomes outmoded. Perhaps it is more important that students learn how to learn. It would probably be more useful in the long run to develop individuals who know how to raise the "right" questions and know where to go to get answers than to learn the "right" answers for a limited period of time. Goal statements were developed along these lines.

A special concern of another subgroup was with values. This group, which included several parents, felt that schools ought to help individuals to clarify their values—to know what they believe and why. The home is a fundamental source of values development, but the school is a proving ground in formative years. Therefore, a goal statement about values clarification was added. In the affective area, a special plea was made for developing appreciation for aesthetic aspects of life. This goal was also included.

Human relationships was another concern. Everyone agreed, without much discussion, that one goal statement ought to deal with the development of human relations.

So much emphasis had been placed on the cognitive and affective goals that the teachers representing physical education and vocational training asked that at least one goal be directed at developing motor skills both in physical development and in manipulation of various tools. After much discussion the validity of goal statements in these two areas was accepted and separate statements were developed; one, dealt with developing and maintaining the body and also included an appreciation of recreational activities which would lead to satisfactory use of leisure time; the second, was concerned with abilities to use a variety of tools commonly used in daily living and also included an orientation to vocational career opportunities.

Once the goals were written, edited, and again discussed, they were accepted by all who had worked upon them—teachers, administrators, parents, board members and student representatives. Even then the overwhelming feeling was that goals have to be open to change; they should not become so rigid and fixed that new circumstances could not bring about needed changes. The goal statements thus became tentatively-held beliefs about what education ought to be at East Hills. These statements now serve as the basis for curriculum development, resource allocation, media acquisition, teacher recruitment, and a host of other activities which require an agreed-upon starting point.

Its Community

Racial minorities comprise less than 10 percent of the community's population. There is a dominant middle class but about 15 percent of the students come from lower-middle-income homes and about 25 percent come from upper-middle-class families. Like all communities, about one family in five moves each year so many of the students come with backgrounds from other communities. The community supports its schools. Since the district was established about twenty years ago there has never been a defeat of a bond issue for new construction nor of an annual budget.

Students

Most of the students come from all the elementary schools in the district and most will go on to the senior high school. The students generally reflect the values of their parents. At this time about two-thirds of them aspire to some post-secondary school or college. They enjoy the opportunities for extracurricular activities in athletics, music, recreation, and content-related clubs. The range of intelligence could best be described as a normal distribution.

Administration

East Hills Middle School is one unit within a larger system which includes four elementary schools (K-5) and a senior high school (9-12). Each school is authorized to have a principal and an assistant principal. East Hills convinced the District's superintendent and board of education to reallocate the assistant principal's position to create the position of "coordinating teacher" in each of the three "houses" in the middle school. The house plan is an attempt to break down the relatively large enrollment of 1,100 students into smaller units which include all three grades. Each house has a coordinating teacher who serves as a curriculum leader. The principal is involved primarily with matters of budget, personnel, and public relations. The principal has a secretary and each coordinating teacher has a clerical assistant who also works with all the teachers in that unit.

Teaching Staff

The teachers were carefully selected for their competence in the subject matter fields they represent; for their openness to innovation; for their commitment to students; and for their willingness to work with others. Each house includes a cadre of teachers from the major fields: social science, language arts, mathematics, and the sciences. In addition, a counselor is employed for each house. Two sets of teams were formed immediately: one representing subject matter fields for the purpose of curriculum planning and the other on a grade-level-basis to insure communication about each learner's progress across fields.

Support Staff

Teachers of physical education, home economics, industrial arts, art, and music are employed to work with all houses. The nurse-teacher, likewise, serves across the entire school. Two media professionals, one with primarily library preparation and the other with an educational technology background, were hired to work cooperatively with all teachers within the school. Each house employs two or three aides and the media center has two aides.

Building

East Hills Middle School was converted from an elementary school which had a low enrollment. Most of the renovation consisted of removing many of the walls which constituted self-contained classrooms to open up the building and provide larger spaces. The media center was located in the center of the building to permit easy access from each house. All the floors were carpeted and new lighting was installed. New electrical service and a conduit for television were added. The large classroom areas use dividers which double as storage units, bulletin boards, chalkboards and acoustical separators. The media center installed clusters of carrels, each of which has electrical current. Small work areas were placed around the periphery of the media center for project work by students and teachers. A special area in the building was set aside for teachers' offices, a teacher's workroom and a faculty lounge. The cafeteria was reoriented to double as a small auditorium for large classes, dramatic presentations and musical recitals.

Resources

Aside from the special facilities for art, music, home economics, industrial arts, physical education, and science, the learning resources emanate from the media center. Based on the commitment to help each student become increasingly responsible for his or her own learning, a wide range of resources is made available through the media center. Many resources are dispersed throughout the school, near the place where they are most likely to be used. A decentralized pool of audiovisual equipment is deposited in each house including a 16mm motion picture projector, a filmstrip projector, a slide projector, a record player, a reel-to-reel tape recorder, and screens. Each instructional area has its own overhead projector. In the media center there are collections of filmstrips, slides, audiocassette and disc recordings, and some videotapes. Books, periodicals, and reference works are supplemented by vertical files and a rather large collection of microfilms of major periodicals and newspapers. Films and videotapes are borrowed from a central collection in the district office and from a regional film and videotape library.

One special feature of the media center is a large area where media may be produced. There is a videotape recorder for recording programs within the school and off the air. Copystands for photographic production, a transparency maker, and a dry mount press permit students and teachers to create their own visual materials. There are several cameras and audiocassette recorders which are loaned to students and faculty. A copy machine, a spirit duplicator, and a mimeograph machine allow for reproduction of printed materials.

All of these factors—and many others—combine to make this school what it is—a dynamic and innovative environment for teaching and learning. A similar profile could be developed for any school, but the facts would necessarily change. The school described here may seem to be ideal, but it is not uncommon. The description incorporates many of the features which can be found in schools today. The point of this narrative is that the media professional must know the context in which he or she will be working. To develop a media program without an appreciation for all the forces which impinge on the total school is like wearing blinders. The description of East Hills Middle School should help you to know what questions to ask about the environment in which you will be working and should provide some insights into the direction in which your media program should be moving.

THE SCHOOL AS AN INFORMATION CENTER

Call it a library, a media center, an audiovisual center, a learning resources center, or an information center—the important factor is that the functions of identifying, acquiring, storing, retrieving, and making available information in a variety of formats are performed. Whether the personnel have professional preparation in librarianship, audiovisual communications or educational technology—the important factor is that media professionals (as we shall call them in this book) are resource people—curriculum and instructional developers. They are members of a team of teachers, curriculum specialists and, on occasion, administrators. In this ideal situation the entire school functions as an information center with the media program providing many of the specific resources.

One of the basic commodities of education is information. This is a staple for teaching and learning. Information, as it is used here, is more than "facts" or "knowledge." Information is that which reduces uncertainty. One definition, which was developed after a year-long study on information and education is: "Information is a symbol or set of symbols which has a potential for meaning." [1] The potential for meaning is attained when the uncertain becomes certain. Students seek information to answer questions and to solve problems. Teachers attempt to provide information which will help students to have the tools to cope with their questions and problems. Media professionals assist in meeting information needs.

It should be pointed out that information exists in many formats. It may be oral—words from one person to another; it may be written—as in books and articles; it may be on film, magnetic tape, or pictures. It may come from a computer, a microfilm reader or a television screen. Media professionals

Information exists in many formats. Students should have access to
a variety of media.

[1] Sylvia G. Faibisoff et. al., *An Introduction to Information and Information Needs: Comments and Selected Readings* (Syracuse, N.Y.: Center for the Study of Information and Education, 1973), p. 10.

are expected to provide information regardless of the format in which it is packaged.

Sources of Information Within the School

One of the most efficient ways to provide information in the school is through a coordinated program with professional personnel and facilities which handle, store, produce, and distribute that information. The expanded concept of a library—the media center—manned by media professionals is one of the best ways to accomplish the goals of easy access to information for every user.

But within the school there are additional resources not normally considered as information. There is the complete staff—teachers, administrators, and support staff. These people can offer rich resources in areas in which they possess some interest and competence. The students themselves can often offer information which teachers and other adults cannot provide. The facilities can be used as information resources—the school yard, the halls, the offices, the kitchen, the special rooms—all should be considered as resources. The local environment is surprisingly full of information, if only it is sought.

Sources of Information Outside the School

The resources available in any community are so extensive that it would be impossible to list them here. An excellent approach to community resources is presented in *The Yellow Pages of Learning Resources*.[2] This comprehensive guide is an invitation to discover the community as a learning resource. So pervasive are local resources that several alternative schools, such as the Parkway in Philadelphia, have oriented their entire curriculum around nearly two hundred city institutions, organizations, and agencies. In the Parkway project there is no school building; rather, there are four home bases for students who are carrying out their program at various locales in the city. When one stops to think of the obvious resources—public libraries, museums, galleries, then expands to governmental offices, business, and industry, the magnitude of these resources seems endless. Consider also all the people— their interests, jobs, experiences, and abilities—and you discover the richness of this source. To marshal the resources requires some sort of clearinghouse. The media center is a logical coordinating point for information regarding community resources.

Arranging for Access and Use of Information

The media professional serves as an information broker; that is, the link between a user's expressed information need and the information which

[2] Richard Saul Wurman, *The Yellow Pages of Learning Resources* (Cambridge, Mass.: The MIT Press, 1972).

will fill that need. This book is about the competencies required of media professionals to reach this objective.

In serving as an information broker, the media professional must provide *access* to resources. Access is probably the key word for the media professional. People who have studied information users have discovered that most individuals use that information which is most readily at hand. The more difficult information is to obtain, the less likely it is that the person will seek it and use it. This apparently simple maxim is really one of the fundamentals. of the media program and it is the task of the media professional to make appropriate information available in a variety of formats at the time the user requires it. This book is about the ways in which the access goal can be met.

A second fundamental base of the media program is concerned with *use* of information. This aspect goes beyond access and, for many media professionals, is a new dimension. For some users, access to requested information is all that is required. But for many others, help is needed to make optimum use of information.

The media professional participates in the design of instruction as a member of a curriculum development team. Not only is assistance given in suggesting available resources, but suggestions regarding the production of new materials are given; recommendations are given for use of media by individual students, by small groups, and by teachers. In this role the media professional recognizes the need for systematic design of instruction which incorporates media use in a variety of ways. This new dimension of the media professional requires additional competencies and an understanding of this role by fellow teachers, administrators, students, parents, and school board members. In many ways it is the real "pay-off" for the media program.

REFERENCES

ARMSEY, JAMES W. and NORMAN C. DAHL. *An Inquiry Into the Uses of Instructional Technology*, pp. 7-74. New York: The Ford Foundation, 1973.

Commission of Instructional Technology. *To Improve Learning: A Report to the President and Congress of the United States, Committee on Education and Labor, House of Representatives*. Washington, D.C.: U.S. Government Printing Office, 1970.

DALE, EDGAR. *Buiding a Learning Environment*, pp. 1-50. Bloomington, Ind.: Phi Delta Kappa, 1972.

FAURE, EDGAR et al. *Learning to Be*, pp. 51-86, 116-44. Paris: UNESCO, 1972.

ILLICH, IVAN. *Deschooling Society*, pp. 103-50. New York: Harper & Row, 1971.

Improbable Form of Master Sturm. 16 mm, motion picture, sound, color, 13 min. Dayton, Ohio: I.D.E.A., 1968.

LEONARD, GEORGE B. *Education and Ecstasy.* New York: Dell Publishing Co., 1968.

Make A Mighty Reach, 16 mm, motion picture, sound, color, 45 min. Dayton, Ohio: I.D.E.A., 1967.

POSTMAN, NEIL and CHARLES WEINGARTNER. *The Soft Revolution.* New York: Dell Publishing Co., 1971.

Remarkable Schoolhouse. 16 mm, motion picture, sound, color, 25 min. New York: McGraw-Hill, 1967.

SILBERMAN, CHARLES E. *Crisis in the Classroom,* pp. 265-369. New York: Random House, 1967.

What's New at School? 16 mm, motion picture, sound, color, 45 min. New York: Carousel Films, 1972.

2 The Philosophy and Rationale of a Media Program

The school media program has not always existed in its present and emerging form. It grew out of common elements in library and audio-visual programs and was fostered by changing educational philosophies. As book and nonbook media began to be considered together as learning resources, administrative arrangements and facilities had to be adapted to reflect new directions. Integrated media programs have developed benefits which earlier separate programs could not provide.

Increasingly, information is found in numerous and diverse formats. A school media center has the responsibility to provide information to users in any appropriate format, whether that format is in print or in audio or visual form such as films, filmstrips, slides, audio tapes, video tapes, phonograph records, or digital tapes.

The National Commission on Libraries and Information Science has issued a proposal for "A New National Program of Library and Information Services" [1] which states:

> Information, whether in the raw form of empirical data or in the highly processed form we call "knowledge," has come to be regarded as a national resource as critical to the nation's well-being and security as any natural resource like water or coal. The wealth of popular, intellectual, scholarly and research resources in its libraries and information

[1] National Commission on Libraries and Information Science, *A New National Program on Library and Information Service* (Washington, D.C.: October 1973), p. 1.

centers is one of the great strengths of the nation. . . . Only the judicious use of knowledge resources gives us power to solve the complex social and economic problems that will free our nation in the future. . . . But like many natural resources, knowledge resources uncoordinated in growth and usage, are in danger of being wastefully utilized.

School media centers are an eminently valuable part of this natural resource. A unified program which integrates both print and audiovisual materials and related services exemplifies an effective and economical program for organizing knowledge resources for optimum utilization. From the viewpoint of the user, a unified media program fulfills all of the user's information needs in one place. Users (teachers and students) can call or visit one physical location to find answers to their educational, recreational, and information needs. If a student wishes to read a book, listen to an audiotape, look at slides, or at a film on Shakespeare or on ecology, all of these information formats should be equally accessible in a school media center.

Many schools have old facilities which make it difficult to totally implement this integrated concept. The experience and judgment of many authorities in the fields of librarianship and educational technology support the philosophy of the integration of all media formats in one center in so far as it is physically possible.

The concept of the unified center is a relatively recent one. Even though in some geographical areas of the country this concept was implemented earlier than in others, one of the first nationally accepted statements referring to the unified concepts was made in the national standards which were published in 1960.[2]

The American Association of School Librarians believes that the school library, in addition to doing its vital work of individual reading guidance and development of the school curriculum, should serve the school as a center for instructional materials. Instructional materials include books—the literature of children, young people and adults—other printed materials, films, recordings, and newer media developed to aid learning.

Teaching methods advocated by leaders in the field of curriculum development and now used in elementary and secondary education call for extensive and frequently combined use of traditional along with many new and different kinds of materials. Since these methods depend for their success upon a cross-media approach to learning, a convenient way

[2] *Standards for School Library Programs* (Chicago, Illinois: American Library Association, 1960), p. 11. Reprinted by permission of the American Library Assoc. © 1960 by the ALA.

of approaching instructional materials on a subject or problem basis must be immediately at hand in each school. Historically, libraries of all types have been established to provide convenient centers for books and reading and for locating ideas and information important to the communities they serve. The interest a modern school now has in finding and using good motion pictures, sound recordings, filmstrips and other newer materials simply challenges and gives increased dimension to established library roles.

Historically, libraries developed many years in advance of audiovisual programs. The very earliest school libraries in the U.S. performed the function of serving as a basic reference collection for the community or township in which the school was located. The next developmental stage was to have the collection of books in the school library serve as supplements to the single text used for teaching each class. The library was established on the "storage" concept and served as a depository of printed material to be held until students came to use them. As technology developed, audiovisual equipment and materials came to the attention of educators. Phonograph records, slides, and films probably were the earliest formats used extensively. As collections of audiovisual equipment and materials were built up in schools it is interesting to note that the persons who had responsibility for these collections were much more aggressive in "selling" their product than most librarians had been. Audiovisual specialists enthusiastically sought out teachers and encouraged them to use films and other types of audiovisual materials to enhance and enrich their classroom presentations.

Then came a transition in educational philosophy. No longer was the major focus on classroom presentations, but the attention was shifted to individualizing and personalizing instruction. In response to this change, the library focused on meeting the needs of individual students by providing materials to meet their special interests and their special abilities. As a part of this change of focus greater emphasis was placed on audiovisual materials as they can be used to facilitate individualized learning.

Educators became more sophisticated in their understanding of learning theory and came to the realization that each student learns best through differing modes which may be visual, aural, or kinesthetic. To meet these needs most adequately, librarians and audiovisual specialists came to the realization that all materials must be made equally accessible to all students. The service to teachers changed too in that librarians took on the responsibility of "reaching out" to the faculty to assist them in the selection of the entire range of materials, to work with them on curriculum committees, and to plan with them to make appropriate materials available to students. Audiovisual specialists started to work directly with teachers in the early stages of curriculum planning to give the most appropriate type of audiovisual support to classroom presentations. As audiovisual specialists became more sophisticated in their educational background and became knowledgeable about systems analysis, curriculum design and education, this field became identified as educational technology. Currently, most persons who call themselves educational technologists have completed a doctoral degree and work at the university level in planning and evaluating curriculum design. However, elements of this sophisticated approach can be found in well-developed programs at the school and district level. This brief historical overview delineates what elements and forces combined to shape the school media center as we know it today. Librarians traditionally performed certain activities; they ordered books (plus newspapers and pamphlets), processed them for the shelves, classified and cataloged the materials, stored them, and circulated them to students and teachers. Audiovisual specialists traditionally, previewed films and filmstrips, ordered phonograph records and audio tapes, actively encouraged teachers to use these materials in teaching, and checked out materials and equipment.

Clearly, none of these services was comprehensive and many activities were redundant or overlapping. However, critical elements were missing. It is dangerous to generalize, but an overview and analysis of a great number of separate library programs and audiovisual programs would likely reveal the following patterns of operation. *Ordering* of materials would be done in both programs, creating an ineffective method of handling records and an inefficient utilization of clerical help in typing and checking invoices. *Selection* tools are numerous and readily accessible to librarians, but the ordering of audiovisual materials was done mainly through producers' catalogs. The use of these catalogs is difficult as they are numerous and the purchaser must rely on the publisher's description rather than on an authoritative evaluation. Selection tools available for ordering books are quite comprehensive in that they include almost every publication, and in addition many of these selection lists include evaluative statements developed by accepted authorities. This information makes it possible to have some prior evaluative assessment of a book before it is ordered. By contrast only a limited number of tools have been developed to give evaluative information about audiovisual materials. This will be discussed in greater depth in Chapter 14, The Evaluation Function.

Processing has been developed into a highly routinized practice in the handling of books. Most school districts coordinate their purchasing and have developed system routines for pasting in card pockets, putting labels on spines of books, and putting on plastic jackets. Many commercial companies have identified needs in this area and will now, for an additional charge, supply books with the processing already completed. Partly because of the great diversity of format, and the greater difficulty in handling, many media centers have procrastinated about developing processing procedures for audiovisual materials. In some cases this was delayed until an overwhelming backlog of materials made the task seem formidable. In other cases, some librarians have resisted the idea of handling these more complex materials and have refused to face the problems posed by these materials. Commercial companies have also been challenged by these problems and have developed ingenious methods of attaching pockets and labels and have developed specialized techniques that make the packaging of the materials more uniform in size and shape in order to facilitate handling and shelving.

The activities of *classifying and cataloging* are traditionally associated with book collections. Classification is the process of assigning code letters and/or numbers to books for the purpose of organization. Cataloging is the process of describing books according to bibliographic information for the purpose of selective retrieval. Librarians have often been criticized for devoting a disproportionate amount of time and energy to these processes in order to avoid working directly with students and teachers. As with processing, commercial companies have become very active in supplying classifying and cataloging services for an additional charge when materials are purchased. Personnel directing audiovisual programs can probably be characterized as being less interested in classifying and cataloging materials than in any other activity related to the program. There may be many reasons for the reluctance to make progress in this area. First of all, in the early stage of the program the numbers of materials in the audiovisual collections were relatively small and the persons who worked with them kept a mental inventory. Second it was easy to adopt a simple method of organizing and many collections simply used accession numbers. This process was and is quite acceptable for many collections, however it does not organize materials by subject, therefore it does not permit browsing by subject. It does prove to be economical of space, as all formats of materials can be shelved together. As collections of audiovisual materials expanded in number and type of format, and as increasing attention was focused on the individualization of instruction, it became imperative to have the entire range of materials classified and cataloged to make them readily accessible. At first, many audiovisual specialists were extremely skeptical and insisted that audiovisual materials had to be classified and cataloged in a manner different from books. That argument has subsided and almost disappeared, as many total collections are now organized in an integrated fashion. Commercial companies are alert to the pressing needs of organizing audiovisual materials in collections and are moving ahead to develop ways to supply this service commercially.

The activities related to the *circulation* of materials appear to be quite similar for both print and nonprint materials. There are some unique problems, however, in that audiovisual materials usually require special listening or viewing equipment. Circulation procedures also have developed in different ways because of the fact that initially audiovisual materials were much more costly than books, and there was a great reluctance to circulate these materials.

Even though the costs have been reduced in many instances, this reluctance remains rather widespread.

In the matter of services provided to the user, librarians have often been characterized as being "protective of their books" while audiovisual specialists were viewed as aggressive in "selling" their materials to teachers and students. These images must be interpreted as stereotypes and may be totally inappropriate when describing individuals. Nevertheless as attention has shifted to the individual student it has become incumbent on the director of a media center to become actively involved in the "outreach" type of programs and to function in a much more aggressive manner when working with students and teachers.

Production of instructional materials has been almost exclusively related to the audiovisual programs. This service of providing instructional support materials particularly designed to fulfill the needs of an individual instructor has been one of the outstanding and valuable contributions of the audiovisual program. This activity is increasingly becoming a major responsibility of the media center. With the current focus on individualizing instruction, this service will take on increasing importance.

From the traditional service of developing instructional materials has come the more complex process identified as instructional design. The term instructional design connotes total planning of a course of study through the work of cooperating team members. The team members could be the teacher, the curriculum supervisor, the director of the media center, the graphic artist, the television specialist, and probably the resource specialists. These persons cooperate to plan a course of study. To accomplish this task they must identify student interests and abilities, identify goals and objectives, select appropriate commercial materials, identify teaching methodologies, suggest alternative modes of presenting audiovisual materials, produce materials particularly for these students, develop criterion-referenced means of evaluating competencies, and specify alternative means of evaluating the entire course. Persons in the audiovisual (educational technology) field have provided much of the leadership in developing the field of instructional design. The personnel of the media center must assume greater responsibility in the process of instructional design, as this is where it "all gets put together."

Evaluation has often been interpreted differently by these two fields. Audiovisual personnel have tended to evaluate the effect of the product and the process on the student, while the librarian has tended to evaluate books in a more or less isolated fashion, as though the values were inherent in the book, rather than its use by the student. Both of these approaches must be reassessed, amalgamated and expanded.

It is hoped that this brief examination of traditional roles will help to provide perspective. Very frequently persons who have been employed in a certain position for a length of time tend to develop "blinders" and believe that the way they are doing their job is the only way it can be done. Also, persons just entering the field have no opportunity to compare their work with others and usually don't have the authority to experiment with alternatives. This is a retrospective overview of how personnel functioned in traditional settings, based on the education they received. This education usually did not teach the philosophy of integrating print and audiovisual programs so this description will provide a contrast to a visionary perspective which includes an effective merger of all formats of information, programs, and services which can be provided through a totally integrated center.

Several important questions must be answered. First, what is a contemporary media center like? It is a facility that houses all kinds of print materials including books, pamphlets, newspapers, paperback books, clippings, and microforms and every kind of format of audiovisual materials such as films, filmstrips, audiotapes, videotapes, games, puzzles, models, realia, charts, graphs, art prints, and study prints.

There must be access to all of the equipment necessary to use the materials. Some devices permit small groups to preview materials together.

In addition there must be access to all of the equipment necessary to use the materials. These materials should be housed together for convenient access. In some instances it is possible to have all formats shelved together by subject, but in facilities where less space is available, formats such as filmstrips are all shelved together. The personnel of the center should collectively represent all of the skills and abilities necessary to provide a total range of services to the users. In each case the staffing patterns might vary, according to the education and background of each staff member, size of the center, needs of the school, and budget. Until quite recently most authorities writing or speaking about a school library referred to it as the "heart of the school" or the "hub of learning" and invariably described it as being physically located in the center of the school. For that time, educationally speaking, these descriptions were appropriate. However, current educational programs are developing many cooperative relationships with community activities, with adult education programs, and with public libraries. These cooperative efforts require that media centers be accessible before and after school hours, and on week ends, so architectually it is being recommended that media centers be located in a place that provides easy access to users. Security is possible by locking off the rest of the school building, and the media center should have an outside exit close to a main street and parking lot. All of these factors add to the optimum use of the centers.

What are the values of a totally integrated center? The first assumption must be that the media center exists for one purpose—to fulfill the needs of the users. A total range of materials and related services can unquestionably meet the needs of the user in a more adequate and effective way. In addition, an integrated program allows a much more efficient use of space, of personnel, and of budget. Because of this demonstrable and measurable effectiveness the program is more "salable." With current stress on accountability it is more important than ever before to be able to substantiate that there is no overlap in the responsibilities of any staff member, that no jobs are performed twice (e.g., the ordering process for audiovisual materials does not take place separately from the ordering of book materials), that there is no wasted effort in locating different formats of materials for teaching, and all programs and services are accessible in one physical location. This arrangement provides greater emphasis on accountability. Programs are more visable, identifiable, and less disparate.

Philosophically, information is information regardless of its format. There are no differences between information in print or in audio and visual formats, therefore it is a disservice to users to establish artificial dichotomies that separate formats.

The greatest challenge evolving from this "merger of media" is that those who are responsible for developing the programs must have a sensitivity to changing definitions and concepts. It is imperative that the persons who make up the staff of a media center have an attitude of openness and flexibility. There must be an acceptance of the total range of media, a willingness to work with all programs related to all forms of media. The director of the media center must provide the leadership of the program by creating this kind of atmosphere and taking positive action to establish this ambience. It is not enough just to agree with these ideas, but they must be implemented. It is sometimes possible to find a situation in which these ideas are articulated, but every action and even the atmosphere contradicts implementation. In addition, there must be the acceptance of innovation, the establishment of an atmosphere that encourages creativity and experimentation. This sense of visionary acceptance of change and permissiveness to try new approaches must be established by the director of the center and must pervade the entire staff. Of course it is extremely helpful if the administration of the school and district share these attitudes, but oftentimes it becomes the responsibility of the staff of the center to demonstrate the value of this approach and by so doing, "sell" it to others.

In an integrated program, many other aspects also change, or take on a new significance. By being able to provide information and materials relating to the entire range of media formats, the development of media personnel in curriculum planning becomes increasingly important. It is even more important that the personnel be able to work cooperatively to make materials and services available to teachers and also to students.

Because they have specialized training in selection, evaluation, production, design, and instruction, media professionals are able to contribute to the process of instructional design. The highest priorities of media center personnel should be to work with a curriculum committee to develop instructional goals, describe behavioral objectives, identify appropriate commercial materials, both print and audiovisual, to draw up specifications and produce original materials and assist in the evaluation process.

Even though the philosophy and rationale for an integrated program have been stressed thus far, common sense demands that some modifications be stated. It would be ridiculous for anyone to be so narrow-sighted to believe that there is only one means of achieving a set of goals. Even though the authors have tried to emphasize the many variants of a media program that must be considered in reaching the educational goals, in some instances physical facilities absolutely prohibit an integrated program. In some cases the rigid stance and objections of one person inhibits implementation of an integrated program. In other cases separate library and audiovisual programs have been so firmly established that it would take a great physical and psychological upheaval to make a change. In all of these cases, sound judgment and consideration for human involvement should take some priority. It is recommended that the ultimate objective—that of most adequately fulfilling the needs of the users—be identified and accepted as a goal. Decisions must be made by a careful assessment of the best way to use available facilities, personnel, and budget to meet this goal.

Another caution is that as transitions to these new programs or new organizational arrangements take place no one in the profession should feel threatened. Jobs or job opportunities will not disappear. Even though role definitions may change slightly or certain jobs may be given changed titles, the entire range of tasks must be performed. These tasks may be clustered in different ways or in changing configurations, but they will still need to be done. For example, an audiovisual professional may have functioned in a program in which all audiovisual materials were separated from print materials. Under this arrangement that person would have had the responsibility for identifying appropriate filmstrips, previewing them, doing all of the ordering work, receiving them, processing, organizing, and circulating them. Under an integrated program many of these tasks could be incorporated with other similar tasks. For instance, the previewing would be done through a team arrangement. The team could consist of teachers, students and other media specialists. The ordering could be combined with other materials. Likewise, cataloging and processing tasks would be handled along with other materials. These different work configurations, and the delegating of responsibilities to technicians and aides, would leave a staff member with more free time to perform higher priority responsibilities—working with teachers and other professionals in instructional design and working directly wth teachers and students. Even though change may be demanding, it does not have to be threatening or frightening in any way. Focusing on the advantageous outcomes may help to lessen the apprehensions about a new kind of program.

A question that has been the cause of concern among professionals in both the library and the audiovisual field is, if a new program has no director, should the person appointed have a background in librarianship or be an audiovisual specialist? Everyone is hoping that educational programs will develop rapidly enough to make this question moot and outdated. Professional education programs and state certification requirements should soon be geared for providing a comprehensive background in the total media field. Until this happens, the selection of a director should be based on the premise that the person most competent to do the job should be selected. In every case where separate programs exist, surely one of the persons will emerge as having had more administrative background, as being more competent in dealing with others, in developing rapport with teachers and students, in providing strong leadership and the ability to develop budgets and work with the administration. The person who can perform these tasks best should be chosen. There should be no hard and fast rule that the person who serves as director must have cataloging skills as a librarian or must have production skills as an audiovisual specialist. The person must have management skills and must be able to identify and hire other staff members who can perform the necessary tasks to make the program complete and comprehensive.

In summary, the entire focus of a program—its identification of staff abilities and areas of expertise, development of facilities, and the planning of services and programs—must be on the needs of the user, or the entire program is in vain.

REFERENCES

American Association of School Librarians. *Standards for School Library Programs*. Chicago: American Library Association, 1960.

At the Center. 16 mm, sound, color, 20 min. Chicago: American Library Association, 1971.

Learning With Today's Media. 16 mm, color, sound, 35 min. Chicago: Encyclopaedia Britannica Corp., 1974.

Media Center in Action. 16 mm, color, sound, 13 min. Chicago: Coronet Films, 1972.

National Commission on Libraries and Information Science. *A New National Program on Library and Information Service*. Washington, D.C.: Oct., 1973.

3   The Emerging Role of the Media Professional

This chapter discusses the activities which characterize the operation of a media center. The levels of personnel (aide, technician, specialist, generalist) are introduced and the training required for each is outlined. The ten functions performed by media personnel (organization, management, personnel management, design, information retrieval, logistics, production, instruction, evaluation, research, and utilization) are presented with a brief discussion of their derivation and applications.

It's day number one on the new job and the media professional wonders where to begin. The courses have been completed; some on-the-job experience has been gained; and practicing media professionals have been observed on the job. Yet, there is the uncomfortable feeling about what to do first. As the media professional looks around the new location, there are shelves and storage spaces holding books, filmstrips, disc and tape recordings, pictures, microforms and all the associated equipment for using them. There may be films and videotapes, a computer terminal and a television receiver. There are people—media center staff, students, and teachers. There is space for using the vast array of resources which is now the domain of the new professional. And there are the files in the office with such labels as "budget," "policies," "research findings," and "media sources." Where does one begin?

A quick flashback recalls the job interview with the chief administrator who stressed the need for a person who could provide not only access to all learning resources, but assistance in the selection and use by students and teachers. "In our goal of gearing innovative programs to meet individual needs of our students," he said, "I except the media professional to be a member of the curriculum development team with a special emphasis on providing the instructional materials to attain learning objectives." It was a big order but the brashness of an aspiring candidate brought forth the assurance that the job could be done. But . . . where does one begin? What does the media professional do?

DETERMINING WHAT A MEDIA PROFESSIONAL DOES

The profession itself has not always been clear as to what its practitioners do. Even though media professionals (librarians, audiovisual specialists, educational technologists or others with similar job titles) have been employed in schools and colleges for the best part of the twentieth century, a complete analysis of the tasks performed by these professionals has never been done. In order to identify the multiplicity of media-related tasks performed in schools and colleges today and the types of staff performing them, two projects were undertaken: (1) the American Association of School Librarians (AASL), a Division of the American Library Association (ALA), received support from the Knapp Foundation of North Carolina, Inc. to conduct the *School Library Manpower Project* (SLMP) (2) the Association for Educational Communications and Technology (AECT), received a grant from the Division of Vocational Education of the United States Office of Education (USOE) to conduct the *Jobs in Instructional Media Study* (JIMS). The products of these two studies have contributed substantially to the answering of the question: "What does the media professional do?"

THE RANGE OF TASKS

One of the first findings of both the studies was that there rarely is one single media professional. Even in schools where only one person has the full-time appointment as the media professional, there often are clerks, aides, pages, projectionists, and other types of support personnel from the student body, from parents organizations, and the community. Much of this assistance is volunteer although some personnel may be paid. Other assistance "in kind" comes from contracted services, e.g., book processing and equipment maintenance, whereby commercial organizations outside the school are hired to do some of the work which would ordinarily be performed by staff members of the media center if there were sufficient demand for full-time personnel. Even with the part-time help and contracted "staff" the media professional may be alone in a one person center within an individual building and be expected to perform many tasks which would ordinarily be performed by assistants, clerks, technicians, and other help. Such practices should not be endorsed but it should be recognized that they do exist. Media professionals who are dedicated to make their program work are usually not afraid to perform mundane tasks in order to move the program ahead. An early objective ought to be to define the tasks which can be performed by others and to seek ways to recruit personnel to assist in accomplishing some of the more routine services so that the professional can be released to work at the highest level possible.

The anomaly of the single building appointment is that the media professional is frequently expected to perform (or be responsible for) all the tasks which are normally part of larger operations which have more staff members with a variety of specializations. The generalist is expected to be informed about a lot of things since he or she is the only person in that building. A further paradox is that the single building appointment is usually given to the new graduate who has less experience while the more experienced professional who could probably better handle the job often joins a larger staff or seeks a specialized position.

The point is that most of the major tasks performed in a media center will have to be accomplished whether there is one professional or several; whether there is additional clerical or technical assistance or not. Obviously, one person cannot do everything and compromise will have to be made in regard to which tasks are done and the quality of the work completed. To provide an overview of what gets done in a media center and who does it, let us consider the levels of positions as determined by the *Jobs in Instructional Media Study* and the *School Library Manpower Project*.

Three Levels

The Jobs in Instructional Media Study (JIMS) conducted over 125 on-the-job task observations which yielded more than 2,000 discrete task statements ranging from the very simple to the extremely complex. The tasks were analyzed and coded according to a scale of Worker Instruction.

The Worker Instruction scale measures the amount of instruction required by media personnel to complete their tasks. Low-level tasks (Worker Instruction Level 1) have procedures that are completely specified. Almost everything the person needs to know is contained in the job assignment. At the highest level (Worker Instruction Level 8) the individual makes decisions regarding courses of action to take in order to complete tasks.

The advantage of the Worker Instruction scale is that it permits tasks to be classified according to complexity and responsibility. The tasks observed are grouped into three basic clusters—beginning, middle and advanced. These

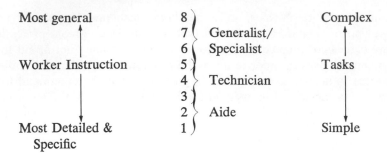

Figure 3-1   The Worker Instruction Scale

are also described as the aide level, the technician level, and the specialist level. See figure 3-1 above.[1]

Further descriptions of each level help to explain the nature of the simple to complex continuum.

AIDES have specific instructions about the tasks they perform. The task may be only part of a process, the other parts of which the aide cannot or does not control, e.g., running the ditto machine, but not necessarily preparing the stencil or collating the pages run off. Aides can be trained for a task in a relatively short period of time since everything they need to know is contained in the task. Aides are not required to solve problems external to the task. If something happens which is not covered by the instructions, the aide asks for help and cannot be held responsible for solving the problem.

TECHNICIANS have instructions which deal more with a cluster of tasks leading to a specified output. The technician may have a choice of routines to reach a given output. He has a broader view of the situation and is expected to generalize more from task to task than is the aide. The technician is responsible for the product as long as all of the routines necessary to reach the output have been specified and made available to him. For example, a technician might be told to produce six 8″ × 10″ prints from a given negative.

SPECIALISTS do not have tasks specified. They are responsible for a general problem and must determine what the product should be as well as how to achieve it. Having defined the goals, they are often forced to develop the routines or tasks necessary to achieve the goals. They deal with a broad process approach.[2]

The three levels determined by the JIMS were congruent with the levels

[1] C. James Wallington, "The Media Specialist: A Task Approach to Certification," *Guidelines for Certification of Media Specialists* (Washington, D.C.: AECT, 1972), pp. 42, 43.

[2] Freda D. Bernotavicz et al., *Training Programs for Media Support Personnel: An Annotated Directory* (Washington, D.C.: Association for Educational Communications and Technology, 1970), pp. 2-3.

determined by the SLMP except that the specialist level included three distinct positions: "Head of Library Media Center," "Assistant Librarian," and "Audiovisual Specialist." It should be noted that these are job titles which are examples of the more generic term—generalist. In the scope of this book, we are primarily concerned about the generalist—the media professional who is responsible for the entire program. Most of our discussions will focus on this job role. It will be necessary, however, to discuss specialists, technicians, and aides since they constitute a large portion of each generalist's staff and the responsibility for their supervision rests with the generalist.

Differentiated Staffing

The variety of tasks which must be performed in a school media center can best be accomplished by a staff of individuals who possess a variety of abilities. The worker-instruction analysis on p. 30 offers a scheme for assigning tasks to individuals according to the complexity of the task and the amount of instruction or training required to perform it. While it is difficult to classify people according to ability and educational attainment (since there are always exceptions to the rule) the following pattern serves as an initial guideline for reviewing the staffing of a media center by complexity of tasks and level of training for individuals assigned to each level.

TABLE 3-1 Guideline for Reviewing Staffing of a Media Center

Category	Examples of Job Titles	General Responsibility	Education Background
Generalist	Director of Media Center Head Librarian Director of Learning Resources	Over all organization, supervision and leadership	Graduate study in library-media
Specialist	Television Coordinator Catalog Librarian Director of Computer Assisted Instruction	Emphasizes one aspect of many media center functions	Graduate study in specialty area
Technician	Graphic Artist Chief of Equipment Maintenance	Provides services and/or creates materials according to specifications established by others	Training in area of specialization (not necessarily at collegiate level)
Aide	Reproduction Operator Charging Desk Clerk Typist	Provides services according to standards set by supervisor	On the job training

MEDIA AIDE   The person who holds this position usually possesses some basic skills at the time of initial appointment. Examples of such skills are typing, bookkeeping, and mechanical operations. There is an on-the-job training period when the media aide is taught procedures which are unique to the operation of the media center. With certain innate abilities, some entering skills, and on-the-job training, an individual is usually prepared to handle tasks related to ordering, receiving, taking inventory, producing, circulating, and utilizing materials and equipment. Media aides work under the direction of the media professional or, in some cases, under a media technician.

Although the media aide appears to be "the low person on the totem pole," this individual is often the key to the successful day-to-day operation of the media center and is a vital link between students and teachers and the media professional. The status which is attributed to this position reflects the less complex tasks and the minimal education and training required before filling the position. It is conceivable and possible that with high motivation an aide could gain useful experience while on the job and additional competencies through advanced education and move up to a position as a media technician,

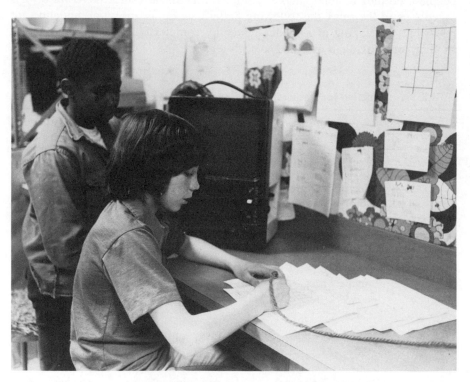

Aides can assist the media professional with such routine tasks as charging out materials and equipment.

specialist, or professional. Such career ladders have been proposed and closely parallel vocational and professional education programs.

Media aides would probably enter the field with a high school diploma and perhaps a one year post secondary school certificate from a business school, for example. Media aides come from a variety of settings. They may be full time or part time. High school and college students often serve as aides. Housewives and mothers sometimes serve in this capacity on a volunteer basis. The common requirement of each person is the ability to follow instructions and to learn how to handle routine tasks. Training occurs on the job and assumes a certain basic intelligence and a positive attitude toward the goals of the media center. Individuals who are dedicated to serve and who demonstrate an ability to get along with others are highly desirable.

Media aides often perform tasks which technicians and professionals have been performing in the past. For example, charging out materials and equipment, reserving, booking, and scheduling have been done by professionals because there was no one else to do it and it had to be done. Job analyses revealed that there were many tasks performed in media centers which do not require professional training. These tasks continue to be identified and individuals with lesser training are hired at lower wages to handle routine matters thus releasing the technician and professional to do those things for which he/she has been trained. This procedure is simply a good use of human resources. Other examples of tasks performed by media aides include:

1. Maintaining records, inventories and accounts
2. Typing correspondence, reports and bibliographies
3. Locating and retrieving materials and equipment
4. Assisting in the production of transparencies, slides, tapes and other non-book media
5. Assisting in the maintenance and minor repair of equipment
6. Operating reproduction equipment

The media aide is a vital member of the media center team. The media professional needs to carefully analyze the tasks which are performed each day in the center and then determine which duties can be assigned to others. Capable personnel who possess the necessary skills, a positive attitude toward the media center program, and an ability to work with people should then be selected. A formal training program must be carefully planned and carried out to insure that the duties are performed at the expected level. Some supervision will be required to monitor performance.

The media professional is sometimes placed in an uncomfortable position in relation to the media aide. The professional must know enough about the various tasks in the center to be able to teach the aides how to perform them. Since the professional already possesses many of the competencies which could be handled by the aide, there is a tendency among some professionals to do the routine things. There are probably many reasons why individuals choose to do certain things themselves rather than to turn them over to others

Media technicians work under the direction of the media professional.

but the danger is that day-to-day tasks could eventually consume the professional and leave very little time and energy to exert the leadership and management functions which are necessary for a strong media program. The media aide offers the potential for release from repetitive and time-consuming tasks and therefore should be perceived as a major personnel asset.

MEDIA TECHNICIAN   Individuals who hold positions in this category usually have completed specialized training or extensive, successful experience. They provide essential services that require a general knowledge of the media program's goals and operations as well as specific skills related to their specialty. Areas in which technicians serve include photography, graphic arts, materials processing, electronics and certain types of instruction. Media technicians work under the direction of the media professional or a supervisor who may be a specialist, such as a director of television. The media technician may, in turn, have media aides as staff members for whom supervision is necessary.

Media technicians would most likely hold an Associate of Arts (AA) or an Associate of Science (AS) degree from a two year community or junior college program. Media technicians sometimes come from vocational and technical programs such as commercial art, electronic maintenance, photography, and business. However, there are a growing number of programs in the United States and Canada that are preparing individuals to serve as media technicians through two year post secondary curricula. The more established programs exist at:

Anne Arundel Community College Arnold, Maryland	(Multi-Media Technicians)
City College of San Francisco San Francisco, California	(Audio-Visual Services)
Columbus Technical Institute Columbus, Ohio	(Audio-Visual Technology)
College of Dupage Glen Ellyn, Illinois	(Media Consultants)
Grossmont College El Cajon, California	(Instructional Media Technician)
Humber College Rexdale, Ontario, Canada	(Instructional Materials Centre Technicians)
Macomb County Community College Mount Clemens, Michigan	(Audio-Visual Technicians)
Mesa College Grand Junction, Colorado	(Audio-Visual Technicians and Graphic Communications Technicians)
Monroe Community College Rochester, New York	(Audio-Visual Technicians)
Portland Community College Portland, Oregon	(Instructional Materials Aides)*
Richmond Community College Richmond, Kentucky	(Instructional Media Technology)
Seneca College Willowdale, Ontario, Canada	(Educational Resource Technicians)
SUNY—Alfred A & T College Alfred, New York	(Audio-Visual Technicians)
SUNY—Farmingdale Farmingdale, New York	(Audio-Visual Technology)*
Thornton Community College Harvey, Illinois	(Educational Media Technicians)

* One year programs

Media technicians are hired because they possess certain competencies which will permit them to perform specialized functions within the media center's program. There should be minimal on-the-job training required. An orientation to the policies and procedures of the center is necessary. Specific duties and standards of performance will be outlined soon after employment. Essentially, the technician comes prepared to do what he has been trained to do and there should be only a brief period necessary for an individual to adapt to the new situation.

Since the nature of the media technician's responsibility is largely specialized, it is unlikely that the media professional will have a thorough knowledge of the technician's specialization. The professional will realize what type of work has to be done and will know that the technician ought to be able to do it. But the professional will have to trust that the technical ability of the technician will meet the general specifications stated for any given job.

What does the media technician do? The list of specific tasks is in the thousands but generally these tasks can be clustered into three areas dealing with production, support services, and instruction. The examples given are illustrative of the variety of tasks performed by technicians in the media center.

Production
1. Performs photographic production work in still and motion picture formats; processing; editing
2. Performs graphic art production and display tasks such as transparencies, original art work, posters, charts, graphs, exhibits, and publications
3. Performs television production work such as scripting, planning, and directing instructional TV programs

Support Services
1. Assists in the technical processing of materials by performing such tasks as bibliographic searching, processing of materials, location of materials, and handling.
2. Performs maintenance and repair of all electronic and mechanical equipment.
3. Coordinates data processing related to media center activities.

Instruction
1. Provides instruction in the operation and use of instructional equipment
2. Trains media aides to perform production and support service tasks

In smaller media centers with limited budgets, media technicians may not be hired but the services they normally perform can be obtained through contracts and purchased services. For example, it is usually more economical to turn over audiovisual equipment maintenance to a good dealer who has a convenient and reputable service shop. Photographers and graphic artists who do free lance work in a community can be hired for short term projects. Colleges often have students who have highly developed competencies of a technical nature. Such students can be hired on a part-time basis to handle tasks normally done by media technicians. There is no reason why every media center should not have access to services of media technicians even though they may not be hired on a full-time basis.

MEDIA SPECIALIST This category requires individuals with more education to handle tasks which are more complex than those accomplished by the aide or technician. The label, *media specialist,* has been used in some publications to designate the person who holds general responsibility for operation of the media center. However, in this book, we want to make a distinc-

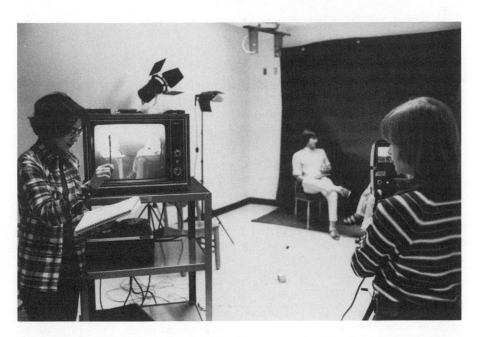

A media specialist has highly developed expertise in one distinct area such as television.

tion between the professional who has a highly developed expertise in one special area (e.g., computers, television, cataloging) and the professional who possesses a broader knowledge of an entire operation. Therefore, we shall use the term, *media specialist* to identify the professional who demonstrates competence in one special area or cluster of related areas; the *media generalist* will identify the professional who has a broad background involving all of the functions performed in the media center. Both may be identified by the generic term, *media professional*. The media generalist will have some competence in the management area.

A medical analogy might be helpful. All doctors receive a general medical education but some decide to specialize. Those doctors who do not choose to specialize become general practitioners. Their broad preparation permits them to consider all parts of the human body in their practice. Those doctors who choose to specialize usually concentrate their efforts on one aspect of medicine. Their expertise in their chosen area is so extensive that they would find it difficult to change to general practice. The general practitioner often refers patients to specialists as problems intensify in the area which can no longer be handled by the generalist. In a media center the generalist has the broad perspective and can sense the totality of the operation. The specialist is an expert in one specific area. The training for both professionals is likely to be comparable in time, but each one's emphasis is quite different.

The media specialists employed by an institution or school system are almost always unique to the program emphasis. For example, if a school system is dedicated to the development and use of television for teaching and learning, it will probably be necessary to have a television specialist who can work with teachers in planning programs relevant to curricular objectives and coordinate a staff of technicians and aides in a facility especially designed for television. The television coordinator will probably serve on the media center staff under the direction of the media generalist. A similar analysis could be made for a specialist in computer assisted instruction. A librarian specializing in cataloging would also be an example of a specialist. This person is first a librarian but has chosen to emphasize cataloging as a primary specialty.

The professional education of specialists is usually equivalent to that of generalists. After baccalaureate study in the arts and sciences, an individual enters a professional program on the graduate level to prepare for a more specific career. Individuals who eventually are appointed as directors of media centers or media specialists usually come from graduate schools of library and information science;[3] graduate programs in educational technology;[4] or combinations of both.[5] It is during the period of graduate study that specializations most often occur. By concentrating course work, field experiences, and independent study in one specific area, the individual tends to select a position which meets the chosen specialization. Education continues on-the-job and through association with like-minded professionals.

It is important to note that these persons are almost always equivalent in professional preparation to the media generalist who more often manages the entire enterprise. Like the generalist, their tasks are not specified even though the area of specialization is known. They develop or interpret goals and then develop routines necessary to achieve the goals where the area of specialization can contribute. This book is devoted to the media generalist, but most of the concepts and procedures discussed here are applicable to the concerns and responsibilities of the specialist as well as the generalist.

MEDIA GENERALIST This professional is the coordinator, conductor, ringmaster and presiding officer of the media program. As the "Number One Generalist," all functions come within the purview of this person. This individual establishes the climate in which a program can flourish. The philosophy of the chief executive officer permeates all that is done within the center. It's a big order and an exciting opportunity.

[3] "Graduate Library Schools Accredited by the American Library Association," *The Bowker Annual of Library and Book Trade Information 1973* (New York: R. R. Bowker Co.), pp. 415-17.

[4] L. C. Larson, *Instructional Technology Graduate Degree Programs in United States Colleges and Universities 1969-71* (Washington, D.C.: Association for Educational Communications and Technology, 1971).

[5] Robert N. Case, "Experimental Models for School Library Media Education," *School Library Journal* 96, No. 22 (December 15, 1971): 4151-56.

The remainder of the book is devoted to the media generalist and the functions which are performed so nothing will be said here regarding operational responsibilities. Rather, a few comments regarding professional education of media generalists and their place in the administrative hierarchy seem to be in order.

The educational level and process described for the media specialist also includes the pattern of professional preparation for generalists. The major difference between the preparation of the specialist and generalist is breadth and depth of study in various areas of graduate study. While the specialist probes one specific area in depth, the generalist acquires knowledge across a variety of areas relating to media in schools. But one area, more than any other, needs to be emphasized—management. The overarching responsibility of the media generalist who serves as the executive officer of a media program is in managing the program and its personnel. Unless an individual has the interest, aptitude, and ability to organize, administer, and evaluate all those factors which make a media center work, it would be best to consider another line of work.

The education of the media generalist can be viewed from several standpoints: (1) the graduate program—courses pursued for a degree; (2) the requirements for certification of professionals by state education agencies; and (3) the competencies a person must acquire to perform those functions which are unique to a media center.

The graduate program.   The most common preparation of media generalists is a one or two year Master's degree in a program accredited by the American Library Association [6] or through a graduate program in educational technology, educational media or audiovisual education.[7] There are other options, of course. Some individuals may complete an undergraduate program in library science or instructional media since there are several programs of this type in North America. Some individuals may come from related fields such as education, psychology, and computer science, and acquire necessary courses to become qualified to serve in a media center. Still others may choose to go beyond the Master's degree and pursue doctoral degrees. However, the Master's degree has become the professional degree and will probably continue to be the *sine qua non* for work in the field. One major change that appears to be forthcoming is a systematic plan for continuing education of all professionals. The Master's program usually provides the essential or core knowledge and skills a person needs to manage a media center. But in a changing world, the need for continuous education is vital for one's professional well-being. Such programs are now beginning to emerge through existing academic programs.

Certification.   The media professional who decides to locate in a public

[6] "Graduate Library Schools," pp. 282-83.
[7] L. C. Larson, *Instructional Technology Graduate Degree Programs in United States Colleges and Universities 1969-71* (Washington, D.C.: AECT, 1971).

school system will require certification in most states. The certificate is a license to practice a profession. Award of a certificate by a state department of education indicates that a person has completed certain requirements that would permit him/her to practice that profession. Teachers and administrators are the most typical personnel for whom certificates are issued. In nearly every state there are certification requirements for librarians; in twenty-two states there is audiovisual certification (and nineteen states are in process). Some states issue "unified" or combined "print/nonprint" certificates. Of nine new certification programs adopted since 1970, five require or recommend that courses be taken in print and nonprint areas (Florida, Illinois, Oregon, South Dakota, and Texas). Since that time many other states are moving in this direction. Prior to 1970 only two states required or recommended work in both areas (Indiana and North Dakota).[8]

Since we are concerned with the unified program administered by personnel at the generalist's level, it should be useful to look at those certification requirements to verify the adequacy of professional preparation and to identify what appears to be a national trend. Within the certification requirements for generalists in unified programs, four states issue certificates at two levels, and three states at three levels. The others are at one level. The pattern for certification, where levels are used, is to offer a *basic* certification which states the minimum requirements and an *advanced* certification which adds additional course work and/or evidence of experience on top of the basic standard. Because certification patterns in states differ so widely, it is difficult to generalize. However, it is important to point out that some states have superviser's certificates, which are beyond the advanced certificates just described. Where several levels exist, the top level is an exemplary preparation—far beyond the basic and advanced. It is usually reserved for someone with the equivalent of a doctoral course of study and is recommended for an individual serving at a district, regional, or state level.

The competencies discussed in this book are aimed at persons preparing for basic and advanced levels. Certification is a reality which must be faced by most professionals. At the present time certification requirements are stated most commonly in terms of course titles and credit hours to be completed although some states are beginning to move toward *competency-based* requirements. The authors believe that the demonstration of competencies hold more promise as evidence of potential performance on-the-job than any other measure.

The Competency Approach

There is a movement toward competency-based professional education in many fields, most notably in teacher education. The trend has begun to

[8] *Guidelines for Certification of Media Specialists* (Washington, D.C.: AECT, 1972), pp. 20-36.

include media personnel. The concept of *competency* emphasizes the ability to do something as contrasted to the traditional emphasis on the ability to demonstrate knowledge. Competency-based instruction stems from recent concerns for individualization of instruction and the use of explicitly stated learning objectives. Thus, a competency-based approach might be followed in a graduate program or might be the basis for certification. In either case, the functional areas in which individuals are expected to demonstrate competencies must be named and the specific competencies in each area must be spelled out. In specifying competencies, it is necessary to state a discrete behavior, and also the conditions within which the behavior will be demonstrated, and the degree of acceptable performance. Since professional education for competency is "the wave of the future," the concept has been incorporated into the basic design of this book and will be discussed at the end of this chapter.

FUNCTIONS OF A MEDIA CENTER

What gets done in a media center? Plenty! It is often referred to as the pulse of the school. Many new schools have been designed so that teachers and learners will have ready access to all resources. But what happens there? The best way to describe what gets done is through a functional analysis of the activities which occur within the center. Several research studies in recent years have systematically investigated the functions of media personnel in schools and colleges.

The Media Guidelines Project was funded by the Bureau of Research, U. S. Office of Education to produce guidelines and other information for planning media training programs.[9] The ultimate goal was to insure that professional training programs develop plans and procedures for competency-based education to meet future needs of the field. One aspect of the Media Guidelines project was concerned with a conceptual organization of the domain of media. After much field research and testing, nine functions were determined to be the domain of the media field.[10]

The functions within the domain of media were developed primarily by Dr. Kenneth Silber who also served as a major consultant to the Jobs in Media Study (JIMS). The Jobs in Instructional Media Study, funded by the Division of Vocational Education, of the U. S. Office of Education, used Silber's functions, with minor modifications, and field tested the functions by

[9] Dale Hamreus (ed.), *Media Guidelines: Development and Validation of Criteria for Evaluating Media Training* (Final Report) (Monmouth, Oregon: Teaching Research, 1970).

[10] This list of functions is comparable to those developed in similar projects and can be seen on pages 43-44.

observing more than one hundred workers according to a standard procedure known as Functional Job Analysis. The format for each task statement followed this pattern: "(1) Upon what instructions (2) who (3) does what (4) in relation to what or whom (5) to accomplish what immediate result (6) with what tools, equipment, or work aids?" [11] After this study the function list was modified.

About the same time, the Knapp Foundation of North Carolina had funded the School Library Manpower Project. One of the first steps in this project was to identify the tasks performed by school library personnel in unified service programs at the building level. A Task Analysis Survey Instrument [12] was prepared using 300 tasks performed by library media center personnel. Previous studies had generated the information from which specific task statements were derived. The 300 task statements were clustered into twelve categories which correspond roughly to the lists of functions developed by the two other studies.

After considerable field testing of the task statements in five training programs [13] the clusters were refined and collapsed into seven competency-based job functions.[14]

The functions identified from each of these projects are compared in Table 3-2. From this table it can be seen that the functions are grossly comparable from project to project and the ones selected for this book are consistent with the research. There is probably no one best list of functions. Those used in this book seems to be practical, comprehensive and exemplify the unified media concept.

It should be made clear that there is a difference between a function and a job. An individual is employed for a job and the job is composed of a set of interrelated functions. The concept of "function" was developed by the United States Department of Labor to classify what people do on a particular job because job titles tend to be ambiguous descriptors of activities. For example, the term "librarian" sheds little light on a librarian's duties. Such a person could be an administrator of media services, a specialist in reference services, or a cataloger. *Function refers to a group of interrelated tasks engaged in by media personnel to attain a specific outcome or purpose.* Seldom, if ever, is a job composed entirely of one function.

---

[11] C. James Wallington et. al., *Jobs in Instructional Media Study,* Interim Report, November, 1969, p. 23.

[12] *Task Analysis Survey Instrument* (Chicago: American Association of School Librarians, 1969).

[13] Anna Mary Lowrey, "School Library Manpower Project Launches Phase II," *Audiovisual Instruction* 15, No. 1 (January, 1970): 25-28.

[14] Robert N. Case and Anna Mary Lowrey, *Behavioral Requirements Analysis Checklist* (Chicago: American Association of School Librarians, 1973).

TABLE 3-2 Functions Performed by Media Personnel: A Comparison

Media Guidelines[a]	JIMS[b]	SLMP[c]	Chisholm & Ely
Research	Research	Research	Research
Evaluation	Evaluation-Selection	Planning & Evaluation	Evaluation
Design	Design	Human Behavior	Design
Production	Production	Media	Production
Logistics	Support-Supply		Logistics
Utilization	Utilization	Learning & Learning Environment	
Organization Management	Organization Management	Management	Organization Management
Information Management	Utilization/ Dissemination		Instruction
Personnel Management	Personnel Management	Professionalism	Personnel Management Information Retrieval

[a]Dale Hamreus (Ed.) *Media Guidelines: Development and Validation of Criteria for Evaluating Media Training.* (Monmouth, Oregon: Teaching Research, 1970) pp. 11-4, 11-5.
[b]Kenneth Silber, "Domain of Instructional Technology." *Jobs in Instructional Media* (Washington, D.C.: Department of Audiovisual Instruction, 1971) pp. 298-301.
[c]Robert N. Case and Anna Mary Lowrey, *Behavioral Requirements Analysis Checklist.* (Chicago: American Library Association, 1973) p. vii.

The functions discussed in this book include:

Organization Management—to plan, establish and maintain the policies and procedures for the operation of a media service.

Personnel Management—to hire, interact with, and supervise the media service personnel.

Design—the development of a plan for teaching and learning which takes into account as many variables as possible (such as, media, people, content, method) and orders them in a systematic fashion. The purpose of design is to assist teachers and learners to achieve stated objectives in the most effective and efficient manner.

Information Retrieval—to organize knowledge and to order information in all formats in a systematic fashion for the purpose of making the information accessible to the user.

Logistics—the mechanics of acquisition, storage, retrieval, distribution, and maintenance of information in all formats.

Production—the design and creation of an instructional product.

Instruction—the process of communicating information to defined audiences.

Evaluation—to examine and judge the worth, quality and significance of specific media and programs of instruction.

Research—the process of generating and testing theory; it is inquiry, examination, or experimentation having for its aim the discovery of new facts or their correct interpretation (in this book, as related to the use of media in the context of teaching and learning).

Utilization—to employ media for the purpose of achieving individual and group objectives.

Each function will be discussed in a separate chapter. Tasks related to each function will be be described in detail. It is important to remember that functions are not jobs, but rather a cluster of related tasks. Any person on the media staff usually performs more than one function.

A graphic interpretation of the ten functions performed by media personnel at differing levels of service is shown in Figure 3-2. Note that all personnel engage in the performance of each function.

At times a diagram or paradigm can serve better than words to develop a concept. This diagram is presented to illustrate the role of the media professional and to graphically present many relationships. The major point toward which everything focuses is user needs. The entire intent of establishing

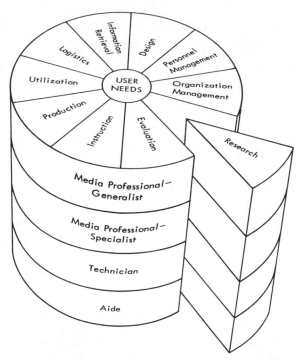

Figure 3-2 Functions Performed By Media Personnel in Relation to the User

the service of a media program is to fulfill the information needs of the users. The approach used in this book is that the role of the media professional— all of the tasks which he or she performs—can be clustered and fit into categories called functions. These functions are organization management, personnel management, design, information retrieval, logistics, production, instruction, evaluation, research, and utilization. Each of these functions contributes toward the major goal of fulfilling user needs.

All or parts of each of these functions can be carried out by a media professional who is able to perform the competencies which together make up the function.

The layers in the cylinder labeled media professional/generalist, media professional/specialist, technician, and aide, show graphically that there are some aspects of each function that can be done by personnel with different training and expertise. This shows the opportunities for differentiated staffing. Note that the media generalist and media specialist can both be media professionals and in most states would meet certification requirements.

The major points illustrated by the diagram are:

1. The focus of the entire media program is to fulfill user needs.
2. The role of the media professional is comprised of functions which he or she performs.
3. Each function is important, but all functions are essential for providing optimum service.
4. Each function is interdependent on the other functions to provide a total program.
5. Each function can be analyzed separately to assess the competencies which comprise that function.
6. Responsibilities for various levels of performance of each function can be assumed by a media professional, a technician, or an aide.
7. The total media program functions deal with both print and audiovisual materials and treats them all as formats for transmitting information.

The purpose of the model in Figure 3-2 is to explain how *user needs* can best be fulfilled. Basically, man is an information-seeking organism. He usually seeks information in a more or less random fashion. But in the domain of media, an attempt is made to organize information so that it can be made available in a more systematic and useful fashion. As institutions are built to provide information to users, the basic question must be: "How does this function or service help to fulfill user needs?" In other words, on what basis will any given service answer an information need of a user? Why does the media center exist? Who is it serving? What are their unique information requirements? To what extent should assistance be given in helping to identify problems and to what extent should the center be responsive to perceived problems? These are fundamental questions and must be the touchstone for all further analyses and research.

The Concept of Competency

Professionals can often describe their jobs and what it is they do (or ought to do) but the difference between *knowing* what to do and actually being able to do it is best described by the term *competence*. Competence means "adequacy for a task"—the possession of necessary knowledge, skills, and abilities to achieve an acceptable level of performance.

Within the school media program there are functions which must be performed. These functions are composed of hundreds of tasks. Each task requires a specific competency or several competencies to adequately perform it. For example, receiving an order for a film is a task within the logistics function. If the title and source of the film are known, the competency required is largely clerical and can be carried out by an aide or clerk. The competency is that the aide must be able to receive an order from a user by telephone or in writing, obtain all relevant information (title, source, use date, location of use) and complete an order form. If the title and source of the film are not known but a user wants a film in a certain subject area, a technician who possesses competencies with the use of all the media indexes can, when given a subject area, identify titles and sources of films in that area through use of all relevant media indexes. If a user comes to the media center with some idea that help with media selection can be obtained, the media generalist will probably be called upon to demonstrate competence in consultation (to help the user identify the behaviors desired as a result of using the medium); evaluation (to select appropriate titles for all those which are potentially useful); and utilization (to suggest strategies for use of the media to enhance the liklihood of achieving the desired behavior).

The nature of each request requires different competencies to satisfy it. In this example the competencies were assigned to staff members at three different levels. In some cases, when personnel are limited, one staff person might have to fulfil all the competencies. The important idea here is that someone is able to perform the required task. In each case, the competency required was named (in behavioral terms) but the acceptable level of performance was not. The ability to measure and assess outcomes is essential in any statement of competency. In the case of the film order, successful completion would be the sending of a correct order; in the second case, success could be measured by the list and source of films generated; and in the third instance, the user's satisfaction could be evaluated by the degree to which his expectations were met. A complete statement of competency, then, requires (1) a description of the behavior to be performed (2) the conditions under which it will be performed and (3) the degree of acceptable performance.

Houston and Howsam provide a useful framework for considering competency-based instruction.

Competency-based instruction differs from other modes of instruction, not in its goals, but rather in the assumptions that underlie it and in the approaches that characterize it. . . . Two characteristics are essential to the concept of competency-based instruction. First, precise learning objectives—defined in behavioral and assessable terms—must be known to the teacher and learner alike. . . . The second essential characteristic is accountability. The learner knows that he is expected to demonstrate the specified competencies to the required level and in the agreed-upon manner.

Other characteristics of competency-based instruction include: (1) provision for one or more modes of instruction pertinent to the objectives, through which the learning activities may take place; (2) public sharing of the objectives, criteria, means of assessment, and alternative activities; (3) assessment of the learning experience in terms of competency criteria; and (4) placement on the learner of the accountability for meeting the criteria.[15]

The concept of competency will be used in this book as a way of describing what a media professional ought to be able to do. As each function is described, clusters of competencies will be named. In essence, each competency should trigger several rhetorical questions: "Can I do this?" "How well?" "Can I expect someone else (on my staff) to do this?" "How can I assess the outcome?" "Will the outcome adequately satisfy the user's need?"

Your professional education for a media career may use competency-based instruction. Some states are moving toward competency-based certification procedures. Many teacher education institutions are investigating or implementing a competency-based program. Clearly this is the era of competency-based programs. This movement is an outgrowth of the concern for accountability. Many competencies can be stated, observed, and measured. Armed with evidence, individuals feel that they can defend or justify what they are doing if they are called upon to do so. Each reader should realize that many movements and emphases come and go on the educational scene and perhaps the newness of the concept of competency will wane as it becomes accepted practice. But there is an enduring satisfaction in knowing that one possesses a competency or a cluster of competencies. It is reassuring to be able to say, "I can do it." There seems to be no substitute for competency in any area of life or work.

One way to view competencies in relation to functions and levels of staff is shown in Figure 3-3. The solid blocks represent competencies or clusters of competencies which are performed within each function. The levels of work, determined by the complexity of the tasks and the amount

[15] W. Robert Houston and Robert B. Howsam, *Competency-Based Teacher Education* (Chicago: Science Research Associates, 1972), pp. 3-6.

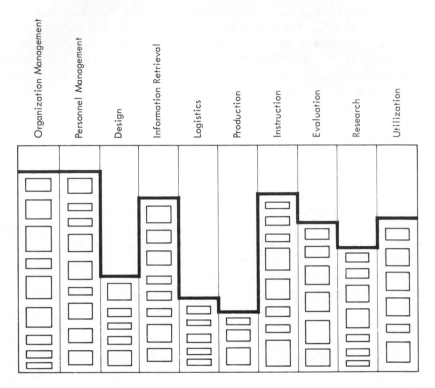

Figure 3-3. An Example of Competencies Needed by a Media Generalist

of instruction required to master each task, are shown on the vertical column. The competencies which might be required for a media generalist are shown by the solid line.

Figure 3-3 shows the combination of competencies needed by one hypothetical media professional, in this case a media generalist. This example indicates that strengths in organization management, personnel management, information retrieval, and instruction are expected while fewer competencies are needed in design, logistics and production. The combination of competencies needed varies from place to place because of differing curricular emphases and size and abilities of staff.

Figure 3-3 can be used in a variety of ways. It can represent the competencies which actually are in the repetoire of each staff member in a media center or it can serve to define those competencies which ought to be represented on the staff. It can also be used to assign responsibility. For some, it can be used as a guide to planning an individual curriculum for graduate study or for a graduate media program to design a curriculum.

Of course the solid areas, which represent statements of competency, have to be filled in with actual statements of competency. As the entire list of competencies for each function is considered, one might ask whether or not the professional (at the highest level) ought to possess the competencies of all personnel who work at the other levels. The best answer is that the professional should probably be able to demonstrate most of the competencies at all levels if required to do so, but better, the media professional should be able to teach others to attain the competencies and be able to describe in very specific terms what is expected of others.

REFERENCES

BERGESON, CLARENCE. "Accreditation of Educational Media Personnel: A Developmental Look." *Audiovisual Instruction* 18 (May, 1973): 23-25.

BERNOTAVICZ, FREDA D., PAMELA KENYON and C. JAMES WALLINGTON. *Training Programs for Media Support Personnel: An Annotated Directory*. Washington, D.C.: Association for Educational Communication and Technology, 1970.

BROWN, JAMES W., KENNETH D. NORBERG and SARA K. SRYGLEY. *Administering Educational Media*, pp. 17-34. New York: McGraw-Hill, 1972.

CASE, ROBERT N. and ANNA MARY LOWREY. *Behavioral Requirements Analysis Checklist*, pp. VI-XI. Chicago: American Library Association, 1973.

CASE, ROBERT N. and ANNA MARY LOWREY. *School Library Manpower Project*, Phase I, Final Report. Chicago: American Library Association, 1970.

ERICKSON, CARLETON W. H. *Administering Instructional Media Programs*, pp. 1-33. New York: Macmillan, 1968.

GRADY, WILLIAM F. "Certification of Educational Media Personnel: A Developmental Look." *Audiovisual Instruction* 18 (May, 1973): 26-32.

Guidelines for Certification of Media Specialists (Extended Version), pp. 5-8; 37-44. Washington, D.C.: Association for Educational Communication and Technology, 1972.

HAMREUS, DALE G. (ed.) *Media Guidelines*, Part 2. Monmouth, Oregon: Teaching Research, 1970.

LARSON, L. C. *Instructional Technology Graduate Degree Programs in U.S. Colleges and Universities 1969-71*. Washington, D.C.: Association for Educational Communications and Technology, 1971.

PRIGGE, WILLIAM C. "Certification and Accreditation of Educational Media Personnel: A Frame of Reference." *Audiovisual Instruction* 18 (May, 1973): 16-21.

PROSTANO, EMANUEL T. and JOYCE S. PROSTANO. *The School Library Media Center*, pp. 48-69. Littleton, Colo.: Libraries Unlimited, 1971.

School Library Personnel Task Analysis Survey. Chicago: American Library Association, 1969.

SILBER, KENNETH H. "What Field Are We In, Anyhow?" *Audiovisual Instruction* 15 (May, 1970): 20-24.

Task Analysis Survey Instrument. Chicago: American Library Association, 1969.

WALLINGTON, C. JAMES, ANNA L. HYER, FREDA D. BERNOTAVICZ, PRYOR HALE and KENNETH SILBER. *Jobs in Instructional Media,* pp. 6-13. Washington, D.C.: Association for Educational Communication and Technology, 1971.

4 User Needs: The Basic Concern

The purpose of this chapter is to examine the major goal of the media program—to serve the needs of the user. Consideration is given to the historical development of responses to user needs. Limited populations have been studied to assess their needs and these first steps are described. The relation of these studies to the school media field is examined.

The raison d'etre for any media center is to fulfill the needs of the user. If the needs of the user are not being met there is little or no justification for the existence of such a center. Therefore the fulfillment of the needs of the user becomes a fundamental concern.

This book is concerned with a very specialized type of library, a school media center, which is located in a particular setting, the school or another educational environment. This media center functions in a specialized environment and serves a specific and select clientele, comprised of students and teachers, and on occasion, people in the community. The task of identifying the needs of the users becomes relatively circumscribed by the setting, the environment, and the specialized clientele.

To view this problem within a broad context it is essential to establish a historical perspective. One encyclopedia defines a library as a collection of graphic materials (such as books, films, magazines, maps, manuscripts, and phonograph records) designed for use.[1] This article on libraries points out that the phrase "for use" given in the definition is vitally important. This distinction is crucial as books and other materials can be brought together

---

[1] "Libraries" *Collier's Encyclopedia* (New York Crowell-Collier Educational Corporation, 1968), vol. 14, p. 558.

for some purposes in which they would not constitute a library. For example, copies of books in a publisher's warehouse or phonograph records for sale in a store are not libraries. By contrast, a shelf of books on coin collecting maintained by a numismatist would qualify as a library. Ordinarily a shelf of books would not be considered a library, but this illustrates the point that *purpose* rather than size is the factor that determines whether or not a collection is a library. To summarize—the idea of "use" or serving the needs of the user is a fundamental part of the concept of the library.

As a part of the introduction to the study of libraries, Gates states that in considering the historical development of libraries certain facts of significance become clear: (1) libraries are essential ingredients of a civilized society; (2) they come into being to meet certain recognized needs and these needs determine their forms, purposes, functions, programs, and services; (3) certain conditions—economic, technological, scientific, geographical, cultural, or social—encourage their development, and when such conditions do not prevail, libraries decline and may disappear.[2]

So, in a historical context what were some of the needs which led to the development of libraries? Scholars commonly believe that civilization began in the fertile valleys of the Tigris and Euphrates rivers. As an agricultural economy developed, nomadic tribal settlements grew into towns and cities. Governmental, religious, social, and economic institutions developed, and commerce and industry expanded in cities. It is conjectured that writing on clay tablets was invented about 3500 B.C. as a tool for keeping accounts, recording transactions, issuing receipts, making wills, and developing land contracts. As these written records developed it became essential that they be preserved so that they could be used when needed, and so that they could be handed on. These early accumulations of clay tablets stored in temples became the first libraries. Scribes had to learn to draft commercial documents so schools were established. As knowledge increased among these Sumerian priests and scribes other information was recorded. These Sumerian temple repositories contained grammatical exercises for the scribes, mathematical texts, treatises on medicine and astrology, commercial accounts, collections of hymns, prayers and incantations, and the beginnings of literature.

So in actuality, it could be said that the first libraries were established in response to user needs—the economic and social needs of both the individual and the community led to the founding and perpetuation of the earliest libraries.

In Egypt, the first library of consequence has been attributed to Rameses II (c. 1304–1237 B.C.). This was a library of sacred literature as were most of the records preserved in the temples. They were probably administrative and liturgical documents produced by the priests.

One of the best known of the early libraries was located at Nineveh,

---

[2] Jean Key Gates, *Introduction to Librarianship* (New York: McGraw-Hill, 1968), p. 7.

the capital of ancient Assyria. The library at Nineveh consisted of clay tablets and leather and papyrus scrolls which contained information on agriculture, government, poetry, medicine, and catalogs of minerals, plants and animals. During the reign of the monarch Assurbanipal the library contained about 20,000 volumes and was maintained in his palace at Nineveh "to meet the need of instructing his subjects." [3]

There is some historical evidence that small libraries were owned by authors and statesmen of Greece, but the first truly extensive library in Greece was founded and arranged by Aristotle (384–322 B.C.). He founded a private library of great importance which he used in the preparation of his writings. His example of how his library served his needs demonstrated for his contemporaries the value of such records.

About 300 B.C. the Ptolemies established the library at Alexandria in Egypt to preserve and extend the civilization of the old Greek world throughout Egypt. This library served only a group of wealthy patrons who were interested in preserving all books in the Greek language. The collection was secured by obtaining copies of all books on board ships which docked at Alexandria and by acquiring from Athens all official state copies of plays of the Greek playwrights.

In Rome it was Julius Caesar who first planned a public library. He did not accomplish his goal, but one of his intimate friends Asinius Pallio did achieve success and was said to be "the first to make men's talents public property." [4] By the beginning of the fourth century A.D. twenty-eight public libraries existed in Rome to meet the public needs.

In the early middle ages monasteries often housed libraries. Volumes in the form of the "codex" or the block form of book were used for studying and for copying and were also loaned to other monasteries.

During the later Middle Ages, as trade and manufacturing developed in the cities the rising middle class required books for amusement and instruction. In response to this need the professional men and civic leaders of medieval German towns commonly owned small collections of books and made them available. As cities grew, universities were founded. These, in turn, needed books and libraries. In addition, the nobility collected private libraries to fulfill the needs of their families and privileged subjects.

The introduction and spread of printing in the fifteenth century gave great impetus to the development and growth of library collections. As the use of the printing press increased the number of books in collections grew and new physical arrangements were made to meet the needs of the users more adequately. When manuscripts were hand-copied and rare they were often secured with chains. As books became more accessible the volumes were shelved vertically in bookcases along the walls around the library.

---

[3] *The Story of Our Libraries* (New York: Crowell-Collier Educational Corporation, 1969), p. 1.
[4] *The Story of Our Libraries,* p. 3.

When the collections grew, bookcases were built to the ceiling and again the needs of the patron were considered, and balconies were constructed to provide easy access to these upper shelves.

During the seventeenth and eighteenth centuries experimental science began, and scientific and learned societies were established. Scholars of different countries entered into the exchange of information and publications. This intellectual activity and scholarship established the need that gave libraries a new direction and purpose. For the first time libraries were fulfilling the need to advance the work of scholars and the first functional research library of modern times was opened in 1602, the Bodleian at Oxford University.

During the eighteenth century there developed increased faith in logic and science and an even stronger belief in the value of education; thus universities and libraries increased in importance.

The Industrial Revolution ushered in the great social upheaval of the nineteenth century. Before the Industrial Revolution, popular education was a democratic ideal, but it now became a real possibility and a need. This new mode of life in cities created increased demands for libraries. National libraries were established to promote nationalism, circulating and mercantile libraries were established for the improvement of workers, and public libraries for the education and entertainment of adults, and special libraries were established for government bureaus, industries, historical studies and research.

The twentieth century saw library collections grow at an unprecedented rate. The needs of new client groups were recognized and services were established to meet the needs of children, industry, business, and the special needs of large corporations and government bureaus and agencies. Philanthropists developed collections of rare books. During this time county and state libraries were organized to meet the needs of legislatures and residents of rural areas. This period also saw the establishment and growth of school libraries.

As technology develops it is becoming possible to be more and more precise in meeting the needs of the user. For example, when moveable type came into use the dramatic increase in the number of books made it possible to meet the needs of more specialized groups of clients. Today as computer capabilities develop it is becoming increasingly possible to meet the needs of individuals with greater specificity according to totally individualized criteria.

School libraries, secondary, junior high school, and elementary were established in response to a need for their resources and services. The first steps in the development of the school library movement began in the early nineteenth century. The responsibility for developing a system of public education lies with individual states. Both New York and New Jersey adopted a series of laws providing that small collections of reference books be established in schools. It is interesting to note, in light of future developments of multi-media collections, that New Jersey's first specifications for purchase included *Webster's Unabridged Dictionary,* William E. Sackett's *History of New Jersey,* Lippincott's *Pronouncing Gazettes* and the nonbook medium

Arnold H. Geryot's *Physical and Descriptive Map of the United States.* Within thirty years, nineteen other states had passed similar laws, but these libraries were intended primarily for the use of adults throughout the entire school district. Public libraries gradually superseded these early school libraries.

During the later part of the nineteenth century and the beginning of the twentieth century educational goals concentrated on the mastery of subject matter; stress was placed on the use of a single textbook, and on the lecture and recitation methods, so libraries were not considered highly essential. During the early twentieth century there was a move toward educational experiments which shifted the emphasis from the subject matter to the learner. The Dalton plan, the Winnetka plan, and the Platoon school systems attempted to develop each child's potential and were based on the utilization of a variety of information sources. These educational developments encouraged and gave impetus to the development of school libraries.

Other factors have had an influence on the growth of the library media centers: the impetus provided by professional organizations such as the American Library Association, American Association of School Libraries, and Association for Educational Communication and Technology, the development of standards which served as guidelines (in 1920, 1945, 1960, 1969 and 1974), and both state and federal programs of funding for expanding facilities, equipment, and materials.

But above all, there have been curriculum developments which have stressed the idea of meeting the individual needs, interests, and abilities of each student. Concomitant with these curriculum developments have come the technological developments in audiovisual equipment and materials and computers. All of these elements combine to make it possible for each individual student's needs to be met in ways which were never possible before. It becomes possible for listening and viewing to be the preferred means of acquiring information. By the 1970s the major thrust in education became the movement toward individualized instruction. It then becomes imperative for students to have access to a great diversity of materials, both print and nonprint to meet their individual information and recreational needs. To meet these needs a comprehensive library media center is essential. The challenging question is, how can a school media center be organized, stocked, and staffed to most effectively meet the diverse needs of the users?

We have seen how libraries developed in response to the needs of a culture or of groups within a culture. There has now developed an entire field of study within library and information science that has to do with assessing the needs of the user. These studies use two approaches: one type of assessment is usually done by librarians and is concerned primarily with the library who uses it and for what purpose; another type of study is done by social scientists, usually psychologists and sociologists who look at user's information gathering habits, whether they use libraries or other sources. Usually included in these studies are the use of catalogs, reference services, circulation, browsing, and the use of library facilities. There also have been studies on the information gathering habits of the general public, the differences between users and non-users of the library, of scientists, and other specialists, assessing their knowledge of the library, its accessibility, and the attitude of the librarians toward them.

Bates has completed a selective review entitled *User Studies: A Review for Librarians and Information Scientists.*[5] This bibliographic essay describes and assesses empirical user need studies conducted from about 1930 to the present and provides a much needed comprehensive summary. A review of user studies reveals that there have been a very limited number of studies done in the school library setting, and then only as a part of a larger study. However, an evaluation of the methodology and design used in these studies would help to determine which would be most appropriate for future studies to be conducted in the school setting or in the educational environment. Although some of the findings of these studies might have relevance for the school media center, new studies are desperately needed. There are some distinct advantages in conducting user studies in the school settings, as the clientele is much more homogeneous, hours of use are controlled, and the objectives and goals of the users are probably less diversified.

Another approach to the problem has been developed by Dr. Edwin E. Olson in an instrument entitled "Questionnaire for Survey of Library User Service Policies".[6] His theory is that current practices in describing library user services rarely cover the full spectrum of services and do not delineate precise services in detail or with clarity. In addition, it is frequently difficult to evaluate the various internal operations of the library, those of selecting, acquiring, and organizing materials when there is so little information as to how much these technical procedures contribute to actually serving the user. Another weakness which Olson identifies is the overemphasis on assessing the quantities of resources or materials which he claims are only a rough index of the library's function. He stresses the assessment of specific services to users which means placing the emphasis on the *end* rather than on the *means*. The assessment instrument he has developed for evaluating libraries places an emphasis on *output* rather than on *input* (on services rather than on the storage of materials).

Olson's survey instrument employs a technique for evaluating the range and depth of library services to major user groups. It approaches the library from the user's viewpoint and classifies services according to the functions performed for the user, such as provision of materials, information, work space, with the entire spectrum of user services listed for assessment. The

[5] Marcia J. Bates, *User Studies: A Review for Librarians and Information Scientists* (Educational Resources Information Center [ERIC] ED 047738, 1971).

[6] Edwin E. Olson, "Questionnaire for Survey of Library User Service Policies" (College Park, Maryland: University of Maryland, 1969).

resulting data give a comprehensive picture of what a certain library does or does not offer its users, including any significant differences in its policies as related to different user groups. An additional feature of this tool is that each section can be analyzed through a weighting device which permits library staff or users to indicate those services which, according to user requirements, should be given priority in planning and financing.

Topics covered in this instrument are: access to materials, staff delivery, forms of request, requests when user is away, delivery when user is away, reservations and notifications, interruption of processing, subject collections, bookmobile service, facsimile copying, requests for facsimiles, translations, individual collections, check-out procedures, borrowing limitations, routing services, renewals, overdue notices, recall, return of loans, provision of materials not in the collection, requests, use of interlibrary loan materials, charges, verification of citations, subject searches, screening aids, alerting services, library as agent, answer services, advisory services, informal instruction, formal instruction, directional services, exhibits, group programs, program planning services, instruction services, organization of the library, work space, audiovisual materials, and user areas for special groups, working accessories, editing services, parking and transportation, babysitting, and identification of special user groups.

This instrument is being revised and adapted to be particularly appropriate for use with school library media centers.

Another approach has been developed by Johnson in a study entitled *A Feasibility Study for Establishing an Information Switching Center at Hamline University.*[7] The premise on which this study is based first identifies all the information needs of certain professors in teaching their classes and makes a parallel assessment of the information needs of students taking certain classes. Then a plan is developed for fulfilling these needs. An inventory of the needs of the professors and students is developed. Concomitantly, an inventory is made of the library's holdings which appropriately fulfill these needs. The switching center idea evolves from the need for identifying sources of information outside of the university library to fill the specified needs of the students and professors more adequately. The library serves as a switching center, or a link in an information chain, to identify other sources of information to fill the needs of the clients. These other sources could be public libraries, museums, special libraries, government agencies, school libraries— or any other available source of information. This plan holds great promise for school media centers since each aspect of the plan could readily be implemented and would surely be a significant move in the direction of more adequately fulfilling user needs.

[7] Herbert F. Johnson, Jack B. King and Anne S. Mavor, *A Feasibility Study for Establishing an Information Switching Center at Hamline University* (St. Paul, Minnesota, Hamline University, 1970), PB 192944 (available from National Technical Information Services, Springfield, Virginia).

Many educational institutions and commercial organizations have developed plans designed to provide individualized instruction. Some of these are packaged units of multi-media materials and some are computer based, accompanied by supplementary reading, viewing, and listening materials. One example of such an individualized learning system was PLAN devised by Westinghouse Learning Corporation. One major problem which evolved as the teaching-learning units were developed was the problem of locating both the print and nonprint materials that were needed. This is particularly difficult in the nonprint field, as bibliographic control has not developed adequately in this area to make it easy to retrieve materials. As a result, Westinghouse Learning Corporation has published *The Learning Directory,* a comprehensive listing of 200,000 items of both print and nonprint materials with basic information to aid in identifying and ordering. This is one first step in solving some of the problems related to retrieval of audio and visual materials.

Individual learning differences must be considered in the field of audiovisual materials. Educators appear to be in unanimous agreement that students learn according to different learning styles. Research in the audio and visual fields substantiates that some students learn better through listening, some through viewing, and some most effectively through reading. Much work had been done in the audiovisual field to determine the criteria for selecting a certain audiovisual medium for an individual student at a specific time under certain learning conditions. This problem is still unresolved. Research is being done at Oakland Community College in Michigan to identify the different learning styles of students.[8]

One of the most sophisticated and exciting developments in this area is the CBRU, Computer Based Resource Units for Special Educators. The headquarters is at State University College, Buffalo, New York. It is a procedure which has been developed to match teaching units to the specific needs of the users. These resource units are a collection of suggested learning activities and materials organized around specific objectives on a given topic which the teacher may use as help in preplanning a teaching unit. The use of the computer makes it possible to store and select for a given student or group of students all the subject matter, activities, materials, and evaluation devices related to a teaching objective. The computer serves as the storehouse of this information. The printout provided by the computer has to be adapted and used creatively by the teacher in the classroom environment.

In order for the computer to generate a Resource Guide the teacher must designate educational objectives since all resource materials are related to objectives. In any teaching-learning situation a teacher must have instructional objectives stated which indicate an expected behavior to be displayed by the student when the objective is achieved. Each CBRU contains a large number

[8] Derek N. Nunney and Joseph E. Hill, "Personalized Educational Programs," *Audiovisual Instruction,* Vol. 17, No. 2, Feb., 1972, pp. 10-15.

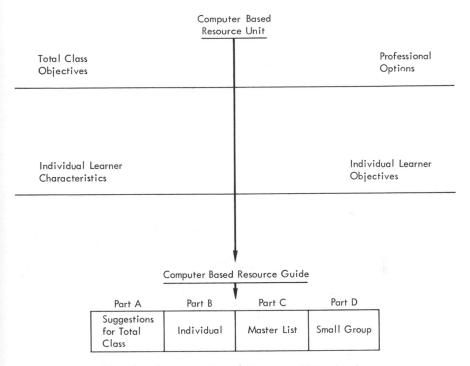

Figure 4-1   **The Computer Based Resource Unit: An Attempt to Meet User Needs** *

of behaviorally stated objectives. The teacher chooses up to five objectives from the master list and writes them in for each child in the class.

The next important input to the computer is the listing of variables from the pupil profile sheet. This consists of seven parts; general interests, occupational interest, sex, reading level, mental age, chronological age, and special considerations. The special considerations include physical handicaps, residential status, and learning environment.

A Computer Based Resource Unit consists of a great number of suggestions for instructional strategies. Each of these suggestions is coded to the objectives in that particular unit as well as to appropriate learner characteristics and professional variables.

This plan has great potential for future planning as it is a breakthrough combining the idea of individualized instruction and the objective of fulfilling user needs.

Another mechanism that has importance for media centers is SDI, or selective dissemination of information. This is a plan that functions very

* Used by permission of SUNY College at Buffalo, N.Y.

Research and Development Complex
State University College at Buffalo

COMPUTER-BASED RESOURCE GUIDE: REQUEST FORM

Unit Title_____

Unit Number _____

School Name_____

Address_____
       (street)   (city)   (state)   (zip)

PART A

Teacher's Name:_____   Group Objectives: _____
          (please print)

Class Mental Age Range: (Circle the consecutive numbers which best describe the M.A. Range of your class - typically a 4 - 5 year range)*

194-195-196-197-198-199-200-201-202-203-204-205-206-207-208-209-210-211-212-213-214-215-216-217-218

*See unit instructional variables for appropriate M.A. code numbers.

PART B

VARIABLE CATEGORIES

1 Student Name	2 Individual Objectives	3 Student Interests	4 Devel. Tasks	5 Reading Level	6 Age M.A. C.A.		7 Physical Handicaps	8 Learning Environment

INSTRUCTIONS FOR REQUESTING A COMPUTER BASED RESOURCE GUIDE:

A.   Necessary Materials:

1.   "Computer Based Resource Guide Request Form"
2.   Objectives List.
3.   Variables List for the unit being requested (found on reverse side of Objective List).

B.   Directions for completing the Request Form:

1.   Indicate complete mailing address.
2.   Indicate unit title and unit number.
3.   Part A: Group Request: After indicating "teacher's name", you may select from the objectives list as many as five (5) objectives which you plan to utilize with the entire class. Indicate the numbers of the "Group Objectives" selected on the lines provided. Utilizing the information indicated on the Variables List under "Mental Age", circle all of those numbers which would indicate the mental age range of the students in your class. In most cases, this would include at least 4 or 5 consecutive M.A.s.
4.   Part B: Individual Student Request: List in Column 1 identifier (first name or other designators, e.g. initials, student number) for each student in your class. For each student select one or two appropriate objectives from the Objectives List and indicate the number(s) of each objective in Column 2. The individual student objectives may be the same as those selected in Part A or they may be different.
5.   All variables categories are optional. You may provide in Columns 3 through 8 as much or as little information as you wish concerning student characteristics, keeping in mind that the information which you do provide for each student will serve to screen the activities, materials, and measuring devices which he or she will receive.
6.   Note the following additional instructions and suggestions:
    a.   In listing variables, use only code numbers taken from the Variables List. You need not fill in the same categories for each student.
    b.   If you plan to provide information related to Interests and/or Developmental Tasks, it is suggested that you indicate approximately 3 to 5 items in any combination of the two categories, i.e., 5 Interests or Developmental Tasks, 4 Interests and 1 Developmental Task, 3 Interests and 2 Developmental Tasks, etc.

Return completed forms to: Research and Development Complex-State University College-1300 Elmwood Avenue-Buffalo, N Y. 14222

COMPUTER-BASED RESOURCE UNITS DEVELOPED IN PART BY THE RESEARCH AND DEVELOPMENT COMPLEX STATE UNIVERSITY COLLEGE AT BUFFALO, N.Y. WITH FUNDING FROM THE N.Y. STATE EDUCATION DEPARTMENT AND THE U.S. OFFICE OF EDUCATION effectively for specialists in a variety of professional fields, particularly in special libraries. Clients of the library develop profiles of their special interests; the library staff identifies materials that are particularly relevant to those identified interests of the user. The materials are sometimes automatically sent to the client, or a notice is sent and the user comes to pick up the materials. This plan has been developed to a high degree of sophistication in some libraries and information centers. Some school media centers are using adaptations of SDI on a small scale.

All of these plans have potential for helping to solve problems of the future. With these capabilities of the computer it is certainly within the realm of feasibility to develop comprehensive profiles of individual students. It is also possible to develop data banks which are stored in computers which make materials and information easily accessible through their retrieval systems. It is also possible to establish computer based switching systems—to inform the user as to where certain information is available, such as at a museum.

Even though the emphasis on meeting individual user needs appears to be somewhat visionary now, the extensive use of computers, two-way cable television, the innovative use of the switching center concept, and SDI (selective dissemination of information) systems will make it a reality probably much sooner than most of us anticipate.

REFERENCES

BATES, MARCIA J. *User Studies: A Review for Librarians and Information Scientists.* Educational Resources Information Center [ERIC] ED 047738, 1971.

GATES, JEAN KEY. *Introduction to Librarianship.* New York: McGraw-Hill, 1968.

JOHNSON, HERBERT F., JACK B. KING and ANNE S. MAVOR. *A Feasibility Study for Establishing an Information Switching Center at Hamline University.* St. Paul, Minnesota: Hamline University, 1970, PB 192944 (available from National Technical Information Services, Springfield, Virginia.)

"Libraries." *Collier's Encyclopedia,* vol. 14, 558. New York: Crowell-Collier Educational Corporation.

OLSON, EDWIN E. "Questionnaire for Survey of Library User Service Policies." College Park, Maryland: University of Maryland, 1969.

NUNNEY, DEREK N., and JOSEPH E. HILL. "Personalized Educational Programs," *Audiovisual Instruction* 17 (February, 1972): 10-15.

The Story of Our Libraries. New York: Crowell-Collier Educational Corporation, 1969.

5 Functions— What and Why?

Media professionals are generalists and specialists. They are supported by technicians and aides. Together they perform thousands of tasks which can be clustered into ten functional areas: organization management, personnel management, design, information retrieval, logistics, production, instruction, evaluation, research and utilization. Academic programs for preparation of media personnel exist at several levels depending on the amount of responsibility expected.

There are literally thousands of tasks performed in a media center regardless of the number of personnel or the size of the program. A task is a logically related set of actions which involves data, people, and things. Tasks have been observed, recorded, and classified by the Jobs in Instructional Media Study (JIMS) [1] and the School Library Manpower Project (SLMP). [2]

Procedures for defining tasks have been developed by the United States Department of Labor using a technique called Functional Job Analysis. Functional Job Analysis was modified for the Jobs in Instruction Media Study which actually observed 110 media personnel on the job in 55 locations [3] to determine what the worker does and what gets done. All tasks observed were related to data, people, or things. "In performing any task, the worker usually deals with all three of these areas—Data, People and

[1] C. James Wallington et. al., *Jobs in Instructional Media,* Washington, D.C.: Department of Audiovisual Instruction, 1971.

[2] *School Library Personnel Task Analysis Survey,* Chicago: American Library Association, 1969.

[3] C. James Wallington et. al. *Jobs in Instructional Media,* p. 20.

Things. However, in *most* tasks the emphasis is only on one orientation—either towards Data *or* People *or* Things. . . . Some examples of tasks and their orientation follow.

Writing an article or a budget is primarily oriented toward Data. Things (pencil, paper) may be involved as may People (who give instructions about the article) but the emphasis of the task is upon Data.

Persuading a teacher to use an overhead projector is basically a People-oriented task although Data (information about the overhead projector) and Things (the overhead projector itself) may be involved.

Once tasks have been classified according to Data, People or Things, they can be further classified as to *how complex they are.*[4] Figure 5-1 outlines the

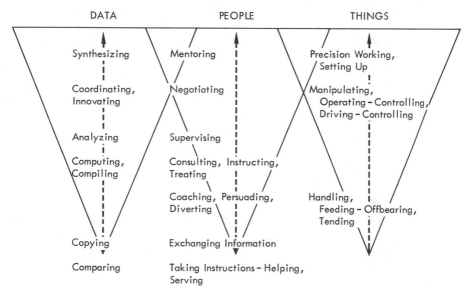

Note: Each successive function reading down usually or typically involves all those that follow it. The functions separated by a comma are separate functions on the same level separately defined. They are on the same level because empirical evidence does not make a hierarchical distinction clear.

The hyphenated functions: *Taking Instructions-Helping, Operating-Controlling, Driving-Controlling,* and *Feeding-Offbearing* are single functions.

Setting Up, Operating-Controlling, Driving-Controlling, Feeding-Offbearing, and *Tending* are special cases involving machines and equipment of *Precision Working, Manipulating,* and *Handling,* respectively, and hence are indented under them.

Figure 5-1   Summary Chart of Worker Function Scales

[4] Freda D. Bernotovicz and Jim Wallington, "Act I of JIMS," *Audiovisual Instruction* (May, 1970): 26-27.

levels of complexity for each orientation—Data, People and Things. The arrow from its shaft to its tip, demonstrates increasing complexity. Figure 5-1 is a summary of the scales developed for each orientation.[5]

FUNCTION

The logical procedure for handling large quantities of data about jobs is to group related tasks into categories which are sufficiently inclusive to accommodate a large number of tasks yet exclusive enough to distinguish one cluster of tasks from another. The term *function* seems to be most appropriate for this purpose. Throughout this book we use the term *function* to mean the cluster of closely related activities which relate to a single unifying idea. Functions are performed in a media program by the various members of the staff regardless of level.

It is important to note that functions are neither jobs nor people. It is only when the tasks within several functions are combined that job roles or people can be defined. Elliott describes the concept in this fashion:

> An individual holds a job, and a job is composed of a set of inter-related functions. The concept of "function" was developed by the United States Department of Labor in order to classify what people actually do on the job because job titles tend to be somewhat inaccurate as descriptors of activity. For example, the term instructional technologist sheds little light on what a person really does. He could run an instructional television studio, be in charge of audiovisual services for a school district, or serve as the graphic artist for a team of instructional developers. "Function" is used to refer to a group of interrelated activities engaged in by an instructional technologist in order to obtain a particular outcome or purpose. Seldom, if ever, is a job composed entirely of one function.[6]

Functions can be used as organizing concepts with which to group tasks and thus serve as guidelines to: (1) plan curricula for the media profession, (2) help develop certification requirements, (3) serve as the basis for competency statements and (4) prepare job descriptions.

In the previous chapter we learned of the ten functions which serve as points of departure in this book. Since this concept is so basic to the re-

---

[5] Sidney A. Fine and Wretha W. Wiley, *An Introduction to Functional Job Analysis,* Kalamazoo, Mich.: The W. E. Upjohn Institute for Employment Research, 1971, p. 31.

[6] Paul H. Elliott, "The Logistics Function in Instructional Technology," *Audiovisual Instruction* 18 (March, 1973): 74.

mainder of the book, it seems worthwhile to explore one function a little further as an example of how all the functions can be analyzed and used.

The Logistics Function: An Example

This function is described as the acquisition, storage, retrieval, distribution, and maintenance of information in all formats. It involves all those activities which support the media program. Three levels of tasks, all part of the logistics function, are shown below:

AN AIDE

Operates spirit duplicator to produce duplicated copies
Operates tape recorder to check on reported defect
Makes list of schedule cards to compile inventory
Logs in materials to have record of return [7]

A TECHNICIAN

Discusses with client to clarify details of assignment
Writes equipment specifications to equip closed circuit TV studio
Inspects audiovisual equipment to determine readiness for use
Locates information to order preview materials [8]

A MEDIA PROFESSIONAL

Reads curriculum guides to classify materials in curriculum areas
Analyzes usage figures to project equipment needs
Confers with teachers to determine needs and objectives
Designs new forms to improve record keeping [9]

Uses of Functions

None of the tasks described thus far, at whatever level, are sufficient for the description of one job or one person. They describe a variety of activities carried out at a particular level. It may be that some tasks, which are considered to be appropriate at the aide or technician levels, may in some cases be done by the media professional simply because they need to be done and no one is available for the job. If a media professional realizes that an inordinate amount of time is being spent on tasks in the logistics function which ought to be done by aides and technicians, steps should be taken to recruit such personnel on a paid or volunteer basis.

Another use of the functions and tasks is to develop statements of

[7] C. James Wallington et. al., *Jobs in Instructional Media Study* p. 239.
[8] Ibid. pp. 238, 245, 254.
[9] C. James Wallington, *Guidelines for Certification of Media Specialists,* p. 56.

competency. As specific tasks to be performed are named, the use of behavioral language helps to turn a task statement into a competency. For example, a media professional usually decides how all media should be physically stored. To be able to make this decision (perform this task), the media professional must be able to describe the alternative types of media storage components and, using established criteria, select the best storage for that particular center.

The media professional will have to develop a training program for new aides who perform logistic tasks. In order to do this, it will be necessary to list the tasks which need to be performed and the competencies required to adequately do each task. This list of tasks can be reviewed in existing studies [10, 11, 12] or might be generated locally by observing present activities of the staff, conferring with the staff regarding their perceptions of the job, or by a combination of all three procedures.

The difficult aspect of transferring tasks and functions to job descriptions is that the tasks do not always fit neatly into one function. Consequently, when there is a job which is largely composed of tasks in the logistics function, there may be several other tasks which come from the functions of production, organization management, and selection.

The utility of the functional approach to media center operations is that it provides an organizing concept for looking at what gets done and what the worker does.

At first glance, the two viewpoints might seem identical but they can be quite different. For an example, consider a task such as 'makes a photographic print.' From one point of view, 'what gets done,' this is an acceptable task statement. In terms of what the worker did, it is not acceptable. Did the worker operate an enlarger? Did he put the film in a contact frame? Did he operate an automatic stabilization processor to make the print? Or did he develop it by inspection? The statement 'makes a photographic print' does not tell us what the worker does. And if there is vagueness about what the worker is to learn to do, there cannot be a specific curriculum which can be expected to teach competencies.[13]

The ten categories offer a starting point for describing jobs and competencies which fall *primarily* in one category or another. It is highly likely that a

[10] C. James Wallington et. al. *Jobs in Instructional Media Study,* pp. 237-277.
[11] *Guidelines for Certification of Media Specialists,* pp. 45-58.
[12] *School Library Personnel Task Analysis Survey,* pp. 19-84.
[13] Freda D. Bernotavicz and C. James Wallington, "Act I of JIMS," *Audiovisual Instruction,* 18 (May, 1970): 26.

person will perform most of his job within one or two functional areas even though tasks from other functions will be included in the total job role. The head of a media center will have most of the tasks derived from the Personnel Management and Organization Management functions but will certainly have to possess competencies in the other functional areas if only to properly supervise the personnel who actually perform other tasks.

Functions Performed by a Media Professional

What does a media professional do? To properly answer this question we must consider the differences between a *specialist* and a *generalist*. The specialist will most likely perform one function in depth while the generalist will have competencies in all functions, but none in sufficient depth to be a specialist. Figures 5-2 and 5-3 illustrate this difference.

THE MEDIA SPECIALIST   This individual has chosen to specialize in one aspect of the media field which means that one function will dominate and others will be secondary. For example, the producer or director of television

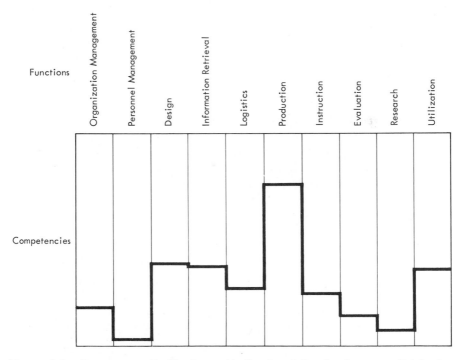

Figure 5-2 Competency Profile for a Media Specialist Serving as a Production Supervisor

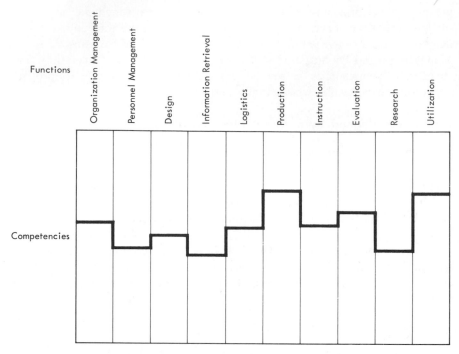

Figure 5-3 Competency Profile for a Media Generalist Serving as a Director of an Instructional Materials Center

for a school system should have developed extensive competencies in *production*. There are hundreds of tasks which make up the competency statements in the production function, including some that relate to the production of graphic materials, photography, film, and audio components. In addition to the primary function, a TV producer-director would be expected to have competencies in *design* (to determine how TV is part of the larger plan of instruction), in *evaluation* (to select existing materials for use on TV and to assess the impact of TV productions), in *utilization* (to help teachers and learners to achieve their objectives in an optimum fashion) and in *instruction* (to communicate information about using TV). To a lesser extent competencies may be needed in *management* (to organize a TV operation and to supervise personnel) and *logistics* (to distribute TV signals to requested locations on time). Perhaps minimal competencies would be required in *research* (to understand the results of TV research) and *information retrieval* (to assist in classifying film clips and videotapes).

This case study illustrates the idiosyncratic nature of each media professional. The competencies of a professional and the classification of these competencies into the ten functional areas are unique for each individual. No two people have had exactly the same education and experience and even if this were the case, the ability to perform would vary from individual to individual.

By the same token, no professional position is so specific that all competencies will be spelled out in detail. This is where functional areas take on a more important descriptive role. A school or college seeking a television producer-director will most likely look for a person with education and experience in the production function, specifically TV production. In seeking such a person the employer usually assumes some competencies in the other functions and may even spell out those which are desired by certain specifications in the job description, e.g., "must be able to supervise a technical staff of three"; "must be able to work with teachers in preparing and using locally produced television"; and "must be able to justify the TV program to the community."

Employment of an individual in a professional position is usually the result of the best "match" between competencies the individual has demonstrated (or believes he/she possesses) and the expectations an employer has stated in terms of functions. In almost every case an adjustment between the media professional and the position is necessary. There will be certain aspects of a job which an individual cannot do but, because they are part of the performance expectations, they will be learned through some type of formal or informal training program. But adjustment works two ways. The employer often does not find an individual who fulfills every expectation and therefore settles on a person who most closely fits the original job description. At this point the employer decides whether the missing competencies are sufficiently important to make additional training a condition of employment or to accept the individual as is. In rare cases an individual can persuade a prospective employer to change the job description to meet the particular competencies of that person. The concept of functions serves as a reference point from which positions are described and training programs are designed.

Actual job descriptions from schools and colleges seeking media specialists indicate the nature of expectations and, to some extent, the competencies required. Note the dominant function in each description.

WANTED: MEDIA DESIGNER (in a state education department) To design formats of instructional modules, detail major points and general interpretation of curriculum content; act as liaison between instructional designers and script writers. Experience in media evaluation

—emphasis on materials design; proficiency in writing and in organization of materials.

WANTED: MEDIA PRODUCER (in a district media center)
To assist faculty in the planning, production and implementation of self-instructional audiovisual resources. More specifically: (1) prepare behavioral objectives; (2) prepare instructional specifications in accordance with established objectives; (3) plan and prepare production scripts in programmed format; (4) specify all graphic visuals (to be prepared by a graphic artist); (5) supervise the productions (may take the form of video or audio tape, still and motion pictures, photography, etc.); (6) field test resources for validity; and (7) prepare evaluations and required reports.

WANTED: FILM LIBRARIAN (in a regional education center)
To select and evaluate titles to be added to an existing film collection in cooperation with selection committees in the schools; to publish an annual catalog and to keep teachers posted on current additions to the collection. This person will supervise a staff of film bookers, inspectors and shipping personnel; will be responsible for the preparation and operation of a budget; and will serve on the curriculum planning board.

THE MEDIA GENERALIST   This person needs to know something about many things. Some competencies in all functions should be within the repertoire of the media generalist. Since this is the person who usually directs the media program, extensive competencies in the *management* functions are required. The tasks which make up the management functions are concerned with organization and operation of the media program and supervision of personnel. Many activities are not specific to media programs but are generic to administration. Some formal training and experience outside the media field is probably an asset to anyone who aspires to direct a media program. Beyond the management function, the other functions will dominate depending on the emphasis of the program. If there is a strong commitment to providing a full range of resources to users, competencies in *information retrieval, logistics, instruction, evaluation* and *utilization* will be highlighted. If there is an emphasis on instructional development within a curriculum context, there will be more demand for competencies in *design, production, evaluation* and *research*. In each case, however, competencies in *all* functions are required.

The demands on the media generalist would appear to be rather extensive. The required broadness raises several questions: *Why* does the media generalist need to know something about everything? *How extensive* must knowledge of each function be? *What type of academic program* would best prepare an individual to serve as a media generalist?

1. *Why?* There are literally thousands of tasks which must be performed in a media program. Whether the staff is composed of one person or a staff of several dozen these tasks must be done. If only one person is available, that person is responsible for the full range of activities and consequently must be able to perform most of the tasks at some minimal level. If there is a staff, paid or volunteer, full-time or part-time, the director must write the job descriptions, hire the personnel (and fire them when necessary), supervise their activities, train them in local procedures, and make plans for continuing growth and development of the staff. Unless there is a basic familiarity with all the job functions and many of the tasks, much of the staff performance cannot be adequately guided and evaluated.

2. *How extensive?* A good rule of thumb is that a media professional ought to know enough about each function to evaluate the adequacy of performance when done by someone else. The director of a media program has to assign responsibilities to other individuals. In doing so he/she must be able to state specifically what is expected of each person in each position. Such job specifications must be realistic and feasible. If the professional does not have sufficient knowledge regarding the nature of the tasks to be performed, there is little likelihood that the individual staff member can meet job expectations. Sometimes, through fortunate coincidences, an employee is especially perceptive and can determine an employer's wishes with minimal guidance or can steer the job to meet his/her competencies. For comprehensive preparation, a media professional should be able to demonstrate competencies in one of three ways:

a. The media professional should be able to perform the competency and usually does;
b. The media professional should be able to perform the competency but usually assigns the tasks to someone else; and
c. The media professional should be able to describe what tasks need to be done, but usually cannot perform the tasks.

To illustrate the differences among these three operations, let's look at a media generalist on the job. A teacher asks to see someone in the media center about selecting materials which could be used in a forthcoming unit. The media generalist is the initial point of contact. The first meeting is spent probing the objectives of the unit, the content area and special emphases, and matters pertaining to the students' sophistication and readiness. (This media generalist believes that this should be the first contact. The media generalist has competencies which permit identification of the problem and the ability to come up with alternate solutions.) The media generalist then asks for lists of materials—in all media formats—to be developed for review by the teacher. (The media generalist could have developed the list of materials, but this person preferred to use a staff member who was assigned this responsibility.)

The media generalist is the initial point of contact for a teacher seeking assistance.

A check with the graphic artist is made to determine availability of time should it be necessary to create special materials. Later it is determined that a series of overhead transparencies should be prepared by the graphic artist. (The media generalist was able to describe what was needed but could not easily do the design and production of the transparencies with a professional touch.)

The extent of knowledge regarding each function will vary from individual to individual. There is no agreement at the present time as to a "core" content for all professionals. Although there is agreement on the ten functions, further delineation of tasks within each function are more difficult to agree upon. Each chapter on each function will spell out the major competencies included in that area. It will be up to the reader to determine the level of competency (or incompetency, if the Peter Principle [14] is followed) he/she

[14] Lawrence J. Peter, *The Peter Principle* (New York: William Morrow and Co., 1969). Dr. Peter studied the competence-incompetence phenomenon which led to the formulation of the Peter Principle: *In a hierarchy every employee tends to rise to his level of incompetence.*

wishes to attain. Further guidance can be obtained from media faculty and practitioners in the field.

3. *What type of academic program?* The media generalist requires broad academic preparation. Ideally, each person seeking to serve in the field should possess some background in each function. Below are possible academic areas for study and experience possibilities within each function:

Logistics—the mechanics of acquisition, storage, retrieval, distribution, and maintenance of information in all formats. Courses in "administration of media programs," "data processing," (used as a management tool) and "information handling" should provide sufficient background for the media generalist. In addition, experience at the service desk of any type of a library or a media center would aid in gaining specific knowledge about the various logistics tasks.

Information Retrieval—to organize knowledge and to order information in all formats in a systematic fashion for the purpose of making the information accessible to the user. Courses in "classification," "cataloging," "fundamentals of documentation," "development of thesauri," and "development of indexing languages" would help an individual to gain competencies in this area. Persons who work in a technical processing center, such as those who type catalog cards or file the completed cards, often gain some understanding of the cataloging process through observation and constant exposure to the practices and procedures.

Design—the development of a plan for teaching and learning which takes into account as many variables as possible and orders them in a systematic fashion. There are courses in "instructional systems," "instructional design," and "instructional development" which come closest to the competencies in this area. In some cases courses in "curriculum development" might be appropriate. In some institutions there are courses in individualized instruction or in the preparation of learning modules which would relate to this function. Experience in design can be gained only by doing it. Such experience can be acquired through personal trial-and-error or by association with an instructional development team in a school, school district or a college. Design always has to have a context of operation and therefore can be done only in relation to content and objectives which have been determined.[15]

Production—the design and creation of an instructional product. For a general production background, courses in "instructional graphics" or "preparation of teaching materials" usually provide an overview of several production processes. A course in "message design" would focus on the

---

[15] Vernon S. Gerlach and Donald P. Ely, *Teaching and Media: A Systematic Approach.* (Englewood Cliffs, N.J.: Prentice-Hall, 1971), Chapter 1.

development of specific instructional products to be used within an instructional system. A basic course in "still photography" is an essential since it is the basis for all other photography including motion picture and television production. The use of lenses, lighting, and related equipment applies to several types of production. Courses in other production areas include "television," "radio," "publications design," "programmed instruction," and "computer-assisted instruction." It is not difficult to gain experience in the production area since materials and equipment are often inexpensive. Opportunities to work in radio, television, film, and still photography exist on nearly every college campus. Production competencies are skills needed to accomplish larger educational goals and the production specialist must be cautioned not to get involved in the specifics of making things while losing the broader perspective of attaining learning objectives.

Evaluation—to examine and judge the worth, quality and significance of specific media and programs of instruction. To gain competencies in evaluating media there are courses in the "selection and evaluation of media"—books, films, records, filmstrips, and others. Courses in "literary criticism" and "criticism of mass media" should be considered as useful and substantive dimensions to the evaluation function. Individuals can join evaluation committees and participate in the process. Reviews in the periodical literature can be compared with personal assessments of films, TV programs and plays seen. Book reviews can be compared with personal judgments.

A second facet of evaluation is a more comprehensive assessment of larger segments of instruction—a class session, a unit, a course, a curriculum. This type of evaluation requires a different order of skills usually gained from courses in "evaluation of instruction" or "program evaluation." Experience is gained slowly and painfully by working on a one-to-one basis with a master evaluator. Evaluations of instruction can be seen in the publications developed by students in colleges and universities which essentially report student opinions of courses taught. Evaluation of accreditation teams which review specific academic programs (such as the American Library Association's accreditation process) and entire institutions (such as the North Central Association and other regional bodies) are often made available at each institution. Reviewing these documents provides some insight into the evaluative process as done by others.

Management (Organization and Personnel)—to plan, establish and maintain policies and procedures for the operation of a media service; to hire, interact with, and supervise the media services personnel. Courses in the "administration of media programs" should provide some specific assistance with problems and issues peculiar to media center management. More general competencies could be acquired through courses in educational administration, business management, public administration, and administrative engineering. However, be sure to check the content and objectives of these courses before enrolling in them. Field work and internship opportunities provide some of the best experience in the management area. There are many aspects of management that cannot be learned in the classroom and theories which make sense intellectually often seem inappropriate in the real world.

Since the media generalist is most likely to need more competencies in the management function than any other function, the field work and internship is an essential component of the professional program. Just as student teaching is required of all persons preparing to teach, so should a media generalist be required to demonstrate those management competencies which can best be acquired from a formal period of internship.

Utilization—to employ media for the purpose of achieving individual objectives. Courses in the "selection and use of instructional media," "foundations of instructional technology," and, occasionally, "audiovisual materials in teaching" are found in departments or colleges of education. The emphasis is on the use of media to enhance learning. There are courses such as "survey of nonbook media" and "audiovisual materials in libraries" which are offered by library departments and schools which may help to prepare for the utilization function. Supporting work in learning and learning theory in departments of educational psychology offer major assistance in this area. To gain experience in utilization, one must do some teaching. It may be that the media professional has prepared to teach and has gained classroom teaching experience prior to graduate study in media. For those who have not had this type of experience, there are opportunities to serve as a teacher aide or assistant. Observation of teaching is also possible. This may occur prior to employment in the media field or after beginning in a new position. The reason for stressing academic preparation and experience in utilization is that this is the ultimate purpose and context for media. If all other functions are operating at peak efficiency and utilization is neglected, all the effort is for nothing. Unless the staff and resources of the media program facilitate learning and help each student achieve the objectives which the individual and the teacher have established, it is difficult to justify a program.

Instruction—the process of communicating information to defined audiences. To gain competencies in instruction, courses in "communication," "public relations," "general teaching methods," and "advertising" might be considered. The essential thrust of this function is to reach users and potential users of media with useful information. The purpose of the information may be to motivate individuals to use services, to assist users in locating and using resources, or to report on services rendered. Experience comes from helping media professionals with instructional tasks such as preparing news releases for publications, writing for internal newsletters, and creating a display within the school building. Conducting a media center orientation program and training student projectionists would be additional ways to gain experience in the instructional function.

Research—the process of generating and testing theory. A media generalist ought to be able to read and understand research reports and, on occasion, design research studies which are appropriate within the context of the job. To acquire competencies in this area, courses in "research methods" or "introduction to research in libraries" or "educational research" should provide the basic research competencies. Serving as a research assistant to a professor who is doing research or performing small pilot research studies would yield useful experience. Browsing through research journals such as *AV Communication Review* and the *British Journal of Educational Technology* would provide some insight into this function.

The reason for the broadness of professional preparation can be readily seen in the job descriptions for media generalists which are sent to placement offices. The term "media generalist" is seldom used, but the desire for a broad professional background with emphasis in management is clearly evident. The following example is taken from actual job descriptions listed with a placement service.

> WANTED: DIRECTOR OF MEDIA SERVICES (in a school system). . . . It will be the responsibility of the Director to provide leadership in melding library and instructional resources policy, and to coordinate the development and expansion of normal library services with radio and television production (all phases), instructional materials (audiovisual equipment use, purchase, service and maintenance), Film Rental Library, and self-instruction laboratories. The position requires supervision and evaluation of the professional and clerical staff and serving on various district committees.

FROM FUNCTIONS TO COMPETENCIES

Up to this point we have been exploring the role and functions of media personnel, especially the media generalist. We have seen a new setting —a new environment—in which media programs will operate in the near future. We have documented the tasks and functions which are performed by the media professional and his staff. Our concern has been with what gets done within the school media center and not so much with who does it. Our position has been that there are certain tasks which must get done and that these tasks can be clustered and labeled as functions. There is a staff of individuals, each of whom possesses certain competencies. The staff should be organized in such a way that tasks of less complexity are handled by aides, tasks requiring specialized training should be the responsibility of technicians, and some distinctive tasks should be handled by media specialists. Media generalists have the broad overview and usually manage the enterprise.

We must now turn our attention to the competencies required by media professionals and explore the relationship between the users and the media professional. The user is, after all, the *raison d'etre* for the media program and, therefore, special care and attention should be devoted to this all important human being. In focusing on the user, it seems appropriate to consider the competencies which media professionals must possess in order to adequately meet the needs of users. First, we must understand what is meant by competencies and how they can be acquired and measured. Then, we can look at the competencies required for each function.

REFERENCES

CASE, ROBERT M. and ANNA MARY LOWREY. *Behavioral Requirements Analysis Checklist,* pp. 3-53. Chicago: American Library Association, 1973.

ELLIOTT, PAUL H. "The Logistics Function in Instructional Technology." *Audiovisual Instruction* 18 (March, 1973): 74.

FINE, SIDNEY A. and WRETHA WILEY. *An Introduction to Functional Job Analysis.* Kalamazoo, Mich.: The W. E. Upjohn Institute for Employment Research, 1971.

Guidelines for Certification of Media Specialists (Extended Version), pp. 45-58. Washington, D.C.: Association for Educational Communication and Technology, 1972.

HAMREUS, DALE G. (ed.) *Media Guidelines,* Part 3. Monmouth, Oregon: Teaching Research, 1970.

WALLINGTON, C. JAMES et al. *Jobs in Instructional Media,* pp. 56-173. Washington, D.C.: Association for Educational Communication and Technology, 1971.

6 Assessment of Competencies

The increasing use of competency-based programs in teacher education has led to the use of this concept in related fields such as the media profession. Competencies required for media professionals can be identified, acquired, and assessed. The approach followed in this book is based on competency. The competencies can be acquired in a variety of ways and can be measured for the purpose of certification.

Throughout this book we will be focusing on competencies. Competence means "adequacy for a task"—the possession of necessary knowledge, skills and attitudes to achieve an acceptable level of performance. A series of competencies have been derived for each function. Each competency, in turn, is composed of several tasks. A graphic representation of the conceptual organization is seen in Figure 6-1.

WHY COMPETENCIES?

There is much talk and activity today in educational circles regarding competency-based professional education whether it be for teachers, school administrators or media professionals. The move toward competency-based (or performance-based) programs is a direct outgrowth of the accountability movement in the United States. Parents and the public want to be certain that the schools are achieving what they say they are; school administrators want to know that their teachers have certain knowledge, skills, and attitudes and are applying them in the classroom; students who are preparing to teach want to be certain that they graduate with the necessary knowledge, skills,

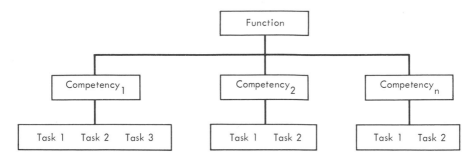

Figure 6-1   Relationships Between Function and Competency and Between
Competency and Tasks

and attitudes to perform well in their first position. This press toward specificity and need for evidence has given rise to the competency-based movement. State education departments have joined the movement and are establishing competency-based requirements for teacher (and administrator) certification in many states. In the media field, competency-based certification requirements are established or are being considered in North Carolina, Maryland, Alabama, New York, Utah, Oregon, and Georgia.

The attraction of competency-based programs is that performance objectives are specified and agreed upon in rigorous detail before the learning process begins. The individual who is preparing to be a media professional must be able to demonstrate the ability to perform each competency. The individual is held accountable not for passing grades but for attaining a specified level of competency in performing the essential tasks in each function of the media field. The institution which prepares media professionals is held accountable for preparing professionals who can demonstrate the competencies required for a wide variety of positions in the field. The individual and the institution must "prove" competence by evidence that the graduate of the program can do certain things. The emphasis is on a demonstrated product or output.

There are several advantages of competency-based programs for the preparation of media professionals. Among the most promising are its attention to individual abilities and needs; its focus on objectives; its emphasis on the process by which program goals and objectives are formulated and used as the basis of evaluation; its efficiency, enhanced by the use of appropriate technology; and its accountability features.

The media field seems to be a strong candidate for using a competency-based concept in its professional education programs, in its certification processes, and in its continued self-evaluation.

ESSENTIAL ELEMENTS

The bulk of the work in the competency-based movement has been accomplished in the field of teacher education. It is appropriate, therefore, that we look to that literature to discover the characteristics which are common to most competency-based programs. These characteristics are summarized in a useful pamphlet, *A Résumé of Performance-Based Teacher Education:* [1]

1. Competencies (knowledge, skills, behaviors) to be demonstrated by the student are derived from explicit conceptions of teacher roles, stated so as to make possible assessment of a student's behavior in relation to specific competencies, and made public in advance.
2. Criteria to be employed in assessing competencies are based upon, and in harmony with, specified competencies; explicit in stating expected levels of mastery under specified conditions; and made public in advance.
3. The student's rate of progress through the program is determined by demonstrated competency rather than by time or course completion.
4. The instructional program is intended to facilitate the development and evaluation of the student's achievement of competencies specified.

There appear to be two additional characteristics which are related to the above list: (1) most programs are personalized in ways that take into consideration the needs of the learner; and (2) media are often part of competency-based programs. These two factors are somewhat interrelated. Media may be used as an alternative means of learning. Such alternatives are, in fact, individualized and personalized. While media is not essential to competency-based programs, they are employed to facilitate personalization. [2]

Two Views of Competency

There are two major approaches being taken in contemporary competency-based programs. The first is a highly behavioristic approach with emphasis on planning curricula on the basis of well-defined, specifically stated, behavioral objectives. These behavioral objectives would relate to the task statements shown in Figure 6-1. There may be subtasks in some programs

[1] Stanley Elam, *A Résumé of Performance-Based Teacher Education* (Washington, D.C.: American Association of Colleges for Teacher Education, 1972), p. 4.
[2] Gaston Pol Paccieri, *Competence Required for the Principalship: A Methodology Applied to the Urban Education Setting* (Unpublished doctoral dissertation, University of Utah, 1973), p. 16.

which attempt to be highly specific and delineate almost every activity performed by a professional. The second approach recognizes the importance of defining and measuring performance, but bases its educational program on the broader view of competence as a larger entity. This approach includes the totality of qualities needed to adequately function in a professional role. The competency statements in Figure 6-1 would be an example of this approach.

The authors of this book have chosen to emphasize the second approach. In essence, each competency statement throughout this book is a cluster of tasks which are amalgamated to form one competency statement. It is still possible to measure the performance, but perhaps without some of the precision of the purely behavioral approach. The authors felt that attempts to measure each task would be self-defeating because of their specificity and because the information load would be unnecessarily excessive.

In order to blend tasks into competency statements, the tasks gathered by the Jobs in Instructional Media Study (JIMS) and the tasks discovered in the School Library Manpower Project (SLMP) were used. Each of these studies did a careful analysis of tasks performed by media professionals (generalists and specialists), technicians, and aides.

Components of Competency

There appear to be three broad components in any competency-based program: (1) knowledge; (2) skills; and (3) attitudes. The three components appear simultaneously and are interactive. It is difficult to separate the three elements in actual settings but for the purposes of discussion here, each component is discussed separately.

KNOWLEDGE   This is the body of facts and information that is required of each media professional in order to operate on a day-to-day basis. Knowledge, in this case, is a tool for performing on the job. There are some facts which always ought to be available on recall. To look them up every time the occasion demands would be highly inefficient and frustrating. While a premium is not placed on knowledge for its own sake in competency-based programs, it is a vital part of the total educational effort. Knowledge is seen as a facilitating or enabling tool to assist the media professional to function in an efficient and effective manner. Knowledge is fairly easy to measure; indeed, it has been the mainstay of most professional programs over the years. The next thrust is to consider knowledge as only one prerequisite element to performance.

SKILLS   The word, "skill" implies the ability to do something. Most frequently it is the application of knowledge to solve a particular problem.

The ability to do something which can be observed and judged by another person is performance of a skill. The media field is highly skill oriented. One look at most of the functions in this book suggest a host of skills: logistics, management, production, evaluation, etc. The measurement of a skill is accomplished by observing a performance or the product of a performance. In some cases it is possible for an individual to judge his/her own performance. In most competency-based programs, an outside evaluator makes the judgment. Even better is the agreement of two or more persons that the trainee has indeed achieved the competency as stated according to the criteria for judgment which have been adopted.

ATTITUDES   It is much more difficult to determine the attitude which one holds. Attitudes have to do with feelings and approach or avoidance tendencies. It is sometimes possible to infer a person's attitude by watching performance over a long period of time. Attitudes also are sometimes expressed overtly in statements made during conversations. In most cases the evaluation of attitudes is a subjective act which is often colored by the person who is observing. Even with this difficulty in judging the nature and extent of a media professional's attitude, it must be considered as an important dimension of the competency-based program.

Components of Judgment

Some mention has already been made of judging the three components of competency. Without the ability to judge performance, the competency-based movement would not be possible. After all, what good is a competency statement if it cannot be assessed? The nature of the assessment is, therefore, a critical task. It should be approached with some care.

Schalock points out the differences among measurement, evaluation and assessment. He proposes that "measurement refers to the assignment of numerals to objects or events according to rules . . ." and "evaluation refers to the assignment of worth or value to objects and events according to standards. . . ." [3]

The term, assessment, according to Schalock, should be used "to refer to the identification, collection, reduction, analysis and use of information in service of targeted, adaptive decision making." [4] In this context, the term

---

[3] H. D. Schalock. "Notes On A Model of Assessment That Meets The Requirements of Competency Based Teacher Education." In W. Robert Houston (ed.), *Exploring Competency Based Education* (Berkeley, Calif.: McCutchen Publishing Co., 1974), p. 212. Reprinted by permission of the publisher.
[4] Ibid.

assessment becomes more inclusive than either measurement or evaluation. In regard to the use of these terms in a competency-based teacher education (CBTE) program, Schalock notes:

> Two requirements of CBTE programs encourage the view of assessment as a targeted, decision serving information system: (1) the requirement that designated teaching competencies be demonstrated as a basis for graduation from a teacher education program and (2) the requirement that a program be continuously adapted, updated, or "renewed" on the basis of information on cost and effectiveness. Both requirements depend upon data to be collected (measurement), judgments to be made in relation to standards held (evaluation) and utilization of the information generated through measurement and evaluation in adaptive decision-making (assessment).[5]

These three components of judgment can be used in relation to programs for the preparation of media professionals. When judging the performance of a competency, data must be collected—often using instruments that employ scales for judgment or other numerical or check-off procedures. This is the *measurement component*. Data thus collected must be analyzed by comparing them to criteria or standards which have been previously established. This is *evaluation*. The combined use of collected and analyzed data permits decisions to be made based on the interpretation of those data for a specific purpose. This is *assessment*. The important outcome here, regardless of how the labels are used, is a decision as to whether or not an individual has performed satisfactorily and to acknowledge that competency has been completely achieved or achieved to some degree. Without this activity, competency-based programs are hollow exercises.

COMPETENCY AS USED IN THIS BOOK

As indicated earlier, the competency statements which are the organizing concepts of each chapter on functions, were derived from existing task analyses made by research teams from the American Association of School Librarians and the Association for Educational Communications and Technology. These statements represent, in the opinion of the authors, the best single expression regarding a cluster of tasks. They are an attempt to look at competencies in discrete yet manageable proportions. Each competency statement is expressed

[5] Ibid., pp. 213-14.

in terms of what the media professional should be able to do. These are not behavioral objectives in the strictest sense, but they do emphasize the expected behavior to be performed.

After the competency statement has been made, there is a discussion of the nature of this particular competency. At this point terminology is clarified, relationships are drawn, and examples are given. After reading the description of the competency, the learner should be able to express the desired behavior in his or her own words.

The section, "Resources for Gaining Competency" points out the variety of resources which can be used in attaining that competency. Books and audio-visual media are listed as obvious and relatively accessible sources of information. Comprehensive information regarding each resource is provided, including source. Other activities are also described. The use of field experience, internships, observations, simulations, games, and other direct and vicarious experiences are noted. It is likely that many of the resources, particularly in the area of experiences, are repetitive from competency to competency. There are a finite number of activities from which individuals can derive useful experiences so these are necessarily repeated. Since there is no one best way for all people to gain any particular competency, a variety of alternatives are presented with the hope that individuals will seek out those resources which are most compatible with their own learning styles and which are accessible wherever that person happens to be.

The "Mastery Item" is an example of the many possible mastery items which could be used to "test" the ability of the individual in regard to one specific competency. Of necessity, these items measure *knowledge* rather than skills or attitudes. It is much easier to test knowledge because we are dealing with cognitive facts and information, not the actual performance which would be measured as a skill. These items are intended for self-analysis of ability to perform a given competency. It should never be inferred that a correct answer on the mastery item will guarantee that the person will be able to perform that competency on the job. Satisfactory completion of a mastery item is an *indicator* that the individual is on the right track and *should* be able to perform that task on the job. It should not disturb the reader if his or her answer is not exactly the same as that proposed by the authors. There are a variety of possibilities for each item. While there are often several options for a "correct" answer given, it may be that the creative reader will come up with still another. The mastery items are the closest opportunity for dialogue between the reader and the authors. Even though these items may not be used as "questions and answers," they should be read as thoroughly as the body of the text since there are important principles imbedded in most of the "answers."

ASSESSMENT IN EXISTING COMPETENCY-BASED PROGRAMS

Project LIBRA

Project LIBRA at Auburn University was one of the programs in the Knapp Foundation School Library Media Project of the American Association of School Librarians. Its entire curriculum is competency-based and is still in the process of evolving its statements of competency and its methods of assessment. Several examples from their *Objectives, Content, and Strategies* [6] publication illustrate one very good attempt to achieve a competency-based curriculum for media professionals. The one area of ambiguity in these early attempts is in such criterion statements as; "Work judged against a prepared model," "Objective measure," and "Observed performance." Unless we know what is in each of these procedures, we know only the proposed method, not the content. Table 6-1 presents five examples from a twelve-page list of forty-seven performance objectives.

Utah's Certification Program

The State of Utah has moved to a competency-based certification program. Their publication, *Requirements for Instructional Media Endorsements* [7] is probably one of the first and most comprehensive attempts to specifically spell out performance and criteria in behavioral terms. Utah offers two levels of media endorsements after completion of a bachelor's degree and the awarding of a teaching certificate. The basic media endorsement can be obtained by demonstrating proficiency in: cataloging and classifying, selection of media, utilization of media, media production, and media administration. The advanced endorsement is comparable to a master's degree in the field and includes, in addition to the areas designated for the basic endorsement, information retrieval and data processing; human relations, leadership and supervision; and communication theory.

A few statements from the list of proficiency criteria will give an idea of the nature of this certification program. [8]

---

[6] *Objectives, Content and Strategies,* (Unpublished manuscript, Project LIBRA, Auburn University, 1971).

[7] *Requirements for Instructional Media Endorsements,* (Salt Lake City, Utah: Utah State Board of Education, 1972).

[8] *Requirements for Instructional Media Endorsements,* pp. 8-10.

TABLE 6-1 Objectives, Content, and Strategies (Project Libra)

Sample Performance (behavioral) Objective	Sample Content (skills)	Suggested Strategies
1.1 The student will prepare a bibliography of tools essential for the selection of media for a specified segment of the curriculum. CRITERION: Work judged against a prepared model.	determine criteria, select tools, identify function of each tool, weed out inappropriate selection tools, organize tools identified	curriculum laboratory, demonstration, self-check, written project, independent study, small-group discussion
1.2 Given a series of information requests related to 1.1, the student will locate and select appropriate sources of information. CRITERION: Work judged against a prepared model.	define problem, identify key words, select information sources, find information, prepare information for user	simulation, small-group discussion, curriculum laboratory, study guides
1.3 The student will participate on a curriculum planning and materials selection committee. CRITERION: Quality of contribution judged by a student-teacher designed checklist.	acquire knowledge of media appropriate to curricular problem, demonstrate ability to work with other professionals, offer suggestions for use including weaknesses and strengths of specific media	committee work, field-centered activity

1.4 Given the objectives of a learning sequence, the student will be able to classify the objective and select media appropriate to the class (verbal, discrimination, motor performance, affective). CRITERION: Objective measure.	discriminate between types of objectives, identify potential media, select media which will best accomplish the learning task, design appropriate criterion items	independent study, written activity, small-group critique, programmed instruction
1.5 The student will develop a plan for the acquisition system in the student's field center. CRITERION: Work evaluated by a student-faculty committee against standards identified and utilized.	formulate policies, identify procedures, develop a plan to check effectiveness	charrette, seminar, independent, study, field-based experience

Objective Number 1: . . . select teaching and learning materials

Selecting Media
1. Using selection tools of his choice, the candidate will:
   a. Identify the tools he has selected and include a rationale for the choice of each.
   b. Make a list of three titles from each of four of the following categories as selected by the examiners at the time of examination. Include full information for ordering and indicate the reasons for selecting each item: i.e., for whom and why.
      (1) Programmed materials
      (2) Study prints
      (3) Slides and filmstrips
      (4) Prerecorded audio tapes
      (5) Motion pictures (16mm sound)
      (6) Instructional television programs
      (7) Overhead transparencies
      (8) 8mm loop films
      (9) Fiction books
      (10) Reference books, including one set of encyclopedias
      (11) Non-fiction books
      Note: The list of tools and rationale, the lists of materials, and the ordering information will be evaluated.
2. The candidate will:
   a. Identify five professional journals for the media specialist and five others for the teacher.
   b. Identify those useful for selection because they contain annotations or reviews of material.
3. The candidate will explain six techniques for involving faculty and students in selection.
4. The candidate will differentiate between jobbers (distributors) and publishers (producers) by giving two examples of each and enumerating types of materials not usually available through jobbers.
5. The candidate will select a medium of his choice, identify the necessary elements of an evaluation, and develop an evaluation form for that medium. The form should include sufficient information to completely describe the medium.

Oregon's Proposed Certification Program

The Oregon Educational Media Association developed a proposal for competency-based certification in that state in 1974. As a comparison between the Auburn and Utah statements, the following excerpt is taken from the Oregon proposal in the area designated as "Selection and Utilization of Educational Media":

Demonstrate an ability to select and utilize materials and equipment according to the needs of the users, school curriculum, and recognized standards of quality.

A. Demonstrate the ability to evaluate and select educational media based upon established criteria.

   1. Given an actual or simulated situation in the selection of educational

media in any common format, the media specialist will be able to write and apply:

  a. Standards of technical quality appropriate to the format.
  b. Procedures for determining content accuracy
  c. Principles relating to the age and maturity levels of the intended users.
  d. Standards of organizational quality appropriate to the format.
  e. Principles relating to the intended curriculum usage.
  f. Principles relating the appropriateness of the format in conveying the content.
  g. Principles of learning theory appropriate to evaluation of the item.
2. Given an actual or simulated situation on the selection of specific items of educational media, the media specialist will be able to specify in writing whether the objectives established by the producer or publisher have been achieved.
3. Given an actual or simulated situation requiring the selection of educational media the media specialist will be able to list standard selection tools containing information appropriate to the situation.[9]

North Carolina's Guidelines

In 1972, the State of North Carolina adopted a set of guidelines for the preparation of media personnel. Graduate level preparation is required for persons who intend to serve as Media Coordinator (Master's degree), Advanced Media Coordinator (a sixth year program), and Media Specialist (a sixth year program). The catalog of competencies required for both the Media Coordinator and the Media Specialist lists the following in the area of "Evaluation and Selection of Media":

  a. An awareness of the varied needs of the student body being served.
  b. An awareness of the organization pattern of the school program and the effect this pattern has on the use of materials.
  c. Ability to provide for the curriculum needs of the entire school (system) including the staff.
  d. Knowledge of and ability to use selection guides.
  e. Ability to identify and apply appropriate criteria for assessing and evaluating materials and equipment in terms of their purported function and the needs of the potential users.
  f. Ability to involve the staff and students of the school in the process of evaluation and selection.
  g. Ability to maintain a collection free of worn, unattractive, and obsolescent (providing inaccurate information) materials.
  h. Knowledge of the content of a broad range of print and audiovisual materials.
  i. Ability to coordinate the formulation of a media selection policy.
  j. Ability to identify and involve community resources, including people.[10]

[9] "Oregon Basic Educational Media Now . . . Any Comments, Questions, Feedback?" *Interchange*, Vol. 3, No. 4, Summer, 1974, p. 9.
[10] *Guidelines for Media Preparation,* (Raleigh, North Carolina: State Department of Public Instruction, September 7, 1972).

While these competency statements do not appear to be as specific as those developed at Auburn University and by the Utah State Board of Education, they do provide a point of departure. With more specific criteria and a clarification of the performance expected, these statements can serve as a useful standard for media professionals in that state.

The patterns being established for certification and for professional education in the media field are consistent with programs in related fields within professional education. The emphasis on the ability to perform at a specified level is a far cry from the completion of a given number of credit hours in defined areas of specialization and then pronouncing the person qualified for service. Competency-based programs demand proof in performance, judged by a qualified jury before permitting an individual to practice. Many of the guidelines and criteria which presently exist are but a first stage in moving toward a rigorous assessment procedure which will guarantee at least a minimal level of performance on the job. However, we must be careful not to place all our confidence in one procedure. The history of education has shown that no one material, method, or philosophy has ever revolutionized or even substantially improved the process of teaching and learning. It is the mix of materials, messages, machines, methods, and persons in a facilitative environment which helps to bring about most of the goals we are seeking. Competency-based programs offer an approach to improve the performance of practitioners.

ACHIEVING COMPETENCY

If competency-based programs are going to be prevalent in the future, the aspiring media professional and the practicing media professional should be aware of ways in which competencies can be acquired and tested. Fortunately, there are ways for individuals to gain competencies without taking courses, going back to school, or attending extensive in-service workshops. One of the features of competency-based requirements is that the proof is in the performance on the job, in a simulated environment, on a test or combination of all these procedures. It does not matter where or how an individual has attained the competency; the test is that he can demonstrate that he can do it. Competency-based programs do not demand a given number of courses or credit hours at an accredited institution of higher education. If an individual has learned the competencies by self-study, on the job training, and through using good common sense, the test is in the performance and the manner of preparation for that examination is unimportant. This does not mean that there will be a mass exodus from library schools and schools of education where media professionals are being trained. Many people feel that this is still the most efficient way to gain competencies. The emphasis on competency-based programs will probably cause many graduate programs to emphasize competency-based curricula to insure certification of their graduates and eventually their employment. There will be some states that will review academic programs at institutions of higher education and certify the program as being equivalent to attainment of the competencies required for state certification. This procedure is often called program approval. Graduates of such certified programs will be automatically certified without further examination since their entire academic program is considered to be the equivalent of the competency-based examination procedures. Some states may require both professional education in an accredited school and an examination. Some states will give temporary certification until there has been sufficient time to perform on the job. After one, two, or three years experience, permanent certification will be awarded. Each state will have its plan; many already do. Check to determine what the state in which you will work requires in the way of certification for media professionals.

As measurement of competencies becomes more of a routine matter, a combination of procedures will be used to test each competency. Some competencies are best tested by paper and pencil tests while others demand the demonstration of a skill using a piece of equipment. There are more subtle measures of competencies which are concerned with interpersonal relationships. These must be observed on the job, during an internship, or during the initial months of employment. There are some rather sophisticated simulations which permit evaluation of interpersonal competencies. In some cases, interviews may be used to evaluate the readiness of a person to embark upon a job which requires a specified set of competencies. Probably a combination of all these measurement and evaluation procedures is necessary for a comprehensive assessment of one's ability to perform. There will be further developments and refinements of these procedures as time goes on and professionals determine what combinations best measure and evaluate each competency.

Self-Assessment

One of the useful attributes of competency statements is their lack of ambiguity. This clarity permits individuals to conduct a self-assessment of their ability to perform. When a statement is clear and criteria are stated or implied, it is possible to determine the degree to which you are able to meet the criteria. After self-assessment (using the mastery items in this book, for example) you might turn to friends in the same field (to test each other), to professors (with whom you can carry on dialogue), and to media professionals (who *really* know). While the criteria for successful attainment of each competency may vary from person to person, one of the best ways to insure your correct performance is to submit yourself to the judgment of others.

Long-term assessment of competencies can be observed through such factors as retention in the position, a merit increase in salary, promotion, and offers from other school systems which have noted your abilities. Each one of these indicators would confirm that you have gained many of the competencies which others feel are important. The ultimate assessment must be done by the individual. It is only in the individual's own understanding of his professional competency that genuine assessment can be made.

Indicators of insufficient competency would be: inability to explain a task to an employee; finding continuing satisfaction in repetitive tasks; being defensive about what you do; constantly saying that you have insufficient time to do everything you should do. There are other "danger signals" but these show the nature of the feelings which only you can completely observe. If you recognize these symptoms, it would be well to consider ways in which they can be corrected. Some may stem from lack of competency; some may dwell within as problems of personality.

EXTENDING COMPETENCIES

There are many suggestions throughout this book regarding the attainment of competencies. The suggestions included in "Resources for Gaining Competency" in each section provide specific procedures for attaining that competency. The recommendations made here are more general and could apply to almost any of the competencies the media professional is seeking to gain or improve upon.

Some of the most logical resources are close at hand. Seek opportunities to talk with other media professionals and other colleagues. Such opportunities may arise on the job or during coffee break. A person usually likes to talk about his/her job and the problems and achievements related to it. Your questions, therefore, will be welcome. Most media professionals pride themselves as being good counselors.

Seek out professional meetings. There are often formal organizations in the area in which you live. Local groups of media professionals meet about once a month in metropolitan areas. There are often regional groups which include one section of a state and, of course, there are state associations which hold annual meetings. All of these meetings should be within the geographic and financial reach of most media professionals who see the opportunity for professional development through active participation in professional organizations. National meetings are the *sine qua non* for professionals but they are not always accessible. The national meetings provide opportunities to meet the people who are involved in the issues of the field at a national level. Through prominent speakers and meetings of the committees of the association, a professional can begin to sense that he or she is part of a movement that goes beyond local boundaries. Since most national meetings move from one region of the country to another, check the professional publications to see if one will be held within a reasonable distance of your home sometime in the future—and plan to attend.

One word in regard to professional associations in the media field is necessary. This is a field in transition. Several segments of the educational world are drawing together to represent the field. Some areas and states move more rapidly than others. It is well to know the state of professional associations so that opportunities can be identified. There is a segment of the field which stems from librarianship and is represented nationally in the American Library Association (ALA) and in one of the divisions, the American Association of School Librarians (AASL). Another major segment comes from the audiovisual-educational technology movement and is represented nationally by the Association for Educational Communications and Technology (AECT). Another strand, of somewhat lesser concern to school people, is the American Society for Information Science (ASIS), which is concerned with information retrieval, documentation, and systematized information systems. In education, the Association for Supervision and Curriculum Development (ASCD) provides a broad overview of matters related to the planning of curriculum and the relationships among teachers and specialists in the school setting.

At the state level, many of the school library and audiovisual-educational technology associations have merged into one statewide media group because of the recognition that they have common purposes and that to be divided leads to less effectiveness.

A person can gain as much from an organization as he/she is willing to put into it. After listening to speakers, observing multimedia presentations, looking at the exhibits, and conversing with individuals in hotel lobbies and coffee shops, many persons ask: "How can I become active in this organization?" One of the best ways to start is to volunteer for committee work. There is almost no organization that does not welcome requests to be placed on committees. During the first year on the committee volunteer to do something that no one else wants to do. Your efforts will usually be "rewarded" with more work, but that is how people begin to be active in any organization. From such work comes recognition and nominations to serve in other capacities. As you move along in an association, you will become more discriminating in your goals. Make these organizations work for you. They are gateways to professional growth. Your professor should be able to give you the name and membership chairman of the associations in your state and region or you may write to the state director of media.

Another resource for gaining competency and for continued self-renewal are the publications of the professional associations. You will receive these with your membership in most cases. The state associations have newsletters or small magazines. The American Library Association sends *American Libraries* to its membership and the American Association of School Librarians publishes *School Media Quarterly*. All members of the Association for Educational Communications and Technology receive *Audiovisual Instruction* and, for an additional fee, *AV Communication Review*—a research journal. These journals and others keep the media professional up-to-date on current happenings and issues within the field. They are vital in one's professional growth.

From time to time there are books published for the professional. Select those titles which help to update and upgrade your competencies. Many of the books published relate directly to the various functional competencies presented in this book. One of the popular formats these days is the programmed text. Using the principles of programmed instruction, the reader is guided through a series of steps with immediate feedback of information so that learning is virtually guaranteed. Most of the publications in this format deal with specific skills such as production techniques, statistics, equipment operation, and management procedures.

Enrolling in formal courses sponsored by colleges and universities and continuing education workshops is a good way to learn new competencies. Two- and three-week workshops in the summer are commonplace in colleges and universities. From time to time the Office of Library and Learning Resources of the U.S. Office of Education provides funds to institutions and organizations to conduct institutes for pre-service and in-service personnel. These special courses are often advertised in the professional journals.

During professional preparation many individuals seek opportunities for experience. Some schools offer field work or internships to provide real world contexts during study. Individuals on their own can volunteer for work in media centers as apprentices, aides, or clerks. These experiences are rich in providing opportunities to observe professionals solving actual problems and exercises which can never be provided in formal courses.

There is a rich body of information available in audiovisual resources— films, videotapes, sound filmstrips, cassettes, and simulation games. Many libraries are adding these media to professional collections so that individuals and groups can see what is happening in the field. Comprehensive listings of such audiovisual materials may be found in *Audiovisual Resources for Teaching Instructional Technology* (3rd ed.) (Syracuse, N.Y.: Area of Instructional Technology, 1971) and *Audiovisual Materials in Support of Information Science Curricula: An Annotated Listing With Subject Index* (Stanford, Calif.: Educational Resources Information Clearinghouse on Information Resources, 1971).

Keeping up-to-date and creating conditions for self-renewal are the marks of a professional. The activities will vary from time to time. An appropriate mix of some of the above activities will help the media professional maintain currency in the field. The suggestions made here relate directly to the profession since the bulk of current knowledge is contained in these resources. There are other resources which are commonly used by all people who need to renew themselves and should not be neglected by media professionals. Since media professionals deal with so many people in so many fields, it is important to be familiar with ideas from a variety of disciplines. Reading widely helps to broaden one's horizons. Viewing entertainment films and television helps to keep one fresh on what is happening in the world of which we are a part. Vacations and travel help to sensitize people to other people. Time for rest and relaxation is just as much a part of professional self-renewal as reviewing professional literature and going to conventions. The media professional must be humane above all and activities which help to develop this quality are a vital part of one's life style.

REFERENCES

CARRUTH, JAMES W. "North Carolina Moves Toward Competency-Based Media Preparation Programs." *Audiovisual Instruction* 18 (May, 1973): 33-34.

Certification Requirements for Educational Media Personnel. Baltimore, Maryland: Division of Certification and Accreditation and Division of Library Development and Services, Maryland State Department of Education, 1974.

ELAM, STANLEY. *A Résumé of Performance-Based Teacher Education.* Washington, D.C.: American Association of Colleges for Teacher Education, 1972.

GORMAN, DON A. "Mastery Based Instruction in Educational Media: A Prototype for Change." *Educational Technology* 14 (August, 1974): 36-38.

Guidelines for Media Preparation. Raleigh, North Carolina: State Department of Public Instruction, 1972.

HOUSTON, W. ROBERT and ROBERT B. HOWSAM (eds.) *Competency-Based Teacher Education,* pp. 1-33; 56-74, 102-142. Chicago: Science Research Associates, 1972.

QUIRK, THOMAS J. "Some Measurement Issues in Competency-Based Teacher Education," *Phi Delta Kappan* 55 (Jan., 1974): 316-19.

Requirements for Instructional Media Endorsements. Salt Lake City, Utah: Division of Instructional Support Services, Utah State Board of Education, 1972.

ROSNER, BENJAMIN (ed.) *The Power of Competency-Based Teacher Education: A Report,* pp. 3-34. Boston: Allyn and Bacon, 1972.

ROSNER, BENJAMIN and PATRICIA M. McKAY. "Will the Promise of C/PBTE Be Fulfilled?" *Phi Delta Kappan* 55 (Jan., 1974): 290-95.

SCHALOCK, H. DEL. "Notes on a Model of Assessment That Meets the Requirements of Competency Based Teacher Education." In W. Robert Houston, ed., *Exploring Competency Based Education.* Berkeley, Calif.: McCutchen Publishing Co., 1974.

7 The Organization Management Function

The basic concepts of media center organization are presented in this chapter. The competencies presented cluster around six focal points: program planning; budgeting; planning and managing facilities; organizing access and delivery systems; and conducting program evaluations.

Management is the executive function of planning, organizing, coordinating, controlling, and supervising an administrative unit with responsibility for the results. It is a function with many facets. Whether a person is called "manager," "director," "coordinator," or "supervisor," the tasks performed are more or less the same.

As a media professional there is a strong likelihood that you will spend a substantial portion of your time performing management tasks. This is especially likely if you plan to coordinate or direct a school or district media program. Even the media specialist who is concerned primarily with one area, such as television or production, performs certain management tasks.

Management (or administration) is a major responsibility of any media professional. In the *School Library Personnel: Task Analysis Survey*[1] there were eighteen categories of duties which media center staff performed. The head of the library media center (the person we have been calling the media professional) spent 50.5 percent time with administrative duties at the secondary level and 41.8 percent time at the elementary level. The closest category to administration was "general media services" which consumed 28.8 percent

[1] *School Library Personnel: Task Analysis Survey* (Chicago: American Library Association, 1969) p. 20.

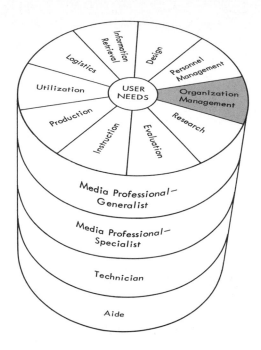

COMPETENCY 1   Establishes goals of the media program.

COMPETENCY 2   Develops and maintains a longe range plan.

COMPETENCY 3   Prepares and administers a fiscal plan based on operational needs.

COMPETENCY 4   Seeks information regarding supplemental funding from governmental agencies and other sources.

COMPETENCY 5   Organizes services to achieve goals.

COMPETENCY 6   Plans media facilities; allocates and monitors space according to program needs.

COMPETENCY 7   Assesses the degree to which the operations meet the program goals.

of the secondary school's media professional's time and 32.6 percent for elementary personnel. "General media services" could include several management tasks. These figures are averages and need to be interpreted for each school.

Any organization which provides service to people must be organized to satisfy the needs of its clients. The school media center is no exception. The ultimate client is the *learner!* There are factors which influence the student in the process of learning. These factors are

messages (content), *man* (persons who present messages to learners), *materials* (software or media in which messages are stored), *machines* (hardware or equipment to display messages), *methods* (procedures or techniques to transmit messages) and *settings* (the environment in which the message is presented).[2]

The factors which impinge upon the learner are created, acquired, manipulated or handled in order to make them available in the best form for the learner and to help attain an instructional objective. These steps are taken within the several functional areas performed by the media generalists, media specialists, technicians, and aides. For example, the function of *production* takes the message specifications for materials to be developed for use by teachers (man) and to be displayed by a device (machine) following predetermined procedures (methods) in a classroom (setting).

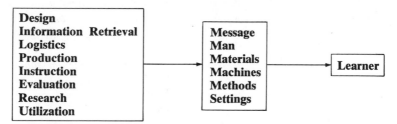

The functions include: *design* (preparing the specifications for producing learning resources); *information retrieval* (arranging materials in a systematic fashion to make them accessible to the learner); *logistics* (performing support and supply operations to provide learning resources; *production* (translating specifications into an actual product); *instruction* (communicating information to a specific audience); *evaluation* (choosing and assessing the worth of learning resources and their use with learners); *research* (investigating and testing the use of learning resources); and *utilization* (bringing the learner into contact with the learning resource).

[2] The model used here is adapted from C. James Wallington and Carol Bruce, "Educational Media: A Field of Work" *Training Programs for Educational Media Technicians* (Washington, D.C.: Association for Educational Communications and Technology, 1972), pp. 7-16.

But there is another function which is part of all the functions just mentioned—management. The management of the organization itself and the management of the personnel constitute a major responsibility of the media

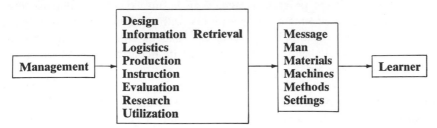

professionals. There are aspects of management which relate to each function in some way. For example, any research project needs to be planned, organized, controlled, and assessed. The use of a systematic approach to instructional design calls for a management system to be sure that all of the diverse elements are brought together at the proper time and place to insure that the conditions of success are established.

Management is an all-encompassing function. There are courses and degrees in management. There are books and manuals. In the media field itself there are several useful books which emphasize management.[3,4,5] The question we will address here, however, deals with competencies—*What management tasks does a media professional need to be able to perform?* Second— *How does a person gain those competencies?*

The competencies cluster around five areas: program planning; budgeting; planning and managing facilities; organizing access and delivery systems; and conducting program evaluations. For each area there are several task competencies which each person should be able to demonstrate.

COMPETENCY 1   Establishes goals of the media program.

"Would you tell me, please, which way I ought to go from here?"
"That depends a good deal on where you want to get to."
Alice in Wonderland [6]

[3] James W. Brown, Kenneth D. Norberg and Sara K. Srygley, *Administering Educational Media* (New York: McGraw-Hill, 1972).

[4] Carleton W. H. Erickson, *Administering Instructional Media Programs* (New York: Macmillan, 1968).

[5] Ruth Ann Davies, *The School Library Media Center: A Force for Educational Excellence*, (2nd ed.) (New York: R. R. Bowker Co., 1974).

[6] Lewis Carroll, *Alice's Adventures in Wonderland*, Macmillan Classics Series (New York: Macmillan, 1963), p. 59.

A statement of goals should tell us where we "want to get to." Very often goals are proposed, approved and published as the official *raison d'etre* of the media program. These goals serve as a constant touchstone for assessing the degree to which the program is achieving its mission. Each media center should develop goal statements cooperatively with its constituency—students, faculty, staff, administrators, board members, and parents—as each can contribute. The goal statements serve as a point of departure for all other dimensions of the program.

The director or head of the media program is responsible for implementing the goals of the program. The goals for the media program should be an integral part of the goals and objectives of the larger school or school system of which it is a part. To carry out this responsibility requires a definition of the center's users (usually students, teachers, and administrators but perhaps certain elements of the community as well) and an analysis of the user's information needs. (See Chapter 4 for a comprehensive discussion of determining user needs.) Data collected in this process are used in establishing program goals and objectives, modifying existing goals, and devising ways for reponding to the need.

It is helpful to know the difference between a goal and an objective. A goal is a broad statement of purpose. It is more global than an objective. It points direction rather than specifying behavior. An *objective* is a statement of intent. It is a subset of a goal. It is specific in regard to one aspect of a program. For example, one goal of a school library media center may be "to provide access to a wide range of learning resources"; objectives related to that goal could be "to collect and make available catalogs and lists of audiovisual materials available from local community agencies and business organizations," and "to maintain a list of available resource people in the community."

RESOURCES: ESTABLISHING GOALS

Writing goals is not something one does by formula. Goal statements have to be written and reviewed by someone who is experienced in writing and critiquing such statements. There are a few guidelines which may help. First, goals are reflections of the philosophy of the media center. Unless the director is able to describe and discuss the philosophy of the center, the development of goal statements will be very difficult. Chapter 2 provides a rationale for developing a philosophy from which goals could be derived. Second, there are articles in professional journals which appear from time to time that are helpful in providing substance and direction for goal statements. One excellent example of goal statements is found in "The School Library as a Materials Center." More recently, "Learning Centers: A Working Bibliography," outlines references to sources which might be helpful in developing goal statements. Complete source information for these articles may be found at the end of this chapter.

Third, goal statements which have been developed by established media centers often serve as helpful references or models in creating new statements for new centers. Adaptations will have to be made depending on local circumstances. Goal statements are highly similar in nature but cannot easily be transferred from one school system to another without careful consideration of the local philosophy and the unique needs of local users.

For more detailed information about goals and objectives of the media program, see the entries for Taylor and Erickson in the bibliography at the end of the chapter.

MASTERY ITEM: ESTABLISHING GOALS

Write a statement of goals for a school media center as though it were to be presented to a local school board accompanying a request for additional financial support.

Response: Establishing Goals

There is no one "correct" statement since goals vary from school to school. Your statement should be consistent with the goals of the school and district in which the media program is located. It should be broad in scope but specific enough to permit objectives to be drawn from it. It should reflect a philosophy—a point of view. Sample goal statements could read as follows:

> The goal of the media program is to provide a full range of book and nonbook resources to meet the needs of all users.
>
> The goal of the media program is to provide alternative learning opportunities for each student.
>
> The goal of the media program is to assist each user in the selection and/or design of media and to facilitate optimum use.

For the local school board you would describe specific activities performed which stem from the goal statement and, for the purpose of eliciting additional financial support, you would point out those activities which need to be performed but cannot be accomplished because of limited funds. But remember, each request should be consistent with your stated goal.

COMPETENCY 2   Develops and maintains a long range plan.

Once the philosophy of the media program has been expressed in terms of goal statements (and, perhaps, related objectives) the overall design of the program can begin to emerge. But the design must be long range as well as immediate. Planning is pervasive and guides every aspect and phase of media program development from goal formulation through evaluation of specific program components and operations. It is a cyclical process through which each element of the program is systematically considered and periodically reconsidered.

To plan effectively, the media professional must have one foot in the present and one in the future. Plans often need to be made from day to day or week to week but the leader of a media program must look several years ahead. Short range plans are for one to two years and long range plans are five to ten years away. The five year point seems to be a reasonable projection which maintains the reality of the present yet projects future events which ought to be factored into every planning effort.

RESOURCES: DEVELOPING A LONG RANGE PLAN

Read a long range plan developed by the director of a school media program. Try to write such a plan yourself. Essentially a plan needs to state: (1) present status of the program; (2) future aspirations for a given period of time; (3) recommendations regarding what it will take to get there—in terms of personnel, space, finance, program, policy, etc.; (4) priorities; (5) problems, constraints, and other variables.

Long range plans are usually very specific. Beginning with a reconfirmation of philosophy or a recommended change, goals are presented, objectives stated, data regarding the current operation reported, assumptions regarding future changes (in number of students and faculty, roles of teachers and learners, new technology, new methodologies, etc.) are given, and priority steps to implement the plan are recommended.

Some of the tasks for media professionals in regard to planning were discovered by the Jobs in Media Study when media professionals were interviewed about their responsibilities.

Reads project reports to identify current work
Discusses projects and fiscal resources to identify future priorities
Confers with staff to identify project interests
Confers with colleagues to become involved in new ventures
Compares interests with organizational policy to ensure compatibility
Reads newsletters, fiscal statements to identify possible financial sources
Synthesizes discussions to propose department programs/projects
Writes paper to present department/program projects

Confers with staff to evaluate program/projects paper
Identifies constraints on programs to decide on program feasibility
Selects programs (projects for department to plan work for year) [7]

MASTERY ITEM: DEVELOPING A LONG RANGE PLAN

Circulation figures for a school media center increased by about 20 percent for the past four years but the immediate past year showed only a 2 percent increase over the previous year. In developing a long range plan (for five years), what variables need to be considered?

Response: Developing a Long Range Plan

To look ahead it is sometimes helpful to look back, if only briefly. During the four years in which circulation increased by 20 percent each year were there factors which could be directly associated with the increase, e.g., higher enrollments, an abnormal expansion of the collection by the availability of federal funds, intensive public relations campaigns, or a new facility? If the increase can be attributed to any of several factors, will those factors continue to affect the circulation? But remember, *circulation* is only one variable to consider.

It might be that more targeted consultation with users yields less circulation but better use of materials cooperatively selected by the media professional and the user. Will your long range plan call for different emphasis and *priorities?* If so what are they?

Do you envision *new services* during the next five years? If so, what does that mean in terms of space, personnel and budget? The addition or acceleration of nonbook media services has substantial impact on your resources.

Are the school's *goals and objectives* changing? If so, what are the implications for the media program?

The important thing to remember in developing a long range plan is that change in magnitude (more of the same) is a straight line projection but change in *priorities, new services, goals and objectives* and *philosophy* will dictate different projections.

COMPETENCY 3   Prepares and administers a fiscal plan based on operational needs.

---

[7] *Guidelines for Certification of Media Specialists, Extended Version* (Washington, D.C.: Association for Educational Communications and Technology, 1972), p. 46.

A budget is a fiscal plan. Once needs of users have been determined and translated into program objectives, then details of resources required to fulfill these objectives are stated. From the resource requirements (personnel, facilities, materials, equipment, and services) the financial plan or budget is developed.

There are several guidelines which should be considered in the process of budget preparation:

1. The media program is an integral part of the instructional program rather than a support service and the media budget provides the resources for teaching and learning.
2. The director of the district media program is responsible, within established administrative channels, for the design, formulation, justification, administration, and evaluation of the budget for the media program in the district.
3. The head of the building media program works with the principal in creating budget recommendations to submit to the district director.
4. The media program budget is developed cooperatively and is based on program goals and objectives.
5. Budget preparation applies systems theories that emphasize program and accountability.
6. The total media program budget includes funds for both school and district programs, with fiscal responsibility assigned at the appropriate operating level.
7. Where decentralization places budgeting for media program resources under the individual school, the head of the school media program, the principal, and the district media director concur in its approval.
8. The responsibility for identifying or approving funding sources, including state, federal, and local funds, rests at the district level.
9. Implementation of the budget is carried out in accordance with local, state, and federal laws and regulations governing purchases, contracts, bidding procedures, building codes, and standards of operations.[8]

Budgets are presented in a variety of formats. Each school or school system usually requests that its format be followed. Many school systems are now using a "program budget" or PPBS (Planning-Programming-Budgeting-System) which has its own set of procedures. The line items in nearly all budgets will include:

Salaries and wages of personnel
Supplies (office, production)
Communications (telephone, postage)
Instructional Materials
New Equipment

[8] *Media Programs: District and School* (Chicago: American Library Association and Washington, D.C.: Association for Educational Communications and Technology, 1975), p. 39.

Replacement Equipment
Maintenance
Travel

The basis for budget planning should be the outcomes of the teaching/ learning process—the attainment of educational objectives. A budget is justified on the extent to which it promises to reach the objectives of learning. A relationship between each budget item and objectives should be established.

Once the budget plan has been developed, presented, and approved, procedures for allocation and monitoring must be established. The allocation process is another dimension of planning. The funds requested are not always the funds approved. Sometimes amounts are approved for one category, e.g., instructional materials, and must be subdivided into more specific items, e.g., books, periodicals, records, filmstrips, etc. Often one amount is approved for an entire district and must be reallocated to each school within the system. With all these possible changes the allocation process becomes an important instrument of planning and program operations. The practice of dividing materials budgets into print and nonprint categories has been a rather common practice. It is recommended that the budgets be unified so that materials can be purchased where needed and not restricted to categories.

Monitoring a budget is a continuing activity. Just as it is important to know your personal checkbook balance and to anticipate forthcoming expenses, the manager of the budget must know how the accounts stand on a day-to-day basis. After allocations have been made, bookkeeping accounts need to be established for each major budget category. Whether the accounting is handled primarily by manual methods, or by computer, or by a combination of both, it should be possible to know the status of each account; basically, how much has been spent and how much remains as of a specified date. Good monitoring procedures project anticipated expenses so that possible surplus and deficit amounts can be identified early in the fiscal year. Since so many decisions have financial implications, it is imperative that the media professional monitor all accounts pertaining to the media program.

RESOURCES: ADMINISTERING A FISCAL PLAN

Good examples of budgets are presented by Brown, Norberg and Srygley and by Erickson. Complete source information is listed in the bibliography at the end of the chapter.

Ask to see the budget for the school system in the area where you live. It is a public document which offers details on amounts allocated to each budget category. You might probe to determine how dollar amounts are assigned to reach objectives of the educational system. Particularly note the amounts assigned to the media center, instructional materials, equipment, and personnel to gain some insight into the amount allocated for the media program. The general guideline given for district and local media programs is ". . . at least 10 percent of the national Per Pupil Operational Cost (PPOC), as computed by the United States Office of Education." [9] Total operational cost includes administration, instruction, attendance services, health services, pupil transportation services, operation of plant, maintenance of plant, and fixed charges.

Probably the best courses in this area are offered through the department of educational administration or the school of business or management in a university. In the professional education of media personnel the budgeting process is discussed as a unit within a media administration course.

For the actual monitoring of budgets, you might visit the business office of the school district and ask to see their monthly report forms which are usually sent to supervisors and administrations to inform them of budget status. Media professionals might share their reports with you as samples of the forms they use.

Talk with individuals who have to prepare and administer budgets. Ask them how they do it; what frustrations they encounter; and how well their system is working.

MASTERY ITEM: ADMINISTERING A FISCAL PLAN

One of the major objectives of a secondary school media program is to provide more alternative resources in nonbook formats in the social studies curriculum area. The budget allocation for new materials acquisitions is $6,000. Last year's budget for the same item was $5,500 with $4,800 being spent for books and periodicals, $400 for records and $300 for filmstrips. What recommendations would you make for this year's expenditure which should include slide sets, transparencies and simulation games in addition to books, records and filmstrips? (If you feel awkward stating specific amounts, what questions would you ask?)

Response: Administering a Fiscal Plan

It is difficult to specify amounts for each type of media initially, but you could begin by deciding to spend one-half the budget on books and periodicals and one-half on nonbook media. You would then have to determine relative costs of each type of media and arbitrarily assign amounts to each medium. This is a crude start which should be open to change based on the information needs of users.

[9] Ibid., pp. 40-41.

A better approach would be to discover answers to the following questions and then move toward a financial plan:

1. In what curriculum areas do teachers and learners need nonbook resources?
2. What is the likelihood of use for each medium? (Do teachers have access to appropriate equipment and do they know how to use it?)
3. What has been the circulation of existing nonbook media?
4. What subject matter is available in each medium and does it correlate with the current curriculum?
5. Are teachers and learners interested in producing their own materials?

There may be other questions, but these would offer a good start in determining need, availability and probability of use. With answers to these questions, it would be possible to begin intelligent budgetary allocations.

COMPETENCY 4   Seeks information regarding supplemental funding from governmental agencies and other sources.

No media program ever has adequate funds to do everything the director would like to do. There are, in fact, many programs operating on marginal budgets which barely keep the program in operation. The alert media professional is one who knows sources of funds beyond the allocation from the school or school system. Awareness of such sources is a never-ending task. The most obvious sources of supplemental funding are the federal and state governments but the perceptive professional will be able to ferret out sources within the community or region as well.

In exploring this competency further, we must assume that the media professional has established specific program objectives and has set priorities. Very rarely does any individual or agency provide money without knowledge of how it will be used and what unique achievements are anticipated. The best first step toward obtaining additional funds is to envision what you want the program to be—the opportunities you see for learners to have access to resources they could not possibly have with only the current level of funding from the schools. We must assume that this plan has been worked out. Now— where are the dollars?

FEDERAL FUNDS   First, it is important to know the area in which you seek funds. Is the money needed for materials? for equipment? for training? for an innovative program activity? for research? for demonstration of a new procedure? Next, who will benefit from the grant of additional money—the learners, the staff, yourself, your community or region, a national audience of media professionals, or combinations of these? You will also have to know how you are going to measure the success (or failure) of your investment. In other words, you must have a plan before federal funds are requested. The plan is usually in the form of a proposal to a federal agency.

There are several federal agencies which have funds available for use by schools but most of the programs are located in the United States Office of Education (USOE) of the Department of Health, Education and Welfare. Each year a list of federal programs is published in *American Education,* a magazine sponsored by the U.S. Office of Education. Reprints are also available. The list, "Guide to OE-Administered Programs," is published in a chart form with information pertaining to type of assistance, authorizing legislation, purpose, amount of appropriation, who may apply and where to apply. Another guide which lists federal programs is the *Catalog of Federal Education Assistance Programs* (An Indexed Guide to the Federal Government's Programs Offering Educational Benefits to the American People).[10]

The media professional who is seeking funds should identify the programs which appear to be appropriate and write to the person or office designated as the contact point. Be sure to determine in this initial screening whether or not the funds in the program are distributed directly by the federal government or through state agencies. The federal offices will usually send more detailed information about the program, guidelines for submission of proposals, and deadline dates for application.

After proposals are submitted, they are read by the staff of the program office in USOE and by a team of "outside" evaluators who are brought in from the field to assess the proposals submitted. Eventually (usually from one to six months after submission) notice regarding acceptance or rejection of the proposal is given. If accepted, there is a final stage of budget negotiation before specific amounts are allocated.

Federal support for media programs comes from a variety of offices depending upon the nature of the request for funds. The broad categories of programs include: research, demonstrations, training, materials and equipment, and construction.

The administrative structure of the U.S. Office of Education changes frequently and therefore it is difficult to specify which offices are the best contact points. The annual list of federal programs is usually up-to-date. At the time this book was written, the Office of Library and Learning Resources offered a rather complete spectrum of funding opportunities involving media concerns. There are, however, other specialized programs such as media development and use for special education administered through the Bureau for Education of the Handicapped.

[10] The 1972 Edition was sold by the U.S. Government Printing Office, Washington, D.C. 20402, for $4.30.

STATE FUNDS   It is common today to distribute funds from national programs on a state-to-state basis. Much of the support for direct categorical aid to schools is the result of federal legislation which mandates distribution by the states. The programs that have been supported over the years are Title III of the National Defense Education Act of 1958 (NDEA) which requires matching funds for the purchase of instructional equipment including audiovisual devices. Title II of the Elementary and Secondary Education Act of 1965 (ESEA) provides funds for acquisition of library materials in all media formats. There are other specialized programs administered through the states including: educationally deprived children (ESEA Title I), vocational education, and public libraries (Library Services and Construction Act, Titles I, II and III).

Applications for funds through the states are made through the state departments of education, each of which have special application forms.

LOCAL FUNDS   Since most of the financial support for a media program comes through local support, it is unlikely that much additional money can be acquired through that route. However, it is a wise media professional who is ready with a "want list" for those occasions when additional money becomes available, usually toward the end of the fiscal year. Sometimes unspent funds are available and a tactful approach to the school's fiscal officer may yield a "windfall" surplus to permit additional purchase of materials or equipment.

There are times when local service clubs or PTA's are seeking opportunities to contribute tangible gifts to the school. The media center's needs should be brought to the attention of these organizations. The basic premise of tax support for educational programs must be maintained so the extra gifts should go for items beyond those which are legitimate requests through the normal budgetary procedures.

Once in a while you may discover a local foundation or company which will make grants to schools for highly visible and innovative programs. Do not overlook this resource.

RESOURCES: SEEKING SUPPLEMENTARY FUNDS

Scan the "Guide to OE-Administered Programs" for the current fiscal year. Single copies are available free from *American Education,* P.O. Box 9000, Alexandria, Virginia 22304. Review the *Catalog of Federal Education Assistance Programs.* Identify the programs which are appropriate to support your needs. Write to the office which monitors the programs in which you are interested and ask for program guidelines, applications, and a list of programs currently being funded. Get to know the programs so that you can determine whether or not your needs can be filled by any of the funding agencies.

Many school systems have a coordinator of federal programs or special projects. The title may vary from district to district and the amount of time spent on this activity may vary from person to person. Sometimes a principal or assistant superintendent will fill the role. The point is that there probably is a person who can help you to identify and interpret the appropriate agencies for supplementary funds.

You might ask to see the proposals developed for other programs in the district since the format followed in making applications is quite similar from agency to agency. To see how someone else has made a case for additional funds is probably one of the best ways to see how the elements of a proposal can be put together.

MASTERY ITEM: SEEKING SUPPLEMENTARY FUNDS

From Table 7-1, identify those programs which would be *primarily* intended for school media programs and those which offer *secondary* possibilities.

Response: Seeking Supplementary Funds

The first key phrase is found under "who may apply." If "local education agencies" or "local school districts" are named, you would be eligible. Eligibility is a first criterion. Purpose becomes a second criterion. If the provisions of the legislation specify certain categories of persons to be served, e.g., bilingual children or deprived children, you would have to determine whether or not your school serves the special population. A third criterion is the quality of the proposal to fit the needs which you define for your school. Obtaining federal money depends upon a proposal which you must make to request funds for a specific purpose. Even though the appropriations are in the millions of dollars, the funds are dispersed only upon application and, usually with a proposal.

There is only one program listed in Table 7-1 which is intended *primarily* for school media centers and that is number 11, School Library Resources and Instructional Materials. *Secondary* possibilities would depend on the resourcefulness of a proposal writer who could associate a particular aspect of the media program with the provisions of each legislative act. Assuming no specialized audience, only number 5 would fall into this category. If a proportion of the school population could be identified as bilingual (number 1), disadvantaged (numbers 8 and 12), or Indians (numbers 6 and 13) then proposals could be prepared.

Remember in reviewing this chart, that it was prepared for the 1974 fiscal year. It is used here only as an example so do not use it as a guide for subsequent years since legislation and appropriations have probably changed. The chart is issued each year and should be obtained on an annual basis.

COMPETENCY 5   Organizes services to achieve goals.

This is one of those competencies which is easy to state but far more difficult to perform. "Organization" as it is used here is the orchestration of such diverse components as personnel, facilities, equipment, and materials to achieve the goals of the program. While goals remain the touchstone of the program, the idiosyncrasies of the people, space, and resources must be taken into account. What does it mean "to organize"? A sampling of the tasks in this category include:

Develops organizational model
Defines functions to be performed by each person
Drafts policies for operation of program
Recommends arrangement of facilities
Monitors operation of the center
Recommends procedures for improved communications
Designs financial structure

All of these tasks can be further broken down into subtasks. The number of subtasks is almost infinite. In one sense, the organization (and operation) of the media program is at the core of the entire cluster of competencies which media professionals must perform. "It includes the identification, acquisition, organization, administration, supervision and evaluation of the use of funds, personnel, resources and facilities to support a program for utilization of recorded knowledge." [11]

The aspect of the organization function that sets it apart from the other functions is in the formulation and implementation of policy. *Policy* is a deliberate course of action selected from among a cluster of alternatives in light of present and projected conditions. Policy is used to establish procedures and to guide future program directions. Policies are an outgrowth of goals and yield operational guidelines; the following outline shows this relationship.

Goal statement: The media center will provide access to information in all media formats.

[11] *Behavioral Requirements Analysis Checklist,* p. 36.

TABLE 7-1

GROUP I: TO INSTITUTIONS, AGENCIES, AND ORGANIZATIONS
PART A--For Elementary and Secondary Education Programs

Type of Assistance	Authorizing Legislation	Purpose	Appropriation (dollars)	Who may Apply	Where to Apply
1 Bilingual education	Elementary and Secondary Education Act, Title VII	To develop and operate programs for children aged 3-18 who have limited English speaking ability	50,350,000	Local education agencies or institutions of higher education applying jointly with local education agencies	OE Grant Application Control Center
2 Comprehensive planning and evaluation	Elementary and Secondary Education Act, Title V-C	To improve State and local comprehensive planning and evaluation of education programs	4,750,000	State and local education agencies	OE Division of State Assistance
3 Follow Through	Economic Opportunity Act of 1964 (amended by PL 90-222)	To extend into primary grades the educational gains made by deprived children in Head Start or similar preschool programs	41,000,000	Local education or other agencies nominated by State education agencies in accordance with OE and OEO criteria	OE Division of Follow Through
4 Incentive grants	Elementary and Secondary Education Act, Title I, Part B (amended by PL 91-230)	To encourage greater State and local expenditures for education	17,855,000	State education agencies that exceed the national effort index	OE Division of Compensatory Education
5 Innovative and exemplary programs--supplementary centers	Elementary and Secondary Education Act, Title III	To support innovative and exemplary projects	146,168,000	Local education agencies	State education agencies, or OE Division of Supplementary Centers and Services
6 Indian education	Indian Education Act (PL 92-318) Title IV, Part A	To aid local education agencies and Indian controlled schools on or near reservations meet the special educational needs of Indian children	25,000,000	Local education agencies and Indian controlled schools on or near reservations	OE Office of Indian Education
7 Programs for children in State institutions for the neglected and delinquent	Elementary and Secondary Education Act, Title I (amended by PL 89-750)	To improve the education of delinquent and neglected children in State institutions	25,449,000	State parent agencies	State education agencies
8 Programs for disadvantaged children	Elementary and Secondary Education Act, Title I (amended by PL 89-750)	To meet educational needs of deprived children	1,446,338,000	Local school districts	State education agencies

	Authorizing legislation	Purpose	Amount	Administered by	Administering office
9 Programs for Indian children	Elementary and Secondary Education Act, Title I (amended by PL 89-750)	To provide additional educational assistance to Indian children in federally operated schools	15,809,936	Bureau of Indian Affairs schools	Bureau of Indian Affairs, Department of Interior
10 Programs for migratory children	Elementary and Secondary Education Act, Title I (amended by PL 89-750)	To meet educational needs of migratory farm workers	98,331,000	Local school districts	State education agencies
11 School library resources and instructional materials	Elementary and Secondary Education Act, Title II	To help provide school library resources, textbooks and other instructional materials	90,250,000	Local education agencies	OE Division of Library Programs
12 Special grants to urban and rural school districts with high concentrations of poor children	Elementary and Secondary Education Act, Title IV, Part C (amended by PL 91-230)	To improve education of disadvantaged children	47,701,000	Local school districts	State education agencies
13 Special projects in Indian education	Indian Education Act (PL 92-318) Title IV, Parts B and C	To support planning, pilot, and demonstration projects for the improvement of educational opportunities for Indian children and to develop training programs for education personnel	15,000,000	Indian tribes, organizations, and institutions. State and local education agencies and federally supported elementary and secondary schools for Indian children	OE Office of Indian Education
14 State administration of ESEA Title I programs	Elementary and Secondary Education Act, Title I (amended by PL 89-750)	To strengthen administration of ESEA, Title I	18,048,000	State education agencies	OE Division of Compensatory Education
15 Strengthening State education agencies	Elementary and Secondary Education Act, Title V-A	To improve leadership resources of State education agencies	34,675,000	State education agencies combinations thereof and public regional interstate commissions	OE Division of State Assistance

PART B—For Strengthening Organizational Resources

	Authorizing legislation	Purpose	Amount	Administered by	Administering office
16 Library services	Library Services and Construction Act, Title I	To extend and improve public library services, institutional library services, and library services to physically handicapped persons	44,019,000	State library administrative agencies	OE Division of Library Programs

Policy: All media acquired will be classified using the Dewey
                           Decimal Classification System.
Operation: All catalog cards for all items in the collection will be
                           placed in one card catalog.

There will be policies regarding personnel (advertising vacancies, qualifications for jobs, hiring practices, performance analysis, firing, hours, vacations, etc.); facilities (arrangement, hours, purchase of furniture, who may
use, etc.); resources (selection, balance of collection, cataloging, borrowing,
purchasing, processing, etc.); and finances (who may order, purchasing, control, reporting, etc.). Policies help to establish operational procedures which,
in turn, demand coordination among the diverse elements to insure attainment of goals. Policies and operations are as good as the communication and
feedback systems which permit the administrator to know how well the program is working and where modifications need to take place.

RESOURCES: ORGANIZING SERVICES

A good course in basic management techniques is the place to begin.
Such a course should look at administration in an organized and systematic
fashion. In a college or department of business administration or management,
a generalized approach is usually followed. Such a course emphasizes principles which can be applied in a variety of settings. In a school or department
of education, the application of management principles are specific to the
educational enterprise. In a college or department of library science or instructional technology (media), examples are likely to be specific to media
management. While the last option seems to be most immediately useful,
there is insufficient time to cover basic principles of management which are
common to more general courses. Before deciding to take any course, it would
be helpful to discuss the content and approach with the instructor.

A compendium of information about the management function may be
found in the books listed in the bibliography by Brown, Norberg, and Srygley;
by Erickson, and by Emanuel T. Prostano and Joyce S. Prostano. Use these
references as aids in gaining management competencies.

Internships in media centers offer practical on-the-job experience. Internships can vary from a few hours a week to full time over a period of
months. The opportunity to observe a media professional and the staff in
context provides a referent for all the classroom work which has come before
and might follow such an experience. Internships can be arranged by personally volunteering for services or by arranging for credit experience through a
faculty member in your professional program. Some internships offer random
experiences where assignments are given on a day-to-day basis depending on

need. Others are based on contracts or agreements whereby individuals are expected to perform certain duties and thus gain experience in specific functional areas. The latter arrangement is usually preferable since all concerned parties know what is expected and responsibilities are based on agreements from the start. It also permits the learner to determine whether or not the experience will contribute to his or her professional development or will merely repeat experiences already learned.

Another approach is for interns and media professionals to define problem areas which could be studied. The intern collects data and offers potential resolutions to the problem.

There is an increasing use of simulations in professional education. These simulations are generally not available commercially but are designed by the instructor of administration courses. At Ohio State University, the University Council for Educational Administration has developed complete school system simulations for the training of educational administrators. Background material about the community and school system is presented by sound filmstrips. Roles are assigned to individuals. "In-baskets" provide "work" to be completed. References regarding the school are available. "Interruptions" by tape recorded telephone calls provide a sense of reality. This technique permits an individual to become sensitive to the pressures of the "real world."

MASTERY ITEM: ORGANIZING SERVICES

Identify each statement below as a goal; a policy; or an operational procedure.

1. The program will serve the needs of each student and teacher ———
2. Cassette tape recorders are available for students to check out for home use ———
3. No materials will be added to the collection without evaluation and recommendation by a selection committee. ———
4. Non-book media will be shelved with books ———
5. Paraprofessional personnel will be used wherever possible ———
6. Program objectives will be based on user's needs ———

Response: Organizing Services

1. goal
2. operational procedure
3. policy
4. operational procedure
5. policy
6. goal

COMPETENCY 6   Plans media facilities; allocates and monitors space according to program needs.

The media professional must be concerned about the space which houses the program. Whether the base of operations is an existing media center (probably designed as a library), a converted room in a school basement, or a new building designed to meet contemporary standards for a school media program—the allocation of space must be done. What are the types of tasks related to facilities planning and use and where does one begin?

As an example of the tasks which a media professional performs in relation to space and facilities, the *Behavioral Requirements Analysis Checklist* provides the following:

1. Serve as liaison between administrators, faculty and architect to help interpret space utilization of the media center.
2. Arrange and allocate space to permit optimum utilization and accessibility to service, media and equipment.
3. Determine specifications for the purchase of media center furnishings.
4. Select interior furnishings to meet predetermined specifications.
5. Initiate procedures for bids and purchase orders for interior furnishings.
6. Plan and arrange shelving, storage spaces and interior furnishings in terms of their characteristics and potential use.
7. Plan and arrange staff station locations to provide accessibility of media center staff to faculty and students.
8. Identify and recommend maintenance needs of the media center to assure continued upkeep and repair.[12]

These tasks are not exhaustive, but serve to show how deeply involved the media professional can be in arranging and planning facilities.

Where to begin? Assuming that the media center reflects the philosophy and goals of the school or school system of which it is a part, it is then possible to list the activities which must occur to help meet the goals. When activities are defined, the media center can be designed appropriately for the users. In a new facility, the size and shape of the media center will be determined by the functions which take place within the center. In an existing facility, spaces will need to be adapted to make them "fit" into a predetermined area. Since most libraries were designed with large open spaces without walls, a desirable situation for flexibility exists and space reconfiguration is easily accomplished. Most of the principles of designing new spaces apply equally well to the reconfiguration of existing space.

A useful exercise as one begins to plan media center facilities is to list

---

[12] *Behavioral Requirements Analysis Checklist*, p. 44.

the verbs which describe what people will be doing in these spaces. (e.g., listening, reading, talking, viewing, writing, constructing, etc.) If learners will be looking at films or filmstrips, listening to recordings, or drawing on transparent acetate, the program should reflect these activities. How are these activities stated and communicated to the architect or facilities designer?

Generally there are two types of specifications: the *educational specifications,* which define the functions that will occur in the space, and the *architectural specifications,* which are derived from the educational specifications and spell out specific areas within the facility, the materials to be used, and the relationship of one space to other spaces. The local building committee develops the educational specifications in a *building program* and the architect uses these requirements as the basis for the architectural specifications which he develops. . . . The building program is a statement which translates philosophy and goals into specific building requirements. It defines in words and diagrams the functions and people to be accommodated, the kinds of facilities needed, and their relationships to each other. The program, as a written document, appears to be deceptively simple, but its preparation is a complex process.[13]

A brief summary of the components of a building program would include:

1. A clear statement of the school's philosophy and the goals of the media program.
2. A brief description of the activities to be performed in the media center.
3. A list of special requirements for each space:
   a. Type of space and number of occupants;
   b. Tasks to be performed;
   c. Approximate amount of square footage required; and
   d. Furniture and equipment to be used.
4. A description and/or diagrams of how each space should relate to other spaces in the media center and to the building as a whole.

A typical statement from a building program might look like this:

Production Area: remote from storage and user areas; near technical processing area (for access to water) and administrative office area (for staff supervision). Space for up to six individuals standing at counters. Equipment on counters (or tables) will include a Thermofax machine (approximately 18″ x 24″), a dry mount press (approximately 24″ x 36″), a photographic copy stand (36″ x 36″), a spirit duplicator (ap-

[13] Donald P. Ely et al., *Audiovisual Facilities and Equipment for Churchmen* (Nashville, Tenn.: Abingdon Press, 1970), pp. 231-32.

proximately 18″ x 30″) and a paper cutter (approximately 24″ x 24″). Counters should include storage space for materials. One drafting table and chair will be used for graphic art production. Table space for materials, collating, assembly, and related tasks should be 24″ x 48″. Electrical strips fused for 20 amps., should be provided at the back of the counter. Overhead lighting can be at the same level as the overall media center. No special ventilation required.

The major space requirements for a media center include: administration, storage, user, and production. Spaces for *administration* involve office space for the staff, technical processing (shipping, receiving, cataloging) and equipment and material maintenance and repair. *Storage* spaces include card catalog, shelving for books and periodicals, files, and special units for storing audiovisual media. User areas are the circulation desk, carrels, tables, conference rooms, classrooms, and previewing and auditioning spaces. *Production* space includes those areas where materials are copied, photographed, recorded, mounted, and created.

The competency, "to allocate and monitor space according to program needs" requires the media professional to carry out the procedures outlined above.

RESOURCES: ALLOCATING SPACE

Begin by visiting a school media center. Look for the administrative, storage, user, and production spaces. Talk with the media professional about the layout—why it is arranged as it is, how it works, and what changes should be made (if any). Observe how students are using the facilities. Are several activities occurring at the same time? Do people seem to be working independently or are they crowded? What are the activities? (viewing? reading? listening? constructing? etc.) How are various areas defined?

Visit another media center, preferably in a different area and serving different ages or types of learners. Ask some of the same questions. Are patterns beginning to emerge? Visit several more centers if possible. There is probably no better way to assess facilities than by observing them in use or trying to use them. How well does the media center in your college or university serve its clientele? It may be useful to begin the exercise in observation at home before visiting other locations away from campus.

It would be helpful to write a brief critique of each center. If you can ascertain the goals of the media program in each school district visited, you might assess the degree to which the attainment of the goals are being facilitated by the arrangement of space. Compare notes with your colleagues. What generalizations appear to be emerging?

Some people find it helpful to review layouts of traditional libraries or media centers in order to name the adequacies or inadequacies of each layout. Other people like to start from "scratch" attempting to sketch an ideal layout if there were no restraints. Think big! What would you do if you were asked to recommend a layout for a new school media center?

A visit to an architectural firm which has experience in designing schools is often helpful in finding out how educators work with architects. The key to successful planning of a media center is the ability to communicate your ideas to an architect in sufficiently specific terms to help him or her create a design which will meet your requirements.

At the beginning of the planning phase, it would be helpful to review the chapter on facilities in *Media Programs: District and School* [14] for general guidelines and specific space recommendations for each area. An example of the type of recommendations given is as follows:

TABLE 7-2 Recommendations for Planning (1,000 or fewer students)

Area	Relationships and Special Considerations	Space Allocations
Small group listening and viewing	*Relationships*: Small group listening and viewing may be accommodated in open areas of the media center via use of headsets, rear-screen projection, etc. Additional small group listening and viewing areas may be necessary.	Minimum of 150 sq. ft. per area
	Special Considerations: Space provided for listening and viewing areas is in addition to space allocated for conference rooms (which should be equipped also to accommodate this function). The area(s) should have electrical and TV inputs and outlets, permanent wall screen, and acoustical treatment.	

Many states have developed standards for gross space required for school media centers and sometimes specific allocations of space are recommended. Consult the buildings and facilities department of the state education agency and the state library office for assistance.

There are several references which are especially helpful in presenting the procedures for facilities planning and for stating requirements for each

[14] *Media Programs: District and School,* p. 97.

functional area. Even though the publication date is relatively old (1963), Ralph Ellsworth's *The School Library: Facilities for Independent Study in the Secondary School* (New York: Educational Facilities Laboratories) is one of the best publications to show a variety of space configurations for users. Many case studies and sketches open up many possibilities and stimulate further thinking. Support services are also discussed.

In Harold S. Davis, ed., *Instructional Media Center: Bold New Venture,* pp. 64–75 contain layouts and descriptions of five school media centers in various stages of development. In Chapter 7 (pp. 92-107) LeRoy R. Lindeman discusses "The Range of Services" as manifested in the design and use of spaces within a media center.

Very comprehensive discussions of the facilities planning process with illustrations, layouts and case studies are presented in: books by Prostano and Prostano (see Chapter 5, "Facilities for Programming"); Brown, Norberg, and Srygley; and Bowman et. al., all listed in the bibliography for Competency 6.

After following the suggestions listed here for gaining competency in facilities planning, the media professional should be able: (1) to describe the functional areas in media center; (2) to write specifications for each area; and (3) to communicate space needs to an architect.

MASTERY ITEM: ALLOCATING SPACE

Complete each item.

1. In the administration area, people will be doing the following: _____

2. The *storage* area should accommodate _____

3. In the *user* area, people will be doing the following: _____

4. In the *production* space, the following activities will occur: _____

5. Sketch a functional layout for a media center in a school with an enrollment of 1,000 secondary school students. The school is committed to using the full range of instructional resources to achieve its goal of making each individual responsible for his/her own learning.

Response: Allocating Space

1. In the administration area, people will be doing the following: *talking, listening, typing, writing, reading, calculating (and a few other activities which you may have stated).*
2. The *storage* area should accommodate *equipment, books, periodicals, audiovisual materials, file cards and supplies.*
3. In the *user* area, people will be doing the following: *reading, listening,*

viewing, writing, and thinking. (The circumstances might also include constructing, eating, smoking, lounging and other activities—depending upon the designated use of the space.)

4. In the *production* space, the following activities will occur: *drawing, lettering, mounting, laminating, cutting, copying, transparency making (and a host of other activities depending upon the extent of the production program which could include television, audio, and motion picture and still photography.)*

5. There are as many possible designs as there are media professionals and architects. Once again, the unique philosophy and needs (not to mention political and fiscal considerations) of each school will help to shape the media facilities. The guidelines offered in *Media Programs: District and School* will also assist in creating a plan.

   Begin by sketching what you consider to be the optimum space and arrangement that you can justify. That first draft can always be modified later.

   The floor plan on page 122 is *one* way to represent a media center which has incorporated most of the functions that an ideal center ought to perform.

COMPETENCY 7   Assesses the degree to which the operations meet the program goals.

Here we are again! Back to goals. But . . . how do we know whether or not we have arrived unless we know where we are going? It might be useful to quickly review the first competency in this chapter "Establishes goals of the media program." Did you develop a goal statement for the mastery item? If not, try to do it now. We must begin with goals if we are to adequately evaluate.

Evaluation, in the sense that it is used here, refers to an assessment of how well the entire operational program is doing. In Chapter 14, evaluation of media and in Chapter 13, evaluation of instruction, are interpreted differently although, in each instance, many of the same principles apply.

To adequately judge a media program there must be a *standard* for evaluation. That standard may be the goal and objectives of that specific media center. If the objectives are stated in observable terms, this will make the task easier. Beyond the local standards, there are often state standards. National standards do exist. Regional accrediting associations also include "library" standards as part of the evaluation schedules. There is no dearth of standards regarding school media programs.

Whether evaluation is a process of self-assessment to determine "how well we're doing" or a more formal evaluation for accreditation of the school system, it is helpful to the media professional since the results indicate both

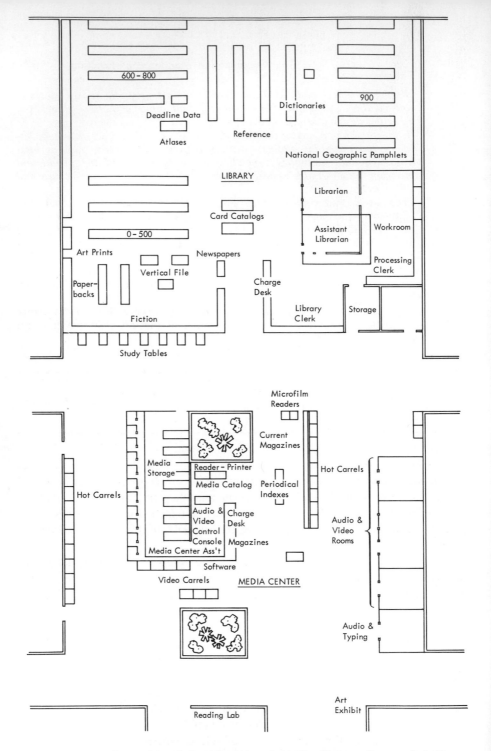

Figure 7-1. Floor plan of the Library and Media Center, Corona Del Mar High School (Square Feet: 14,000).

the accomplishments and the work yet to be done. Standards are often developed as much for providing direction as for making judgments and should be used for both purposes.

RESOURCES: ASSESSING OPERATIONS

Probably the best and most widely accepted standards are those published by the American Library Association and the Association for Educational Communications and Technology: *Media Programs: District and School.* While this publication is not specifically designed as an evaluation instrument, it does provide standards which serve as guidelines for the development of the school media program. The chapters dealing with operations of the program are the most useful in the evaluation context (planning, budget, personnel, collections, production, facilities, access and delivery systems, maintenance, public information and program evaluation).

There are several instruments which have been developed for assessing school media programs. One of the newest and best which considers comprehensive media programs is *An Instrument for the Qualitative Evaluation of Media Programs in California* (Sacramento: California State Department of Education, 1972). The guide was prepared by a joint committee of the California Bureau of Audio-Visual and School Library Education, the California Association for Educational Communications and Technology, and the California Association of School Librarians. The instrument is intended to be used by the local school district itself or by a visiting team who comes to the school to help develop new insights into local objectives, capabilities, and needs.

The Association for Educational Communications and Technology has developed and distributed a self-evaluation instrument for many years. The *Evaluative Checklist: An Instrument for Self-Evaluating an Educational Media Program in School Systems* is available from the Association for Educational Communications and Technology.[15] Since it was developed before the era of integrated library and audiovisual programs it emphasizes those aspects of the program which are concerned with nonbook media.

Evaluative Criteria,[16] widely used for self-evaluation and accreditation purposes by the regional accrediting associations, publishes a revised version every ten years—1960, 1970, etc. Much emphasis is placed on program objectives and qualitative and subjective judgments.

These instruments provide guidelines for assessing what is being done, how well it is being done, and what changes ought to be made.

[15] Association for Educational Communications and Technology, 1201 Sixteenth Street, N.W., Washington, D.C. 20036.
[16] *Evaluative Criteria, 1970 Edition* (Washington, D.C.: National Study of Secondary School Evaluation, 1970).

A thorough discussion of the evaluation process and a variety of instruments is presented in Carleton W. H. Erickson's *Administering Instructional Media Programs* (Chapter 15, pp. 599–628 "Evaluation"). It is probably one of the best summaries of the entire evaluation process with examples of a variety of instruments.

An example of an evaluation study which has been completed is *Services of Secondary School Media Centers: Evaluation and Development* by Mary Virginia Gaver. While this is not a case study of any one school, it does represent the procedures which can be followed when conducting an evaluation and the criteria which are studied. "It is the purpose of this study to provide a means of evaluating the media center program of secondary schools, specifically the variety and balance of services. The selection of outstanding media programs for comparison with a sample that is representative of a single state is one method for such evaluation. In its entire scope this study (1) presents a picture of the status of secondary school media centers in New Jersey; (2) provides one means of objective evaluation of several aspects of programs, especially variety and balance of services; and finally (3) gives some leads on how to turn libraries into media centers." [17]

With these resources, it should be possible to develop a strategy for program evaluation. How well can you do it?

MASTERY ITEM: ASSESSING OPERATIONS

Circle those items which would provide the media professional with information to assist in the evaluation process:

1. Three staff members have resigned in the past two months.
2. The media center has more than half of the user spaces full during all the hours it is open.
3. The center's budget has increased by 20 percent each year for the past three years.
4. There is a decrease in the use of books and an increase in the use of non-book media.
5. Equipment sent out for repair is never returned sooner than one month.
6. There is increasing use of the copy machine by students.

Response: Assessing Operations

1. The resignations themselves would not help, but knowing the reasons for them would indicate whether or not there are internal problems.
2. This fact really doesn't help until you know that the capacity of the

[17] Mary Virginia Gaver, *Services of Secondary School Media Centers: Evaluation and Development* (Chicago: American Library Association, 1971), p. xi.

center meets national standards. It would also help to know what individuals are doing. If they come to the media center as a quiet place to study, mere occupancy doesn't mean much.

3. This fact might make the media professional feel that something is right, but perhaps the increase should have been 50 percent. Perhaps the increase was a routine budget matter with little or no knowledge of needs. An increase does not help in evaluation unless you know why it has happened.

4. This circulation figure does not answer the "why" question. It is of little help in evaluation but could lead to further exploration which might be helpful.

5. This fact would assist the media professional in evaluating the efficiency of the repair service. If *no* equipment is returned sooner than one month, there must be something wrong with the service. Once in awhile it is necessary to send away for parts or there may be a seasonal load, but one month for all equipment is too long. You have enough to begin an evaluation.

6. This may be an indicator of an increased desire on the part of students to have a copy of materials from publications. Or it may have been stimulated by a teacher's request to maintain a notebook or any of a dozen reasons. The important thing here is that this is an *indicator* which merits further investigation before evaluation can occur.

REFERENCES

Competency 1   Establishes goals of the media program.

Davies, Ruth Ann. *The School Library Media Center: A Force for Excellence* (2nd ed.), pp. 409-11. New York: R. R. Bowker Co., 1974.

Erickson, Carleton W. H. *Administering Instructional Media Programs*, pp. 22-25. New York: Macmillan, 1968.

Gaver, Virginia Mary. *Services of Secondary School Media Centers: Evaluation and Development*, pp. 1-16. Chicago: American Library Association, 1971.

Gillespie, John T. and Diana L. Spirt. *Creating A School Media Program*, pp. 32-34. New York: R. R. Bowker Co., 1973.

"Learning Centers: A Working Bibliography" *Audiovisual Instruction* 15 (December, 1970) : 60-62.

"The School Library as a Materials Center" *Library Journal* 81 (February 15, 1956) : 547-51.

Taylor, Kenneth I. "Instructional Media Programs and School Objectives" in Harold S. Davies (ed.) *Instructional Media Center: Bold New Venture* pp. 21-33. Bloomington, Indiana: Indiana University Press, 1971.

Competency 2 Develops and maintains a long range plan.

BOWMAR, CORA PAUL. *Guide to the Development of Educational Media Selection Centers,* pp. 20-25. Chicago: American Library Association, 1973.

BROWN, JAMES W., KENNETH D. NORBERG and SARA K. SRYGLEY. *Administering Educational Media,* pp. 1-14. New York: McGraw-Hill, 1972.

DAVIES, RUTH ANN. *The School Library Media Center: A Force for Excellence* (2nd ed.), pp. 21-31. New York: R. R. Bowker Co., 1974.

DAVIS, HAROLD S. "Organizing an IMC" in Harold S. Davies (ed.) *Instructional Media Center: Bold New Venture,* pp. 55-75. Bloomington, Ind.: Indiana University Press, 1971.

ERICKSON, CARLETON, W. H. *Administering Instructional Media Programs,* pp. 42-54. New York: Macmillan, 1968.

GILLESPIE, JOHN T. and DIANA L. SPIRT. *Creating A School Media Program,* pp. 35-52. New York: R. R. Bowker Co., 1973.

LOHRER, ALICE. "The School Library in Transition," in Harold S. Davis (ed.) *Instructional Media Center: Bold New Venture,* pp. 35-54. Bloomington, Ind.: Indiana University Press, 1971.

Media Programs: District and School, pp. 30–31. Chicago: American Library Association, and Washington, D.C.: Association for Educational Communications and Technology, 1975.

PROSTANO, EMANUEL T. and JOYCE S. PROSTANO. *The School Library Media Center,* pp. 181-213. Littleton, Colo.: Libraries Unlimited, 1971.

Competency 3 Prepares and administers a fiscal plan based on operational needs.

BOWMAR, CORA PAUL. *Guide to the Development of Educational Media Selection Centers,* pp. 64-67. Chicago: American Library Association, 1973.

BROWN, JAMES W., KENNETH D. NORBERG and SARA K. SRYGLEY. *Administering Educational Media,* pp. 359-84. New York: McGraw-Hill, 1972.

DAVIES, RUTH ANN. *The School Library Media Center: A Force for Excellence* (2nd ed.), pp. 95-97; 397-98. New York: R. R. Bowker Co., 1974.

ERICKSON, CARLETON W. H. *Administering Instructional Media Programs,* pp. 544-583. New York: Macmillan, 1968.

GILLESPIE, JOHN T. and DIANA L. SPIRT. *Creating A School Media Program,* pp. 73-99. New York: R. R. Bowker Co., 1973.

Media Programs: District and School, pp. 31-34. Chicago: American Library Association, and Washington, D.C.: Association for Educational Communications and Technology, 1975.

PROSTANO, EMANUEL T. and JOYCE S. PROSTANO. *The School Library Media Center,* pp. 164-79. Littleton, Colo.: Libraries Unlimited, 1971.

Competency 4 Seeks information regarding supplemental funding from governmental agencies and other sources.

Catalog of Federal Education Assistance Programs. Washington, D.C.: U.S. Government Printing Office, 1972.

GILLESPIE, JOHN T. and DIANA L. SPIRT. *Creating A School Media Program,* pp. 20-24. New York: R. R. Bowker Co., 1973.

"Guide to OE-Administered Programs" *American Education,* (issued annually).

Competency 5   Organizes services to achieve goals.

BOWMAR, CORA PAUL. *Guide to the Development of Educational Media Selection Centers,* pp. 26-45. Chicago: American Library Association, 1973.

BROWN, JAMES W., KENNETH D. NORBERG and SARA K. SRYGLEY. *Administering Educational Media,* pp. 35-76. New York: McGraw-Hill, 1972.

DAVIS, HAROLD S. (ed.) *Instructional Media Center: Bold New Venture,* pp. 92-107. Bloomington, Ind.: Indiana University Press, 1971.

ERICKSON, CARLETON W. H. *Administering Instructional Media Programs,* pp. 226-99. New York: Macmillan, 1968.

LINDEMAN, LEROY R. "The Range of Services" in Harold S. Davis (ed.) *Instructional Media Center: Bold New Venture,* pp. 92-107, Bloomington, Ind.: Indiana University Press, 1971.

PROSTANO, EMANUEL T. and JOYCE S. PROSTANO. *The School Library Media Center,* pp. 25-45. Littleton, Colo.: Libraries Unlimited, 1971.

Competency 6   Plans media facilities; allocates and monitors space according to program needs.

Basic Language Laboratory Equipment and Its Use. 16mm motion picture, sound, black & white, 14 min., Pennsylvania State Department, 1966.

BOWMAR, CORA PAUL. *Guide to the Development of Educational Media Selection Centers,* pp. 59-63. Chicago: American Library Association, 1973.

BROWN, JAMES W., KENNETH D. NORBERG and SARA K. SRYGLEY. *Administering Educational Media,* pp. 141-64. New York: McGraw-Hill, 1972.

DAVIES, RUTH ANN. *The School Library Media Center: A Force for Excellence* (2nd ed.), pp. 440-552. New York: R. R. Bowker Co., 1974.

DAVIS, HAROLD S. "Organizing an IMC" in Harold S. Davis (ed.) *Instructional Media Center: Bold New Venture,* pp. 64-75. Bloomington, Ind.: Indiana University Press, 1971.

Designing for Projection. 35mm slides (280), sound (reel to reel tape) and script, color, 80 min., Kodak, 1970.

ELLSWORTH, RALPH E. and WAGENER, HOBART D. *The School Library.* New York: Educational Facilities Laboratories, Inc., 1963.

ELY, DONALD P., EDWARD A. GEORGE and JAMES E. ALEXANDER. *Audiovisual Facilities and Equipment for Churchmen,* pp. 225-306. Nashville, Tenn.: Abingdon Press, 1970.

ERICKSON, CARLETON W. H. *Administering Instructional Media Programs,* pp. 175-225. New York: Macmillan, 1968.

GILLESPIE, JOHN T. and DIANA L. SPIRT. *Creating A School Media,* pp. 111-28. New York: R. R. Bowker Co., 1973.

Media Programs: District and School, pp. 75-89. Chicago: American Library Association, and Washington, D.C.: Association for Educational Communications and Technology, 1975.

Planning for the Language Laboratory. 16mm motion picture, sound, black & white, 13 min., Pennsylvania State Department, 1966.

PROSTANO, EMANUEL T. and JOYCE S. PROSTANO. *The School Library Media Center,* pp. 103-35. Littleton, Colo.: Libraries Unlimited, 1971.

A Room for Learning. 35mm filmstrip, sound (record), color, 14 min., Fairfax, Va.: National Audio Visual Association (NAVA), 1968.

Space is Not Enough. 35mm filmstrip, sound (record), color, 16 min., Fairfax, Va.: NAVA, 1969.

Competency 7   Assesses the degree to which the operations meet the program goals.

BROWN, JAMES W., KENNETH D. NORBERG and SARA K. SRYGLEY. *Administering Educational Media,* pp. 412-17. New York: McGraw-Hill, 1972.

DAVIES, RUTH ANN. *The School Library Media Center: A Force for Excellence* (2nd ed.). pp. 259-306. New York: R. R. Bowker Co., 1974.

ERICKSON, CARLETON W. H. *Administering Instructional Media Programs,* pp. 599-628. New York: Macmillan, 1968.

Evaluative Checklist: An Instrument for Self-Evaluating an Educational Media Program in School Systems. Washington, D.C.: Association for Educational Communication and Technology, n.d.

Evaluative Criteria, 1970 Edition. Washington, D.C.: National Study of Secondary School Evaluation, 1970.

GILLESPIE, JOHN T. and DIANA L. SPIRT. *Creating A School Media Program,* pp. 53-69. New York: R. R. Bowker Co., 1973.

An Instrument for the Qualitative Evaluation of Media Programs in California. Sacramento, Calif.: California State Department of Education, 1972.

KAUFMAN, ROGER B. "Accountability, A System Approach and the Quantitative Improvement of Education—An Attempted Integration," *Educational Technology* 11:21-26 (Jan., 1971).

8 The Personnel Management Function

The second major element of management is concerned with personnel. This chapter presents several ways in which people are assigned responsibilities in a media center. The competencies involve recruiting, hiring and terminating personnel; conducting staff in-service training; assigning job responsibilities; assessing performance; and implementing creative supervision. The emphasis is on human relationships.

"We are in the people business." This motto is often used by media professionals to describe their basic purpose. The reason for emphasizing people is to spotlight the ultimate consumer of the services rendered and to diminish an emphasis on the materials and machines. The message here is that the acquisition, storage, and delivery of products is secondary (but necessary) to the process of dealing with people.

The usual emphasis on people is external—concentrating on those who are served. But there is another dimension of concern about people which is internal—the relationship of the media professional to the staff. It is critical that a qualified staff be hired; that initial training be conducted and continued training be encouraged; that tasks be assigned to appropriate personnel and that work be supervised and evaluated. It is necessary, at times, to terminate ("fire") an employee. And in addition to all these personnel management tasks, the media professional must maintain an *espirit de corps* among the entire staff. It's a big job. Where do you begin and how do you learn how to manage personnel?

We discuss personnel management as if it were a separate entity. It is not. It is an integral part of organization management and plays a role in the operation of each function performed by the media center staff. Handling

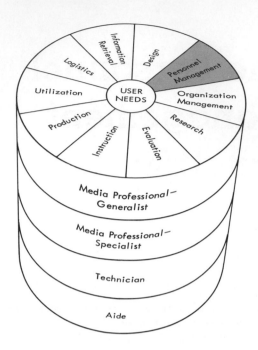

COMPETENCY 1 Writes job descriptions for recruiting and hiring personnel.

COMPETENCY 2 Recruits, hires, and terminates personnel.

COMPETENCY 3 Conducts training for staff.

COMPETENCY 4 Assigns job responsibilities to specific personnel.

COMPETENCY 5 Supervises personnel.

COMPETENCY 6 Maintains job satisfaction of personnel.

COMPETENCY 7 Evaluates employee performance.

personnel in a media center is not substantially different from managing personnel in any organization or agency where there is more than one person. As soon as one more person is hired or volunteers appear on the scene, the media professional has to be prepared to perform personnel management functions. Of course, the size of the staff and the way in which the center is organized will affect the way in which personnel are managed. Three or four full-time staff can report to the director, but more full-time staff and a cadre of part-time workers may create the need for delegating responsibility. For example, the clerical personnel and the technicians may be part-time people, perhaps students, who could report to an assistant director or some other designated person who, in turn, reports to the director. Let's consider how a staff is organized.

PERSONNEL ORGANIZATION

How many staff are needed for a media center? That depends on the size of the school or school system, the number of people being served and the range of services offered. *Media Programs: District and School* provides some helpful guidelines in Table 8-1.

The person who is ultimately responsible for the program is usually designated as "director" and reports to the principal if the center is in a single school building (Fig. 8-1). In a district program, the director usually reports to the Assistant Superintendent for Instruction (Fig. 8-2). This arrangement may vary due to unique situations in school and district organizations.

Some schools and districts separate those responsibilities which involve print media and nonprint (audiovisual) media. This separation may be due to historical circumstances since separate people were hired some time ago to perform each specialized function. Some school administrators believe that the activities of personnel dealing with printed materials and those concerned with audiovisual materials are so different that it is better to have separate units for each. Still others believe that the professional preparation of librarians emphasizes print media while audiovisual specialists are prepared to handle the nonprint media.

The contemporary trend is toward integrated or amalgamated programs with a single library media or learning resources program headed by one competent media professional who is prepared to handle all media. More and more professional education programs in library schools are being extended to include the nonbook media as well as the more traditional media. Some professional programs which have prepared audiovisual specialists are beginning to include preparation in organization and use of print media.

Some of the issues involving "separate" or "integrated" programs are political matters in state and national media organizations. Other issues involve incumbent personnel and job security. Some concerns focus on state certification requirements for media professionals. Whatever the issues or concerns, the important point is that most leadership positions should be filled by personnel who are competent to do the job. The emphasis here is on *competencies* which any media professional ought to possess regardless of the academic department in which he or she receives his or her professional education. What is advocated is an integrated or cooperative program which is

TABLE 8-1 Recommended Base for Media Programs in the School

Size of School	Professional Staff				Support Staff			Total Staff
School enrollment	Head of media program	Other media specialists	Other media professionals	Sub-total	Media technicians[b]	Media sides	Sub-total	
250	1	0	0	1	1[b]	1	2	3
500	1	0-1	0-1	2	1-2[b]	2-3	3-4	5-6
1,000	1	1-2	1-2	3-4	3-5[b]	3-5	6-8	9-12
1,500	1[a]	1-4	1-4	4-6	4-6[b]	4-6	8-12	12-18
2,000	1[a]	2-5	2-5	5-8	5-8[b]	5-8	10-16	15-24

[a]In large schools with fully developed media programs, the professional staff includes both media specialists and other media professionals. The head of the school media program, selected on the basis of managerial competencies, may be a media professional (other than media specialist).

[b]The number and proportion of media technicians on the staff of the individual school media program is influenced by the services provided from the district media program as well as program emphases within the school.

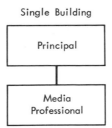

Single Building

Figure 8-1   The Relationship of the Media Professional in a Single School Building

designed to serve users in the most efficient and accessible fashion. A unified program appears to be the best way to accomplish this purpose. Several alternative organizational arrangements are shown in Figures 8-3, 8-4 and 8-5. The examples are for individual schools.

Beyond the organization at the leadership level is the designation of personnel to perform special functions. Positions usually contain clusters of responsibility, rather than one specialization alone. A helpful way to determine what kinds of personnel may be required, is to review the functions discussed in this book and ask yourself, who will perform each. In a relatively small school, one person may have to be responsible for all functions. In some cases,

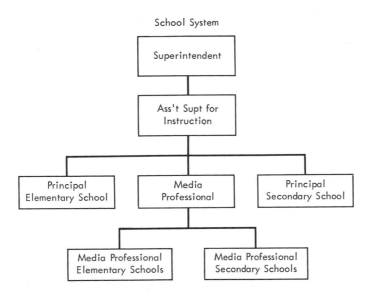

Figure 8-2   The Relationships of the Media Professional in a School District

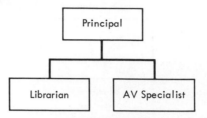

Figure 8-3   **Separate Responsibilities for Media Program**

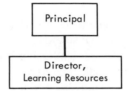

Figure 8-4   **Integrated Program—All Responsibilities Under One Media Professional**

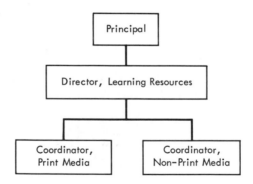

Figure 8-5   **Integrated Program With Specialists Reporting to Program Coordinator**

nonprofessional assistance may come from student help or parent volunteers. In other cases, members of the faculty might assist. For example, the art teacher might help with graphics design and photography. Review the functions to determine who will be responsible for each and which ones will be emphasized:

Organization Management	Production
Personnel Management	Instruction
Design	Evaluation
Information Retrieval	Research
Logistics	Utilization

Positions within the media center should be organized around the functions which are performed there. Further, each function can be broken down into tasks, each with a specified competency. While this approach is easy to understand theoretically, it is usually altered when people are considered and hired for positions. It is unlikely that any one person will ever possess all the competencies you feel are desirable and therefore you will have to compromise. You may even provide training or encourage an individual to obtain further competencies in order to more adequately meet your requirements.

Here is an example of the way in which one media professional analyzed the personnel needs for an integrated secondary school media program. The school has approximately 1100 students and 45 teachers. This media professional decided to find a trained librarian to work part-time initially (because of budgetary limitations) who would gradually become a full-time employee. A person with some training in educational technology (media professional) was already on the staff. Some responsibilities could be performed at the district level. The following arrangement is feasible:

Function:	*Assign to:*
Research	Media Professional (District Office)
Evaluation	Self
Production	Media Professional (educational technology training); student help
Design	Media Professional (educational technology training)
Logistics	Part-time assistant (trained librarian); student help
Information Retrieval	Self
Personnel Management	Self
Organization Management	Self
Instruction	Self; part-time assistant (trained librarian)
Utilization	Self

ACQUIRING COMPETENCIES IN PERSONNEL MANAGEMENT

How does one learn to get along with people? How does one acquire the competencies which are required for leading people? A truthful person would probably reply, "By doing it!" And that would be correct. However appropriate the direct experience approach might be, it is difficult for many individuals who are involved in a formal education program to acquire such real world experience. The problem is compounded by the need for a competent observer to criticize the trainee's performance so that appropriate behaviors are reinforced and inappropriate behaviors extinguished. This approach has been used in student teaching with some degree of success. Trained observers using interaction analysis techniques have helped the student teacher to know how successful human relationships have been.

With media professionals, an internship with a competent professional would seem to be a desirable approach. Unlike teaching situations where performance is confined to a classroom and compressed into a given time period, the activities of the media professional are spread over several areas and involve a variety of people during an entire working day. It would seem, therefore, that an apprentice-like relationship in a media center with commentary about a trainee's performance from the professional would be an ideal training ground for learning how to manage personnel. The assumption here is that the person being observed is a model for personnel management; that time for dialogue is available; and that the nature of the dialogue is perceptive, constructive, and generalizable to other situations. This is an ideal worth striving for.

Other approaches which should be considered include the techniques of simulation, role playing, and personal involvement. A simulation exercise places the individual in a context very much like the real environment. The person is given sufficient information about the situation and is expected to perform an assigned role. Pilots learn to fly in simulators and business people play management simulation games using computers as tools. In training for personnel management, videotaped incidents can present stimuli to which reactions are made.

Simulations must be carefully designed with adequate data to help individuals make decisions. Some simulations require months to prepare and take several days to play. Others are less consuming in time but require extensive planning. The technique is useful because it is close to reality, demands decision-making, and requires interaction among people.

Role-playing is closely related to simulation, but it is usually shorter in duration and often occurs on the spur of the moment. Individuals are asked to assume roles to act out a single incident. For example, for a group that is learning to interview, individuals will be asked to assume the role of the interviewer and interviewee. They would be told about the circumstances of the interview—applying for a job, for example—and would be given just enough information to interact with each other. Sometimes individuals are asked to assume characteristics which they would not normally possess for the sake of the role. After a situation is played out, the group discusses the process and then questions the role players about their actions and feelings while acting. The technique is useful because it is involving, brief and provides a sense of reality.

Simulations and role-playing are reality-based, "let's pretend" exercises which are planned to teach specific procedures. There are other types of activities which help individuals to understand themselves and their relationships with others that do not require the assumption of roles. The human potential movement, sometimes referred to as "sensitivity training," helps individuals to develop more productive relationships with other people. Human potential training programs vary from those which use sensory experiences to develop body awareness to some which use a structural approach to help improve specific skills, such as listening. Also included in this genre are training programs in transactional analysis (the Parent–Adult–Child roles) and achievement motivation. The common thread running through these programs is the attempt to develop a personal openness and frankness which, theoretically, others will respond to in kind. These programs have helped many people to open themselves to new experiences and to appreciate themselves as persons. In some cases the very honesty of the probing and the atmosphere of therapy have caused individuals to break. This is a risk in some of the programs that elicit deep emotional involvement.

In developing personnel management competencies it would be helpful to participate in some of the human potential courses, mini-courses and sessions. They are usually offered on a formal or informal basis on most college campuses. Community groups in adult education centers establish short courses. Churches and community social service agencies sometimes provide opportunities to participate in human relations programs. In checking out these programs, it is wise to ask: (1) Who will be the leader? (2) What is his or her training? (3) What do others say about previous sessions conducted by this leader? (4) Is it possible to drop out at any time? (5) What results are promised? (6) Are these results important to you? Selection of a qualified and successful leader is of critical importance as is finding an approach which you can tolerate. Check each program before you commit yourself.

To best prepare for personnel management it would be wise to opt for an internship with a top flight media professional; sharpen your skills in simulation exercises; and get in touch with yourself and with others through participation in human potential groups. While this ideal may not be achieved, undertaking any part of it is a move in the right direction. Finally, try to consider your day-to-day actions as you talk and work with other people. How effective are you in communicating, in listening, and in responding empathetically and honestly? This is a kind of learning which never stops and must be practiced continually in order to maintain its effectiveness.

COMPETENCIES FOR PERSONNEL MANAGEMENT

There are literally dozens of tasks which are included in the personnel management category, but all of these tasks can be clustered in seven distinct areas. Each competency with its associated tasks will be presented separately. It is assumed in this chapter that actual members and types of personnel have been determined according to the particular needs of a single media center and its unique program.

COMPETENCY 1 Writes job descriptions for recruiting and hiring personnel.

A job description outlines the qualifications for the position and the areas of work in which a person will perform. It sometimes describes the nature of the media center and its administrative organization. Salary range for the position is often mentioned. The job description is almost always stated in terms of the ideal. It lists all of those qualifications which would be ideal for the job and all of the competencies which a candidate should possess in order to perform at the highest possible level.

The job description is developed on the basis of competencies needed for a particular program. The person to be hired will complement the talents of those already employed, and, in some cases, assume responsibilities currently handled by persons who are overloaded. Thus the list of responsibilities will vary from position to position and from school to school.

RESOURCES: WRITING JOB DESCRIPTIONS

It is important to distinguish between professional positions and paraprofessional positions. *Professional* positions possess qualifications which require undergraduate and/or graduate work in media. Minimum qualifications are often specified by state certification requirements and it would thus be wise to review these requirements for school media personnel before writing a job specification. Additional qualifications can be specified depending on the unique requirements of the school or school system. The media specialist, as compared with the media generalist may need special qualifications.

The *paraprofessional* positions include technicians and clerks. The qualifications for such personnel may already be determined by the school district as in the case of secretaries and clerks. Check with the school administrator to see if job descriptions for such personnel already exist. Some specialized training for technicians and clerks is usually required, but can be acquired at a secondary school or junior college level. Some aides and clerks may not require specialized training. In this case qualifications are stated more generally and are often more difficult to assess. For example, a job description may request a person who can "get along with people" and one who "is able to organize materials in an orderly fashion."

A useful outline for preparing a job description is as follows:

Title of position
Location
Qualifications (general and specific)
Description of duties
Salary range
Starting date
Deadline for application

The job descriptions which follow illustrate several formats which have been used to announce positions in the school media field. You may use these or review others as guidelines to prepare job descriptions for your program.

MASTERY ITEM: WRITING JOB DESCRIPTIONS

Write a job description for one of the following positions:

1. You are seeking a professional assistant for your elementary school media center who has competencies in the areas of production, instructional design, and logistics. The salary range will be $9,500-$11,000 for the school year. There are no state certification requirements for this position.
2. The school district in which you are employed is seeking a graphic artist to serve all schools in the system from the central office. The salary is set at $7500 for eleven months.

Response: Writing Job Descriptions

These are sample job descriptions. They will vary depending on the position and the policy for advertising positions by the personnel office of the school district. This is how they might look:

1. Vacancy for: Assistant Director, George Washington Elementary
   School Media Center

Qualifications:

Bachelor's degree in elementary education preferred, but not required
Master's degree in audiovisual education or educational technology
Experience in media production, instructional development and management
Ability to work with teachers and students

Duties:

Organize and maintain production activities in the media center including
graphic arts, photography, transparency making and portable video recording.
Consult with faculty on the design and use of media in all curricular areas
Assist with the distribution of non-book media and equipment

Salary: $9,500 to $11,000 to start depending upon qualifications (Sept. 1–
June 30)

Starting Date: September 1

Deadline for Application: April 1

2. Vacancy for: Graphic Artist, Westerly School District

Qualifications:

Associate's degree in commercial art
A portfolio which reflects appropriate skill for the position
Experience as a graphic artist in school or industrial settings desirable, but
not required

Duties:

Plan and execute graphic designs for instructional materials
Prepare master art work for printing, overhead transparencies, and photography
Consult with media professionals and teachers in the design of instructional materials
Establish and maintain a file of art work for future use

Salary: $7,500 per year; one month paid vacation; health and retirement
benefits

Starting Date: January 1

Deadline for Application: December 15

TABLE 8-2 Examples of job descriptions

Title	Media Specialist
GENERAL STATEMENT OF DUTIES	Responsible for providing extensive training and experience for library technicians. Develop workshops for classroom teachers and administrators in the utilization of multi-media approches in education, such as: (1) application of media in curriculum development, (2) administration of instructional media systems, (3) media research and evaluation, (4) proper maintenance and use of media equipment and materials. To assume the responsibility for production of media materials and services as well as guides for the full utilization. Develop the overall media budget and supervise the expenditures from the media budget.
SUPERVISION RECEIVED	Under direct supervision of Superintendent with cooperation of building Principals.
SUPERVISION EXERCISED	Library technicians, clerical aide, pages, volunteers.
JOB GOAL	To help each student obtain maximum benefit from the educational program through the utilization of diversified educational materials.
EVALUATION	Performance will be evaluated annually by the Superintendent in collaboration with building Principals and in accordance with the provisions set forth in the School Committee policy on evaluation of support personnel.
ILLUSTRATIVE EXAMPLES OF WORK PERFORMED	1. Interprets to the faculty, administration and public the objectives and facilities of the media program. 2. Arranges inservice programs for teachers, support personnel, media center staffs, and volunteers, students, and adults in the use of materials and equipment. 3. Plans and develops a coordinated media program for the school district. 4. Does media research, develops efficient system of distribution and retrieval.

Title	*Media Specialist*

5. Serves as consultant to all curriculum committees.

6. Conducts continuous evaluation of the effectiveness with which media is used by teachers and plans for increasing the educational value of the materials.

7. Coordinates the field trip programs of the district.

8. Coordinates school media needs with the available media of Public Library.

9. Maintains running inventory of equipment and materials.

10. Manages the distribution, repair, and maintenance of equipment and resources.

11. Supervises centralized processing of materials.

12. Supervises production and acquisition of print, non-print and manipulative materials.

13. Coordinates preparation of media materials for use in independent study as well as in classroom instruction.

14. Exercises a high degree of personal initiative, imagination and thorough cooperative planning with the building Principals, strives to accomplish the aims, goals, objectives of the Schools.

15. Develops media objectives and budgets which reflect studied consideration of system-wide needs and usage and supervises the media expenditures.

16. Establishes clearly defined policies, procedures and plans for the system-wide media program, including short and long-range goals.

Title	*Media Specialist*
KNOWLEDGE; SKILLS, CAPACITIES	Possess a thorough working knowledge designed to organize, evaluate, and maintain multi-media/study skills laboratory. Is knowledgeable of the systems of graphics, photography, slide transparencies, video and sound production. Possess the ability to work cooperatively in a service capacity with all personnel of the district. Ability to exercise prudent judgment in all acquisitions.
EDUCATION	Valid teaching certificate. Master's degree or higher, advance graduate study in media preparation. Graduate work to include audio-visual media services. Selection and utilization of instructional materials, learning and communications theory, cataloging and classification of instructional materials, evaluation designs, curriculum development, experience as a media specialist. Such alternatives to above qualifications as the School Committee may find appropriate and acceptable.
TERMS OF EMPLOYMENT	Twelve months. Salary and other benefits as established and contractually agreed to with the School Committee.

COMPETENCY 2   Recruits, hires, and terminates personnel.

Recruiting

Once the job description is written, it must be disseminated to prospective applicants. Jobs may be advertised in professional publications, listed with educational placement bureaus, sent to colleges and universities which have professional education programs in this field, and mentioned to colleagues in other schools and school systems. The objective should be to make the position in your media center as visible as possible so that a large number of applications are received. The rationale behind wide dissemination is that there will be a large number of applicants to choose from thus the probability of locating the most highly qualified person is enhanced. The limitation of this procedure is that you may be flooded with applicants and you must thoroughly review them all and notify each final applicant about your decision.

A useful procedure for recruiting is to ask interested candidates to send a letter of application and a copy of a professional resumé. A professional resumé or vitae usually includes name, address, telephone number, date of birth, and other vital statistics which a person wishes to mention. Also listed are the names of institutions from which degrees have been awarded, identification of the degree, date awarded and field(s) of major concentration. Experience is also listed, usually in chronological order with brief explanations of special aspects of each position. Some resumés list publications written by the individual, professional organizations in which memberships are held and honors received. Very often names and addresses of references are given.

When a letter of application and resumé are received, the job description should be sent to the candidate. If the person appears to possess the necessary qualifications, the next step would be to request the professional placement file (if available) from the institution most recently attended or from the institution which awarded the professional degree. References should be contacted by letter or telephone. Telephone interviews. regarding prospective employees tend to yield more frank statements than those which are written.

Hiring

Once all this information has been gathered, it is likely that several candidates will emerge as superior to the total population of applicants. These persons should be invited to the school for interviews.

The interview is a critical event for both the interviewer and the applicant. For the interviewer it is a time to probe further some of the statements made on the resumé and by the references. It is a time when favorable and unpleasant idiosyncracies emerge. It provides an opportunity for assessing personal qualities which are difficult to describe on professional resumés. The interviewer should aim to set the applicant at ease in a nonthreatening environment, free from possible interruptions, and without undue time pressure.

For the applicant the interview is a time to explain further some of the brief citations of the resumé and to present the personal dimensions of his or her character. It provides the opportunity to raise questions about the job and the performance expectations. The interview is just as much an assessment of the program by the applicant as it is an evaluation of the applicant by the interviewer. It is, in the best sense, a dialogue between professionals.

It is helpful to have the applicant meet and talk with other members of the staff and the administrators in the school. Judgments made by others can augment your own evaluation. It also helps the applicant to understand the broader aspects of your program within the school.

Finally a decision must be made. Which person is best for the job? Review the qualifications and job requirements which you developed for the job description. How well does each candidate match up with your initial expectations on a point-by-point basis? What do others say who have interviewed each candidate? Could you ask these persons to list the candidates in order of preference? What did the references say—particularly the person(s) who knew the individual in his or her most recent position? What affective feelings did you have about the person? Is this a person who is committed to the field? Is the person professionally competent in the areas in which you need help? Is this a person whom you feel you could trust? There are measures for determining the optimum candidate for a position but, in your situation you will factor in all of the above variables and should probably hire the person whom you feel best about, assuming that all the other qualifications are met.

Remember in selecting one person, that you should have reasons why the other applicants have been rejected. You will be asked by the unsuccessful candidates for reasons why they were not selected. Documentation during the interviews helps to provide these answers when they are requested.

There is probably no more important event in the life of a media center director than the hiring of staff. Your staff is an extension of yourself. They represent you. They will relieve you of many tasks which you would otherwise do. Careful, thoughtful, and thorough procedures during the recruiting and hiring phases can lead to a professionally rewarding relationship with a new colleague. The alternative is an uncomfortable, unrewarding, and uninspired relationship resulting from sloppy recruiting and hiring practices which must be endured for a longer period than you ever thought was possible.

Terminating Personnel

The spectre of the poor decision in hiring often leads to that uncomfortable moment of terminating employment. You realize that the person you hired is not "right" for the job; the individual has been performing so poorly that his usefulness has ended; he cannot deal with users in a cordial fashion; or relationships among staff members are becoming frayed because of this person's inability to be sensitive to the feelings of fellow employees. There may be several other reasons for having to fire an employee; funds may run out and not be renewed; there may be general cutbacks in the school budget and those who were hired most recently would be the first to leave; there may be a reorganization of the school media program with subsequent change or elimination of personnel. These reasons, while difficult to explain to an employee being terminated, are more or less beyond the control of the director and the employee. They do not enter the personal realm.

When an employee is being fired for personal and professional inadequacies, it is imperative that there be documented evidence of those inadequacies. For example, records of continued tardiness, evidence of poor work, complaints from users and staff, evidence of incompetence can all be used to indicate why an employee is being fired. There should have been previous "warnings" so that termination is not an abrupt and unexpected event. Reasons must be given for terminating employment.

Employees who appear to be in trouble should receive counsel and advice from the director and other colleagues. Attempts to help a person adjust to the style and procedures of a media center should precede any consideration of termination. Firing is a last resort which takes place only after continued attempts to help the individual have failed.

In some cases, individuals may recognize their own limitations and resign from the position. This is, of course, the less painful route for all concerned. In many cases, however, terminating employment will be left up to the director, and, no matter how unpleasant this task may be, it is part of his job.

RESOURCES: RECRUITING, HIRING, AND FIRING

Some of the procedures recommended in the early part of this chapter provide vehicles for gaining competencies in recruiting, hiring and firing. Consider especially the use of role-playing situations combined with discussions by participants and observers of the role-playing exercise.

MASTERY ITEM: RECRUITING, HIRING, AND FIRING

1. Prepare your personal professional resumé as a model for those you would expect to receive if you were hiring a media professional.
2. Write a list of questions you would ask while interviewing applicants for an assistant director's position in your media center.

Response: Recruiting, Hiring, and Firing

1. Professional resumés are very personal. They reflect the uniqueness of the individual. Be sure that your resumé communicates your strengths and job aspirations. The resumé which follows may be followed for format, but adapt your own to express your individual qualities. Ask your instructor to review it for you.

PROFESSIONAL RESUME

Donald G. McKinny

Address: 40 Ivy Court, Amherst, Mass.
Telephone: Home: (413) 246-8024
            Business: (413) 542-4700
Date of Birth: Feb. 15, 1942
Place of Birth: Philadelphia, Pa.
Marital Status: Married; one child
Health: Excellent

Education

Undergraduate
  Bucknell University, B.A. (American Studies) 1964
Graduate
  Rutgers University, M.L.S. (Library Science) 1967
  Additional graduate study in educational technology, Pennsylvania
  State University, 1970-1973.

Experience

Coordinator for Educational Technology
  Johnson Library Center, Hampshire College, Amherst, Mass.
  1971-present.
Assistant Director of Educational Communications, Media (Pa.) Schools
  1967-1971
Graduate Assistant in Learning Resource Center, Rutgers University
  1966-1967
Videotape Coordinator for Teacher Education Program, West Chester
  State College, West Chester, Pa., 1964-1966
Summer Intern
  WQED-TV, Pittsburgh, Pa., Summer, 1963

Professional Affiliations

American Library Association
Association for Educational Communications and Technology
National Association of Educational Broadcasters

Professional Goals

Instructional development with particular reference to media

Teaching media production, mass communications, selection and
   use of media

Instructional television production

Personal Interests

Ham radio; cinema study, hiking and camping.

2. Questions to ask while interviewing might include:

> What first interested you in the media field as a professional?
>
> In what areas of the media program do you prefer to work?
>
> Are there areas of work which you would rather avoid?
>
> What experiences have you had working with other people?
>
> Would you assess these experiences as successful? (Why or why not?)
>
> In what areas do you feel especially well-prepared?
>
> Have you worked with students? (If so, has this been satisfying? If not, do
> you feel you want to work with students?)
>
> What books have you read recently (television or films seen) that you would
> recommend?
>
> What evidence do you have that your previous work (or professional prepa-
> ration in the case of inexperienced candidates) has been satisfactory?
>
> What would you like to know about our media program?

Of course this is not an exclusive list. There are dozens of other questions which are equally valid. This line of questioning focuses on professional
preparation and satisfactions; human relationships, personal self-renewal, and
perceptiveness in self-appraisal.

COMPETENCY 3   Conducts training for staff.

There are two major types of training conducted within the media center
by the director or designated representative: (1) orientation or initial training
for new staff, and (2) continuing on-the-job training for current staff. Responsibility for such training falls on the director of the media center.

The purpose of *orientation* or *initial training* is to acquaint a new employee with people and procedures within the center. The new staff member
should be able to identify individuals by name and to describe the major tasks

performed by each person. In addition, the new person should be able to locate materials, equipment, and supplies for users or for personal use. This person should be able to follow established procedures and describe policies in his or her area of responsibility. Above all, this individual should be able to express the philosophy and goals of the media center to someone who has never heard them.

Training for new staff is usually a shared responsibility with the director assuming the coordination. It is likely that one person will be trained at a time and that established personnel can work individually with the new person for the length of time necessary to acquire a particular understanding or skill.

Continuing training for current staff is always necessary, particularly in the era of change in which we live. Some continuing education occurs in colleges and universities through workshops, short courses, evening courses, summer programs and federally funded institutes. There is increasing interest in nontraditional studies which do not require long-term attendance at classes on a college campus but, rather, use various types of audiovisual media (slide/tapes, programmed instruction, television, videotapes, audiocassette tapes and films) in remote locations with letters, tapes and telephone used for dialogue between learners and teachers. State, regional and national meetings provide short courses prior to, during, and after conferences. The alert media professional will identify those programs which promise new understandings and skills which are required locally and send staff to these sessions at the school's expense. The director must also consider attendance at such programs as an opportunity for personal self-renewal.

Continuing education does not occur only in formal and nonformal courses and workshops offered by colleges and universities. There are opportunities within the media center which ought to be used. Certain individuals have skills which they can share with one another so that services can be extended. For example, a staff person who can produce overhead transparencies with ease and with a creative flair could help others to do so. The person who reads widely or the individual who views films and television extensively can share criticisms of current titles and assist others in developing their own criteria for evaluating media. As new equipment is added to the media center, it would be wise to have several people trained in its use. A new teletype terminal which is tied into a statewide information network should be familiar to several staff members. A new tape duplicator which makes several copies of audiocassettes at one time should be able to be used by more than one person. New procedures developed by the school district media office can often be better disseminated by a brief training session than by long memoranda. And so it goes. No one should ever stop learning—especially the media professional.

Still another opportunity is offered through courses, workshops, and institutes offered in the school and school district but intended primarily for teachers. Media professionals should be part of the continuing in-service training of teachers since they work so closely together. To separate media professionals from those they serve is a foolish distinction and should not be made.

RESOURCES: CONDUCTING TRAINING

Design for training should follow the principles of instruction design outlined in Chapter 9. The elements that need to be considered when designing training for staff are: (1) the need for the training; (2) objectives; (3) content; (4) entering behavior; (5) strategy; (6) grouping; (7) time; (8) space; (9) resources and (10) evaluation and feedback.

Gaining competencies in conducting training is one of those skills that is best learned by doing it. There really is no simulator or role playing that will help to gain this competency. Active participation in a training program as a presentor of new information may provide a kind of "student teaching" experience. You should, if possible, have your effort evaluated by those you are teaching, whether it is a one-time presentation or a mini-course. Knowledge of how well you are doing with your intended audience will facilitate your improvement.

MASTERY ITEM: CONDUCTING TRAINING

A new mini-computer has been placed in your media center. It is primarily for individual use of students (and teachers) in science and mathematics. With your approval the media center was determined to be the best location for the console since it would be accessible more hours per day and would not detract from group instruction in the classroom. Since a math or science teacher cannot always be available to assist users, you decided that the assistant director, the head clerk, the audiovisual specialist, and yourself should acquire the necessary skills to assist others in using the computer. Which of the following procedures would you recommend for such training once the content and objectives were determined? (Circle as many as you feel are appropriate.)

1. Sign up for a beginning computer course at the local university.
2. Invite the salesmen who sold the mini-computer to the school to train your staff.
3. Ask the science and math teachers to develop a mini-course for your staff.
4. Read the instruction book, observe students' use, try it out on your own and then design the training program.

5. Develop a step-by-step instructional program to guide each person through the operation.
6. Ask students who have mastered the computer's operation to teach members of your staff.

Response: Conducting Training

All of the listed procedures could be followed but some are better than others.

1. A computer course at the local university would probably be interesting but it most likely would be general to all computers, not specific to your mini-computer. It may tell you more about computers than you want to know.
2. The salesman who sold you the mini-computer has the obligation to teach its use. Call on this source for help.
3. Since you are working closely with the science and math teachers, it probably would be helpful to seek their counsel in training your staff. In that way the special concerns of those teachers would be met while your staff became trained.
4. Reading the instruction book and observing is a cumbersome and time-consuming task. It *can* be done and, for some people—to discover by trial and error just what works and what doesn't—may be the best way.
5. Developing the step-by-step program requires knowledge of the computer's operation so this procedure could not be accomplished until mastery of the computer is attained.
6. Students manage to learn the operation of devices in an amazingly brief time. They learn the short-cuts and boil down procedures to the bare essentials. A student who has mastered the computer's operation would probably be an excellent way for you and your staff to learn if you could stand the role reversal and the student did not balk at being the teacher.

COMPETENCY 4   *Assigns job responsibilities to specific personnel.*

This competency is as simple as asking, "What tasks need to be done and who ought to do them?" But it is as complex as the question, "How can I make the best use of available staff to effectively and efficiently perform all the services expected from our center?"

One helpful way of beginning to perform this competency is to start with the ten functions used in this book and to review the competencies listed for each. From the competencies are derived the tasks for which individuals will be held responsible. Using the *logistics* function as an example, we might center on the competency "schedules and distributes audiovisual materials." From this competency stem such tasks as:

Develops systematic procedures for scheduling and distribution

Designs appropriate forms to use with the system

Examines routing system to determine problems

Analyzes circulation records to report usage figures

Analyzes usage figures to determine equipment needs

Such task statements can be gleaned from the *Behavioral Requirements Analysis Checklist* [1] and *Guidelines for Certification of Media Specialists.* [2]

The clusters of tasks which need to be accomplished should then be matched with personnel who are prepared (or could learn) to handle each group of tasks. It is sometimes wise to have a second (or back-up) person also responsible for certain tasks. All tasks which need to be accomplished within the center should be "covered" even though some may occur only once per year or require minimal effort from time to time.

The basic point to remember here is that the media professional who is in charge of the center is ultimately responsible for all that happens there even though many tasks may be delegated to others. Good planning, appropriate designation of personnel, open communication, and creative supervision can make this responsibility challenging and rewarding.

RESOURCES: ASSIGNING RESPONSIBILITIES

A comprehensive, but manageable, list of tasks is found in Chapter 6, "Center Personnel Tasks" in *Guide to the Development of Educational Media Selection Centers.* [3] Each task is listed in a category dealing with policies, planning, budgeting, and administration. The approach is by categories of tasks, not by level or type of personnel responsible for them.

Prostano and Prostano [4] discuss briefly the selection of personnel, reality staffing, and deployment of staff in practical terms which would help any director to face the job assignment responsibility with greater confidence.

In developing the list of tasks and determining who should be responsible for which task, it should be remembered that when there is a staff of only one or two persons, each person may have to perform work in each category. Specialization is difficult in such situations. Staff expansion is often accomplished by hiring part-time staff, securing volunteers for certain activities and contracting with individual firms for repairs, maintenance, processing,

---

[1] *Behavioral Requirements Analysis Checklist* (Chicago: American Library Association, 1973).

[2] *Guidelines for Certification of Media Specialists: Extended Version* (Washington, D.C.: Association for Educational Communicaton and Technology, 1972).

[3] Cora Paul Bowmar, et al., *Guide to the Development of Educational Media Selection Centers* (Chicago: American Library Association, 1973), pp. 54-58.

[4] Emanuel T. Prostano and Joyce S. Prostano, *The School Library Media Center* (Littleton, Colorado: Libraries Unlimited, 1971), pp. 64-68.

and other tasks which might ordinarily be accomplished within a center but can be done more efficiently by this alternative procedure.

MASTERY ITEM: ASSIGNING RESPONSIBILITIES

Assume that you are the director (with library training) of a school media center and your staff consists of another professional (with special training in audiovisual media), an audiovisual technician, an administrative

TABLE 8-3

	Director (Library)	Assoc-Dir. (AV Media)	Admin. Ass't.	AV Tech.	Clerk I	Clerk II	Clerk III
Information Retrieval							
Logistics							
Design							
Production							
Evaluation							
Management (Organ.)							
Management (Personnel)							
Utilization							
Instruction							
Research							

assistant, and three clerk-typists. Further assume that you can divide the time of personnel in percentages. How much time would you allocate for each person in each functional area?

Response: Assigning Responsibilities

You would need more information than you presently have in order to respond to this question. However, even in the abstract, you should be able to make some estimates. For example, the director has library training. As director, he or she would spend more time in organization management and personnel management; with library training it is likely that he or she would be more involved with information retrieval and evaluation than some of the other functions. The assistant director with training in audiovisual media would probably devote a major portion of time to design, production, and instruction. One of the clerk-typists may be assigned to handle most of the logistics while another may be assisting with production. The answer below is a reasonable allocation of staff time based on the given information.

TABLE 8-4

	Director (Library)	Assoc-Dir. (AV Media)	Admin. Ass't.	AV Tech.	Clerk I	Clerk II	Clerk III
Information Retrieval	10	5	20	0	80	10	10
Logistics	0	5	30	60	10	80	20
Design	5	30	5	0	0	0	0
Production	0	20	5	20	0	0	60
Evaluation	10	5	10	5	10	0	0
Management (Organ.)	40	10	20	0	0	0	0
Management (Personnel)	20	5	5	0	0	0	0
Utilization	5	5	5	5	0	10	0
Instruction	5	10	0	10	0	0	10
Research	5	5	0	0	0	0	0
Total	100%	100%	100%	100%	100%	100%	100%

COMPETENCY 5   Supervises personnel.

The supervisory function of the executive deals primarily with the governing and coordinating of human resources and includes the activities of (1) dealing with people, practices, motivation and performance; (2) establishing and coordinating work priorities, and (3) linking technical processes with the managerial functions.[5]

Regardless of what a definition may say, the fact is that supervision is interpreted in a variety of ways. There are those who feel that supervision is what the "boss" does when he or she is keeping track of you. Some people feel that they are under constant surveillance just to insure that assigned jobs get done. At the other extreme is the feeling that supervision is a collegial relationship between the executive in charge and each staff member. This position holds that supervision is a creative and constantly evolving process to bring about maximum contributions by everyone on the staff. There are interpretations in between these extremes as well. In the end, the role of supervisors and the effectiveness of their efforts will depend on the way in which each supervisor perceives himself and each employee who is being supervised.

[5] Norman J. Boylan, "Common and Specialized Learnings for Administrators and Supervisors: Some Problems and Issues" in Leu and Prudman (eds.), *Preparation Programs for School Administrators* (East Lansing, Mich.: College of Education, 1963), pp. 13-14.

Supervision is pervasive since the director of the media program is ultimately responsible for all that happens within the scope of that program. Of necessity, the performance of each staff member is of direct concern to the chief administrator of the program. Job functions have been delegated and therefore need to be evaluated. As individuals prove their abilities through satisfactory performance, the need for supervision decreases.

There are a variety of supervisory techniques which go beyond the scope of this section. As a beginning, however, the director should consider observation, conferences with the employee, reactions from other employees, and comments from users.

RESOURCES: SUPERVISING PERSONNEL

Human relations training is probably one of the best avenues of preparation for supervision since it is based on human interaction—people dealing with people. The variety of human relations programs such as transactional analysis, sensitivity training, and role-playing exercises provide some of the best resources for acquiring skills in human relations. One of the most widely used and effective programs for human development and interpersonal communications has been produced by the Instructional Dynamics Institute.[6] The General Relations Improvement Program (GRIP) is for two people. It consists of ten different sessions lasting from forty-five minutes to one hour each. The two participants take turns reading the specially designed segments or "frames" which guide them through the course from start to finish. Sometimes one person responds to specific questions and at other times they both do. Sometimes they engage in discussion and then explore their interactions together. They look closely into various types of exchanges found in everyday life. Often they share significant events from their own experience, working always to increase the depth of their understanding of themselves and others.

The Basic Interpersonal Relations, designed for five, one and one-half hour sessions with five to six people, is an introduction to the field of interpersonal relations. The entire course is actually a series of guided interactions among the group members, allowing them to begin to connect these experiences to basic principles and interpersonal concepts which they can then apply to their relationships with other people. Those responsible for carrying out such a task are fully aware of the fact that there is no way to force true interpersonal learning or genuine human growth. It comes only when a person assimilates some meaningful event or exchange into his own view of "the way things are." The most we can do is provide an occasion in which such learnings might be able to occur. The Basic Interpersonal Relations program attempts to provide a simple yet suitable setting for such learning to take place.

[6] Instructional Dynamics Institute, 166 East Superior Street, Chicago, Illinois 60611.

The Transactional Analysis in Social and Communication Training (TASC) is a tested self-contained program designed to teach the fundamentals of Transactional Analysis to groups of nine to fifteen participants. TASC teaches by giving participants the opportunity to gain new understanding of themselves and the way they communicate with others, then to test the insights they have gained.

ComPAC, developed for the Leadership Training Institute in Librarianship,[7] is a multi-media kit (16mm film, slide/tape, videotape, transparencies,

ComPAC is a multi-media kit designed to help media professionals with the communication process.

and a manual) which is designed to help increase the understanding of the communications process as it relates to library training and librarianship. ComPAC uses transactional analysis as the basic model for understanding the communications process. Transactional Analysis (TA) focuses on self-

[7] Leadership Training Institute, Florida State University, School of Library Science, Tallahassee, Florida 32306.

understanding and the creation of an "OK" self-image as the vehicle for the improvement of interpersonal communication. To communicate with the "OK" other person, the "OK" self can make a conscious decision to create an atmosphere of openness, trust, and acceptance.

MASTERY ITEM: SUPERVISING PERSONNEL

In each of the situations listed below, circle the course of action you would take and state the reason why you feel that this choice is best.

1. A new clerical employee leaves ten to fifteen minutes before closing time every day.

   a. Issue a warning for insubordination.
   b. Talk with the employee in private to determine the reason for the early leaving.
   c. Ask a fellow employee if he/she knows any reason for the early leaving.
   d. Wait another two weeks to see if the practice continues.

2. Your new associate in charge of audiovisual media is taking you at your word when you said that he could change anything around to suit his purposes. All the audiovisual media are now located in one end of the media center and are completely separated from all the other materials by high book shelves which have been moved to establish a divider.

   a. Wait to see how things work out.
   b. Retract your original comments and state more specifically what you really meant.
   c. Arrange to have things moved back when he is out of the media center.
   d. Discuss the reasons for the change with the employee to determine the purpose of the move and how far he intends to go.

3. A student volunteer has, on several occasions, permitted individuals to have direct access to the 16mm film collection. Your procedure, which was spelled out during training, is to obtain the film through a staff member since arrangements for equipment must be made at the same time. The reason for the procedure is that films could become damaged if untrained people try to use them on projectors which they cannot operate.

   a. See how direct access works; the current procedure may be unnecessary.
   b. Reprimand the student and reassign to another area.
   c. Talk with the student to see why he has not followed the procedure.
   d. Check with other students to see if they understood the procedure when presented during the training session.

Response: Supervising Personnel

1. In this case, a direct approach would be better than the other alternatives. Talk with the person privately to determine the reason for the early departure. There may be a legitimate reason such as being at home when a child returns from school or participating in a car pool which leaves earlier than the person's finishing time. An adjustment might be made, or instructions could be given to make other arrangements since all employees must remain until the end of the day and that an exception for one would mean exceptions for all. The important thing here is to take a personal approach and in private.

2. It would probably be best to "discuss the reasons for the change." Your associate is new and you have given him authority to make changes. There may be some very good reasons for the change. On the other hand, he may have gone too far and then it becomes your job to clarify what you feel is in the best interests of the users. It would probably be useful, in this case, to discuss your philosophical position in regard to integrated media programs in order to create a rationale for your actions—and your associate's.

3. You should talk with the student to see why he has not followed the procedure. He may have misunderstood. He may have encountered unique circumstances not covered in your training. Tell him why the procedure must be followed. Clarify the procedure once again.

COMPETENCY 6   Maintains job satisfaction of personnel.

After analyzing hundreds of jobs held by individuals in America today, Studs Terkel concluded that "to survive the day is triumph enough for the walking wounded among the great many of us." [8] There is no one reason why people are generally dissatisfied with their work; there are a host of reasons, some of which can be considered in relation to working in a media center.

Perhaps the best place to start is with the media professional because the attitude demonstrated by this person usually pervades the entire environment. If the director or person-in-charge does not generate enthusiasm and dedication for the job, then it will be difficult for others to express excitement for their jobs. If the media professional does not demonstrate competence and leadership, it is difficult for the staff to do their best. If the executive officer does not invite participation of the staff in planning and decision-making, it is unlikely that they will suggest improvements in the operation or develop an

---

[8] Studs Terkel, *Working* (New York: Pantheon Books, 1974), p. xi.

esprit de corps. The style and ambience of the media center is very much a reflection of the person-in-charge. These qualities must be demonstrated by the leader; they cannot be delegated.

A good place to start developing this competency is in the recruiting and hiring of new personnel. During the interview it is important for the media professional to point out expectations for job performance to the candidate so that there will be no ambiguities later on. As a prospective staff member is interviewed, it should be possible to determine the values he or she holds, the nature of his or her personality, and the probability of the individual "fitting" into the current staff. Other staff members should meet and interview prospective staff members so as to provide inputs to the media professional who ultimately must decide on the person to be hired. Involvement of staff in such decisions is not easy because people very often have different perceptions of an individual's capability and personality. The media professional has to factor in all the comments of the entire staff and then make the decision. The reason for the decision should be communicated to each person who has provided inputs since the selection of a person other than the one recommended by a staff person may lead to the feeling that the initial comments were not heard or taken into consideration.

Job satisfaction is a very personal thing. Many factors contribute to this feeling: physical facilities, colleagues, salary, responsibilities, status, the "boss," fringe benefits, the sense of contribution and many others. If the media professional can control some of these factors, an attempt should be made to do so. Some factors are not directly controllable, such as physical facilities and fixed salary amounts in a budget.

RESOURCES: MAINTAINING JOB SATISFACTION

Since job satisfaction is such an idiosyncratic feeling, the media professional will have to try to determine those factors which impinge on job satisfaction and attempt to control them. As for learning how to do this, the best advice is to observe media centers, talk with media professionals and try to determine what has been done to create conditions where individuals want to be and are happy in their work. Look for the following indicators:

1. *The general appearance of the media center:* Is it inviting? Business-like? Orderly without appearing to be painfully rigid? Light, bright and colorful? Are there a variety of work areas to permit various activities to occur?
2. *Personnel:* Is there an open and free exchange of ideas? Do people generally like each other? Are conversations pleasant and constructive? Are users treated warmly and receptively? Do staff members appear to know what they are doing?

3. *The media professional:* Is the leadership unobtrusive? Is the presence of the media professional felt without being dominant? Are the conversations between the media professional and the staff, the faculty, and the students empathetic and constructive?

Consciousness of the need for creating the conditions for job satisfaction is the best start a media professional can make. Beyond this, a sensitivity to the people and the environment is the primary prerequisite for achieving this competency.

MASTERY ITEM: MAINTAINING JOB SATISFACTION

Visit (or recall a visit) to a school media center. Assess the extent to which job satisfaction is evident according to the following scale:

TABLE 8-5

Facilities	Repulsive	Sterile	Pleasant	Inviting
Personnel	Negative	Evasive	Approachable	Cordial
Media Professional	Rigid	Routine Practitioner	Facilitator	Leader

Response: Maintaining Job Satisfaction

Your rating of a media center you have visited will vary according to that center. This is a highly subjective and personal judgment. The key to this response is to first consider *job satisfaction* and then to determine reasons for this satisfaction. You are not evaluating the facilities, personnel, and media professional per se. Evidence of job satisfaction can be observed by the manner in which individuals speak with other staff, teachers, and students. Another indicator is the appearance of the desk or location where an individual spends the greatest amount of time. In conversation with the personnel you can raise questions regarding their satisfactions and frustrations; the things they like to do; and their commitment to the program.

COMPETENCY 7   Evaluates employee performance.

Once individuals have been hired and descriptions of responsibilities have been outlined, there will be times when the performance of each individual will have to be assessed. This evaluation may occur for many reasons: (1) as a vehicle for assisting an individual to adjust to the expectations of a new position; (2) to create a continuing record of employee performance for later use in recommending salary increase, promotion, or tenure. (In some cases the information may be used as evidence for dismissal. Some evidence of performance must be available in most such cases.) And (3) to fulfill policy requirements of the school system which often requests periodic personnel reviews. Some evaluations occur at specified times, e.g., after three months or six months; some are made annually. Still other assessments occur on no regular basis—perhaps as the need arises or informally during a coffee break or after school. Whenever such evaluations take place and for whatever purposes they are conducted, the media professional and staff members must know why they are being done and the way in which the information acquired will be used.

Performance is best evaluated by direct observation. The media professional should have some basic criteria for making judgments. These criteria may be written and shared with the staff; they may be the basis of evaluation instruments which are used; or they may be loosely-held concepts in the mind of the executive officer. In any case, they should be known by the entire staff. There is nothing quite so demoralizing as being judged by unknown criteria. In centers which use a high degree of staff participation, criteria may be cooperatively developed between the director and the staff.

Most evaluation occurs when the media professional is observing the work of a staff member and when comments regarding employee actions come from other staff and users. Interpretations of these data occur in personal conversations or formal interviews between the director and the staff person. Sound personnel evaluation procedure calls for a statement of evaluative criteria, agreement on the job functions to be performed, a statement of judgment supported by observed evidence, and a summary of the employee's status. After such an assessment, the person should know what areas seem to be going well (and why); what areas of responsibility need improvement (and why); and what the prospects are between the present time and the next review. If a person is to be terminated that fact should be communicated (with reasons); if a person continues to be on probation, that condition should be stated; if the person has gained a permanent standing on the staff, that should be known. This is no time for ambiguity.

RESOURCES: EVALUATING PERFORMANCE

Evaluating the performance of other people is a paradox in that although we evaluate people every day as we interact with them some individuals feel that they cannot assess persons on the job. How does one gain the ability to evaluate the performance of another person?

There is a host of conventional wisdom which has been brought together in books on personnel administration. Most of the work has been derived from business, industry, and government. There are guidelines for job descriptions, help in stating criteria for evaluations, sample instruments, and useful hints in dealing with problem personnel. There are case studies which report on successful and unsuccessful management of employee relations. Although not specifically related to media centers, all of these resources provide some background information.

Some of the training mentioned earlier in this chapter in regard to developing sensitivity to others through techniques acquired from one of the human potential programs, should be considered. One of the most critical human relationships which a director must face is the evaluation of performance and subsequent reporting of that evaluation to each employee. The "truth" (as perceived by the media professional) is sometimes difficult to handle and consequently avoided. The best preparation for handling these situations is to have gone through a program which emphasizes openness, honesty, and frankness in interpersonal relationships. This approach is required for useful employee evaluations.

MASTERY ITEM: EVALUATING PERFORMANCE

Indicate how each of the observed behaviors listed below could be used in an evaluation of an employee's performance. Choose one of the three possibilities for each behavior.

Behavior	*Action*
_____1. The employee is permitting books, materials and equipment to be taken out of the media center without checking out items to individuals.	a. Write a note for the person's file; discuss during next scheduled evaluation. b. Discuss this privately with the employee as soon as possible.
_____2. The new secretary is completing only about half as much work as you anticipated each day.	c. Wait a while; it may be atypical behavior.

_____3. The technician is buying parts on his own without using the school business office and submitting bills for reimbursement.

_____4. Neither teachers nor students ask the new aide for help; she just sits there.

Response: Evaluating Performance

Each of these behaviors, except the secretary's minimum work output, require immediate attention. You should talk privately with the person involved to determine reasons for the behavior and to recommend corrective action. In the case of the new secretary, you might attribute her low work output to her newness on the job so you could note the behavior and discuss it during the employee's next evaluation. By that time she would have had the opportunity to improve her performance and no action would be required. If she continues the low-level performance, you could recommend termination since the first two or three months is usually a probationary period.

REFERENCES

Competency 1   Writes job descriptions for recruiting and hiring personnel.

DAVIES, RUTH ANN. *The School Library Media Center: A Force for Excellence.* (2nd ed.), pp. 319-22. New York: R. R. Bowker Co., 1974.

ERICKSON, CARLETON W. H. *Administering Instructional Media Programs,* pp. 339-45. New York: Macmillan, 1968.

Competency 2   Recruits, hires, and terminates personnel.

BROWN, JAMES W., KENNETH D. NORBERG and SARA K. SRYGLEY. *Administering Educational Media,* pp. 396-97. New York: McGraw-Hill, 1972.

DAVIES, RUTH ANN. *The School Library Media Center: A Force for Excellence.* (2nd ed.), pp. 312-17. New York: R. R. Bowker Co., 1974.

Employment Interview. 16mm motion picture, sound, color, 11 min., New York: McGraw-Hill, n.d.

ERICKSON, CARLETON W. H. *Administering Instructional Media Programs,* pp. 336-39. New York: Macmillan, 1968.

PROSTANO, EMANUEL T. and JOYCE S. PROSTANO. *The School Library Media Center,* pp. 64-67. Littleton, Colo.: Libraries Unlimited, 1971.

Competency 3   Conducts training for staff.

GILLESPIE, JOHN T. and DIANA L. SPIRT. *Creating A School Media Program,* pp. 44-45. New York: R. R. Bowker Co., 1973.

Competency 4   Assigns job responsibilities to specific personnel.

BOWMAR, CORA PAUL. *Guide to the Development of Educational Media Selection Centers,* pp. 54-58. Chicago: American Library Association, 1973.

BROWN, JAMES W., KENNETH D. NORBERG and SARA K. SRYGLEY. *Administering Educational Media,* pp. 388-96. New York: McGraw-Hill, 1972.

DAVIES, RUTH ANN. *The School Library Media Center: A Force for Excellence.* (2nd ed.), pp. 319-22. New York: R. R. Bowker Co., 1974.

ERICKSON, CARLETON W. H. *Administering Instructional Media Programs,* pp. 347-53. New York: Macmillan, 1968.

GILLESPIE, JOHN T. and DIANA L. SPIRT. *Creating A School Media Program,* pp. 100-107. New York: R. R. Bowker Co., 1973.

Guidelines for Certification of Media Specialists: Extended Version, pp. 45-58. Washington, D.C.: Association for Educational Communication and Technology, 1972.

Media Programs: District and School, pp. 16-26. Chicago. American Library Association, and Washington, D.C.: Association for Educational Communications and Technology, 1975.

PROSTANO, EMANUEL T. and JOYCE S. PROSTANO. *The School Library Media Center,* pp. 57-62, 67-68. Littleton, Colo.: Libraries Unlimited, 1971.

Competency 5   Supervises personnel.

Basic Interpersonal Relations. Chicago: Instructional Dynamics Institute, n.d.

BROWN, JAMES W., KENNETH D. NORBERG and SARA K. SRYGLEY. *Administering Educational Media,* pp. 397-98. New York: McGraw-Hill, 1972.

ComPAC, multi-media kit (16mm motion picture, 35mm slides, cassette audio tape, reel-to-reel videotape, manual). Tallahassee, Florida: Florida State University, School of Library Science, 1973.

DAVIES, RUTH ANN. *The School Library Media Center: A Force for Excellence.* (2nd ed.), pp. 307-11. New York: R. R. Bowker Co., 1974.

ERICKSON, CARLETON W. H. *Administering Instructional Media Programs,* pp. 93-95, 117-126. New York: Macmillan, 1968.

General Relations Improvement Program. Chicago: Instructional Dynamics Institute, n.d.

Transactional Analysis in Social and Communication Training. Chicago: Instructional Dynamics Institute, n.d.

Competency 6   Maintains job satisfaction of personnel.

Competency 7   Evaluates employee performance.

DAVIES, RUTH ANN. *The School Library Media Center: A Force for Excellence.* (2nd ed.), pp. 322-31. New York: R. R. Bowker Co., 1974.

9 The Design Function

This chapter emphasizes the analysis and planning of instruction. The term *design* refers to activities which are performed to create an instructional system whether it be for a single lesson, a unit, or a complete course of study. This chapter considers the competencies which are required to perform the design function: (1) analysis and description of learning objectives; (2) determination of learner characteristics; (3) determination of teaching-learning strategies and techniques; (4) recommendation of the most appropriate medium to attain the objective; (5) recommendation of the environment in which the learning ought to occur; and (6) evaluation of the design. The product of the design effort is a series of specifications for each component of the system: (1) persons; (2) message; (3) materials; (4) devices; (5) techniques; and (6) settings. Specific design competencies with illustrative tasks are also described.

The fact that learners differ in intelligence, aptitudes, experiences, and a variety of other factors is sufficient justification for differential instructional treatments. These differences indicate the need for planning, the need to "bridge the gap" between actual practice in a learning environment and what is known about learners, mediating forms, subject matter, thinking processes, settings, and techniques.

In addition to attending to the needs of a diverse learner group, the use of media may be judged on two other criteria, efficiency and effectiveness. The criterion of *efficiency* is based on the assumption that the time of both

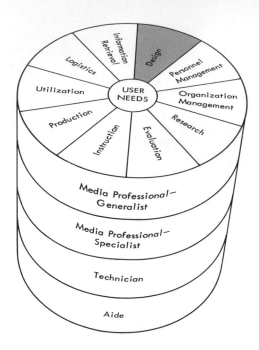

COMPETENCY 1 Elicits and clarifies objectives of the teacher and/
or learner.
COMPETENCY 2 Analyzes learner characteristics.
COMPETENCY 3 Assists in determining teaching/learning strategies
and techniques.
COMPETENCY 4 Considers alternative media formats and recom-
mends most appropriate medium.
COMPETENCY 5 Recommends alternative learning environments.
COMPETENCY 6 Evaluates and modifies teaching/learning designs.

teachers and students is important and should be utilized in the most advantageous manner. The criterion of *effectiveness* assumes that "mastery" is desirable. In combination, efficiency and effectiveness imply the necessity for
some sort of human intervention in order to separate the "essential" from the
"related" and "nice-to-know."

Viewing the learner as central and using the criteria of efficiency and
effectiveness to define a frame of reference, it is possible to construct a syllo-
gism which places design at the heart of the process of providing instruction
to learners.

THE SYLLOGISM

If it is possible to increase the amount of student learning through the systematic application of knowledge about learners, and

If students learn because of their contacts with the various components of the instructional system, and

If these components can be predetermined, planned, and implemented,

Then it is possible to apply knowledge about learners and the various components of the instructional system in order to increase student learning by systematically arranging the various components of the instructional system.

Because of their belief in this conclusion, media professionals engage in design tasks. Briefly, design is justified to the extent that individual learner performance is of primary importance and that efficiency and effectiveness are valued.

DESIGN FUNCTION

In the process of solving instructional problems, a unique set of tasks emerges. The uniqueness of these tasks is based on the purpose for which they are performed: to translate general theoretical knowledge about learners and the various components of the instructional system into specifications for those components.[1] This means that when a media professional prepares specifications for any instructional system, he or she is performing design tasks. For example, some of these tasks are: formulating instructional goals, establishing priorities, analyzing and describing learners, analyzing and describing subject matter domains, sequencing learning tasks, deciding on instructional strategies, selecting appropriate media forms, and writing specifications for instructional media or systems.[2] The sum of these and similar tasks is the design function.

Design tasks can be viewed from two different perspectives: what gets done (outcomes) when an individual performs tasks for the purpose of design, and what a media professional does (activities) to produce design outcomes.

Design Outcomes

The outcome of performing design tasks is a set of specifications[3] for one or more of the components of an instructional system. The components

[1] C. James Wallington et. al., *Jobs in Instructional Media* (Washington, D.C.: Association for Educational Communications and Technology, 1970), p. 298.

[2] Ibid.

[3] The purpose of the specifications is to guide the process of creating the component (as is the case with Materials, Devices, and Settings) or preparing a set of directions or procedures (as is the case with Persons, Message, and Technique). The process of creating is a production function and as such is the topic of Chapter 12 in this book.

are *Persons, Message, Material, Device, Technique* and *Setting.*[4] These components comprise a mutually exclusive and exhaustive classification of all elements of an instructional system. The utility of such a scheme is obvious: *these are all of the resources which can be designed, used, and combined in a systematic manner with the intent of facilitating learning.*

The following paragraphs treat each component separately in order to clarify each element. In practice, the media professional would be dealing with an instructional situation (problem), thus part of the job is to decide which components are necessary to a solution and to write specifications for them. The following section on design activities will deal with that perspective in greater detail.

Persons: People who are acting to store and/or transmit messages. Where it is necessary to specify the tasks performed by people—students as well as teachers—"Person Specs" are written. For example, in an intensive in-service training institute for teachers, it was deemed desirable to prescribe what the leader is to say, what he or she is to have the institute participants do, and how long they are to continue the activity. The result of these concerns is a set of instructions for the leader which is part of the training package.

Message: Information to be transmitted by the other components; takes the form of ideas, facts, meanings, data. "Message Specs" specify the content/subject matter/processes which the student is to learn, the teacher is to teach, or the material is to contain. The "message spec" may be a generalization such as the law of supply and demand. From this general statement, other content is derived which may be the data which the students are to analyze or it may be the basis for the teacher's lecture or demonstration depending on the technique to be employed.

Materials: Items (traditionally called software) which store messages for transmission by devices; sometimes combined in one unit with the appropriate device. "Material specs" describe the characteristics and qualities of components such as motion pictures, audio recordings, and instructional programs.

Devices: Items (traditionally called hardware) which transmit messages stored on materials; sometimes combined in one unit with the appropriate material. "Device Specs" describe the characteristics and qualities of components such as motion picture projectors, tape recorders, and computers.

Techniques: Procedures for using materials, devices, and man to transmit messages. "Technique Specs" describe the ways and means of bringing learners into contact with messages. Programmed instruction, discussion, simulation, and independent inquiry are techniques.

Setting: The total environment in which the messages are transmitted and/or received. "Setting Specs" describe the characteristics and qualities of

[4] This chapter treats these components only in the framework of the design function. For greater detail, or to see the entire scope of the scheme, see Silber, *Audiovisual Instruction* 15, No. 5 (May, 1970): 21-24.

the environment (e.g., lighting, heating, acoustics, colors, furniture, physical arrangement of things, etc.).

Design Activities

In order to write specifications for the various components of an instructional system, the media professional performs a variety of activities. Learners must be analyzed and described in terms of aptitude, previous achievement, and ethnic and socio-economic background; subject matter must be described in terms of processes, structure of the discipline, level of behaviors desired, and specific objectives; learning tasks must be sequenced and decisions regarding instructional strategies and media forms must be determined.

The list seems endless. A frame of reference or model is needed to classify such activities. Listing activities out of context is not a very useful way of describing what a media professional does. By imposing a frame of reference for the activities, the purpose served by these activities becomes clear. Because the goal of the design function is the use of the various components of an instructional system to solve instructional problems, a problem-solving procedure would be one way to classify what a media professional does.

Initially the media professional must recognize that a problem exists. Although little is known about how people recognize problems, it appears to involve noting discrepancies between "what is" and "what might be." In reading the next section, it should be assumed that such a discrepancy has been observed. The following is a general description of what the media professional does next and the competencies which are required to perform the design function.

It is also assumed that the media professional operates at a level of responsibility which requires him or her to initiate productive courses of action without being told to do so.

COMPETENCY 1   Elicits and clarifies objectives of the teacher and/or learner.

To effectively perform the design function, it is absolutely essential that the media professional knows what needs to be learned. The popular terminology is "to state objectives behaviorally." If the media professional knows what a learner should be able to *do* at the conclusion of the lesson, unit, or course, then it is possible to perform the other aspects of instructional design. Without such a statement, almost anything that is designed would be appropriate. An easy way to remember the characteristics of a behavioral objective is the use of the A-B-C-D formula:

*A*udience needs to be specified;
*B*ehavior has to be described so that it can be observed;
*C*onditions under which the behavior is to occur should be stated; and
*D*egree of acceptable performance should be indicated.

The media professional, or staff member designated to serve the instructional design function, will often have to help the teacher or learner to clearly formulate the behavioral objective. Most students and teachers will not come to the media professional with well-stated behavioral objectives. They must be developed cooperatively. Sometimes teachers will have statements which are somewhat broader and are more appropriately called *goals*. Or some teachers will have objectives, but closer scrutiny will show that they are overly general and need to be sharpened before the design process can begin. There are times when the media professional will have to observe the teaching of an instructor and from that observation infer the objectives which are being sought. If this is the case, the objectives written by the media professional will have to be confirmed by the teacher.

Learners often come to media centers with specific questions. These queries tend to be more behavioral than some of the teacher's attempts at formulating objectives. "I need to find out about air transportation in Alaska" or "Could you help me find poetry written by authors during Shakespeare's time?" It is often easier to help learners to state objectives behaviorally than it is to help teachers to do so.

RESOURCES: ELICITING AND CLARIFYING OBJECTIVES

Competency in "eliciting and clarifying objectives" means that the media professional who performs the design function must be able to identify a behavioral objective from a group of behavioral and nonbehavioral objectives. This person should also be able to write behavioral objectives according to the criteria for a good behavioral objective and help others to do likewise .

Many good books have been written in this area. Several are published in programmed format for self-instruction. Probably the single most helpful source is Robert F. Mager's *Preparing Instructional Objectives*.[5] It is well-written, full of examples, and the participation required by the programmed format makes it relevant for anyone who has not mastered the writing of behavioral objectives.

[5] Robert F. Mager, *Preparing Instructional Objectives* (Palo Alto, Calif.: Fearon Publishers, 1962).

In the book, *Teaching and Media: A Systematic Approach* by Vernon S. Gerlach and Donald P. Ely,[6] many examples of objectives are given which relate to the use of media in teaching and learning. A programmed format is used so that each individual may actively participate in the formulation of objectives and check immediately after completion to confirm responses.

There are dozens of other articles, books, and monographs which discuss the writing of behavioral objectives. Some of the best and most frequently used are:

RORERT L. BAKER and RICHARD H. SCHUTZ (eds.). *Instructional Product Development*. (New York: Van Nostrand Reinhold, 1971).

A handbook for developing research-based, quality-verified instructional systems using replicable procedures.

NORMAN E. GRONLUND. *Stating Behavioral Objectives for Classroom Instruction*. (New York: Macmillan, 1970).

Describes the methods used in identifying and defining instructional objectives as learning outcomes.

Instructional Objectives Exchange Catalog. Los Angeles: Instructional Objectives Exchange. (Center for the Study of Education, University of California at Los Angeles, 145 Moore Hall, 405 Hilgard Ave., Los Angeles, Calif. 90024).

A continually updated catalog of behavioral objectives contributed from various sources for an array of subjects.

ROBERT J. KIBLER, LARRY L. BECKER, and DAVID O. MILES. *Behavioral Objectives and Instruction*. (Boston: Allyn and Bacon, 1970).

Identifies functions which behavioral objectives can serve in improving instruction. Describes the nature of objectives, assists teachers in writing them and provides examples of well-written behavioral objectives.

W. JAMES POPHAM and EVA L. BAKER, *Establishing Instructional Goals*. (Englewood Cliffs, N. J.: Prentice-Hall, Inc., 1970).

The focus of this volume is on instructional goals: how to select them, how to state them, and how to establish pupil performance for such goals.

MASTERY ITEM: ELICITING AND CLARIFYING OBJECTIVES

A media professional who can "elicit and clarify specific objectives of the teacher and/or learner" should be able to apply the A-B-C-D rule: the

[6] Vernon S. Gerlach and Donald P. Ely, *Teaching and Media: A Systematic Approach* (Englewood Cliffs, N.J.: Prentice-Hall, 1971).

*A*udience must be specified (or implied); the *B*ehavior has to be described; the *C*onditions of demonstrating the behavior should be stated; and the *D*egree of acceptable performance should be indicated. With this guideline in mind, answer the following questions.

1. Is the learner the audience for each objective? (yes or no)

   a. To name the capital city of each of the New England states. _____
   b. To construct a working model of the Wankle engine. _____
   c. To cover the concept "propaganda" in the first lecture. _____
   d. To discuss the causes of the energy crisis. _____

2. Does each statement express (or imply) audience and behavior?

   a. To punt a football forty yards or more on every attempt without opposition. _____
   b. To master the skills involved in hand lettering. _____
   c. To learn the one hundred multiplication facts. _____
   d. To name the basic elements involved in music appreciation. _____

3. For each of the following objectives indicate whether or not all three criteria of a well-stated objective (audience, behavior, conditions) are stated.

   a. To identify a well-balanced meal, given the foods to be eaten and the amount, within 10 seconds. _____
   b. To name the four stages of an internal combustion engine cycle. _____
   c. To name twenty-five out of thirty North American mammals, given pictures of all thirty, within ten minutes. _____
   d. To identify the twelve months and the seven days. _____

4. Does each objective contain a statement describing the fourth criterion: degree of acceptable performance? If it does, *underline* those words. If it does not, indicate "No."

   a. To run the 100 yard dash in 11 seconds or less, on an AAU approved track, given a wind velocity of 5 mph or less.
   b. To name each primary and secondary color, given an example of each in a geometric shape, within two seconds of the presentation of the color.
   c. To construct a graph showing the population growth of Syracuse from 1900 to 1960, given graph paper and the census reports of New York cities for each decade since 1860, and given three days time.
   d. To sink putts of three feet or less on the Cavalry Club putting green with 80 percent accuracy.

Response: Eliciting and Clarifying Objectives

1. a. yes	2. a. yes	3. a. yes
b. yes	b. no	b. no
c. no	c. no	c. yes
d. no.	d. yes	d. no.

4. a. Underline "in eleven seconds or less."
   b. Underline "within two seconds."
   c. No.
   d. Underline "with 80 percent accuracy."

COMPETENCY 2   Analyzes learner characteristics.

Traditionally, educators have noted the importance of individual differences among learners. They have recognized, over the years, that pupils come to school with varying abilities and from a wide range of family circumstances. In planning instruction for groups of learners it is difficult to plan for each individual pupil so the best strategy seems to be to present information for the "average" student and to set performance expectations at an "average" level. Most of the well-intentioned concerns for individual differences have to be compromised because of the number of pupils who are assigned to each teacher, the lack of time available to prepare for each, and the inability to assess all the variables which each pupil possesses. The general principle which underlies this type of instructional design is the *greatest good for the greatest number.*

The advent of new media and technology has brought about a revived interest in individual differences. As new options for learning emerge in the form of instructional media, the reality of preparing and presenting information through a variety of media to meet the unique needs of individuals becomes evident. The possibility of engaging several groups of students and many more individuals in purposeful activity has been a direct outcome of having more media available. At the same time, the different learning styles of individuals can be accommodated without compromising the intellectual integrity of the information being communicated. Some learners can accomplish more by reading while others achieve more by listening. Some are receptive to simultaneous audio and visual stimuli and some require a mix of several different formats. Some pupils require systematic, orderly and programmed approaches to learning while others prefer more ambiguity with opportunities for self-searching and learning.

Now that a wider variety of resources are necessary for the design of instruction, the media professional plays a more active role in the process of curriculum planning and instructional design. As a member of the instructional design team, the media professional now raises questions about the nature of the learners so that appropriate resources can be located or developed to meet the unique needs of learners on the local level. Therefore, the ability to "analyze learner characteristics" is one important element of the design function and it is an ability which the media professional must possess.

In analyzing learner characteristics, there appear to be three areas of concern: (1) those characteristics which have to do with intellectual activities —the ability to reason, verbalize and use quantitative data; (2) those characteristics which have to do with socio-cultural backgrounds; and (3) those characteristics which involve certain personality variables—attitude, leadership, anxiety. In some cases it may also be necessary to know the psychomotor abilities which an individual possesses—the ability to use one's hands and body.

The purpose of determining all these facets of an individual's background, ability, and feelings is to better select the instructional mode that would be most likely to insure learning for that individual. Likewise, the selection of the most appropriate resources for achieving that learning are another dimension of the same activity. The media professional should be able to assist in determining learner characteristics by knowing what questions to ask, how to get the answers to those questions, and then to be able to interpret them in terms of instructional strategies and resources required for each. The new principle has become *the best for each.*

RESOURCES: ANALYZING LEARNER DIFFERENCES

Learner characteristics can be determined in three ways: (1) by using available records; (2) by designing pretests; and (3) by counseling with individuals.

Use of available records The student's cumulative record probably shows the results of several standardized tests which he has taken. Intelligence tests reveal general information about the student's ability to reason, to verbalize, and to use quantitative data. This information coupled with the data from personality scales provides a general indication of a student's potential. His grades show performance in courses over his school career. Any information concerning a student's potential or his past performance may be useful.

Teacher-designed pretests The teacher will probably want to design a pretest to determine the student's achievement in the subject to be pursued. This screening device might indicate a student's ability to define basic terms in the subject area. The ability to describe basic concepts will also be tested. The fundamental question which must be answered prior to formal instruction is, "To what extent has the student learned the terms, concepts, and skills which are part of this course?" It is good practice to organize the course in units and to administer a pretest before each unit. This procedure serves as a check on previous learnings as well as a guide for the teacher and the student in planning future learning experiences.[7]

Individual counseling This provides a more personal approach to assessing the individual's interests and preferred communication formats. Counseling occurs on a person-to-person basis. It involves the determination of a learner's information needs and media preferences. From this personal approach stems recommended media and materials which often cannot be discerned through the other approaches.

For a comprehensive treatment of the concept of entering behavior see Chapter 3, in John P. DeCecco's *The Psychology of Learning and Instruction: Educational Psychology.* DeCecco is particularly strong on four elements of entering behavior: readiness, maturation, individual differences, and personality.

The communication approach to analyzing learner characteristics is discussed by David K. Berlo in *The Process of Communication* (pp. 40–50). His orientation is the communication process in which the "source-encoder" colors the message (and that of the "decoder-receiver") by communication skills, attitudes, knowledge level, and position within a social-cultural system. The discussion of these variables is helpful in determining the status of the individual for whom messages are to be designed.

A similar position is taken by John Ball and Francis C. Byrnes (Eds.) in *Research, Principles, and Practices in Visual Communication* (pp. 31 and 47–50). Here the emphasis is on the "receiver" of messages—the learner in our terms. Complete listings for these books may be found in the bibliography at the end of this chapter.

MASTERY ITEM: ANALYZING LEARNER DIFFERENCES

You are assisting in the development of instructional materials for a unit on community helpers for the second grade. In an attempt to provide alternative resources for all of the learners, you have undertaken an assessment of the learner's characteristics in relation to this specific topic.

1. Place a check in front of the items in the student's file which would be of some help to you:

Previous evaluations of first grade teachers in all subjects
Scores on Iowa Reading Tests
Scores on SRA arithmetical reasoning test

---

[7] Vernon S. Gerlach and Donald P. Ely, *Teaching and Media: A Systematic Approach* (Englewood Cliffs, N.J.: Prentice-Hall), pp. 14-15.

Parents' responses to teacher evaluations during first grade
Doctor's report of physical examination

2. Place a check before the items you would recommend including in a pre-test:

Name the principal industries of our town.
Name the services of our town which are also necessary in every town.
What does your father do? your mother?
What would you like to be in the future?
Distinguish between products and services.

3. Place a check before the information you would seek in an interview with a student:

How often do you watch TV? What are your favorite programs?
Do you get a daily paper at your house? Which one?
How often do you take a library book home?
Do you prefer to work alone or with others?
If you had a question about something you want to learn, where would you go and who would you ask?

Response: Analyzing Learner Differences

1. You should have checked all but "scores on the SRA arithmetical reasoning test" in the first group. Knowledge of the first grade teacher's evaluation and reading scores might help you to design materials on an appropriate level.

2. In the second group, all items would be useful for you to know. Answers to these questions would provide you with a knowledge of each student's current awareness of occupations in relation to himself and to the community.

3. All of the third group of questions would assist you in selecting an appropriate format for each individual learner and help to determine the teaching methods which might be used.

COMPETENCY 3   *Assists in determining teaching/learning strategies and techniques.*

Once the content, objectives and entering behaviors have been determined, it is then possible to select appropriate teaching (and learning) strategies and techniques. "In the systematic approach to teaching and learning, *strategy* is concerned with the way in which content is presented in the instructional environment. It includes the nature, scope, and sequence of events which provide the educational experience. The strategy must take into account the objectives that have been defined, and the entering behaviors of the learners." [8] "*Techniques* are the ways and means adopted by a teacher to direct the learners' activities toward an objective. Techniques are the tools of the teacher. The effective teacher has a multitude of techniques at his disposal and must be prepared to select the ones which will be most efficient in leading the learner to the desired terminal behavior." [9]

What does the media professional *do* when "assisting in determining teaching/learning strategies and techniques?" The Jobs in Instructional Media Study discovered some of the following tasks which fall within this category:

Analyzes behavioral objectives to select method of instruction
Extrapolates from content and objectives to define teaching strategies
Researches literature to locate examples of simulations
Designs role plays to meet training need
Analyzes subject matter to identify segments for programming
Designs sample lesson plans to provide model for instruction
Synthesizes objectives, sequence, content, media to develop presentation outline [10]

The *Behavioral Requirements Analysis Checklist* (BRAC) also describes some of the media professional's responsibility in this area:

Modify and adapt learning activities, media and equipment for the appropriate learning level [11]
Encourage students to practice self-inquiry through the utilization of a wide variety of media and equipment [12]
Involve the student in the development of his own learning activities
Utilize student peer groups to help design learning experiences
Utilize adult models to assist in the development of positive student attitudes toward learning [13]

The media professional who demonstrates this competency must possess a repertoire of strategies and techniques that can be employed by teachers

[8] Ibid., p. 207.
[9] Ibid., p. 219.
[10] *Guidelines for Certification of Media Specialists, Extended Version* (Washington, D.C.: Association for Educational Communications and Technology, 1972).
[11] *Behavioral Requirements Analysis Checklist* (Chicago: American Library Association, 1973) p. 3.
[12] Ibid., p. 4.
[13] Ibid., p. 8.

and learners to achieve the stated objectives. This is the how of teaching or communicating. The person, the message, the material, and the device may be known and available, but it is *technique* which will insure the attainment of the objective. There is more than one technique. Given a wide range of differences among learners, there are a variety of ways in which each student may be reached. It is here that the pluralism of media plays an important role. And it is here that the creative ability of the media professional is most evident.

RESOURCES: SELECTING TEACHING AND LEARNING STRATEGIES

Teaching is probably one of the best ways to attain this competency. The experienced teacher has some knowledge of dealing with a variety of individuals in any one class and handling the day-to-day pressures. The experienced teacher has had the opportunity to try techniques, some of which have worked and some of which have been failures. The experience approach to gaining comptency is long and difficult—and very inefficient. Fortunately, there are alternate routes.

For a good orientation to the basic concepts of strategy and technique, read Chapter 11, "Strategies for Teaching" in Gerlach and Ely.[14] Two major approaches, expository and inquiry teaching, offer points of departure for the design of a systematic instructional strategy. The strategy then points to the ways in which a variety of techniques might be used. The techniques described in this chapter include: lecture, discussion, demonstration, doing, field trips, role playing, simulation and gaming, student reports, and audiovisual materials. Techniques, as described in this chapter, are the *means* for reaching an objective and can be used in both expository and inquiry teaching.

There is no hard and fast formula regarding the selection of an appropriate strategy and technique. Much depends on the nature of the content, the needs of individual learners and the objectives that are being sought. Therefore, it is important for a media professional to be alert to a wide range of techniques which may be applicable in many settings. A book like Edgar Dale's *Audiovisual Methods in Teaching* (3rd ed.) (New York: Holt, Rinehart and Winston, 1969) is rich with examples of techniques employing the full spectrum of instructional media. Of particular help is Part II in the book where each medium and method is discussed following the cone of experience model which posits "direct, purposeful experiences" as one of the richest types of learning (at the base of the cone) and "verbal symbols" as one of the most abstract means of communication (at the pinnacle of the cone).

Another useful reference regarding techniques is *AV Instruction: Media and Methods* (4th ed.) (New York: McGraw Hill, 1973) by Brown, Lewis, and Harcleroad. The entire volume is rich with specific examples of media

---

[14] Gerlach and Ely, *Teaching and Media*, pp. 207-29.

being used in context. Each case study is enhanced by extensive illustrations and supported by additional references. The encyclopedic nature of this book makes it a needed reference for media professionals who are concerned with the determination of teaching and learning strategies and techniques.

One of the most recent and useful volumes in the same general category is *Instructional Technology: Its Nature and Use* (5th ed.) by Wittich and Schuller (Harper & Row, 1973). The presentation of all media and recommended applications to teaching and learning is enhanced by an extensive discussion of the way in which the systematic design of instruction is related to the selecton of appropriate strategies and techniques.

MASTERY ITEM: SELECTING TEACHING AND LEARNING STRATEGIES

Given the following techniques, which one(s) would be used to achieve the stated objective?

audiovisual materials	lecture
demonstration	role playing
discussion	simulation and gaming
doing	student reports
field trips	programmed instruction

Objective: The learner will be able to measure dry and liquid chemicals in the high school chemistry laboratory with 100 percent accuracy, given an analytic balance, weights, and an unknown quantity of a dry substance and a container of liquid.

Response: Selecting Teaching and Learning Strategies

The techniques which most approximate the behavior should be used. Therefore, a "demonstration" first and then "doing" would probably predict success in reaching this objective. Audiovisual materials (a film, videotape or sound filmstrip, or slides) would be the next most satisfactory procedure. The other techniques are fairly remote from the actual behavior and would probably not be used.

COMPETENCY 4   Considers alternative media formats and recommends most appropriate medium.

If content and objective have been defined, the entering behavior of the learner determined, and the strategy and technique selected, then it should be quite simple to select the best instructional medium to accomplish the objective. It *should* be quite simple, but such is not the case. There is no one medium which is inherently best for any purpose. Combinations of media seem to be required to achieve the kind of instruction which is effective and which exploits the unique properties of each medium to the fullest extent. What then does the media professional do when asked to recommend the most appropriate medium to achieve a defined learning objective?

There are a series of questions which must be addressed after the learning objective has been defined. The combined answers to these questions help to determine the most appropriate medium.

1. *Appropriateness:* Is the medium suitable to accomplish the defined task?
2. *Level of sophistication:* Is the medium on the correct level of understanding for my students?
3. *Cost:* Is the cost worth the potential learning from this particular medium?
4. *Availability:* Are the material and equipment available when I need them?
5. *Technical quality:* Is the quality of the material acceptable: readable? visible? audible? [15]

Performance of this competency also requires a working knowledge of the full range of media including: (1) the physical characteristics of the medium and its associated equipment; (2) the unique advantages and disadvantages of the medium; (3) sources of the medium; and (4) ideas concerning its utilization.

The media professional usually performs this task as a member of an instructional design team. As plans are developed the media professional recommends possible media alternatives and when the final design is established recommends the medium or combinations of media which are most appropriate considering all of the variables of that specific situation.

RESOURCES: RECOMMENDING MEDIA FORMATS

There have been several attempts to develop formulas or guidelines for the selection of media. These are, for the most part, efforts to match objectives with media. While each scheme is useful as a general recommendation and would help to avoid gross errors, specific recommendations are almost always dependent on local conditions and persons involved. It would be helpful, however, to have several of the guidelines in mind as vehicles for achieving this competency.

The *Handbook and Catalog for Instructional Media Selection* by Boucher, Gottlieb, and Morganlander offers a media selection system which is ". . . designed to assist media specialists, curriculum designers, and teach-

[15] Ibid., p. 291.

ers to arrive at informed decisions regarding the use of currently available educational hardware. It presents a step-by-step process of analyzing learning objectives, determining appropriate generic media types, and selecting specific instructional devices to aid in meeting those objectives." [16] Also useful are the complete descriptions of each medium and lists of advantages. Two helpful instruments are included: "Media Requirements Worksheet" and "Media Capabilities Matrix."

A similar listing of media, including definitions, illustrations, physical characteristics, advantages and disadvantages, and sources is in Chapter 15, "Media Facts" in Gerlach and Ely.[17]

Beyond these two comprehensive listings of media are several attempts to chart the process of media selection beginning at different points. Each example is included here for reference purposes but the original articles should be read for comprehensive treatments.

William Allen's synthesis of the research on the use of media is the basis for the correlation between media type and learning objectives in Table 9-1.[18] His interpretation of the HIGH, Medium, and low values assigned to each relationship is a guide to the relative value of each meduim for attaining each type of objective.

Another example of objective-based selection is the series of steps recommended by R. Irwin Goodman in his article "Systematic Selection." [19] The list of tasks, reproduced in Figure 9-1, is enhanced by lists of "preliminary information required" and "products developed" for each step.

Jerrold Kemp, in his article, "Which Medium?" [20] uses grouping as a basis for media selection. He contends that "Independent Study for Individual Students" (Figure 9-2) requires one selection procedure while "Small Group Interaction" (Figure 9-3) and "regular size class to large size" (Figure 9-4) need to follow somewhat different paths. The questions raised here deal primarily with variables of each media format, e.g., visual characteristics, audio characteristics, motion quality, etc.

Once the media professional feels that this competency has been acquired, the difficulty is in knowing that media decisions are "correct." Since there is no objective means of measuring one's ability in this area, the ultimate test must come with actual practice in a real or simulated situation.

[16] Brian G. Boucher, Merrill J. Gottlieb and Martin L. Morganlander, *Handbook and Catalog for Instructional Media Selection* (Englewood Cliffs, N.J.: Educational Technology Publications, 1973). p. iv.

[17] Gerlach and Ely, *Teaching and Media*, pp. 322-92.

[18] William H. Allen, "Media Stimulus and Types of Learning," *Audiovisual Instruction*, Vol. XII, Jan., 1967. pp. 27-31. By permission of Assoc. for Educational Communications and Technology.

[19] R. Irwin Goodman, "Systematic Selection," *Audiovisual Instruction*, Vol. XVI, Dec., 1971, pp. 37-38. By permission of Assoc. for Educational Communications and Technology.

[20] Jerrold Kemp, "Which Medium?" *Audiovisual Instruction*, Vol. XVI, Dec., 1971, pp. 32-36. By permission of Assoc. for Educational Communications and Technology.

TABLE 9-1 Instructional Media Stimulus Relationships to Learning Objectives

INSTRUCTIONAL MEDIA TYPE:	LEARNING OBJECTIVES:					
	Learning Factual Information	Learning Visual Identifi-cations	Learning Principles, Concepts and Rules	Learning Procedures	Performing Skilled Perceptual Motor Acts	Developing Desirable Attitudes, Opinions & Motivations
Still Pictures	Medium	HIGH	Medium	Medium	low	low
Motion Pictures	Medium	HIGH	HIGH	HIGH	Medium	Medium
Television	Medium	Medium	HIGH	Medium	low	Medium
3-D Objects	low	HIGH	low	low	low	low
Audio Recordings	Medium	low	low	Medium	low	Medium
Programed Instruction	Medium	Medium	Medium	HIGH	low	Medium
Demonstration	low	Medium	low	HIGH	Medium	Medium
Printed Textbooks	Medium	low	Medium	Medium	low	Medium
Oral Presentation	Medium	low	Medium	Medium	low	Medium

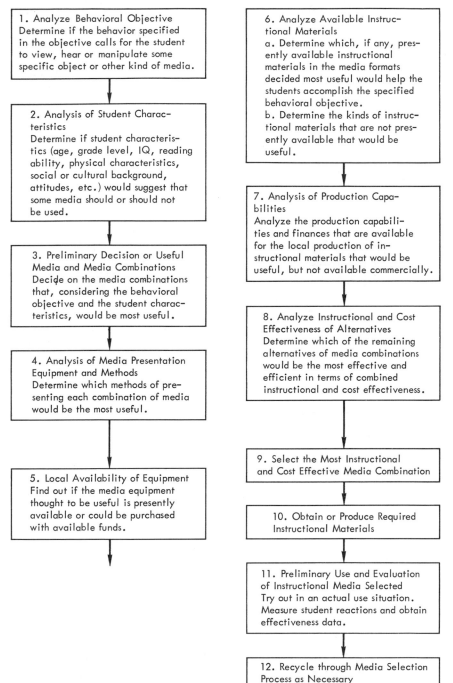

1. Analyze Behavioral Objective
Determine if the behavior specified
in the objective calls for the student
to view, hear or manipulate some
specific object or other kind of media.

2. Analysis of Student Characteristics
Determine if student characteristics (age, grade level, IQ, reading
ability, physical characteristics,
social or cultural background,
attitudes, etc.) would suggest that
some media should or should not
be used.

3. Preliminary Decision or Useful
Media and Media Combinations
Decide on the media combinations
that, considering the behavioral
objective and the student characteristics, would be most useful.

4. Analysis of Media Presentation
Equipment and Methods
Determine which methods of presenting each combination of media
would be the most useful.

5. Local Availability of Equipment
Find out if the media equipment
thought to be useful is presently
available or could be purchased
with available funds.

6. Analyze Available Instructional Materials
a. Determine which, if any, presently available instructional
materials in the media formats
decided most useful would help the
students accomplish the specified
behavioral objective.
b. Determine the kinds of instructional materials that are not presently available that would be
useful.

7. Analysis of Production Capabilities
Analyze the production capabilities and finances that are available
for the local production of instructional materials that would be
useful, but not available commercially.

8. Analyze Instructional and Cost
Effectiveness of Alternatives
Determine which of the remaining
alternatives of media combinations
would be the most effective and
efficient in terms of combined
instructional and cost effectiveness.

9. Select the Most Instructional
and Cost Effective Media Combination

10. Obtain or Produce Required
Instructional Materials

11. Preliminary Use and Evaluation
of Instructional Media Selected
Try out in an actual use situation.
Measure student reactions and obtain
effectiveness data.

12. Recycle through Media Selection
Process as Necessary

Figure 9-1 **The Steps for Systematic Selection of Media**

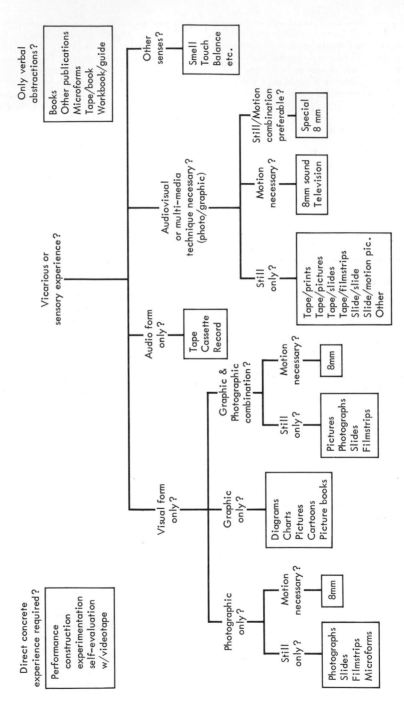

Figure 9-2 Media Selection for Individual Use

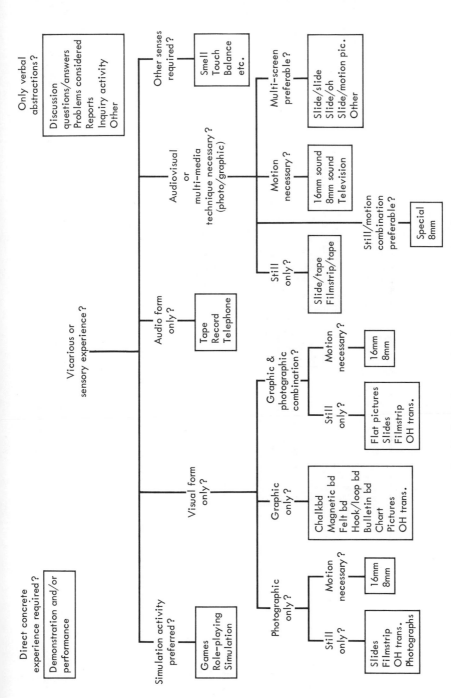

Figure 9-3 Media Selection for Presentation to Small Groups

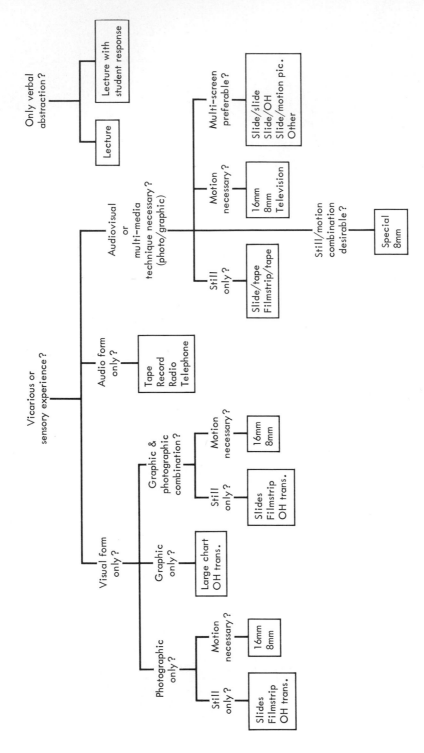

Figure 9-4 Media Selection for Presentation to Large Groups

MASTERY ITEM: RECOMMENDING MEDIA FORMATS

1. The objective is for each fifth grade student to identify Zambia, given a map of the world, in less than ten seconds. What media alternatives would you recommend?

2. The objective is for each eighth grade student to describe the events which caused World War II, given all the resources of a media center, within a forty-five minute class period. What media alternatives would you recommend?

3. The objective is for each first year Spanish student to correctly respond in Spanish to questions regarding personal biographical information when asked the question in Spanish, in less than ten seconds. What media alternatives would you recommend?

Response: Recommending Media Formats

1. The response to this question depends partly on where you are teaching and on the size of the group. It also depends on whether or not the learners have discussed the location of Zambia. If we can assume that this is a class of 32 fifth graders and that you are reviewing the nations of Africa after studying them, then you might turn to the textbook, which is readily accessible. If there is a wall map in the room, you might use it. The availability of an overhead projector and a set of transparencies on the geography of Africa would permit you to consider that option. But if Zambia is labeled on all these maps, you may not be able to achieve your objective because students may respond to the label on the map rather than the location or shape of the country. Perhaps an outline map, in any of the above formats or run off on a spirit duplicator could help each student to identify Zambia, given a map of Africa. There are other alternatives.

2. Two types of resources are required here. First, resources to *gain* the information—such as textbooks, reference books, recordings, films, and filmstrips. Second, resources to *present* the information during a forty-five minute class period. The information gained must be translated into notes to be given orally or in duplicated form, images to be projected with the overhead or slide projectors and perhaps appropriate excerpts from the recordings, films or filmstrips. The objective specifies that each student will *describe* and therefore the stimulus material should help students to be able to describe the events which caused World War II.

3. The response required is an oral statement. A person-to-person dialogue would probably be the best approach but teachers cannot always be available for such personal attention. Perhaps students could tutor each other if less than perfect speech models are permissible. An audiotape with the teacher's voice (or the voice of a native speaker) could also provide the

stimulus to which the student could respond and record. It is then possible for the learner to listen to the original speaker and the response for the purpose of comparison.

COMPETENCY 5   Recommends alternative learning environments.

The term, "learning environment" includes the way in which groups are arranged for optimum learning; the way in which time allocations are made; and the type of space required for the teaching/learning situation. All of these factors must be the concern of the media professional who is a member of the instructional design team. The variables of environment are determined by the content and objectives specified, the entering behavior of the students, the strategy and techniques selected, and the type of media resources which have been recommended. All these concerns must be factored into the decisions regarding whether or not learning ought to take place individually in an isolated setting or in a group. The size of the group is likewise important as is the time which is allocated to the event. The trend is for learning time to be open-ended and based on the ability of each individual to achieve the objective without regard to a specific amount of time. However, it may be necessary to allocate a block of time for certain events. Finally, there is the actual space which has to be made available for the learner(s). The number of individuals pursuing an objective may limit the space and resources available. The grouping of students means that spaces have to be found in which all groups can meet. All of these factors are vital elements of the instructional design process.

There are some who say that the student's learning environment is the total life space of the individual and ought to be considered in any design for instruction. While it is true that persons do not stop learning when they leave learning environments (these could be schools, laboratories, or museums) the designer must remember that the environments which can best be incorporated into the instructional design are those which can be controlled.

Our concern here is with those environments which can provide fairly predictable conditions for insuring optimum learning for a particular type of individual. The three environmental factors are: organization of groups; allocation of time; and allocation of space.

RESOURCES: RECOMMENDING LEARNING ENVIRONMENTS

Chapter 12, "Organization of Groups and Allocation of Space and Time" in Gerlach and Ely offers a comprehensive overview of the three major variables to be considered in recommending alternative learning environments. The chapter is written around three questions which assist in the design process:

1. Which objectives can be reached by the learner on his own?
2. Which objectives can be achieved through interaction among the learners themselves?
3. Which objectives can be achieved through formal presentation by the teacher and through interaction between the learner and teacher? [21]

Gardner Swenson and Donald Keys, *Providing for Flexibility in Scheduling and Instruction,* discusses flexible scheduling at Brookhurst Junior High School in California and provides the rationale for its adoption. Also described are the mechanics of flexible scheduling, its promise as an innovation, procedures for breaking lock step instruction, and providing instruction for groups of various sizes. A companion volume, *How to Organize a Non-Graded School* by Eugene R. Howard and Roger W. Bardwell describes present uses of nongrading, emerging concepts of nongrading, the types of facilities required, procedures for implementing and operating nongraded programs, and what nongrading can and cannot do.

Two monographs describing procedures for grouping are especially useful. *Grouping Students for Improved Instruction* by Dorothy Westby-Gibson describes origins of present grouping practice, research findings, and criteria relevant to making decisions about grouping. Innovations that aid effective grouping and problems that administrators face in grouping are also discussed. In *How to Organize an Effective Team Teaching Program,* Harold S. Davis and Ellsworth Tompkins discuss team teaching—its definition, rationale, and use in elementary and high school. Planning for large group, small group, and independent study, and procedures for evaluating the results of team teaching are also discussed.

The availability and the utilization of space is another element of the learning environment that must be considered. We are not concerned here with the architectural design of facilities but rather with the use of various types of spaces. It is difficult to separate the physical qualities which make a space usable for learning and the way in which a space is used. Brown, Norberg and Srygley discuss matters of space utilization in Chapter 8, "Designing Instructional Facilities," in *Administering Educational Media* which treats matters of design factors for large-group, medium-group and small-group facilities, independent study facilities, and space for teachers. The Educational Facilities Laboratories' publication, *The School Library* (New York: Educational Facilities Laboratories, 1963) discusses both the design and the use of space in areas which are now designated as school media centers. While

[21] Gerlach and Ely, *Teaching and Media,* p. 234.

this publication may appear to be dated by title and copyright date (1963), it is still one of the best references available.

To practice this competency, you might analyze the use of grouping, the allocation of time, and the use of space in the courses in which you are enrolled. What alternatives are there to your present arrangements? What appears to be the advantages of those alternative arrangements? Would you recommend them to your professor or to others?

MASTERY ITEM: RECOMMENDING LEARNING ENVIRONMENTS

1. Check appropriate alternatives for grouping learners:

   _____ large group   _____ by ability
   _____ independently   _____ by age
   _____ by interest   _____ by subject matter
   _____ by projects   _____ teams
   _____ medium group   _____ small groups

2. Check appropriate alternatives for grouping teachers:

   _____ by departments   _____ by subject matter
   _____ by teams   _____ by ability
   _____ differentiated staffing   _____ medium groups

3. Describe flexible time scheduling.

Response: Recommending Learning Environments

You may group learners in any of the above ways—and in several other ways which you may have mentioned. Grouping will depend on the nature of the objective, the tasks involved in performance, the supervision or assistance required, and the space available.

You could group teachers by departments, by subject matter interests, by teams, and by a differentiated staffing plan but it would be difficult to group them by ability. A "medium group" has no significance with teacher grouping.

Flexible time scheduling is a procedure for organizing the school day into modules (usually five to twenty minutes in length) for the purpose of permitting students to achieve instructional objectives on a variable time schedule.

COMPETENCY 6   *Evaluates and modifies teaching/learning design.*

Does the design work? How well? With which learners? How long does it take? To what extent have the defined objectives been achieved? What needs to be improved? These questions (and others) are necessary to evaluate the total instructional design effort. Answers to the questions provide indicators as to how well the design has accomplished its purpose. Areas for revision are identified so that the next cycle will be better and perhaps more efficient. Without this step, the rest of the design process can never be assessed.

The media professional is an evaluator in many senses. In Chapter 14 on the evaluation function the competencies and tasks of evaluation are spelled out. Some of the same principles of evaluation apply here, but to a specific product which has been developed through the design process.

Evaluation here signifies the overt act of determining how well an instructional unit has achieved its purpose. The media professional may try out prototypes with small groups representative of the population for which the instruction was designed. There may be written tests, oral tests, or observations. There may be simulations of actual events. There may be interviews with the representatives of the target group. In short, there are many ways to evaluate instruction which has been designed for a specific audience to achieve specific objectives. There are a few ways to obtain this competency but the best, by far, is to actually do it!

RESOURCES: EVALUATING THE TEACHING/LEARNING DESIGN

Evaluation is a fine art. However, it is an art which begins with a description of desired learner outcomes. Before we begin instruction we want to know whether or not the student already possesses the desired behaviors. If so, there is no need for instruction. If not, we make decisions concerning the entry behavior—does the learner possess the necessary prerequisite behaviors, or readiness, to profit from instruction?

At every point in the teaching/learning process we use information to evaluate. We decide whether the methods, the media, the grouping, the time and space allocation are contributing to the specified outcomes. If these factors are functioning properly, we have increased our knowledge about teaching, and we push on. If not, we go "back to the drawing board" to reformulate our hypotheses—to try other methods, to select different media, to group students differently, to use space and time in yet another way. Evaluation is a process by which we discover whether our instruction is adequate, not whether our students are adequate.

Some of the basic principles of evaluation of instructional design are presented in Gerlach and Ely, *Teaching and Media: A Systematic Approach,* Chapter 14, "The Evaluation Process." The concept of feedback and its use are basic ideas in this chapter. Case studies of evaluation are presented for analysis.

Testing of instructional prototypes usually occurs at three levels:

1. *Development tryouts*—an attempt to look for major flaws; a run-through
2. *Validation* tryouts—to determine how well learners achieve objectives
3. *Field testing*—to see how replicable the materials are with other teachers and/or students

These trial formats for instructional prototypes are presented especially well in Baker and Schutz, *Instructional Product Development.* A broader context is provided in "The Product Development Cycle" (pp. 132–165) of which product tryout and revision are but two parts.

A good summary of the evaluation component of instructional design is given in Bela H. Banathy's Chapter 6, "Implementation and Quality Control" in *Instructional Systems.*

One of the very best publications on evaluation of instructional design is Chapter 6, "The Evaluation Component," in Diamond *et al., Instructional Development for Individualized Learning in Higher Education.* Even though the emphasis is on design of instruction for post-secondary schooling, the principles and examples are useful across all levels of education. A variety of instruments serve as illustrations of specific evaluation case studies. There is probably no other publication currently available which presents equally well the practical background for evaluation with a sound conceptual base.

MASTERY ITEM: EVALUATING THE TEACHING/LEARNING DESIGN

DIRECTIONS: Which is the best interpretation of the following sets of data? Circle the appropriate letter.

1. The average score on a posttest was 52 percent. There was no pretest.
   (a) The class was dull and unable to profit from good instruction.
   (b) The strategy and technique should be altered.
   (c) No judgment can be made.
2. In a representative group of five students, four achieved the objective during a field trial of a new instructional module.
   (a) The module can be installed without further refinement.
   (b) A complete revision is in order since 100 percent attainment of the objective was not achieved.
   (c) The module is almost ready for use but the one student who did not achieve the objective should be interviewed to determine why errors were made.
3. After presentation of a new concept to twelve learners, feedback should be obtained by:
   (a) a written test

(b) discussion with the entire group of learners
(c) discussion with individual learners
(d) all of the above

Response: Evaluating the Teaching/Learning Design

1. No judgment can be made (c). There are no comparative data. Percentages mean nothing unless there is a basis for comparison.
2. Eighty percent is reasonably good, but as long as this is a field test you ought to interview the one student who did not achieve the objective (c). You may learn why that person did not achieve the objective and it may be caused by your materials or methods.
3. All of the above (d) could be used, but one approach may be better than another for a specific purpose. A written test will give you data quickly which can be analyzed later. Discussion with the entire group provides the conditions for interaction and dialogue which may help you to know just how stimulating the material is. Discussion with individual learners insures a response from each person and often provides an opportunity for the quiet person's ideas to emerge. The answer to this question depends upon what you want to discover from your feedback and how much time you can devote to it.

The design function is at the core of the teaching/learning process. While the total function can be separated into discrete components, it is the interactive nature of the components which combine for the ultimate purpose of helping students to learn more effectively and more efficiently.

REFERENCES

Competency 1   Elicits and clarifies objectives of the teacher.

BAKER, ROBERT L. and RICHARD E. SHUTZ (eds.) *Instructional Product Development,* pp. 1-64. New York: Van Nostrand Reinhold, 1971.

BROWN, JAMES W., KENNETH D. NORBERG and SARA K. SRYGLEY. *Administering Educational Media,* pp. 130-132. New York: McGraw-Hill, 1972.

Classification of Objectives. 35mm filmstrip, sound (reel to reel audiotape), color, 61 frames. San Raphael, Calif.: General Programmed Teaching, 1969.

DeCECCO, JOHN P. *The Psychology of Learning and Instruction* (2nd ed.), pp. 24-43. Englewood Cliffs, New Jersey: Prentice-Hall, Inc., 1974.

Educational Objectives. 35mm filmstrip, sound (reel to reel audiotape), color. Los Angeles, Calif.: VIMCET, 1969.

General Goals, Affective Objectives, Cognitive Objectives. 35mm filmstrip, sound (reel to reel audiotape), color. San Raphael, Calif.: General Programmed Teaching, 1969.

GERLACH, VERNON S. and DONALD P. ELY. *Teaching and Media: A Systematic Approach,* pp. 43-75. Englewood Cliffs, New Jersey: Prentice-Hall, Inc., 1971.

GRONLUND, NORMAN E. *Stating Behavioral Objectives for Classroom Instruction.* New York: Macmillan, 1970.

KIBLER, ROBERT J., LARRY L. BECKER and DAVID O. MILES. *Behavioral Objectives and Instruction.* Boston: Allyn and Bacon, 1970.

Learning Objectives. 35mm filmstrip, sound (cassette audiotape), color, 30 min. East Lansing, Mich.: Michigan State University, 1974.

MAGER, ROBERT F. *Preparing Instructional Objectives.* Palo Alto, California: Fearon Publishers, 1962.

Main Components of an Objective. 35mm filmstrip, sound (reel to reel audiotape), color, 64 frames. San Raphael, Calif.: General Programmed Teaching, n.d.

Objectives for Instructional Programs. 35mm filmstrip, sound (cassette audiotape), color, 43 min. Orange, Calif.: Insgroup, 1974.

POPHAM, W. JAMES and EVA BAKER. *Establishing Instructional Goals.* Englewood Cliffs, New Jersey: Prentice-Hall, Inc., 1970.

Competency 2   Analyzes learner characteristics.

BALL, JOHN and FRANCIS C. BYRNES (eds.) *Research, Principles, and Practices in Visual Communication,* pp. 31, 47-50. Washington, D.C.: Association for Educational Communications and Technology, 1960.

BERLO, DAVID K. *The Process of Communication,* pp. 40-50. New York: Holt, Rinehart and Winston, 1960.

DECECCO, JOHN P. *The Psychology of Learning and Instruction* (2nd ed.), pp. 47-69. Englewood Cliffs, New Jersey: Prentice-Hall, Inc., 1974.

Determining Entry Level. 35mm filmstrip, sound (reel-to-reel audiotape), color, 58 frames. San Raphael, Calif.: General Programmed Teaching, 1969.

GERLACH, VERNON S. and DONALD P. ELY. *Teaching and Media: A Systematic Approach,* pp. 14-15. Englewood Cliffs, New Jersey: Prentice-Hall, Inc., 1971.

Competency 3   Assists in determining teaching/learning strategies and techniques.

GERLACH, VERNON S. and DONALD P. ELY. *Teaching and Media: A Systematic Approach,* pp. 207-229. Englewood Cliffs, New Jersey: Prentice-Hall, Inc., 1971.

Learning through Inquiry. 16mm motion picture, sound, color, 31 min. Dayton, Ohio: Institute for Development of Educational Activities, n.d.

Competency 4   Considers alternative media formats and recommends most appropriate medium.

ALLEN, WILLIAM H. "Media Stimulus and Types of Learning," *Audiovisual Instruction* 12 (Jan., 1967): 27-21.

BOUCHER, BRIAN G., MERRILL J. GOTTLIEB, and MARTIN L. MORGANLANDER.

Handbook and Catalog for Instructional Media Selection. Englewood Cliffs, New Jersey: Educational Technology Publications, 1973.

BROWN, JAMES W., RICHARD B. LEWIS and FRED F. HARCLEROAD, *AV Instruction: Technology, Media and Methods* (4th ed.). New York: McGraw-Hill, 1974.

DALE, EDGAR. *Audiovisual Methods in Teaching* (3rd ed.) pp. 107-135. New York: Holt, Rinehart and Winston, 1969.

GERLACH, VERNON S. and DONALD P. ELY. *Teaching and Media: A Systematic Approach,* pp. 281-300. Englewood Cliffs, New Jersey: Prentice-Hall, Inc., 1971.

GOODMAN, R. IRWIN. "Systematic Selection," *Audiovisual Instruction* 16 (Dec., 1971): 37-38.

KEMP, JERROLD, "Which Medium?" *Audiovisual Instruction* 16 (Dec., 1971): 32-36.

WITTICH, WALTER A. and CHARLES F. SCHULLER. *Instructional Technology: Its Nature and Use* (5th edition). New York: Harper & Row, 1973.

Competency 5   Recommends alternative learning environments.

BROWN, JAMES W., KENNETH D. NORBERG and SARA K. SRYGLEY. *Administering Educational Media,* pp. 141-53. New York: McGraw-Hill, 1972.

Charlie and the Golden Hamster: the Nongraded Elementary School. 16mm motion picture, sound, color, 15 min. Dayton, Ohio: Institute for Development of Educational Activities (I.D.E.A.), n.d.

DAVIS, HAROLD S. and ELLSWORTH TOMPKINS. *How to Organize an Effective Team Teaching Program.* Englewood Cliffs, New Jersey: Prentice-Hall, Inc., 1966.

GERLACH, VERNON and DONALD P. ELY. *Teaching and Media: A Systematic Approach,* pp. 234-70. Englewood Cliffs, New Jersey: Prentice-Hall, Inc., 1971.

HOWARD, EUGENE R. and ROGER W. BARDWELL. *How to Organize a Non-Graded School.* Englewood Cliffs, New Jersey: Prentice-Hall, Inc., 1966.

Small Group Learning. 16mm motion picture, sound, color, 21 min. I.D.E.A., n.d.

The Strategies of Small Group Learning, 16mm motion picture, sound, color, 27 min., Dayton, Ohio: I.D.E.A., n.d.

SWENSON, GARDNER and DONALD KEYS. *Providing for Flexibility in Scheduling and Instruction.* Englewood Cliffs, N.J.: Prentice-Hall, Inc., 1966.

Team Teaching in the Elementary School. 16mm motion picture, sound, color, 22 min., Dayton, Ohio: Institute for Development of Educational Activities, n.d.

WESTBY-GIBSON, DOROTHY. *Grouping Students for Improved Instruction.* Englewood Cliffs, New Jersey: Prentice-Hall, Inc., 1966.

Competency 6   Evaluates and modifies teaching/learning design.

Analyzing Learning Outcomes. 35mm filmstrip, sound (reel-to-reel audiotape), color, 26 frames. Los Angeles, Calif.: VIMCET, 1969.

BAKER, ROBERT L. and RICHARD E. SHUTZ (eds.) *Instructional Product Development*. pp. 151-57. New York: Van Nostrand Reinhold, 1971.

BANATHY, BELA H. *Instructional Systems,* pp. 77-86. Palo Alto, California: Fearon Press, 1968.

DIAMOND, ROBERT M., PAUL E. EICKMANN, EDWARD F. KELLY, ROBERT E. HOLLOWAY, THOMAS RUSK VICKERY, ERNEST T. PASCARELLA. *Instructional Development for Individualized Learning in Higher Education,* Chap. 6. Englewood Cliffs, New Jersey: Educational Technology Publications, 1974.

Evaluation. 35mm filmstrip, sound (reel-to-reel audiotape), color, Los Angeles, Calif.: VIMCET, 1969.

Evaluating Learning Systems. 35 mm filmstrip, sound (cassette audiotape), color. East Lansing, Mich.: Michigan State University, 1974.

Validation. 35mm filmstrip, sound (reel-to-reel audiotape), color. San Raphael, Calif.: General Programmed Teaching, 1969.

10 The Information Retrieval Function

Materials in collections must be organized in a way that makes each item readily accessible to the user. Policy decisions must be made and procedures established that will accommodate the efficient handling and storage of materials for retrieval. The advantages and disadvantages of several alternatives in cataloging and classification are presented to provide guidelines for facilitating information retrieval.

One of the basic premises on which a media center is founded is that information appears in many different physical forms. For example, *Hamlet* may appear in the form of a book, a film, or a record. The intellectual content will be the same, but the format is vastly different. It is the important responsibility of the media center to provide this variety of formats to meet the needs, interests, and abilities of all users. This variety of formats is one of the reasons for needing a locating key (or classification scheme) for the materials in the center.

In primitive societies individuals served as the repository of knowledge and served to pass on information from one generation to another. Obviously, the amount of information which can be passed on in this manner is extremely limited, and when more complex societies began to develop, various kinds of information began to be recorded in a variety of permanent forms for the purpose of transmitting knowledge. Today the quantity of new information being generated is so overwhelming that no individual can possibly keep pace with even a small portion of it. The library has developed as a corporate store of knowledge and instead of depending on one person's memory for retrieving information we now depend on catalogs and bibliographic tools.

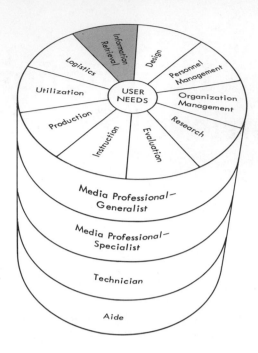

COMPETENCY 1 *Determines classification systems to be used for organizing materials.*

COMPETENCY 2 *Determines and implements policies relating classification to storage and retrieval mechanisms.*

COMPETENCY 3 *Establishes and evaluates procedures for classifying and cataloging materials and implements them.*

COMPETENCY 4 *Determines policies for cataloging of materials.*

COMPETENCY 5 *Organizes and maintains accurate and current retrieval mechanisms such as the card catalog and book catalog.*

COMPETENCY 6 *Organizes and maintains accurate and current accession and inventory records of materials as appropriate.*

COMPETENCY 7 *Assesses and implements automated retrieval systems as appropriate.*

COMPETENCY 8 *Develops indexes and thesauri for organizing special collections.*

This chapter is entitled "Information Retrieval," yet it could equally as well been called "Organization of Knowledge" or possibly "Cataloging and Classification." There is almost a cyclical relationship between organization of knowledge and information retrieval. If information is to be retrieved or located, then it must first be organized in a systematic fashion which facilitates retrieval. The title of the chapter "Information Retrieval" was selected to identify this function, as it is the end or the goal for which the organization takes place. There is a paradox here in that the organization of materials is actually the work performed within the media center by media personnel, while the action of retrieving information is most usually performed by the user, the student, or teacher. However, media personnel do very frequently retrieve materials. If the titles "Organization of Knowledge" or "Cataloging and Classification" had been used; that too is somewhat misleading. These terms clearly indicate the activities performed by the media personnel, but they fail to indicate that these activities in themselves serve no purpose, unless students and teachers use the system for retrieving information. The term "Organization of Knowledge" is much broader in scope than "Cataloging and Classification." Organization of knowledge as it relates to school library media centers usually includes cataloging and classification, which may range from relatively simple systems to the complex and comprehensive. In addition, organization of knowledge implies that the entire range or scope of knowledge has been considered and the plan of organization is the one most appropriate for that particular collection and the needs of the users. It also includes consideration given to the storage plans and arrangements. Cataloging and classification are the activities that serve as the means for getting materials organized. It could be said that cataloging, classifying, and organizing of materials are the means by which materials and information are made available to the user in the most effective and efficient manner.

To be able to retrieve information, one important technique is that of classification. Organization of knowledge is a comprehensive term expressing that function served by classification. Organization of knowledge provides the means of pinpointing specific items of information, and also demonstrates the complete range of subjects available in the library or media center and their relation to each other. The term, organization of knowledge, was most commonly used twenty to thirty years ago, but modern writers usually substitute the terms *information retrieval* or information storage and retrieval. Significant developments in retrieval techniques have come about since the use of the computer has become so widespread.

Classification, as used here, will be defined as the grouping of materials by subject or form usually according to a scheme utilizing numerals and/or letters, and assigning a subject symbol to a work.[1]

Books and other items in a collection can be physically arranged consistently and usefully by one factor only. This usually would be by subject, or

---

[1] Esther J. Piercy, *Commonsense Cataloging: A Manual for the Organization of Books and Other Materials in School and Small Public Libraries* (New York: H. W. Wilson, 1965), p. 168.

in the case of fiction, by the author. It could just as well be by size, format or by color. Each user of the media center may use a different approach in that one person may know only the title, another only the author, or still another only the subject. The catalog, then, is the instrument which must provide, by means of a multiple sequence of entries, access to the entire collection through all the channels by which the user seeks access to the collection. The catalog should be an instrument equipped to provide successful identification of all forms of information and provide for retrieval no matter what pattern of arrangement is provided for storing the materials on the shelves.

Shera and Egan [2] have made a succinct statement of the objectives of the catalog: "The conclusion from both experience and analysis seems inescapable that there are two basic functions of the catalog that are of outstanding importance: 1) accurate and speedy determination of whether or not an item known by author or title is in the collection, and, if so, of where it may be found, and 2) what materials the library contains upon a given subject and where they may be found."

Needham provides a challenging summary:

> All societies depend for their very existence on the communication of knowledge. The more complex the society and the more complex its knowledge, the more complex does this matter of communication become; an ever increasing amount of information must flow smoothly and accurately, not only between the members of the society, but between one society and another and from generations past. Accordingly, the means of communication also become more complex: primitive sounds and signs give way to highly developed spoken and written languages, invention and technical skill produce varied media—printed books, telecommunications, films, sound recordings, and so on, education becomes a matter of increasing importance; conferences proliferate. By these and other means is knowledge communicated and the proper organization of these means is one of the most pressing problems of today.[3]

Bibliographic organization, if developed into a fully integrated system, would be concerned with the publication or production of materials, the means for identification, selection, housing and retrieval of all materials. In most subject areas the systems are only partially developed, and in many cases portions of the system are poorly developed. For totally effective access to materials, all aspects of the system need to be developed.

[2] J. H. Shera and M. E. Egan, *The Classified Catalog; Basic Principles and Practice* (Chicago: American Library Association, 1956), p. 9.
[3] C. D. Needham. *Organizing Knowledge in Libraries.* (London: Andre Deutsch Limited, 1964), p. 9.

COMPETENCY 1   Determines classification systems to be used for organizing materials.

The most important consideration underlying all aspects of classification and cataloging is to make materials readily accessible to the user. Historically, a number of classification systems have been developed, each of which has certain advantages and disadvantages.

These systems are usually referred to as codes, as they are based on systematic codes of rules drawn up so that decisions can be uniform and that each time the professional is confronted by a decision point he or she does not make a decision which differs from his previous one. The following are the classification codes which have had the greatest acceptance:

S. R. Ranganathan. Colon Classification introduced in 1933.

Melvil Dewey. Decimal Classification and Relative Index first published in 1876.

Universal Decimal Classification. First produced as a result of the Brussels Conference on Bibliography in 1895 and the first edition in French was published in 1905.

H. E. Bliss. A Bibliographic Classification. Preliminary version of the scheme appeared in 1935.

Library of Congress Classification. Detailed classification scheme instigated by Herbert Putman, who was Librarian of Congress from 1899 to 1939. Most of the scheme appeared between 1899 and 1920. Though this scheme was designed for a single large library it has been adopted by many other libraries. Each main class is published separately.

J. D. Brown. Subject Classification first published 1906 and the only English general scheme.

In making a selection of classification systems there are certain aspects of the entire program that must be taken into consideration such as:

The size of the collection and the potential size.

The depth to which the collection will be developed in certain subject areas.

Whether all media will be integrated into one system.

The sophistication of the students using the collection.

The number of users to be served.

The organizational pattern of the library, and the relationship to a larger system.

The type of circulation system used.

The restrictions under which the program functions. For example, are accession records required?

The types of service to be provided.

The other information resources of the community.

The policies that would relate to classification such as shelving policies, buying, gifts, special collections, discard, duplication.

The professional must think through all of these factors, collect appropriate data and then make the decisions that will most effectively accommodate all of these aspects and provide the best service to the users.

It is most unlikely that any school media center would give consideration to using any of these codes other than the Dewey Decimal Classification and Relative Index or the Library of Congress Classification scheme. However, it is important to know about these codes, to recognize their main classes, understand how the code handles facet analysis, the notation used in the code and the type of index used. All of these elements relate to the theory of classification and assist in understanding the rationale behind the decisions that must be made in organizing materials in a library.

The classification scheme that is used most often in media centers is the Dewey Decimal Classification scheme. It is the most widely used of all general schemes of classification and can be used very effectively in media centers as there is an abridged edition published especially for use in schools.[4] Some characteristics of the Dewey Classification scheme that account for its immediate acceptance and success are the following features:

1. Relative location. At the time it was introduced this was a new idea which overcame the disadvantage of a fixed location meaning the reservation of certain shelves for specific subjects.
2. The simplicity and hospitality of the decimal notation.
3. The relative index. The index is detailed and it gives collation information, e.g.:
   Ships
canal transportation	386.22
construction and engineering	623.8
ocean transportation	387.2

Its continued use is largely due to the fact that it is so firmly established in a large number of libraries, its permanent revision organization was established in the Library of Congress, and many centralized cataloging projects use it, such as Wilson publications and Wilson cards. Another reason is that there is a lack of any other general scheme that is good enough to convince librarians to reclassify their entire libraries. The scheme does have its limitations, but it is still the most popular.

The Dewey Decimal Classification system would be the one normally

---

[4] Melvil Dewey, *Dewey Decimal Classification and Index*. (10th Abridged Ed.) (Lake Placid Club, N.Y.: Forest Press, 1971). Also distributed by H. W. Wilson Co., New York.

used in school media centers. Some of the reasons for selecting this scheme are:

1. It is used in most public and many academic libraries so students will benefit from being familiar with the system.
2. It is relatively simple so it can be readily understood by users.
3. Because the system is based on the decimal system, the numbers used can be kept relatively simple or can be expanded according to the size and complexity of the collection.
4. The system brings together all materials on a certain subject which facili- tates ready access and also browsing.
5. Catalog cards that are printed commercially are readily available in this classification system, and many bibliographic tools and reviewing sources use this system.
6. It has proven to function effectively for retrieval purposes.
7. It can be used equally well for audiovisual materials as well as for books.

The other scheme that is most likely to be considered is the Library of Congress Classification scheme. This scheme has several distinctive features such as the separate publication of classes and the lack of common subdivisions within classes. This situation has occurred because the Library of Congress is organized on a subject department basis and to a large extent the main classes can be viewed as separate special schemes, although they do incorporate the same fundamental principles and practices. Some persons defend this scheme because they say it was developed from an actual existing collection, rather than having the scheme develop from theoretical principles. Most authorities agree that there are parts of this scheme that show particular appropriateness for special categories.

Some media professionals make the decision to use the Library of Congress classification scheme if they anticipate that their collection will become very large, or develop comprehensively in one special area, if many of the other libraries used by the students all use this system, and, if for some reason, it is easier to obtain Library of Congress printed catalog cards.

In some cases, particularly if the collections are expected to remain very small, or if they are comprised mainly of audiovisual materials, accession numbers could be used in place of a classification system. This plan requires that a chronological number be assigned to each item. The major advantage of using the accession number and keeping the record in an accession book is the simplicity of the system. It requires no decision making, and does not require the time and attention of a professional as other classification systems do. One method frequently used is to assign blocks of numbers to certain kinds of materials, e.g. 1000–1999 could be used for records, 2000–2999 could be used for filmstrips. This plan allows materials of similar format to be located together on the shelves. The major problem with this plan is that the number assigned has no relationship to the subject so all users who wish to locate materials by subject would have to locate them through the catalog.

RESOURCES: DETERMINING CLASSIFICATION SYSTEMS

College courses in cataloging and classification are the appropriate sources for acquiring this competency. More advanced courses in information retrieval and indexing are also helpful in understanding the related problem in organization and retrieval. Some may argue that there are aspects of classification and cataloging that can be done by paraprofessionals, and in some cases this might be true. However, to make decisions that are appropriate and are based on a thorough knowledge of the total situation, the decision-maker must have a background in the theory of classification as well as knowing the basic fundamentals in order to make knowledgeable recommendations. Unquestionably, experience is helpful, and it would be useful in developing competency in these areas of classification and cataloging to work in a large technical processing center to be able to observe an efficiently organized system. Work in the various sections would provide both broad and in-depth experience in every part of the process.

It is also important to keep up-to-date on new developments in the area of classification and cataloging, so media personnel are encouraged to keep constantly aware of new professional books and articles in journals relating to this subject. This is particularly true in the area of working with audiovisual materials, as constant changes are taking place.

For background information see Esther J. Piercy, *Commonsense Cataloging: A Manual for the Organization of Books and Other Materials in School and Small Public Libraries.* For more detailed and thorough discussion of comparative schemes see works by Arthur Maltby or J. Mills or Ernest Cushing Richardson, all of which are listed in the bibliography at the end of the chapter.

MASTERY ITEM: DETERMINING CLASSIFICATION SYSTEMS

You are faced with deciding which classification schemes will be adopted in a new high school media center. Select the factors which should be taken into consideration in making your decision.

1. The collection is expected to have 75,000 holdings within two years.
2. The entire collection, both print and audiovisual materials will be integrated as far as shelving is concerned.
3. The community college in the city uses the Library of Congress Classification system.

4. More than half the seniors expect to enroll in the Community College.
5. The public library uses the Dewey Decimal Classification system.
6. Cataloging and classification are done centrally for the entire district.
7. You intend to have a divided catalog, with the subject catalog separate from author and title.
8. You have hired a clerical aide who has had experience keeping accession records.

Response: Determining Classification Systems

Factors 1, 3, 4, 5 and 6 should be considered in making your decision.

COMPETENCY 2   Determines and implements policies relating classification to storage and retrieval mechanisms.

These must be constantly kept in mind that all decisions relating to classification and about related policies must be made with the ultimate goal in mind—to retrieve the appropriate materials for the user.

Many decisions must be made that relate to the actual process of classification. One major decision is whether or not the total collection will be integrated as far as shelving or storage is concerned. In other words, will all audiovisual materials be intershelved with the books? There are many advantages to be found in this arrangement. The major advantage is probably the convenience to the user. If the user wishes to determine what materials are available on a subject, such as the Navajo Indians, the entire range of materials, in whatever format, would be located together on the shelves. There could be books, maps, pictures, films, filmstrips, realia, records and videotapes all on this subject. To be able to browse through an integrated collection is usually an extremely rewarding experience for the user. This system brings to the attention of the user materials in many formats that may not be so appealing when they are only described on a catalog card. An integrated shelving system simplifies the process of returning materials to the shelves, as the classification number would be all that would be necessary to indicate location.

There are some obvious problems. First and foremost, integrated shelving takes more shelf space, as the variety of sizes and shapes does not make for economy of storage. Next, to facilitate on-the-shelf storage, storage containers need to be somewhat uniform, sturdy, easy to label and to handle. A number of commercial companies have recognized this problem and have developed such storage containers. Another problem that deters many from using totally integrated shelving is the apprehension that expensive films, filmstrips, videotapes or records will be damaged if they are made so readily accessible to all users in an open-shelf arrangement.

If other storage or shelving arrangements are going to be used, then the users either must be expected to learn them through inquiry or the location will have to be indicated in some manner on the catalog card. Sometimes codes are developed to indicate locations of materials. If integrated shelving is not used, the normal practice would be to shelve materials in like formats together, such as all films together, all audiotapes together, etc. Decisions affecting shelving or storage need to be made at the same time that decisions are made about classification. These decisions are interrelated as part of the purpose of classification is to serve as a locating device.

Another decision that must be made is whether or not to use accession numbers for any part of the collection. It has already been pointed out that it does not require the time of professionals to assign accession numbers, as once the system has been established it is a simple process. Numbers are assigned chronologically, but may be assigned to different media formats in blocks. The assignment of numbers in blocks assures that each medium will be shelved together. The location of each format can be posted in some strategic place so that all users will have ready access to all materials. Each one of these processes entails a whole series of steps too lengthy to be explained in detail here. These would include the processing of the materials, keeping appropriate accession records and any other steps that would be required to make the materials accessible. The point that must be made is that all of these policies must be identified and the decisions must be made and implemented at the appropriate time, as it is usually difficult to undo or change basic policies after a major portion of a media center is organized under one plan.

RESOURCES: RELATING CLASSIFICATION SYSTEMS TO STORAGE AND RETRIEVAL

College courses, internships and working with experienced professionals are all appropriate here. The books listed in the Reference section at the end of this chapter are recommended. They are James W. Brown, Kenneth D. Norberg, and Sara K. Srygley, *Administering Educational Media;* C. D. Needham, *Organizing Knowledge in Libraries;* and Derek Langridge, *Approach to Classification.*

MASTERY ITEM: RELATING CLASSIFICATION SYSTEMS TO STORAGE AND RETRIEVAL

Choose one of the following that best matches the descriptive phrase.

A. Library of Congress Classification scheme

B. Dewey Decimal Classification scheme
C. Accession numbering plan

1. Most appropriately used for collections that are developed in-depth in certain areas
2. Most commonly used by the greatest number of libraries
3. Most simple to use with a small audiovisual collection
4. Was developed from an actual collection
5. Can be implemented readily by clerical assistants
6. Accommodates shelving of media formats together
7. An abridged version has been developed to use with small collections
8. Within this plan, blocks of numbers can be reserved for each media format.

Response: Relating Classification Systems to Storage and Retrieval

1. A   5. C
2. B   6. C
3. C   7. B
4. A   8. C

COMPETENCY 3   Establishes and evaluates procedures for classifying and cataloging materials and implements them.

This competency is difficult to describe as it can be so different in each situation. Nevertheless, each media center operation requires that this process take place. The following examples demonstrate the different range of complexity of this competency. For some schools, the processes of classifying and cataloging are handled in a centralized operation and are done for the entire district. In such cases it is only necessary for the personnel in the media center to understand the processes, cooperate in the decision making, and follow through on the steps of the operation that must be carried out in each school. For instance, some centralized processing centers handle every aspect of the process and the only task that remains is for each individual center to file the cards that they receive. In other cases, the cataloging is completed in a centralized location but accession numbers are assigned in individual schools, as the chronological sequence may differ in each school (e.g., one school may have purchased 549 filmstrips, while another newer school may only have 325). In districts which have established centralized processing, the responsibilities relating to this competency will be minimal. By contrast, if all of the classifying and cataloging is done in each individual media center, then the responsibilities relating to this competency become demanding. The procedures would include making the decisions as to who does what, when, where, how, and with what priority. The following are examples of questions that must be answered:

1. Which of the personnel in the media center is to perform each aspect of the range of tasks to be completed in the classifying and cataloging process?
2. Is one person to be responsible for all print materials, and another responsible for all the audiovisual materials? Or are the tasks to be divided according to the various areas of expertise of the staff, one to do the classifying, one to check the filing?
3. When are these responsibilities to be completed? During certain hours of the day? As the materials arrive? Only after students have left?
4. Are certain areas of the media center going to be arranged in a manner that would physically facilitate these functions? Arrangements such as, typewriters, typing tables, storage shelves, spaces arranged to handle the "assembly line" processing of the materials, would all be appropriate.
5. Is each aspect of the process assigned to a specific person and does that person thoroughly understand the process?
6. Has a priority been established?

Because of the great number of tasks that must be performed in a media center, problems seem to arise with respect to the classification and cataloging processes. Some professionals go to one extreme and spend a large proportion of their time handling cataloging and classification responsibilities. They are often accused of spending so much time at this task that they neglect the more important tasks of working with the students and faculty members. On the other hand, some media personnel look on the tasks related to cataloging and classification as an intrusion that keeps them from the parts of their job that they enjoy more, and so they neglect this aspect of their responsibility. Cataloging and classification must be looked at as a means to an end. The major objective is to make all materials readily accessible. If the cataloging and classification of materials is not kept up-to-date, this keeps materials from being used. No matter what methods are used to get the tasks of cataloging and classification completed, these processes must undergo constant scrutiny and assessment. It must be determined whether all aspects of the process are carried out in the most economical way as far as expenditure of time and money are concerned. One approach that is used extensively is to purchase commercially printed catalog cards. From some companies, cards can be ordered commercially printed to certain specifications so that they are adaptable to the specific needs of a particular media center. Other companies have a standard format that is appropriate for most typical media centers. The Library of Congress also prints and sells catalog cards. They can be ordered without classification codes so that Dewey numbers or other appropriate numbers or letters can be typed in for call numbers.

RESOURCES: EVALUATING PROCEDURES FOR
CLASSIFYING AND CATALOGING

Once again, the best way to gain this competency is through college classes and experience. Those persons who have had the opportunity to visit media centers and closely observe their functions, will be able to develop a large repertoire of alternative patterns of handling the responsibilities of organizing materials. All media personnel should be encouraged to visit other school districts in their own geographic region, and also in other states, as it is only through a knowledge of a diversity of patterns that one is able to make good judgments about optimum arrangements. It is particularly important for the media personnel to be knowledgeable about the advantages and disadvantages of centralized processing, the initial costs and on-going costs, as in many cases centralized processing solves many problems that are difficult to handle in any other manner.

In general, it can be expected that there will be an additional cost when centralized processing is first established, as there is the need to provide facilities and personnel. In many smaller school districts these costs would be minimal. For instance, one professional cataloger and a secretary could comprise the initial staff. Another problem is to get consensus among the media center personnel of the district on ways in which specific decisions should be handled. In most cases this requires that these persons be flexible and willing to accept minor changes in the way some aspects of the cataloging and classification are handled. In return, by having these processes handled centrally, the redundancy and repetitiveness are eliminated. The cataloging and classification processes are done once for a specific item and do not have to be repeated at each school. Another great advantage is that the media center personnel in each school are released from these tasks and are able to spend much more time working with students and teachers.

Besides reading about various models in the professional literature it is often helpful to write directly to another media professional to ask specific questions or to visit in order to investigate another process at first hand.

The books listed in the bibliography by Piercy; Akers; and Weihs, et al. can also offer help.

MASTERY ITEM: EVALUATING PROCEDURES FOR CLASSIFYING
AND CATALOGING

You are a director of a media center in a high school of 1500 students. Yours is the only high school in the district and you do not have centralized processing. Your background and training relates to the entire range of media. You have one assistant who has a bachelor's degree and has had twenty-four credit-hours in educational technology. You have a full-time secretary.

In this simulated situation answer the following questions:

1. Which personnel perform the tasks of cataloging and classifying?
2. What time schedule would you recommend?
3. What priorities would you establish?

Response: Evaluating Procedures for Classifying and Cataloging

1. One possible allocation of responsibility would be as follows:

a. Order commercially printed catalog cards for as many of the items as possible. Instruct the secretary as to the appropriate procedures for ordering.
b. Assign the responsibility for classifying all audio and visual materials to the assistant.
c. The director will assume the remainder of the responsibility for classifying other materials and completing the cataloging.
d. The secretary will complete all typing and initial filing.
e. The director will check all typing and filing before integration into the catalog.

2. Allocate time for cataloging and classifying responsibilities before and after the time when the center is open for use by teachers and students.

3. First priority for handling should be those materials requested for class use by teacher. A next priority would be those materials requested by students. The third priority would be those materials not especially requested, but identified as important for purchase to extend the collection for general use.

COMPETENCY 4   Determines policies for cataloging of materials.

Cataloging is the process by which the information about the material is recorded in a succinct and consistent manner to provide a guide to the user.

Every aspect of the cataloging process requires decisions. One of the first decisions is to determine whether all catalog cards are going to be filed together or whether there will be a divided catalog. To facilitate the use of all media it is probably very important to have catalog cards for all books and audiovisual materials filed together. When a user is searching for material on a certain subject this means that information on that subject would be filed together in whatever format it was found. Using this procedure, all users can be informed about all of the alternative formats of information on the same subject.

Other decisions about the form of the catalog might involve the question of dividing the catalog by author, as separated from title and subject, or subject, as separated from author and title. Authorities who recommend separation suggest that this kind of division makes it easier for users to locate materials and makes filing much simpler. Others prefer to have all cards interfiled.

Decisions must be made on the comprehensiveness of the information to be included in the catalog in each of these elements. The personnel, time and funds available also determine the depth to which each center can go in providing added entries for coauthors, illustrators, etc. and to what extent content analysis should be carried out. For example, would it be worth while for your users to have individual essays listed, in addition to the title of the book in which they are included? Other decisions relate to audiovisual materials. How much descriptive information is it necessary to provide for your users about audiorecords? about videorecords? Many of these decisions can be handled expeditiously by making one major decision. That decision is to decide on a specific cataloging manual for handling audio and visual materials.

RESOURCES: DETERMINING CATALOGING POLICIES

Two manuals that are recommended are: Jean Riddle Weihs, Shirley Lewis, Janet MacDonald. *Nonbook Materials, the Organization of Integrated Collections.* (Ottawa: Canadian Library Association, 1973), Also, *Standards for Cataloging Nonprint Materials.* (4th ed.) (Washington, D.C.: Association for Educational Communication and Technology, 1974).

Several helpful publications have been written delineating the strong points of each manual. Many of the sources listed in the bibliography for Competency Four may help you in deciding which manual would provide you with more appropriate guidelines. A thorough coverage of the entire problem is found in works by Grove and Clement; Massonneau; and Piercy.

MASTERY ITEM: DETERMINING CATALOGING POLICIES

The school superintendent of your school district has invited you to his office to discuss whether or not the district should establish centralized cataloging and classification and processing to serve the twenty-four elementary schools, three junior high schools and two high schools in the district. How would you answer the following questions?

1. Will the centralized processing center cost the district more?
2. Will the materials get to the user faster?
3. What will the media center personnel do with the extra time they gain?
4. Of what value is a union shelf list?
5. Would you recommend that the district adopt this plan?
6. What steps must we take to implement this plan?

Response: Determining Cataloging Policies

1. In most cases there will be the cost of the central facility and its up-keep, and the cost of hiring personnel to staff the center. Some districts attempt to staff the center by reallocating personnel from the media centers in the schools. This approach is only recommended as a last resort, as it would most likely create dissatisfactions and also curtail some of the services in those schools.

2. In most cases, if the center is organized efficiently there should be a minimum of time lapse in getting the materials to the user.

3. The great advantage is that media center personnel are freed to work with students and teachers. The classification and cataloging is done once and does not have to be repeated at every school.

4. A union shelf list identifies the location of all materials held at any school in the district. Expensive and little used materials do not need to be duplicated but can be shared.

5. Yes. If after considering all factors there are no insurmountable obstacles. For most districts, centralized processing and cataloging services are by far the most efficient manner of handling these tasks.

6. First the District Supervisor will appoint someone from within the district who is knowledgeable about centralized processing. Next, that person will develop a plan outlining the processings, cataloging, and classification tasks that can be performed. Central-media personnel from each school within the district must agree on the plan to be adapted. Personnel must be hired to implement the agreed upon plan. Finally, the person hired usually would be someone who has expertise in the field of calaloging and classification, plus secretarial knowledge.

COMPETENCY 5   Organizes and maintains accurate and current retrieval mechanisms such as the card catalog and book catalog.

This is identified as a separate and discrete competency even though it is very closely related to the cataloging and classification process. Many media professionals fail to realize the importance of keeping the retrieval mechanisms up-to-date. For example, as materials are received, it is important to get the catalog cards filed as quickly as possible and to get the materials on the shelves so that the users can have access to the materials. One of the most important principles to keep in mind with respect to the card catalog is that it should be extremely accurate in reflecting exactly what materials are in the collection. If materials are lost it is important to remove the related cards from the catalog so that users will not be using erroneous information. It is difficult enough to encourage the use of materials, so extreme care must be taken that users are not disappointed or misinformed, since they can become easily discouraged about using the services.

Some school districts have tried innovative approaches to information retrieval through use of the computer. One of the most common applications of computer technology is to print a book catalog. This can be done if the district has adequate access to a computer or if the school district is co-operating with some large public library network that prints a book catalog. The holdings of the library system are established as a data bank and all new acquisitions are added so that the bibliographic information is kept current. Book catalogs are printed and distributed to all media centers that are cooperating with the network. The major advantage is that the book catalog is very transportable and can be used anywhere, as contrasted to the 3" x 5" cards in a catalog, which is very inflexible and must be used in one location. One major disadvantage is the difficulty in making the initial transition and then keeping it current.

In addition to the card catalog or book catalog, supplementary retrieval tools are essential. The media professional must assume the responsibility for developing the collection so that indexes and thesauri of appropriate nature are available to users. For example, it is important to provide such indexes as the *Play Index,* the *Short Story Index, Book Review Digest, Media Review Digest* and *Readers Guide to Periodical Literature.* There are numerous titles of this nature that serve as information retrieval tools and supplements to the catalogs.

RESOURCES: MAINTAINING ACCURATE RETRIEVAL MECHANISMS

College courses in cataloging and reference are important. A major source of information can be found in current issues of professional journals. The following book is helpful. Esther J. Piercy. *Commonsense Cataloging: A Manual for the Organization of Books and other Materials in School and Small Public Libraries.* (New York: H. W. Wilson, 1965), pp. 75-83.

MASTERY ITEM: MAINTAINING ACCURATE RETRIEVAL MECHANISMS

Assume that you have the opportunity to develop a book catalog as a retrieval mechanism in your school district. List the advantages and disadvantages.

Response: Maintaining Accurate Retrieval Mechanisms

Certain general conditions must be present in order to consider developing a book catalog. The bibliographic information about the holdings must be stored in the computer and computer time must be available at intervals when the catalog is to be printed.

Advantages:

1. Book catalogs are easily transportable and can be made available for use at many locations.
2. It is possible to keep book catalogs updated with relative ease. Book catalogs can be used very advantageously to teach location skills, as a number of students can be taught at once, each having a copy of the catalog.
3. Reproducing book catalogs is quite inexpensive after the holdings are once put in to the computer.

Disadvantages:

1. Many school districts do not have access to the computer initially, or at appropriate times for reproducing the catalog.
2. Many districts do not wish to expend money putting the bibliographic information in a computer.
3. Many districts do not have personnel trained to accomplish this task.
4. Each time the catalog is updated, the entire catalog must be reprinted.
5. By contrast to a book catalog, a traditional catalog, can be used in only one location.

COMPETENCY 6 Organizes and maintains accurate and current accession and inventory records of materials as appropriate.

Practices within different school districts vary markedly with respect to the records that are required or recommended. One of the first responsibilities of media personnel when they begin a new job is to check carefully to ascertain what records are expected. Some states have laws requiring that certain records be kept, while some counties or districts have specific requirements. In other circumstances, depending on the systems of classification you are using, and the other operations that are in effect, it is sound practice to keep a variety of kinds of records.

It has almost become a historical tradition to keep a record of attendance of users in the center and to keep a record of circulation. These are relatively unsophisticated records that initially seemed to indicate actual use. Some districts still require such records. If they do, it is incumbant upon the media professional to provide them. However, since the focus of attention on accountability, some persons have begun to do research on methods of record keeping necessary to assessing cost effectiveness. Both Liesener and DeProspo have made significant contributions in this field. Study of the recommendations of both Liesener's and DeProspo's plans give guidelines as to some of the appropriate data to collect and records to keep.

Dr. James Liesener of the College of Library and Information Services of the University of Maryland describes the role of. the media center director as one who serves to facilitate the interaction between clients and information in order to achieve learning objectives. The optimum goal is to have the media personnel identify and assess the information alternatives available on one hand, and the related client needs on the other, to provide the most efficacious match. If this goal is not reached, it may be because of limitations caused by lack of resources, lack of time, or inadequate techniques or methods. Dr. Liesener has developed a program analysis and planning system based on techniques taken from P.P.B.S. (Planning, Programming, Budgeting Systems) and systems analysis. The conceptual framework is based on defining user services, program outputs or ends as clearly and distinctly as possible. It is essential to distinguish ends, or user services from means, resources and operations. It is also necessary to determine the variety of raw materials, the resources required for the various services, and the staff time necessary to transform the raw materials into user services. The technique requires a nine step process described as follows: 1) Definition of Program Output Alternatives, 2) Survey of Perceptions of Current Services, 3) Determination of Service Preference and Priorities in Relation to Local Needs, 4) Assessment of Resource and Operational Requirements Services, 5) Determination of Costs of Preferred Services and/or Current Service, 6) Calculation of Program Capability, 7) Communication of Preferred Services Currently Feasible to Total Client Groups, 8) Reallocation of Resources and Implementation of Changes in Operations to Provide the Range and Level of Services Selected, and 9) Periodic Evaluation of Services Offered and Documentation of Changing Needs.

This approach to program assessment requires a different process of record keeping, which is explained thoroughly in publications by Liesener and DeProspo listed in the bibliography.

If one of the approaches to organizing the collection is to use accession numbers, then a careful accession record must be kept. These are books for recording chronological numbers, with a listing of each item as it is received, indicating the accession number assigned. If blocks of numbers are assigned to different media, then this plan must be carefully specified in the accession record.

Shelf lists probably are not similar to other items identified in this category, but still they are a record. The shelf list is comprised of a copy of the main entry catalog card for each book, arranged according to classification. The shelf list serves many purposes, but one major purpose is that it serves as an inventory of the holdings. Because the shelf list is arranged as the materials are arranged on the shelves, it is the list to use when taking inventory to assess what materials are lost or misplaced. Concerned professors who teach courses in administration of media centers warn students that if they are in charge of a media center and there is a fire, "save the shelf list first as it is the complete inventory of the holdings."

The frequency with which inventories are taken varies according to the requirements of the district. Sometimes they are requested by administrators. It is usually appropriate to take inventory at least once a year to determine what materials need to be replaced and also to determine the exact holdings to be sure that the card catalog is accurate.

Another inventory that is different in scope and nature is that of the equipment. Even if some equipment, such as record players, are out on permanent loan to certain rooms in a school, records need to be kept centrally so that there is an accurate and current record of all holdings.

Another important inventory, particularly in larger schools, is an inventory of all repair and replacement parts for the equipment. To have the correct parts available for repair or replacement is vitally important to the smooth functioning of the equipment.

Each school or district may have other records and inventories which they find important. It is important to cooperate to fulfill these requests for information.

RESOURCES: MAINTAINING RECORDS

College courses in administration of media centers should touch on many aspects of these record keeping activities. On the job it would be advisable to consult other experienced personnel in the district as they would be able to provide guidelines to follow.

Chapter 15 in Esther J. Piercy's book, *Commonsense Cataloging: A*

Manual for the Organization of Books and Other Materials in School and Small Public Libraries (New York, H. W. Wilson, 1965), would be helpful.

MASTERY ITEM: MAINTAINING RECORDS

Outline the steps that must be followed in taking inventory of a media center.

Response: Maintaining Records

The following steps should be followed in taking inventory:

1. Conduct inventory at a time when it is most likely that the major portion of the collection is in the center so that a minimum of materials are checked out.
2. Contact students and teachers to determine whether or not they have the materials checked out to them.
3. Have student assistants and clerical assistants check the shelves to ascertain that all of the materials are located in correct order.
4. Have one person "read" the shelf list and call out the identifying call number to a person checking the shelf to determine whether they match. Have prearranged flags or clips to put on the shelf cards to identify those materials that are missing.
5. Check equipment according to the records of the holdings.
6. The director of the center will need to review the findings to assess the accuracy of the report.
7. A summary report should be submitted to the principal, if appropriate.
8. The catalog should be revised to reflect the current holdings.
9. Replacement materials should be ordered if appropriate.

COMPETENCY 7   Assesses and implements automated retrieval systems as appropriate.

This competency may appear to some to be too visionary and not realistic. However, for persons preparing to enter the media profession it is probable that sometime in their career they will have experience with automated retrieval systems. As computers and minicomputers develop and become commonly used in school districts it is more likely that they will be avaliable for use in automated retrieval processes. It is important for persons now preparing to enter this profession to become aware of developments in automation, to develop some background and skills in data processing, and to keep up-to-date on what others are doing in the field. Other than the problem of having access to a computer, the major problem in most cases is that the holdings are so limited that automation would not be a justifiable expense. A prediction of what is likely to happen is that many different types of libraries, such as public libraries, academic libraries, and special libraries, may in many cases agree to put their holdings into a common data base and then move to automated retrieval.

Another possibility is to implement more ready access to computerized data bases. For example, many faculty members might be interested in having on-line access to ERIC, the Educational Resources Information Centers. Providing this service could be a beginning of an entire program of automated information retrieval.

RESOURCES: ASSESSING AND IMPLEMENTING AUTOMATED RETRIEVAL SYSTEMS

Courses in data processing are highly recommended as are courses in indexing and information retrieval.

MASTERY ITEM: ASSESSING AND IMPLEMENTING AUTOMATED RETRIEVAL SYSTEMS

List the criteria you would expect to be met by an effective automated retrieval system.

Response: Assessing and Implementing Automated Retrieval Systems

1. Are access points readily available to users?
2. Have users been given adequate instruction to feel comfortable using this mode of access?
3. If computers are used, is the system available to users an adequate number of hours and at convenient hours?
4. Is the data base comprehensive enough to serve users adequately?
5. Is the data base inclusive in its content, including complete information about each item?
6. Are there continuous improvements in the system as appropriate?
7. Is the data base being continuously updated?
8. Is there a minimum of waiting time for printouts?
9. Have convenient arrangements been made to acquire hard copy?

COMPETENCY 8   *Develops indexes and thesauri for organizing special collections.*

There are certain special collections within a media center that are not appropriate to be classified and cataloged in the regular catalog. Examples of these collections would be vertical file materials, including pamphlets, clippings and other ephemeral materials. The very descriptions of these materials as "ephemeral" provides a clue as to the reason for needing special tools for access. The materials are kept for a relatively short time and so it is not appropriate to classify and catalog these materials fully. Yet they do need to be retrieved. Another collection that also falls into this category could be collections of transparencies. (However, sets of transparencies could be classified, cataloged and shelved in an integrated collection.)

In most cases these collections will be identified by subject, so the locating indexes or thesauri will be organized according to subject. The skills required for developing complex thesauri can be very demanding, and some large collections may require highly skilled handling. Other collections will be small and can be handled with relative simplicity. These collections must not be ignored, as in many instances they contain the most current and up-to-date information on current events, and on career information.

RESOURCES: ORGANIZING SPECIAL COLLECTIONS

Units or modules within courses on cataloging and classification would deal with this competency in some depth. Further competency could be developed in courses in indexing and information retrieval. Skill comes through working with small collections and simple problems and then moving on to more extensive collections. The work by Gould and Wolfe listed in the bibliography would also be of help in developing this competency.

MASTERY ITEM: ORGANIZING SPECIAL COLLECTIONS

	Yes	No
1. A thesaurus can be constructed by carefully examining the subject field, collecting all related terms, and structuring these into a thesaurus.	——	——
2. The thesaurus can also be built as the work of indexing proceeds.	——	——
3. In building a thesaurus, if synonyms occur, choose one and refer to it from all others.	——	——
4. Most authorities agree that in building a thesaurus the number of terms in the vocabulary should be strictly limited.	——	——
5. KWIC (Key Word in Context) indexes have developed since the use of the computers.	——	——
6. KWIC indexes depend on the principle of using terms in the title to serve as indexing terms.	——	——

Response: Organizing Special Collections

1. Yes.
2. Yes
3. Yes
4. Yes
5. No (As early as 1856 catalogs were produced by this method.)
6. Yes

REFERENCES

NEEDHAM, C. D. *Organizing Knowledge in Libraries.* London: Andre Deutsch Limited, 1964.

PIERCY, ESTHER J. *Commonsense Cataloging: A Manual for the Organization of Books and Other Materials in School and Small Public Libraries.* New York: H. W. Wilson, 1965.

SHERA, J. H. and M. E. EGAN. *The Classified Catalog: Basic Principles and Practice.* Chicago: American Library Association, 1956.

Tools of the Trade. Audio-cassette, 40 minutes. New York: R. R. Bowker Co., 1973.

Tools of the Trade: Additional Aides. Audiocassette, 40 minutes. New York: R. R. Bowker Co., 1973.

Competency 1   Determines classification systems to be used for organizing materials.

DEWEY, MELVIL. *Dewey Decimal Classification and Relative Index,* 10th abridged ed. Lake Placid Club, New York: Forest Press, 1971. Also distributed by H. W. Wilson Company of New York.

MALTBY, ARTHUR. *Classification in the 1970's; A Discussion of Development and Prospects of the Major Schemes.* Hamden, Connecticut: Linnet Books, 1972.

MILLS, J. *A Modern Outline of Classification* (6th Impression). London: Chapman and Hall, 1968.

PIERCY, ESTHER J. *Commonsense Cataloging: A Manual for the Organization of Books and Other Material in School and Small Public Libraries,* pp. 65-70. New York: H. W. Wilson, 1965.

RICHARDSON, ERNEST CUSHING. *Classification: Theoretical and Practical* (3rd ed.). Hamden, Connecticut: The Shoe String Press, Inc., 1964.

Competency 2   Determines and implements policies relating classification to storage and retrieval mechanisms.

BROWN, JAMES W., KENNETH D. NORBERG, SARA K. SRYGLEY. *Administering Educational Media* (2nd ed.), pp. 179-187. New York: McGraw-Hill, 1972.

LANGRIDGE, DEREK. *Approach to Classification; for Students of Librarianship.* London: Clive Bingley, 1971.

NEEDHAM, C. D. *Organizing Knowledge in Libraries,* pp. 9-157. London: Andre Deutsch Limited, 1964.

Competency 3   Establishes and evaluates procedures for classifying and cataloging materials and implements them.

AKERS, SUSAN GREY. *Simple Library Cataloging* (5th ed.). Metuchen, New Jersey: Scarecrow, 1969.

The Media Center. 35mm. filmstrip, sound (record) color. Wichita, Kansas: Library Filmstrip Center, 1969.

PIERCY, ESTHER J. *Commonsense Cataloging: A Manual for the Organization of Books and Other Materials in School and Small Public Libraries,* pp. 13-29. New York: H. W. Wilson, 1965.

WEIHS, JEAN, SHIRLEY LEWIS, JANET MACDONALD. *Nonbook Materials, the Organization of Integrated Collections,* pp. 3-15. Ottawa: Canadian Library Association, 1973.

Competency 4   Determines polices for cataloging of materials.

DAILY, JAY E. *Organizing Nonprint Materials: A Guide for Librarians.* New York: Dekker, 1972.

GROVE, PEARCH S. and EVELYN G. CLEMENT. *Bibliographic Control of Nonprint Media.* Chicago: American Library Association, 1972.

MASSONNEAU, SUZANNE. "Which Code for the Multimedia Catalog?" *School Media Quarterly* 2 (Winter, 1974): 116-22.

PIERCY, ESTHER J. *Commonsense Cataloging: A Manual for the Organization of Books and Other Materials in School and Small Public Libraries,* pp. 30-63. New York: H. W. Wilson, 1965.

QUIGG, P. J. *The Theory of Cataloging.* London: Clive Bingley, 1966.

ROWLAND, ARTHUR RAY. *The Catalog and Cataloging.* Hamden, Connecticut: The Shoe String Press, Inc., 1969.

Standards for Cataloging Nonprint Materials. 4th ed. Washington, D.C.: Association for Educational Communication and Technology, 1974.

VISWANATHAN, C. C. *Cataloging Theory and Practice.* Bombay: Asia Publishing House, 1965.

WEIHS, JEAN, SHIRLEY LEWIS, JANET MACDONALD. *Nonbook Materials, The Organization of Integrated Collections.* Ottawa: Canadian Library Association, 1973.

WHITENACK, CAROLYN I. and DAVID V. LOERTSCHER. "A Review of Symposium," *Audiovisual Communications Review* 22, no. 1 (Spring, 1974): 91-100.

Competency 5   Organizes and maintains accurate and current retrieval mechanisms such as the card catalog and book catalog.

Information Analysis Center. 16mm motion picture, sound, color, 18 minutes. Columbus, Ohio: Battelle. n.d.

Paper Blizzard. 16mm motion picture, sound, color, 45 minutes. Columbus, Ohio: Battelle, 1970.

PIERCY, ESTHER J. *Commonsense Cataloging: A Manual for the Organization of Books and Other Materials in School and Small Public Libraries,* pp. 75-83. New York: H. W. Wilson, 1965.

Competency 6   Organizes and maintains accurate and current accession and inventory records of materials as appropriate.

DEPROSPO, ERNEST. "Library Measurement, A Management Tool," *Library Journal* (December 15, 1973), 98:3605-3607.

DEPROSPO, ERNEST. *Performance Measures for Public Libraries.* Chicago: American Library Association, 1973.

LIESENER, JAMES W. *A System for Planning and Communicating School Media Programs,* Chicago: American Library Association, 1974.

LIESENER, JAMES W. "The Development of A Planning Process for Media Programs," *School Media Quarterly* 1 (Summer, 1974), 278-287.

LIESENER, JAMES W. *Planning Instruments for School Library/Media Programs,* College Park, Maryland: University of Maryland, 1974.

PIERCY, ESTHER J. *Commonsense Cataloging: A Manual for the Organization of Books and Other Materials in School and Small Public Libraries.* New York: H. W. Wilson, 1965.

Competency 7:   Assesses and implements automated retrieval systems as appropriate.

All About ERIC. 35mm slides or filmstrips, audiotape, 12 minutes. Washington, D.C.: Photo Lab, 1971.

FOSKETT, A. C. *The Subject Approach to Information* (2nd ed.). London: Linnet Books and Clive Bingley, 1970.

JAHODA, GERALD. *Information Storage and Retrieval Systems for Individual Researchers.* New York: Wiley-Interscience, 1970.

LANCASTER, F. WILFRID. *Information Retrieval Systems; Characteristics, Testing and Evaluation.* New York: Wiley, 1969.

The Medlars Story. 16mm motion picture, sound, black and white, 24 minutes. Atlanta, Georgia: National Medical Audiovisual, n.d.

SHARP, JOHN R., *Information Retrieval.* London: Andre Deutsch, 1970.

Competency 8   Develops indexes and thesauri for organizing special collections.

GOULD, GERALDINE E., STHMER C. WOLFE. *How to Organize and Maintain the Library Picture/Pamphlet File*. Dobbs Ferry, New York: Oceana, 1968.

11 The Logistics Function

The quality of any media program is ultimately measured by its ability to provide the materials, equipment and environments for maximum learning. This chapter emphasizes the characteristics of a good support and supply program and the competencies needed for operating such a program. Staff differentiation is highlighted.

Since school libraries began, an emphasis has been placed on service. Many of the activities performed within the school library have been oriented to support the classroom teachers. Tasks performed by the school librarian have traditionally included the processing of books and periodicals, shelving, circulation of printed materials, and repairing books and materials to keep them in good condition. Since these activities were vital in maintaining good library service, the libraries tended to handle most of these tasks. Later, as audiovisual programs evolved in the schools, the coordinator ordered films, purchased records and filmstrips, housed the materials and equipment, distributed equipment with the materials and maintained the collection and hardware in good working order.

As analyses were made of what the media staff does by projects like the School Library Manpower Project and the Jobs in Instructional Media Study, the tasks mentioned above, and others similar to them, were grouped together as "logistics." [1] While the term is new in educational settings, the concept is

[1] The term "logistics" comes from military science where three components are considered: planning; materiél; and facilities.

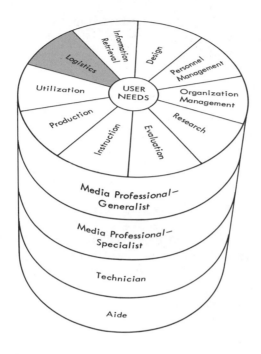

COMPETENCY 1   *Arranges for preview of materials after titles have been identified.*

COMPETENCY 2   *Compiles and organizes orders for materials and equipment; determines most appropriate source after specific materials or equipment have been identified for purchase or rental.*

COMPETENCY 3   *Determines replacement of materials and equipment.*

COMPETENCY 4   *Receives and prepares materials for storage and circulation.*

COMPETENCY 5   *Determines the most appropriate storage arrangements for all materials.*

COMPETENCY 6   *Circulates media and equipment.*

COMPETENCY 7   *Conducts inspection of materials and equipment; arranges for maintenance and repair.*

COMPETENCY 8   *Sets up and operates equipment.*

not. Some authorities have referred to it as the "support-supply" function [2] and others as the "media" function.[3]

The concept of logistics was introduced when the idea of a differentiated staff began to develop. That is, as a variety of individuals performed service tasks at the aide and technician level, rather than at the media professional level, it was observed that these tasks could be handled by personnel with less professional training. The logistics function provided a new way of looking at what gets done in a media program.

Logistics is the backbone for the day-to-day operation of any media program. Tasks related to support and supply for media utilization are critical and form a vital portion of the program. Without these services, the delivery of media to learners would be curtailed.

THE NATURE OF LOGISTICS

The term *logistics* is defined as those activities which directly relate to making materials, equipment, and facilities available to the user. Those activities include portions of acquisition, storage, circulation, maintenance, and retrieval of information in all formats for the purpose of teaching and learning. Provision of support-supply services is one of the most visible activities of a school media program. Therefore, it is useful to consider the competencies which media professionals should possess to adequately fulfil this responsibility.

The logistics function concentrates on performing activities related to acquisition, storage, circulation, maintenance, and retrieval of materials and equipment. It is important to distinguish these specific operations from those which plan, coordinate, control and supervise these activities. The management of logistics activities is usually within the province of the media generalist whether it be in the school building or at a district level and hence falls within the management function. The selection of materials and equipment belongs in the evaluation/selection function while acquisition, as it is used here, is within the logistics function and involves the physical process of ordering, checking on arrival, and referral to the proper person for technical processing.

In the operational sense, the tasks within the logistics function are rather simple and straightforward. Most of the tasks can be accomplished by an aide or technician. There are probably many media professionals who are performing logistics tasks because of insufficient help or day-to-day demands that force priority attention to be paid to these ongoing activities.

[2] Kenneth Silber, "What Field Are We In Anyhow?" *Audiovisual Instruction* (May, 1970): 21.

[3] *Behavioral Requirements Analysis Checklist.* (Chicago: American Library Association, 1973) p. 14.

In a sense, logistics is one of the most important of all the functions because, if it fails, all the other functions have little significance. Logistics is sometimes referred to as the "delivery system" of the media program. If competent personnel are in positions to acquire, store, circulate, maintain, and retrieve the resources which are required for the teaching-learning process, the remainder of the program can be devoted to the other functions. If the logistics area is not operating at an optimal level, attention must be diverted to it since tasks in this area must be performed on an hour-to-hour basis.

Rationale for Logistics

Service has always been a basic premise of the media field. Individuals who have selected this profession are dedicated to helping others to be successful. Satisfaction for the media professional often occurs through someone else's success with media. One of the most direct ways of providing media services is to make materials and equipment available. The materials and equipment must be acquired, stored, and maintained in an efficient manner and handled by competent personnel. Historically, the library and audiovisual fields began with the premise of service. As the fields matured, became more integrated and became more sophisticated in matters pertaining to evaluation, design, production, and utilization, the logistics function continued to play an important role in the total media program. If other functions were de-emphasized or curtailed, the logistics function would have to be continued to serve as the basis of the program. The essential concept here is that for any service to be rendered, support is necessary.

Content

As the tasks included in the logistics function are analyzed, they seem to fall in three categories: (1) obtaining instructional materials and equipment; (2) storing materials and equipment; and (3) providing materials and equipment to teachers and learners. Each of these categories can be further broken down into component tasks, each of which can be described by a competency statement. We will consider the nature of each category first and then the competencies needed to perform each of the tasks.

OBTAINING MATERIALS AND EQUIPMENT   The media staff should assess individual learner and teacher needs for materials and equipment by determining the demand for specific materials and equipment, by informing teachers and learners about available materials and by analyzing curricular areas in which insufficient resources are currently available. Once the need has been established and funds are available, the process of ordering materials for preview, rental, and purchase begins. Equipment required to service requests is also ordered according to established specifications.

STORING MATERIALS AND EQUIPMENT   Once the materials and equipment have arrived, they must be processed, stored, and maintained. Technical processing includes preparation of each material and piece of equipment for shelving or storage. A system for storage should facilitate circulation and, upon return, easy inspection and maintenance, before replacement in the storage location.

PROVIDING MATERIALS AND EQUIPMENT   This category basically involves the loaning and scheduling of materials and equipment; keeping records; managing a reserve system; monitoring the use of materials and equipment; and making necessary scheduling adjustments based on a continuing analysis of the use data.

Competencies

"Because the content of the logistics function is task-oriented and because people trained in this function are usually expected not only to 'know,' but to 'do,' training should be competency-based. That is to say, individuals trained in the logistics function should be able to perform each of the tasks within the function at a high level of competency." [4]

Those individuals who spend a major portion of their time performing tasks in the logistics function should possess an aptitude toward organization. They should value systematic processes and order. They should be able to design and use forms to collect and communicate information. They should like to use machines—typewriters, calculators, audiovisual equipment and the like. Entering skills should reflect these aptitudes and values.

Training for logistics competencies is a combination of formally acquiring skills and on-the-job experience. Some background in business skills, e.g., typing, bookkeeping, accounting, and office practice, acquired in secondary school, business school, the military services or college provides a useful base for adapting these skills to media program operations. Much of the training is acquired on-the-job. Media personnel in training should not only know how to process materials, they should spend time actually processing materials under the watchful eye of an experienced professional.

A competency-based program for acquiring logistics skills must be highly individualized and specific to the location in which the job will be done. This factor alone dictates an individually paced instructional program in a field setting. This experience may be supervised by media professionals from within the organization or from a college or university if the individual is part of an academic degree program. Evaluation of this type of training should be based

[4] Paul H. Elliott, "The Logistics Function in Instructional Technology," *Audiovisual Instruction* 18, No. 3 (March, 1973): 74.

on the trainee's demonstration of acquired competencies. Knowledge-based examinations are useful, but insufficient to measure attainment of training program objectives.

As the content and competencies of the logistics function are considered, it appears that staff members at the aide and technician level might perform most of the activities in this area. This is indeed one of the functions where more tasks can be handled by lesser-trained staff since the tasks are less complex and can be learned relatively quickly on-the-job. It is important that the media professional is thoroughly familiar with the logistics competencies so that hiring adequate staff and optimum training for that staff is accomplished. In certain circumstances, the media professional might have to perform some of the logistics tasks. The media generalist, as manager of the media enterprise, must be able to analyze the logistics tasks which need to be performed and assign staff to handle them. For this reason alone, the media professional must know what these tasks are and what competencies are needed to perform these tasks.

We will use the term *differentiated staff* to indicate the variety of personnel needed to serve in all areas of the media program. The logistics function is an example of the way in which this type of staffing works. The scheduling of materials and equipment can be handled by an *aide* with very little training. The maintenance and repair of equipment requires a *technician* who has had some training and experience in electronics or equipment repair. This person starts with some specialized training. The establishment of policies and procedures for circulation of media falls to the *media generalist* who, as the individual responsible for the entire program, must be sure that it all works.

COMPETENCY 1   *Arranges for preview of materials after titles have been identified.*

In a previous chapter we discovered that the basic concern of any media program is to meet user needs. These needs are determined in a variety of ways and yield lists of alternative strategies and media which might satisfy the needs. At this point the media professional uses a variety of selection tools to identify potential titles of all media which would be appropriate in meeting the defined needs. Once the titles have been identified, one person on the staff must order the materials for preview. To demonstrate this competency the person who orders must be able to:

1. Identify sources of materials for preview by using bibliographic tools and catalogs available in the media center;
2. Prepare letters or forms to order specific titles requested;

3. Schedule space and equipment to be used in previewing;
4. Invite a preview committee composed of appropriate people (teachers, curriculum coordinator, students, community resource people, media professionals);
5. Set up and operate required equipment;
6. Acquire and distribute evaluation forms; and
7. Collate evaluations.

Note that these tasks can be performed by personnel with no formal professional preparation in the media field. They are procedures which implement the established policies developed by the media professional in cooperation with the teaching and administrative staff. However, if no staff person is available, the tasks will fall to others on the staff, perhaps to the media generalist.

The same process is followed in arranging for equipment evaluation. Once a *type* of equipment is identified as needed, e.g., a microform reader, then the same tasks are performed.

RESOURCES: ARRANGING FOR PREVIEW OF MATERIALS

Observation of a competent person fulfilling this function would be one of the best ways to gain competency. On-the-job field experience would extend one's capability in this area. An examination of the materials and equipment catalogs published by producers, manufacturers, and distributors helps to provide orientation for later use. Serving on a preview committee, or assisting with the mechanics of setting up and running a preview session would help a person to learn more about this area. In addition, any experience in organizing, ordering, scheduling and coordinating activities, people, materials, and equipment would be helpful.

A very practical reference is Hicks and Tillin, *Developing Multi-Media Libraries.* Chapter 3, "Selection of Multi-Media Resources" includes a useful section on assistance in choosing media and another on selection procedure. The useful chart shown in Fig. 11-1 is taken from this reference.

MASTERY ITEM: ARRANGING FOR PREVIEW OF MATERIALS

In the space provided indicate by number the order in which the following events take place, e.g., indicate 1 for the first step, 2 for the second, etc. until all items are numbered.

_____   Organize a book review committee
_____   List the purchase sources for each book to be considered
_____   Locate a sufficient number of evaluation forms

_____ Send orders for books
_____ Arrange for a meeting room
_____ Prepare a list of recommended books for purchase
_____ Distribute evaluation forms
_____ Collate evaluations

*Response: **Arranging for Preview of Materials***

1   Organize a book review committee

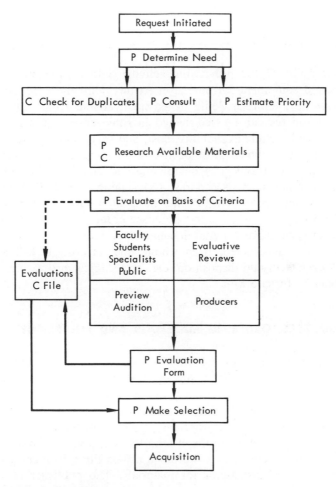

Code: C—Clerical Procedures
P— Professional Procedures
————— Alternate Procedures

Figure 11-1 Selection Work-Flow Chart

2   List the sources for each book to be considered
4   Locate a sufficient number of evaluation forms
3   Send orders for books to review
5   Arrange for a meeting room
8   Prepare a list of recommended books for purchase
6   Distribute evaluation forms
7   Collate evaluations

COMPETENCY 2   Compiles and organizes orders for materials and equipment; determines most appropriate source after specific materials or equipment have been identified for purchase or rental.

The results of the previewing activity yield a "recommended" list of materials and equipment for purchase. At this point the exact source of purchase must be identified. Some items are available from only one source. Alternative sources can be determined in some cases. Criteria for selection of a source will include availability, cost, and service. Then there are several fairly routine steps which must be taken: (1) generating a purchase order using official order forms; (2) completing budget and billing information to comply with established procedures; (3) signing and transmitting the order to the purchasing department or other designated authority for approval; and (4) maintaining a file of all active purchase orders. The records which reflect the status of each order are vital documents. A good system will always show when an item was ordered, from whom, and its cost. It will also indicate arrival of each item and disposition, e.g., to technical processing, to shelving, to maintenance for check-in.

RESOURCES: ORDERING MATERIALS AND EQUIPMENT

The person who does the ordering needs very little additional training if he or she is able to handle routine office matters. The process of generating a purchase order, assigning proper account numbers, and placing it in the hands of the next person in line to handle such orders can be learned on the job. The selection of an appropriate publisher or producer requires more knowledge of the sources and the criteria for selection of a source. A decision regarding purchase-source must be made at this time. In many cases there is only one source or distributor for materials. The publisher of the book is often the primary source or the company producing the film is the only source. However, some materials are sold through dealers or distributors who offer discounts for large orders, special processing of materials, and unique services such as maintenance contracts. It is likely that equipment dealers will offer special services.

To prepare for this competency it would be helpful to scan some of the indexes, lists, and catalogs which list books, films, filmstrips, records, slides, and audiovisual equipment. In addition, check the catalogs of local dealers and distributors of audiovisual equipment, books, and teaching materials. If your instructor or a practicing media professional are not available for help, check the Yellow Pages of the local telephone directory under "Audio Visual Equipment and Supplies," "Motion Picture Film Distributors and Exchanges," "Motion Pictures Film Libraries," "Book Dealers," and "Publishers-Book" to obtain the names of local sources.

There are several standard references which media personnel should have at their disposal for locating sources of materials. These may be found listed in Chapter 14. In addition to the major indexes, every media center should have current copies of producers' and publishers' catalogs for further reference.

Chapter 4 in Hicks and Tillin, *Developing Multi-Media Libraries* describes the "Ways and Means of Acquisition" in complete detail with useful sample forms and practical guidelines and policies. The section on ordering and receiving is especially helpful. Figure 11-2 comes from this reference.

Carleton W. H. Erickson's comprehensive volume, *Administering Instructional Media Programs* discusses the "Acquisition and Deployment of Audiovisual Media" in Chapter 3. Of special help is the section on "Efficient Procedures for the Purchase of Materials" (p. 81) and "The Selection of Media Equipment" (pp. 83–91).

MASTERY ITEM: ORDERING MATERIALS AND EQUIPMENT

You have been given a list of books, filmstrips and recordings (with no publisher or producer named) which have been recommended for purchase by the elementary school social studies curriculum committee. In the space provided, indicate "1" by the first source to which you would go, "2" by the second source, and so on until all items are numbered.

_____ An index which lists materials by medium, e.g., one on books, one on filmstrips, one on tapes

_____ Catalogs of large publishing houses and producers of filmstrips and audiotapes

_____ Catalogs of distributors which handle the products of several publishers and producers

_____ The individuals who first recommended the materials for consideration

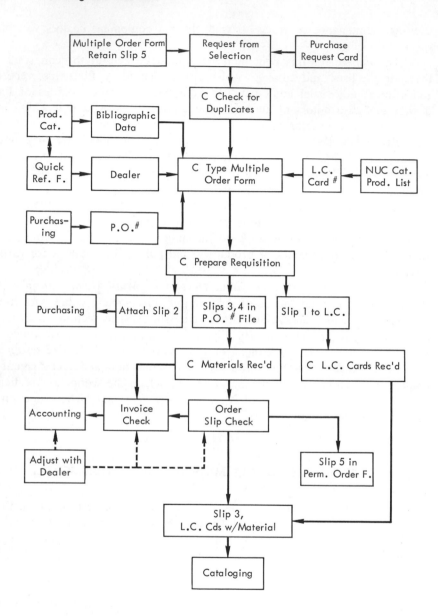

Code: C — Clerical Procedures
       P — Professional Procedures
       ───── Alternate Procedures

Figure 11-2   **Acquisition Work-Flow Chart**

Response: Ordering Materials and Equipment

2	An index which lists materials by medium, e.g., one on books, one on filmstrips, one on tapes
4	Catalogs of large publishing houses and producers of filmstrips and audiotapes
3	Catalogs of distributors which handle the products of several publishers and producers
1	The individuals who first recommended the materials for consideration

---

COMPETENCY 3   Determines replacement of materials and equipment.

Another dimension of the previous competency (to determine sources and to order materials) is to order for the purpose of replacement rather than addition. From time to time the media collection and the equipment must be assessed to determine its current relevancy to teacher and student needs as well as its physical condition. Recommendations for the withdrawal of media and equipment should be made by a group representative of the users who develop the criteria for withdrawal. Once the recommendations are made, the media professional must review them and make decisions regarding which items to withdraw, which to retain, which to repair, and which to replace with updated materials. It is also necessary to decide how to dispose of the media and equipment which is withdrawn. In some cases, it is possible to obtain trade-in value from a used projector on a new model or to purchase a revised edition of a film for a much lower cost if a previous edition is being replaced and the old print is turned in. Some schools and colleges have policies for dealing with the disposal of materials and equipment by declaring items to be surplus and making them available for sale.

The critical element of this competency is to determine the set of criteria which can be used to determine replacement of materials and equipment. The actual act of replacement essentially follows the tasks performed for the previous competency.

RESOURCES: REPLACING MATERIALS AND EQUIPMENT

There are existing policies and "rules of thumb" which are used to guide the media professional in performing the replacement competency. These policies and procedures will vary from location to location.

Replacement is directly related to the maintenance programs for keeping materials and equipment in good condition. Suggestions for maintenance are briefly discussed in James W. Brown, Kenneth D. Norberg, and Sara K. Srygley, *Administering Educational Media* (New York: McGraw-Hill, 1972) pp. 199-201 and pp. 244-247 and Carleton W. H. Erickson, *Administering Instructional Media Programs* (New York: MacMillan, 1968) pp. 551-553. Erickson's cost estimates for replacement of materials and equipment in a single school are especially useful.

MASTERY ITEM: REPLACING MATERIALS AND EQUIPMENT

Indicate the disposition of each item listed below by (1) withdraw; (2) retain and repair; (3) replace with same item; or (4) replace with updated item.

_____ The binding of a book is worn.

_____ The clothing and automobile styles are outdated.

_____ The science book was published prior to 1940.

_____ The equipment uses materials which are no longer produced thus making it obsolete.

_____ The content of the filmstrip is no longer part of the curriculum.

_____ The item has not been used for the past three years.

_____ The projector bulb always blows out after two or three uses.

Response: Replacing Materials and Equipment

2   The binding of a book is worn.

4   The clothing and automobile styles are outdated.

4   The book was published prior to 1940.

1   The equipment uses materials which are no longer produced thus making it obsolete.

1   The content of the filmstrip is no longer part of the curriculum.

1   The item has not been used for the past three years.

2   The projector bulb always blows out after two or three uses.

COMPETENCY 4   *Receives and prepares materials for storage and circulation.*

Materials and equipment which have been ordered eventually arrive and must be inspected to ascertain the quality and correctness of shipment. The systematic process which began with ordering must be followed through so that the dealer is properly paid once the accuracy of the order has been verified. The materials and equipment must be given to the person who is responsible for technical processing, cataloging, routine check-in, or whatever has to be done prior to actual storage and announcement of availability. Records of purchase orders should be maintained for future reference.

RESOURCES: PREPARING MATERIALS FOR CIRCULATION

The process of acquisitioning, accessioning, and arranging materials is described fully in Brown, Norberg and Srygley, *Administering Educational Media.*

The actual procedures used are fully outlined in Hicks and Tillin, *Developing Multi-Media Libraries.* Chapter 7 includes information on procedures, equipment and supplies needed, inventory and also presents sample forms.

There is no substitute for actually observing the process in action. A trip to a media center's receiving and technical processing areas would be more useful than reading many chapters about the process. To observe what the various staff people do and to talk with them about their jobs would be a good substitute for actually doing the job.

MASTERY ITEM: PREPARING MATERIALS FOR CIRCULATION

Describe two actions which must be taken when materials or equipment arrive.

Response: Preparing Materials for Circulation

Your response depends upon how detailed you want to be. Of course, materials and equipment must be unpacked but, beyond that they must be checked for accuracy of shipment, damage, and completeness of all units. Then materials and equipment must be cataloged or accessioned to prepare for shelving. Paper work to verify arrival and correct shipment must be sent to the business office so that payments can be made.

COMPETENCY 5   Determines the most appropriate storage arrangements for all materials.

Storage is a rather colorless word that is used to describe the space and locations where materials and equipment are placed and made accessible to users. Once media and equipment arrive, are checked in, verified for payment, and prepared for shelving, decisions regarding packaging, integrated shelving, and reserve status must be made. When considering storage, one guideline should be paramount—it should *facilitate access to the user*. With this thought in mind the physical location of media and equipment can be determined.

At this point there may be some question regarding the "storage and retrieval systems" used in various types of information agencies. In this case, storage and retrieval refers to the handling of information, usually not a product such as a book, microform, or recording. An information storage and retrieval system may lead to sources of information, e.g., a bibliography or it may provide specific answers to specific questions, e.g., where can a certain

When planning storage, one guideline should be paramount—access to the user.

film be located? Machine readable cataloging (MARC) is one example of a storage and retrieval system which provides information. This concept is fully developed in the information retrieval chapter.

RESOURCES: PROVIDING APPROPRIATE STORAGE

There are several policy decisions which must be made prior to actual storage of media and equipment. The cataloging and classification system used in the media center determines, to a large extent, where materials will be placed. The decision to intermix or integrate media will determine location. To some media professionals it makes sense to locate all media on any given topic in the same location, regardless of format. Others feel that the awkward mix of format sizes is inefficient and requires additional packaging. There is also the issue of what media should be placed in a limited access or reserve area and which items can be open to all users. This question is particularly important in relation to many of the nonprint formats that require equipment. A film or audiocassette is not useful without a projector or an audio cassette playback unit. In many schools, equipment is placed under greater control for security reasons. However, there are schools where equipment is permanently installed in carrels for easy use. Local needs and conditions must be considered in the resolution of these policy issues.

Books that might be helpful are listed in the bibliography. Brown, Norberg and Srygley offers practical advice for processing and storing materials (pp. 187-191). Hicks and Tillin describe "Housing Accommodations" on pages 90-93 and present the issues on "Collection Integration" on pages 60 and 61. Carleton W. H. Erickson, presents a comprehensive description of the space required for storage of media and equipment with several useful illustrations as examples (pp. 317-325).

A visit to several school media centers would provide an opportunity to view the storage arrangements currently in use. Talk with the media professional regarding the rationale for the storage system being used. Try the system yourself. Identify an item or a subject area in which you would like to obtain resources and make a request. How accessible are the materials and the equipment? The first hand experience is probably the best way to gain this competency.

A competency closely related to determining appropriate storage arrangements is conducting periodic inventories. This competency involves the ability to verify the location or status of any equipment or material that has been received and placed in a specific location. For example, the media center owns four, 16mm projectors. At inventory time, the four projectors should be on the shelf in the media center, on loan to a user (whose name and location is known), or otherwise accounted for. The same analysis would apply to any book or nonbook material. A system for inventory must be developed by the media professional, but the actual inventory process can often be assigned to an aide.

MASTERY ITEM: PROVIDING APPROPRIATE STORAGE

Sound filmstrips (a filmstrip with a recording-disc or cassette tape—and usually a manual) pose unique storage problems. List some alternative solutions to storing sound filmstrips and indicate your preference. Give reasons for your selection.

Response: Providing Appropriate Storage

1. Store the filmstrips with the filmstrips; the recordings with the recordings; and let the catalog serve as the source for identification.
2. Establish a separate section for all sound filmstrips; treat them as a separate medium.
3. Repackage sound filmstrips into uniform storage cartons and inter-shelve with the books.
(Justification for each of the above alternatives can be made.)

COMPETENCY 6   Circulates media and equipment.

The term, "circulation" includes the scheduling and distribution of the various audiovisual media and equipment as well as the loaning of books and other printed materials. To be able to circulate all the media and equipment in a media center requires a set of policies and procedures which guide the process. The focus of the circulation or distribution system should be on the user. Procedures which facilitate accessibility to media and equipment should be established whenever feasible. The only controlling factors are the ability to maintain accurate records and the need for security. Files must be maintained to identify the location of media and equipment in circulation. The process should incorporate procedures for handling overdue materials and for handling reserve items.

Since many of the tasks performed within this competency are fairly routine once policies and procedures are established, it should be possible to assign an aide or volunteer to handle most of the daily circulation activities. When procedures become routine and the volume of work expands, it is time to consider the possibility of using electronic circulation systems for media center operations. Electronic data processing offers many alternative options and computers are a distinct possibility for use in large systems.

RESOURCES: CIRCULATING MEDIA AND EQUIPMENT

Have you ever spent a few hours at a library's circulation desk? Here one is able to meet the user and gain some insight into how the circulation system works. It is at this central point that all the policies and procedures seem to focus—access to resources, "where do I find" questions, overdues, reserves, need for equipment to use with audiovisual materials, and so forth. It might be helpful for all neophyte media professionals to serve an internship period at the circulation desk.

You can also read about circulation and distribution. Brown, Norberg and Srygley discuss manual and automated systems with practical suggestions. Carleton W. H. Erickson, emphasizes in his book the distribution of audiovisual materials, especially 16mm films. Lindeman looks at circulation of multimedia resources in his chapter on "The Range of Media Services" in *Instructional Media Center: Bold New Venture.*

You can test the circulation system in an existing media center. Select one title (the children's book *Stone Soup,* for example) and request it in each of several formats: book, filmstrip, recording, and 16mm motion picture. Observe how easy (or difficult) it is to obtain each item. Is it immediately accessible? If so, and it requires a piece of equipment, how readily is that available? Is a wait required? How many minutes? hours? days? weeks? You will soon observe, through this inductive process, what some of the problems of circulation are. Solution to the problems comes from observation of efficient circulation systems and participation in the planning of a system that works.

MASTERY ITEM: CIRCULATING MEDIA AND EQUIPMENT

Place a T in front of those statements which are "true" and F in front of those statements which are "false."

1. In the past a media center often justified its existence by circulation statistics; the prime purpose of a circulation system should be to gather data on use of media and equipment.
2. Procedures for the circulation of audiovisual media must differ from those governing printed materials.
3. One of the major concerns in developing circulation policy is security of media and equipment.
4. The use of electronic data processing or a computer system for circula-

tion of materials is the sign of good logistic management in any media center.
5. Circulation is so important in the day-to-day operation of the media center that a full-time media professional should be stationed at the circulation desk at all times.

Response: Circulating Media and Equipment

1.   F
2.   T
3.   T
4.   F
5.   F

COMPETENCY 7   Conducts inspection of materials and equipment; arranges for maintenance and repair.

Any collection of media and equipment must be in top condition to meet the needs of users. This means preventive maintenance as well as repair. The unique nature of audiovisual materials and equipment makes them more vulnerable to damage than books. Therefore, the program for maintenance and repair refers more frequently to these items.

Within this competency are tasks which involve: (1) the development of policies and procedures for maintaining media and equipment; (2) the decisions regarding local or contract maintenance and repair; (3) the quality control of all work completed locally and on contract; (4) the establishment of a repair area within the media center to perform the maintenance and repair which can be handled locally; and (5) the review of contracts with outside repair agencies to handle maintenance beyond that which can be done internally.

RESOURCES: ARRANGING FOR MAINTENANCE AND REPAIR

It is probably rare that the media professional will actually perform maintenance and repair tasks. As with other competencies and tasks within the logistics function, it is important that the professional in charge insures that the job gets done. This means that this person needs to diagnose a problem sufficiently to know whether or not to handle it internally or to depend on help which is hired from a service agency. In some cases, the volume of maintenance and repair work will dictate the hiring of a technician or a staff of technicians within the media center. A large urban school district or a regional educational service center would most likely have a technical staff on board.

A closer look at this competency will reveal a set of subcompetencies that depend on the types of media and equipment being discussed. Following is a partial list:

    I. Books and printed materials
        A. Placing protective jackets on new books
        B. Repairing torn pages
        C. Repairing bindings of books
        D. Mounting pictures

   II. Audio materials
        A. Cleaning records
        B. Splicing tapes

  III. Film materials
        A. Cleaning film surfaces
        B. Splicing motion pictures

  IV. Equipment
        A. Cleaning areas of heavy use—film gates, audiotape playback heads
        B. Repairing electronic components (audiotape and videotape playback units, audio amplifiers, data processing units)
        C. Repairing mechanical components (projector mechanisms, charging machines)

Each of these tasks can be accomplished by aides or technicians who will have to be trained on-the-job or hired with specific training, for example, in electronics. But the media professional must know what needs to get done and then hire people to perform the tasks either as staff members or on a contractual basis.

One of the basic elements of this competency is the ability to identify a problem, diagnose its probable cause, and direct action to correct it. In the case of torn pages in a book or "dog-eared" pictures in the vertical file, the problem of identification, diagnosis and recommended action are quite simple. Likewise, a broken film or tape and dirty microforms require no extraordinary power of observation to determine what is wrong and what must be done. These steps can usually be handled easily and inexpensively on the spot if the proper equipment and materials are on hand. However, audiovisual equipment is another case and needs to be considered separately.

With equipment it is necessary to determine whether the problem can be resolved immediately (such as replacing a bulb in a projector) or be handled at a later time (such as replacing a simple part which must be ordered). In both cases, the work can be done locally. Another possible decision is whether to send it to a local service representative or back to the factory for more complex repair.

This competency focuses on the ability to inspect materials and equipment; discover the problem; diagnose its cause; and recommend action. It does not emphasize the actual ability to do the maintenance or repair although certain individuals may be able to handle these tasks.

Brown, Norberg and Srygley discuss the dimensions of this competency on pp. 199-201 (on materials) and pp. 242-247 (on equipment). Erickson presents an even more comprehensive description of the maintenance and repair tasks with attention to the details of each audiovisual material and its related equipment.

MASTERY ITEM: ARRANGING FOR MAINTENANCE AND REPAIR

Assuming that your media center has no technicians, what disposition would you make of the following maintenance and repair problems? Your choices are: (a) repair it myself; (b) ask a student, or volunteer (aide) to repair it; (c) send it out for repair; (d) dispose of the item.

    1. The plug at the end of the electrical cord on a microfiche reader is broken.
    2. The folding maps have been worn from use.
    3. The tape in an audiocassette is broken.
    4. The fan in the slide projector doesn't work but the bulb goes on.
    5. Study prints have several thumb tack holes in each corner and the edges are bent from excessive handling.

Response: Arranging for Maintenance and Repair

    1. a or b
    2. a or b
    3. d
    4. c
    5. a or b

COMPETENCY 8   Sets up and operates equipment.

Once again we are dealing with a competency which the media professional may not engage in frequently, but it does fall within the boundaries of the logistics function. It is a job which must be done and it is the responsibility of the media professional to see that it gets done. Many media centers have student assistants, projectionists, or library aides to help perform the equipment operation. However, the media professional often has to train these assistants and, from time to time, needs to set up and operate equipment for preview committees, parents' meetings, and for users when no other help is available. There is no excuse for not being able to set up and operate equipment.

When we discuss equipment here, we are going to refer to the most commonly used types in schools and media centers. We will exclude the office machines, the data processing machines, and the computer terminals even though they are important. We will include audiotape units, filmstrip projectors, microfilm and microfiche units, motion picture projectors, overhead projectors, record players, slide projectors, and videotape units.

The competency, "to set up and operate," includes: (1) removing a unit from its carrying case (if any); (2) plugging in and testing audio and/or video components; (3) inserting the appropriate material in a reasonable time without error; (4) running the materials and making necessary adjustments with minimum distraction (focusing, volume control, framing) and without damage; (5) stopping and starting at any time during presentation; (6) rewinding material (if applicable); and (7) packing up equipment or returning to original status for the next user.

RESOURCES: OPERATING EQUIPMENT

If you do not already know how to operate any of the above equipment, seek out an audiovisual equipment laboratory in a school or college and ask to be taught. In some teacher education programs there are such laboratories set up on a self-instruction basis. Find one; ask permission to use it; and learn. Do not be intimidated by machines. You probably drive a car—and could do more damage with that machine than with a projector! And when you see fourth and fifth grade pupils deftly operating this equipment, you should realize that it is a relatively simple skill. You may have to go to the audiovisual coordinator, or a technician, or a student projectionist and humble yourself by asking to be taught how to operate these devices. Do it. All of the media on the shelves isn't much help if the required equipment cannot be operated. And since this does involve motor skills, the best way to acquire them is by doing them. Books, instruction manuals and demonstrations may provide general guidelines, orientation, and procedures, but actual experience is absolutely necessary.

There are five excellent equipment manuals which are comprehensive and up-to-date. Any of the five would provide useful guidance for the individual who is just learning how to operate audiovisual equipment and provide a reference for those who need to refresh these skills.

In some colleges and universities there are self-instruction laboratories for learning how to operate audiovisual equipment.

These manuals by Bullard and Mether; Eboch; Fulton et al., Davidson; and Oates are listed in the bibliography for competency eight. In the basic media textbook *AV Instruction: Media and Methods* (4th ed.) (New York: McGraw-Hill, 1973) by Brown, Lewis and Harcleroad, there is an extensive reference section, "Operating Audiovisual Equipment" (pp. 462-505) and "Duplicating Processes" (pp. 506-519).

There are two major sources of audiovisual materials to teach equipment operating procedures. Training Services (8885 West F Avenue, Kalamazoo, Michigan 49009) offers more than twenty 2″ x 2″ captioned slide sets which describe step-by-step instructions for operating various models of projectors and tape recorders. McGraw-Hill Text Films (330 West 42nd Street, New York) distributes a series of three to four minute 8mm and super 8mm cartridges on operating selected types of audiovisual materials.

A combination of published references, audiovisual instructional materials and practice on actual equipment will yield optimum competencies in the setting up and operation of audiovisual equipment.

MASTERY ITEM: OPERATING EQUIPMENT

The best way to demonstrate this competency is to set up and operate each type of audiovisual equipment. For this mastery item, arrange the steps of operation in proper order for each type of equipment. Then ask a qualified operator to "check you out" on each piece of equipment.

The Overhead Projector

Focus image _____
Connect power cord _____
Position transparency on
    stage _____
Turn projector ON _____
Adjust image to screen size _____

Record Player

Place record on turntable _____
Set speed control _____
Adjust volume _____
Connect power cord _____
Adjust tone _____
Turn amplifier ON _____
Turn turntable ON _____
Position needle on record _____

16mm Projector

Turn amplifier ON _____
Set up reel arms _____
Thread film _____
Preforms to adjust image
    size to screen _____
Attach belts (if applicable) _____
Connect power cord _____
Rotate manual control to
    insure threading accuracy _____
Turn motor/lamp ON _____
Adjust tone _____
Adjust volume _____
Focus image
Adjust framing _____
Attach speaker plug (if
    applicable) _____

Tape Recorder

Connect power cord _____
Plug in microphone _____
Thread tape _____
Turn power ON _____
Make recording _____
Adjust volume _____
Position supply and take-up
    reels _____
Set tape speed _____
Adjust tone _____
Rewind tape _____
Plug tape _____

Response: Operating Equipment

The Overhead Projector

Connect power cord
Turn projector ON
Position transparency on stage
Adjust image to screen size
Focus image

Record Player

Connect power cord
Turn amplifier ON
Turn turntable ON
Set speed control
Place record on turn table
Position needle on record
Adjust volume
Adjust tone

16mm Projector	Tape Recorder
Connect power cord	Connect power cord
Attach speaker plug (if applicable)	Position supply and take-up reels
Set up reel arms	Thread tape
Attach belts (if applicable)	Turn power ON
Turn amplifier ON	Plug in microphone
Performs to adjust image size to screen	Set tape speed
Thread film	Adjust volume
Rotate manual control to insure threading accuracy	Make recording
Turn motor/lamp ON	Rewind tape
Focus image	Play tape
Adjust volume	Adjust tone
Adjust tone	
Adjust framing	

REFERENCES

Competency 1   Arranges for preview of materials after titles have been identified.

HICKS, WARREN and ALMA TILLIN. *Developing Multi-Media Libraries*, pp. 29-39. New York: R. R. Bowker Co., 1970.

Competency 2   Compiles and organizes orders for materials and equipment; determines most appropriate source after specific materials or equipment have been identified for purchase or rental.

BROWN, JAMES W., KENNETH D. NORBERG and SARA K. SRYGLEY. *Administering Educational Media*, pp. 199-201; 244-47. New York: McGraw-Hill, 1972.

ERICKSON, CARLETON W. H. *Administering Instructional Media Programs*, pp. 551-53. New York: Macmillan, 1968.

HICKS, WARREN and ALMA TILLIN. *Developing Multi-Media Libraries*, pp. 41-56. New York: Macmillan, 1968.

Competency 3   Determines replacement of materials and equipment.

Competency 4   Receives and prepares materials for storage and circulation.

BROWN, JAMES W., KENNETH D. NORBERG and SARA K. SRYGLEY, *Administering Educational Media*, pp. 177-80. New York: McGraw-Hill, 1972.

HICKS, WARREN and ALMA TILLIN. *Developing Multi-Media Libraries,* pp. 85-93. New York: R. R. Bowker Co., 1970.

Competency 5   Determines the most appropriate storage arrangements for all materials.

BROWN, JAMES W., KENNETH D. NORBERG and SARA K. SRYGLEY, *Administering Educational Media,* pp. 187-91. New York: McGraw-Hill, 1972.

ERICKSON, CARLETON W. H. *Administering Instructional Media Programs,* pp. 90-93. New York: Macmillan, 1968.

Competency 6   Circulates media and equipment.

BROWN, JAMES W., KENNETH D. NORBERG and SARA K. SRYGLEY, *Administering Educational Media,* pp. 191-98. New York: McGraw-Hill, 1972.

ERICKSON, CARLETON W. H. *Administering Instructional Media Programs,* pp. 166-73. New York: Macmillan, 1968.

Competency 7   Conducts inspection of materials and equipment; arranges for maintenance and repair.

BROWN, JAMES W., KENNETH D. NORBERG and SARA K. SRYGLEY, *Administering Educational Media,* pp. 244-47. New York: McGraw-Hill, 1972.

ERICKSON, CARLETON W. H. *Administering Instructional Media Programs,* pp. 325-336. New York: Macmillan, 1968.

LINDEMAN, LEROY R. "The Range of Services," pp. 92-107 in Harold S. Davis (ed.), *Instructional Media Center: Bold New Venture.* Bloomington, Ind.: Indiana University Press, 1971.

Media Programs: District and School, pp. 45-46. Chicago: American Library Association, and Washington, D.C.: Association for Educational Technology, 1975.

Competency 8   Sets up and operates equipment.

Audio-Visual Equipment Operation Series. 27-8mm films, silent, color, 3-4 min. ea., 1965.

BULLARD, JOHN R. and METHER, CALVIN E. *Audiovisual Fundamentals: Basic Equipment Operation and Simple Materials Production,* pp. 1-97. Dubuque, Iowa: William C. Brown, 1974.

DAVIDSON, RAYMOND L. *Audiovisual Machines.* Scranton, Pa.: International Textbook Co., 1969.

EBOCH, SIDNEY C. *Operating Audio-Visual Equipment* (2nd ed.) Chicago: Science Research Associates, 1968.

FULTON, W. R., et al. *Programmed Text on the Operation of Selected Audiovisual Equipment.* Dubuque, Iowa: Kendall/Hunt Publishing Co., 1973.

OATES, STANTON C. *Audiovisual Equipment: Self-Instruction Manual* (3rd ed.) William C. Brown, 1974.

Self-Instructional Slide Sets. 21-35mm slide sets. Available in unmounted strips of 81 frames each. Training Services, n.d.

12 The Production Function

The media center can make a major contribution to the teaching/learning process through the production of original materials. The program of the media center should be planned so that it can provide opportunities for teachers, students, and administrators to become active participants in production activities, as well as having the media personnel produce materials. In addition to producing original materials, there may be the need to adapt commercially producted materials and also to reproduce many types of items.

Creative and ingenius audiovisual personnel have become convinced that outstanding contributions to teaching and learning can be made through producing original materials in a school media center. Production is the making of materials and devices to assist or enhance the learning process. Products such as transparencies, graphs, charts, photographic prints, slides, films, videotapes, audiotapes or any appropriate combinations of these or other learning materials have become an important factor in teaching and learning. The desired objectives, the context, the instructional method, and student's needs, interests and abilities all determine the instructional material to be produced.

With the current focus of attention on the individualization of instruction and on independent study there are increased needs for teaching and learning materials that are especially designed to meet the needs of individual students. Because most of the commercially produced materials must be developed for nationwide audiences and cannot possibly be tailored specifically to the immediate needs of the individual student, there is increasing need for production of materials locally.

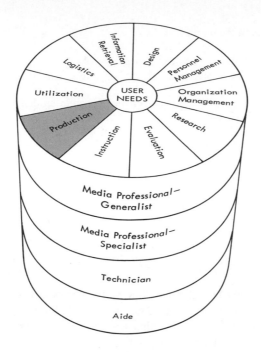

COMPETENCY 1   *Produces audio materials.*
COMPETENCY 2   *Produces graphic and still projected materials.*
COMPETENCY 3   *Produces motion projected materials.*
COMPETENCY 4   *Produces programmed materials.*
COMPETENCY 5   *Reproduces printed materials.*
COMPETENCY 6   *Identifies specific equipment and materials required for production.*
COMPETENCY 7   *Applies rules and standards for evaluation of products.*

There are many advantages to local production:

1. The product most closely matches the particular need of the teacher, students and setting.
2. Parts of the materials can usually be readily adapted to meet changing needs.
3. Production requires understanding of the subject content and often encourages creativity.
4. Students can participate in production activities, which often serves as motivation.

5. Production often encourages students and teachers to work cooperatively.
6. Local production is often less costly, so more students and teachers can be served.
7. Production can often be done even by less able students and so help to develop self confidence.
8. Locally produced materials can be more up-to-date, be more specifically oriented geographically and regionally, and capture local flavor.

There are some disadvantages, namely:

1. There must be someone who can provide leadership in this area to assist and encourage both teachers and students.
2. Local production does take time.
3. Often limited space makes local production difficult.
4. In some cases, the cost could be greater.

Production must be considered from many perspectives. One aspect of production includes certain processes such as the production of slides, audio tapes, and transparencies. There are also the processes which should be described as reproduction. This range of activities includes the reproduction of materials that have already been produced. These processes are much more mechanical in nature and do not usually require creativity. They include reproduction of slides, audiotapes and all varieties of print, including photocopied and mimeographed materials.

In a media center, production services are to be provided for various types of users; therefore, all planning must take into consideration these groups of users:

1. *Media personnel* must have facilities, equipment and materials to be able to provide production services. They have several types of responsibilities: to actually produce the teaching/learning materials to be used by teachers and individual students and to instruct students, teachers and administrators in production skills and techniques.
2. *Students* must have space, equipment and materials accessible to them in such a way that they can illustrate their reports, demonstrate what they have learned and experiment in creative ways of communicating.
3. *Teachers* must have space and materials made available to them so they can conveniently, and with a minimum expenditure of time, produce materials for use in their teaching and for use by individual students or groups of students.
4. *Administrators* must have available to them appropriate equipment to be able to produce those materials which they need for communicating and carrying out their administrative responsibilities.

Each of these groups of users will be producing materials for a variety of purposes, and in addition they will be working at different levels of sophistication for each task. It is important for media personnel to understand the needs and abilities of each of the groups of users and also to be familiar with the requirements for these various levels of production.

The three levels of local instructional media production identified by Kemp are (1) mechanical level: preparation (2) creative level: production and (3) design level: conception.[1]

The *mechanical preparation* is concerned only with the techniques of preparation—or "doing the job as requested." At this level users would be expected to describe the job to be done and supply the specifications for the completion of the product. Examples of this level of activity would be producing transparencies when the content is completely specified, mounting pictures, or reproducing audiotapes.

The *creative level* of production requires additional input on the part of the media personnel, or requires additional decisions relating to the materials involved. Examples of this level of activity would be arranging slides and writing the script to complete a slide-tape presentation, videotaping a sequence if only the script is provided, or making a chart if illustrations need to be developed.

The *design level* of production is required when several sets of related media need to be developed to meet the specifications of predetermined teaching-learning processes so as to accomplish specific objectives that are a part of an overall design for systematic instruction.

It is obvious that the skills and abilities required of the media personnel to perform these services are extensive and diverse. At the same time there is the need for the media personnel to provide enthusiastic leadership in this area of production. It is easy to neglect this area and order commercially manufactured products. However, production is a rich and rewarding part of a fine media program, but it requires creative and inspiring leadership to develop this area optimally.

Before specific competencies are identified, it is important for media personnel to understand that there are certain steps that need to be considered in media product development, no matter what the format is: These steps are: (1) the objectives that are to be achieved need to be specified, (2) the appropriate medium to use must be specified, (3) the preliminary planning must take place, such as script writing, scene planning for video, or sequences and content for transparencies, (4) the actual production of the product, (5) pretesting of the product, (6) actual use of the product, (7) evaluation of the product, (8) storage and dissemination of the product, (9) monitoring and maintaining the product.

The facility that is usually planned for production services is a media production laboratory. As the various competencies are discussed, specific equipment and laboratory facilities will be indicated. Unless otherwise stated

[1] Jerrold E. Kemp, *Planning and Producing Audiovisual Materials* (2nd ed.) (San Francisco: Chandler Publishing Company, 1968), p. 9.

these would usually be found in one conveniently located production laboratory.

According to the publication *Media Programs: District and School,* there are minimal levels for production capability in each school.

> Graphics: the preparation of visuals, including dry mounting, laminating, and transparency production
> Photography: facilities and equipment for black and white photography, 2″ × 2″ color slides, and silent 8mm motion film photography
> Television and radio: the production of videotape recordings
> Audiotape production: the recording and duplicating of audio tapes [2]

There are several textbooks which provide excellent background on production programs and services. The texts listed in the bibliography by Brown, Norberg, and Srygley; Erikson; and Kemp provide general overall background for developing all competencies.

Table 12-1 outlines the basic and advanced components for the production program in an individual school. Resources beyond those listed should be drawn from the district media center.[3]

COMPETENCY 1   Produces audio materials.

The most commonly used means for producing audio materials is through the use of reel-to-reel tape recorders or by using cassette tape recorders. This equipment can be operated very easily and can be used conveniently and creatively in a great number of ways. Both teachers and students are likely to be more familiar with tape recorders than any other type of production equipment. Most schools have had tape recorders for a number of years and many students and teachers own recording equipment. In recent years cassette recorders have become very popular, but reel-to-reel machines are still used extensively in schools. Cassette tape recorders are the most convenient to carry and to operate, but reel-to-reel recorders are usually used in audio production work because they are easier to work with for splicing and editing. Additionally, the recording quality of reel-to-reel recorders is superior to cassettes.

[2] *Media Programs: District and School* (Chicago: American Library Association and Washington, D.C.: Association for Educational Communications and Technology, 1974), p. 47.

[3] *Media Programs: District and School* (Chicago: American Library Association and Washington, D.C.: Association for Educational Communication and Technology, 1974), pp. 50-51.

TABLE 12-1 School Production Capabilities

Format	Basic Components		Advanced Components		Display Technology
	Process	Equipment	Process	Equipment	
Puppet Productions 3-Dimensional Construction	Commercial Hand-sewing Construction	Tools & art materials			Puppet theater Record player Tape recorder
Printing	Hand-lettering Copying Illustrating	Typewriter Spirit duplicator Mimeograph	Preparation of masters Typesetting Layout	Press(es) 8″ × 10″ copy camera Equipment darkroom	
Overhead Transparencies	Direct: Write-on Painted Hand-embellished Thermal Color lift	Thermal copier Laminator	Diazo Photographic	Diazo printer & developer 8″ × 10″ copy camera Equipped darkroom	Overhead projector
Flat Pictures and Posters	Hand-drawing Dry mounting	Dry mount press & tacking iron	Photographic	Cameras Equipped darkroom	Opaque projector Display areas
Slides and Filmstrips	Direct: Write-on Painted Slides Photographic	Simple slide-format camera w/copy stand	Filmstrips, photographic Slides, photographic Sound slides & filmstrips	35mm half-frame camera w/appropriate accessories 35mm single-reflex camera Recorder w/synchronizer	Slide projector Slide viewer Filmstrip projector Filmstrip viewer Tape recorder w/synchronizer
Audiotape Recordings	Reel-to-reel Cassette	Reel-to-reel tape recorder Cassette tape recorder		Soundproof room Audiomixer with monaural & stereo capability	Reel-to-reel tape recorder Cassette tape recorder
Motion Picture Production	Direct: painted Photographic: silent	Super 8mm camera	Photographic, sound	Camera w/sound capability (may use recorder) 16mm camera Film editor	Super 8mm projector 16mm projector Tape recorder
Multi-image Presentations	(May combine any or all of the above process and equipment		(May combine any or all of the above process and equipment		Projection equipment Programmer Dissolve unit
Television Productions	Videotape recording Off-the-air One or two camera operation	Videotape recorder ½″ or ¾″ 1–2 video cameras Switcher, video & audio	Studio productions	Equipped studio Appropriate VTR Film chain Switcher video & audio	Videotape recorder Monitor
Computer Programming			Audio Printed Visual Any combination of above	Keyboard & appropriate computer programming equipment	Computer terminal Display system

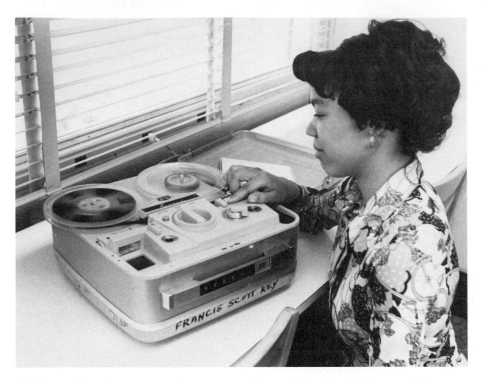

Reel-to-reel audiotape recorders are usually used for production work because splicing and editing are easier than with cassette tapes.

There are so many users for audio materials that the creativity of the user is the only limit to the kinds of materials that can be developed. Tape recorders can be used to record music, voices, and sound effects of any kind or in combinations. Tape recorders can be used in the classrooms, at concerts, lectures, plays or to record radio or television programs or to conduct interviews. The tape recorder can often be used in combination with other audio equipment such as a record player, another tape recorder, a radio, or a television receiver. Oftentimes interesting results occur when several sources are combined on a single tape. Tapes can be made which combine voices and music, or these two can be combined with sound effects on one tape. Audiotapes can also be used in combination with visual presentations, such as slide tapes.

If teachers and students have not yet developed skills and interests in production, the making of audio materials is a good place to start. Reasons for this are that the equipment is inexpensive, easy to operate, and convenient to transport; it is relatively simple to achieve quality productions; playback is simple and the options for use are open to many variations.

RESOURCES: PRODUCING AUDIO MATERIALS

The area of production is one where the adage "you learn by doing" is the most appropriate. Experience in a production laboratory is an effective way to learn. The learning can come through demonstration, watching an 8mm film and following the directions, reading a manual and following directions, or from using a programmed text. Skill comes from continued practice and from working on creative products. A college class in production skills is a basic essential. It is always helpful too, to visit other laboratories to get new and innovative ideas. Attending conventions is another means of developing creative production ideas, as there one can see new products, new combinations of products and new approaches. Books and manuals have been published that are most helpful in developing this competency and three excellent works are listed in the bibliography for competency one.

MASTERY ITEM: PRODUCING AUDIO MATERIALS

List ideas for using audio materials that you might suggest to a ninth grade English teacher.

Response: Producing Audio Materials

1. Record oral reading to assess ways to improve expression.
2. Record speeches for self evaluation by the speaker.
3. Use audio tapes to give individualized assignments.
4. Use audio tapes for teaching listening skills.
5. Use audio tapes to simulate learning telephone techniques.
6. Use audio recordings of drama for study and enjoyment.

COMPETENCY 2   *Produces graphic and still projected materials.*

For anyone just beginning to develop competencies in the production area this may appear to be a broad segment of production skills to master. It will become obvious, however, that many of the competencies are interrelated. The kinds of materials included here would be posters, captions, flash cards, mounted pictures, illustrations, signs, bulletin boards, displays, mobiles, sketches, cartoons, chalkboard messages, graphs, maps, diagrams, time lines, flannel and magnetic boards, hand drawn transparencies, diazo and heat produced transparencies, photographs and slides.

The common goal of all of these products is to communicate visually. The goal of communicating visually can be achieved through clarity, composition, use of color, appropriate brevity or succinctness, legibility, and appropriate emphasis. Even though a variety of techniques must be used, many of the basics—lettering, sketching, arranging pictures, or composing a picture— are the same. Skills that are developed in one area are quite readily transferable to use with other media.

The production of many of these materials requires the use of a variety of tools and equipment. It is important that all these be available in the production laboratory. For lettering, Leroy pens, felt pens, Wrico printers, prepared letters, stencils, and templates are often used. For mounting pictures

One of the basic competencies needed for graphic production is the ability to letter and to sketch.

an electric hand iron or a dry mount press is essential. To make transparencies, acetate sheets, acetate adhering inks and pens, diazo machines, and copy machines are used. The making of slides and photographs requires cameras of various kinds.

RESOURCES: PRODUCING GRAPHIC AND STILL PROJECTED MATERIALS

College classes in graphics and photography would be an appropriate means for gaining competencies. Books by Brown and Lewis, Kemp, and Minor and Frye would be helpful.

Copy machines can be used to make overhead transparencies.

MASTERY ITEM: PRODUCING GRAPHIC AND STILL PROJECTED MATERIALS

How does the diazo process differ from the thermal process for making transparencies?

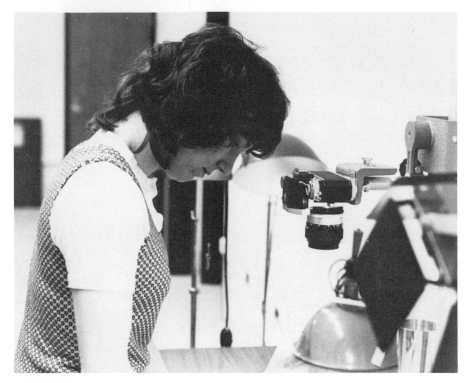

Slides and photographs are often made with a 35mm camera on a copy stand.

Response: Producing Grapic and Still Projected Materials

The diazo process for making transparencies requires a diazo machine, which includes units to provide ultraviolet exposure and ammonia development. The original diagram should be drawn on tracing paper with pen and India ink. The diagram is placed on a sheet of diazo film and the two exposed to ultraviolet light in a printer. The timer on the machine is set to the correct time to make an exposure. The film must then be transferred to a container of ammonia vapor for development. When the image has fully appeared the transparency is ready to be removed and mounted.

The thermal process requires a Thermo-fax copy machine. The diagram can be prepared using India ink, pencil or typewriter. The machine must be turned on to the correct speed and the projection film is placed on the diagram. The two sheets are fed into the machine. When they come out of the machine the papers are separated and the transparency is ready to be mounted for use.

1. The equipment and the material is different for each process.
2. Thermal processes can use pencil or typewriter to make the diagram.
3. Diazo process produces color on the transparency.
4. Color must be added to the finished diagram in the thermal process.

COMPETENCY 3   Produces motion projected materials.

Motion projected materials include 8mm and 16mm films and video-tapes. Although the production of these materials is often a demanding process, is sometimes expensive, and does require special equipment, locally produced materials do have many advantages. Additionally, the activities and processes relating to filmmaking can provide a valuable learning experience for students. Filmmaking often becomes a group process and provides opportunities for students to learn to work together under stimulating and challenging conditions. Student-made films seem to have high motivational value. There have been a number of innovative research projects and federal grants to investigate the values of the use of filmmaking as a means to motivate and teach disadvantaged students.

The 8mm motion picture camera is considered the most simple to learn to operate and requires only rudimentary skills. Other equipment that are required to make films are: tripod, light meter, floodlights, film viewer-editor, rewind, film scaper and splicer. There are certain basic techniques which will give variety to the camera shots; these include the long shot, medium shot, the close up, the pan, the tilt, the zoom, low angle, and high angle shots. There are also special techniques to be learned in editing the film, splicing the film, and putting the completing touches on the film.

Another production skill that is becoming more widely used is the planning and production of videotapes. Videotapes are proving to be extremely flexible as they can be used readily by individual students, small or large groups, and video cameras can be transported easily to most locations. There are innumerable ways in which video recordings can be used for instruction; student performance can be recorded, and television programs can be stored for rebroadcast. Details of demonstrations in laboratories, shops, and in large classrooms can be picked up with a video camera and shown on a television screen to provide close-ups or image magnification. The equipment that is required for learning this competency is a portable television system, which includes a camera and tripod, a television receiver, and reels of videotape. Because the operation of each kind of equipment is somewhat different it is important to have the operating manual for each piece of equipment.

RESOURCES: PRODUCING MOTION PROJECTED MATERIALS

College classes in film or television production would be most helpful in gaining this competency. In addition, practicing and experimenting in a laboratory situation is invaluable. The works listed in the bibliography by Brown and Lewis (eds.); Brown, Lewis, and Harcleroad; and Kemp are all helpful.

MASTERY ITEM: PRODUCING MOTION PROJECTED MATERIALS

Describe some situations in which it would be appropriate to recommend making a videotape rather than to use some other medium. Relate these to general principles.

Response: Producing Motion Projected Materials

1. If a visiting authority were making a presentation, a videotape could be made for replay by students after the visitor had left.

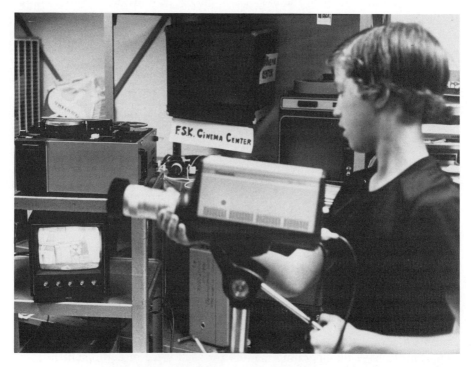

Portable videotaping requires a camera, tripod, recorder, and a television monitor.

2. A videotape could be made of a visit of a first grade class to a farm. The tape could be played, so each child could recall his story of the trip for reading readiness experience.
3. A videotape can be made of a play for evaluation by the cast and director prior to presentation before an audience.

Make videotapes to record action, people, or places that cannot be viewed live by all audiences or which need to be preserved for future reference.

COMPETENCY 4   Produces programmed materials.

The term programmed materials includes a range of different kinds of media, at many levels of sophistication. Some programmed materials are presented in a very simple format resembling a paperback book, others are produced for use on a teaching machine and the more complex are being developed as computer-assisted instruction. Any of these formats lends itself well to self-instruction.

The characteristics of programmed materials are: (1) the content is carefully structured in a sequential learning pattern, (2) the material is presented in a controlled fashion, (3) the learner must interact with the material, (4) cues are presented to prompt the learner to give correct responses, (5) the learner has immediate feedback, (6) the student can proceed at his own rate, (7) the student usually can check his cumulative performance. These characteristics can be built into programmed materials in any of the physical formats; that is, a paperback text or a computer program could each possess these elements.

The programmed materials which have been developed, generally fall into two major groups (1) linear programming and (2) adaptive programming. In the linear type, all students complete all items as they move through the program. The answers are usually based on recognition of information, in which answers are selected from multiple choice items or on recall which requires students to fill in blanks.

Adaptive, or branching programming requires students to answer, but if the student gives evidence that more help is needed, alternative paths are indicated. Some students may move straight through, others must branch extensively. Sophisticated forms of branching have been developed for computer-assisted instruction.

A relatively small number of schools are using computer-assisted instruction although a variety of research projects have been funded to assess the strengths of such programs. One of the findings indicates that computer-assisted instruction may have unusual motivational value with disadvantaged students. Initially, most school systems found the cost prohibitive, but costs are gradually becoming lower for renting equipment and programs, and more school systems are acquiring computers and making them available for use for instructional purposes.

RESOURCES: PRODUCING PROGRAMMED MATERIALS

The developing of programmed materials requires a thorough understanding of behavioral objectives and learning theory in general. A comprehensive background in both these areas can be acquired through college courses. To develop programmed materials requires a special technique so college courses in the development of such materials and in computer-assisted instruction would be essential to becoming highly skilled. Some courses on learning resources include modules, or units that present introductory material on programming. Some books that provide an overview are listed in the bibliography for competency four.

MASTERY ITEM: PRODUCING PROGRAMMED MATERIALS

One important aspect of producing programmed materials is to be informed about those programs which have already been developed so as to prevent duplication. To keep up with this information it is important to be familiar with bibliographies of programmed instruction. Name one major list of programmed instruction.

Response: Producing Programmed Materials

Programmed Learning and Individually Paced Instruction (5th ed.), comp. by Carl H. Hendershot with the assistance of the National Society for Programmed Instruction (Bay City, Michigan: Hendershot Programmed Learning, 1973).

This bibliography lists 3500 program titles with full descriptions under 167 subject areas. The bibliography is a guide to programs, systems, and devices to use on all educational levels from preschool through college. The annotations are nonevaluative.

COMPETENCY 5   Reproduces printed materials.

Another type of production is that of reproducing multiple copies of various typed, printed, or hand-lettered materials. These processes are usually quite routine and demand little or no creativity, but nevertheless are essential in supplying learning materials.

Many kinds of equipment have been developed for reproducing materials, but the four major reproduction techniques used in schools are: spirit duplicating, mimeographing, photocopying, and printing.

Spirit duplicating or hectographing is a much used process that uses a rotating drum machine, a special wood and grain-alcohol fluid and aniline-dye carbon papers. If a good master copy is used and proper grades of materials are used, approximately three hundred copies may be made from one master.

Mimeographing is a process in which a wax coated stencil is placed on the outside of an inked cylinder. As the paper passes through the mimeograph machine the ink flows from the inside of the cylinder through the inking

Reproducing multiple copies of printed and graphic materials is one of the components of the production function.

pad and the stencil to the paper to reproduce the image on the stencil. As many as five thousand copies can be made from one well prepared stencil. Equipment has been developed with which stencils can be produced electronically.

Recently the process of photocopying has improved markedly and these developments have made it possible for teachers to reproduce materials very readily. The two processes most commonly used in photocopying are the electrostatic (Xerography) and the infrared.

The printing most commonly done in schools is the offset printing or a more accurate name would be offset lithography. This printing process can be done by using paper masters or by using metal plates.

All of these methods of reproduction of various items are vital and important in making teaching/learning materials available to teachers and students. Because some of these materials permit very rapid and inexpensive reproduction, great care must be taken not to violate copyright regulations. Media center personnel should be sensitive to this problem and attempt to keep up-to-date on all legal developments relating to copyright.

RESOURCES: PRODUCING PRINTED MATERIALS

The most reasonable way to learn these competencies is to learn by doing. Most school systems have two or more of these kinds of reproduction equipment. A fast and effective way to learn would be to go to a school; spend a short time observing; and then work with these machines to acquire the skills.

The work by Brown, Lewis, and Harcleroad, listed in the bibliography, is helpful. Also, companies who produce the equipment will supply instruction manuals. These are essential for thorough knowledge of all parts of the machines and for instruction in simple repair.

MASTERY ITEM: PRODUCING PRINTED MATERIALS

Fill in the blanks with the appropriate answers chosen from the list on the right.

1. Hectographing is the same as _____.
2. _____ is the process which involves the use of the wax coated stencil through which permanent ink passes.
3. Offset is a term related to _____.
4. _____ is the process developing aniline-dye, carbon papers and an alcohol fluid.
5. Diazo, infrared, dye-transfer, diffusion transfer and electrostatic are all processes involved in _____.

Printing
Mimeographing
Spirit duplicating
Photocopying

Response: Producing Printed Materials

1. Spirit duplicating
2. Mimeographing
3. Printing
4. Spirit duplicating
5. Photocopying

COMPETENCY 6 Identifies specific equipment and materials required for production.

One of the major responsibilities of a media professional is to make sure that all other staff members and all types of users have available the materials and equipment they need. This requires that all of these items be purchased or acquired in some manner. Through this acquisition process the media center should acquire the most appropriate materials and equipment for the tasks to be done. The equipment and materials that could be expected to be found in a production laboratory would generally be the following:

Equipment for producing audio materials:
Record players, tape recorders, tape duplicating equipment (reel-to-reel and cassette), tape erasing device (magnetic field), tape splicer, tape mixing unit, tape signaling unit (subsonic), microphones.

Materials for producing audio materials:
Blank audiotapes (reels and cassettes), tape splicing material, labels, cans for storage.

Equipment for producing graphic and still projected materials:
Dry mount press, Thermo-fax copy machine, diazo machine, cameras (such as instant loading cameras, 35mm cameras, Polaroid cameras), an Instamatic and copy stand, tripods, lights, story board racks.

Materials for producing graphic and still projected materials:
Lettering devices and tools, lettering pens, crayons, colored ink, tag-board, mounting board, felt-board materials, Chartex, muslin, rubber cement, wax paper, masking tape, spray paint, grease pencils, acetate sheets, transparency mounts, film, photographic paper, photographic chemicals, slide mounting tape and glass.

Equipment for producing motion projected materials:
8 mm. motion picture cameras, 16 mm. motion picture cameras, tripod,

light meter, floodlights, video camera, videotape record/playback systems, tape splicing equipment.

Materials for producing motion projected materials:

Videotapes, tape splicing material, reels, cans and boxes for storage, labels.

Equipment for producing printed materials:

Spirit duplicator, mimeograph machine, electronic stencil maker, photocopying machine, (printing press, if appropriate), paper cutters, paper punching equipment.

Materials for producing printed materials:

Dittos, stencils, mimeograph stencils, duplicating paper, staples.

General equipment:

X-acto and matte knives, primary-type typewriters, chalkboards, easels, electric typewriters.

Most media centers must manage their budget efficiently so it is important that media personnel be able to identify quality equipment to get maximum quality work for the money expended.

In addition to providing the anticipated materials and equipment, media personnel should be encouraged to be on the lookout for new and appropriate items as they appear on the market. It is through this sense of pioneering and experimentation that the center takes on an atmosphere of excitement and a sense of development and newness.

Media professionals must accept the responsibility for keeping all equipment repaired. Knowing specifications and the source of repair parts is essential to keeping everything in working order.

Users should be informed of comparative costs of materials, so that the appropriate form of the material can be used for the appropriate product without more expense than necessary. For example, for large numbers of transparencies that are going to be used only once very inexpensive sheets of acetate can be used. The sets that are used repeatedly should be made on heavier acetate and placed in frames for protection and ease of use.

RESOURCES: DESCRIBING PRODUCTION MATERIALS

This competency can probably best be gained by working closely with dealers and sales representatives. They are expected to know their product thoroughly and are pleased to share the information. They are alert to all the newest developments, and changes in repair parts or in prices. They can be contacted through their sales offices or these contacts can be made at conventions. However, be sure that enthusiasm for their product does not allow them to consume a disproportionate amount of your time.

Another source of information is dealers' catalogs. It is important to keep a representative sample of catalogs on hand describing all kinds of equipment and materials so that media personnel, teachers, and students can refer to them.

Courses in production will provide basic information related to this competency, but this information changes so rapidly that other resources are required to keep up-to-date. The *Audio-Visual Equipment Directory,* and the book by Brown, Norberg, and Srygley, both listed in the bibliography, can provide helpful information.

MASTERY ITEM: DESCRIBING PRODUCTION MATERIALS

A district wide committee has been formed to coordinate purchasing of equipment throughout the district. List some basic principles which should be followed as specific items are selected.

Response: Describing Production Materials

1. Equipment should be ordered that meets the need of the students and teachers.
2. The equipment should be sturdy enough to withstand use and its transport from room to room.
3. The equipment should have easily replaceable parts.
4. Equipment should be similar in all buildings.
5. Committees should agree to order identical equipment for most schools because:
   (a) Ordering in large numbers usually cuts down the cost significantly.
   (b) Replacement parts can be ordered to service the entire district.
6. Equipment should be uncomplicated and simple to operate.
7. Equipment should be ordered for which adequate software is available.

COMPETENCY 7   *Applies rules and standards for evaluation of products.*

Standards for evaluation should apply to locally produced products, as well as to those purchased commercially. The criteria for evaluation, should of course be adapted so that they are realistic and appropriate, but the evaluation should be based on the same principles presented in Chapter 14, "The Evaluation Function."

MASTERY ITEM: EVALUATING PRODUCTION MATERIALS

Name two major sources for obtaining evaluative information relating to audiovisual equipment and materials that is impartial and unbiased and which could give you help in making decisions in ordering for a new production laboratory.

Response: Evaluating Production Materials

Library Technology Reports (Chicago, Illinois: American Library Association).

This bimonthly publication started in 1965 provides critical evaluations of equipment and products used in libraries, media centers and educational institutions. These evaluations are designed to enable the librarian and educator to make wise, economical purchase decisions. Testing and evaluation are conducted by nationally recognized independent laboratories.

EPIE Reports (New York: Educational Products Information Exchange).

This organization issues a biweekly newsletter published eighteen times during the school year and six major reports each year, the first of which was issued in 1967. EPIE is an advocate for the educational consumer through an established information and evaluation network run on a nonprofit basis. EPIE has its own testing laboratories and a materials evaluation office, in addition to research laboratories.

REFERENCES

BROWN, JAMES W., KENNETH D. NORBERG and SARA K. SRYGLEY. *Administering Educational Media* (2nd ed.), pp. 251-74. New York: McGraw-Hill, 1972.

Effective Visual Presentations. 160 slides, color, sound, 37 minutes. Rochester, New York: Eastman Kodak Company, 1971.

ERICKSON, CARLETON, W. H. *Administering Instructional Media Programs,* pp. 362-402. New York: The Macmillan Company, 1968.

Handmade Materials for Projection. 16mm motion picture, sound, color, 20 minutes. Bloomington, Indiana: Indiana University, 1955.

KEMP, JERROLD E. *Planning and Producing Audiovisual Materials* (2nd ed.), pp. 23-61. San Francisco, California: Chandler Publishing Company, 1968.

Media Programs: District and School, pp. 108-109, 111-112. Chicago: American Library Association and Washington, D.C.: Association for Educational Communications and Technology, 1974.

Preparing Projected Materials. 16 mm motion picture, sound, color, 15 minutes. Los Angeles, California: BFA Educational Media, 1964.

Competency 1   Produces audio materials.

BROWN, JAMES W. and RICHARD B. LEWIS, eds. *AV Instructional Technology Manual for Independent Study,* pp. 207-31; pp. 469-77. New York: McGraw-Hill, 1973.

BROWN, JAMES W., RICHARD D. LEWIS and FRED HARCLEROAD. *AV Instruction; Media and Methods* (3rd ed.), pp. 117-22. New York: McGraw-Hill, 1972.

KEMP, JERROLD E. *Planning and Producing Audiovisual Materials* (2nd ed.), pp. 129-34, 159-60. San Francisco: Chandler Publishing Company, 1968.

Competency 2   Produces graphic and still-projected materials.

Audio Visual Production Techniques Series. 8mm filmloop, silent, color, 3-4 minutes each. New York: McGraw-Hill Book Company, 1965.

Dry Mounting Press (bw)
Dry Mounting Hand Iron (bw)
Permanent Rubber Cement Mounting (bw)
Mounting: A Two-Page Picture (bw)
Mounting: A Cut Out Picture (bw)
Mounting: Overcoming Dry Mounting Problems (bw)
Mounting: Using Laminating Film (bw)
Cloth Mounting (Roll) (bw)
Cloth Mounting (Fold) Part I (bw)
Cloth Mounting (Fold) Part II (bw)
Mounting: Setting Grommets (bw)
Lettering: The Felt Pen (Basic Skills) (c)
Lettering: The Felt Pen (Applications) (c)
Lettering: Prepared Letters (bw)
Lettering: Wricoprint (bw)
Lettering: Wrico Signmaker (bw)
Lettering: Leroy 500 and Smaller (bw)
Lettering: Leroy 700 and Larger (bw)
Transparencies: Handmade Method (c)
Transparencies: Heat Process (c)
Transparencies: Principle of Diazo Process (c)
Transparencies: Diazo Process (c)
Transparencies: Spirit Duplicator (c)

Transparencies: Picture Transfer I (c)
Transparencies: Picture Transfer II (c)
Transparencies: Making Overlays (c)
Transparencies: Adding Color (c)
Transparencies: Mounting and Masking (c)

Basic Art Techniques for Slide Production. 65-35mm slides with audiotape and script, 8 minutes. Rochester, New York: Eastman Kodak Company, 1972.

Basic Copying Techniques. 78-35mm slides with audiotapes and script, 18 minutes. Rochester, New York: Eastman Kodak Company, 1972.

Basic Educational Graphics. 10 filmstrips, color, 8 records, 4 instructor's manuals, 1 student manual, and materials kit. Austin, Texas: Educational Media Labs, 1967.

BROWN, JAMES W. and RICHARD B. LEWIS, eds. *AV Instructional Technology Manual for Independent Study,* pp. 15-50. New York: McGraw-Hill Co., 1973.

Fundamentals of Layout Design. 2 filmstrips, sound (record) color, Los Angeles, California: BFA Educational Media.

Introduction to Graphic Design: Tools of the Graphic Designer. 2 filmstrips, sound (record) color. Los Angeles, California: BFA Educational Media.

KEMP, JERROLD E. *Planning and Producing Audiovisual Materials* (2nd ed.), pp. 65-90 photography, pp. 91-128 graphics, pp. 137-41 photographic print series, pp. 142-52 slide series, pp. 153-58 filmstrips, pp. 161-86 overhead transparencies. San Francisco: Chandler Publishing Company, 1968.

Lettering Instructional Materials. 16mm motion picture, sound, color, 20 minutes. Bloomington, Indiana: Indiana University.

MINOR, E. and H. FRYE. *Techniques of Producing Visual Instructional Media.* New York: McGraw-Hill, 1970.

Photographic Slides for Instruction. 16mm motion picture, sound, color, 11 minutes. Bloomington, Indiana: Indiana University, 1956.

Projecting Ideas II: Diazo Transparency Production. 16mm motion picture, sound, color, 11 minutes. Iowa City, Iowa: University of Iowa, 1964.

Projecting Ideas III: Direct Transparency Production. 16 mm motion picture, sound, color, 5 minutes. Iowa City, Iowa: University of Iowa, 1965.

The Simple Camera. 12-35mm filmstrips, color, guides. Washington, D.C.: Association for Educational Communication and Technology, 1963.

Competency 3   Produces motion projected materials.

Basic Principles of Film Editing. 16mm motion picture, sound, black and white, 8 minutes. Hollywood, California: American Cinema Editors, 1965.

BROWN, JAMES W. and RICHARD B. LEWIS, eds. *AV Instructional Technology Manual for Independent Study,* pp. 97-98, 149-51. New York: McGraw-Hill, 1973.

BROWN, JAMES W., RICHARD D. LEWIS and FRED HARCLEROAD. *AV Instruc-*

tions: Media and Methods (4th ed.), pp. 179-206; 237-62. New York: McGraw-Hill, 1973.

Eight mm. Film in Education: Its Emerging Role. 16mm motion picture, sound, color, 28 minutes. New York: Du Art Film Labs, Inc., 1966.

The Growing of A Young Filmmaker. 16mm motion picture, sound, black and white, 17 minutes. Washington, D.C.: Association for Educational Communication and Technology, 1969.

KEMP, JERROLD E. *Planning and Producing Audiovisual Materials* (2nd ed.), pp. 187-216 motion pictures, pp. 217-22 television. San Francisco: Chandler Publishing Company, 1968.

Let's Make A Film. 16mm motion pictures, sound, color, 13 minutes. New York: Van Nostrand Reinhold, 1970.

Make a Movie Without A Camera. 16mm motion pictures, sound, color, 6 minutes. Los Angeles, California: BFA Educational Media.

A Movie About Light. 16mm motion picture, sound, color, 8 minutes. Washington, D.C.: Association for Educational Communication and Technology, 1972.

Practical Film Making. 16mm motion picture, sound, color, 19 minutes. Chicago, Illinois: Encyclopedia Britannica, 1972.

Television Series. 26 transparencies, standard size for overhead projector. Ellensburg, Washington: Educational Media, Inc., n.d.

Television Training Films: A Series. 16mm motion pictures, sound, black and white, 13-28 minutes each, n.d.

The Young Art. 16mm motion picture, sound, color, 17 minutes. New York: Van Nostrand Reinhold, 1970.

Competency 4   Produces programmed material.

BROWN, JAMES W. and RICHARD B. LEWIS, eds. *AV Instructional Technology Manual for Independent Study,* pp. 101-4. New York: McGraw-Hill, 1973.

BROWN, JAMES W., RICHARD D. LEWIS and FRED HARCLEROAD. *AV Instruction; Media and Methods* (3rd ed.), pp. 412-14. New York: McGraw-Hill, 1972.

PIPE, PETER, *Practical Programming.* New York: Holt, Rinehart and Winston, 1966.

Competency 5   Reproduces printed materials.

Audio-Visual Production Techniques Series, 8mm filmloop, silent, color, 3-4 minutes each. New York: McGraw-Hill Book Company, 1965.

The Spirit Duplicator: Preparing Masters (c)
The Spirit Duplicator: Operation (c)

BROWN, JAMES W. and RICHARD B. LEWIS, eds. *AV Instructional Technology Manual for Independent Study,* pp. 508-19. New York: McGraw-Hill, 1973.

Competency 6   Identifies specific equipment and materials required for production.

Audio-Visual Equipment Directory. Fairfax, Virginia: National Audio-Visual Association, Annual.

BROWN, JAMES W., KENNETH D. NORBERG and SARA K. SRYGLEY. *Administering Educational Media* (2nd ed.) pp. 223-49. New York: McGraw-Hill, 1972.

13 The Instruction Function

The function of instruction as used in this chapter means "to inform," since there are many aspects of the media center's program about which all users need to be instructed or informed. This chapter examines the diversity of ways in which media center personnel instruct or inform users, such as public relations and in-service training.

The function of instruction must be viewed and interpreted in a special way. Some educators would say that the primary goal of the educational system is instruction. Therefore if the media center is an integral part of the educational system its major goal must be instruction. This is one interpretation of the relationship of the media center to instruction. The function of instruction as it is presented in this chapter is quite different, as the aspects considered will be those initiated within the media center which serve specialized purposes relating to the major goal. Media professionals serve as teachers in many ways. In the function of instruction, they perform the task of educating a variety of publics. It might help to clarify this concept if the word "instruction" were defined as meaning "to inform." The following are some of the publics which need to "be informed." First, the *general community* and particularly the *parents* need to be informed continuously about the goals, programs, and services of the media center. The second group whom the professionals must keep informed are the *school board* and the *personnel of the district administration*. Many might argue that these responsibilities could more appropriately be called communication. Communication skills are absolutely essential; but in many instances these publics have to be educated about many aspects of the media center. Evidence seems to indicate that people are much more positive and enthusiastic in supporting programs about which they

275

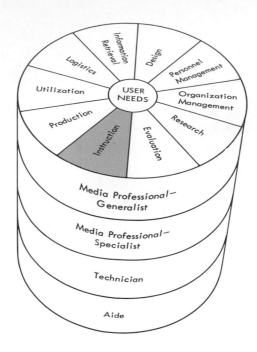

COMPETENCY 1   *Plans and implements a public relations program.*
COMPETENCY 2   *Conducts in-service media training for teachers.*
COMPETENCY 3   *Provides information about media program to administrators and school board.*
COMPETENCY 4   *Develops learning programs to assist individuals in using media center materials and equipment.*
COMPETENCY 5   *Communicates with producers and publishers regarding materials and equipment.*
COMPETENCY 6   *Establishes regular communication channels between media center personnel and users.*

---

are knowledgeable. *Teachers* are another group who need instruction so that they can make optimum use of all services, materials, and equipment available to them in the center.

Publishers and producers make up a special group with whom media center personnel must communicate to keep them informed of the new products and materials needed and also to help them to improve the quality and appropriateness of materials and equipment.

Internally, communication channels must be kept open and functioning among the personnel. Again, many aspects of this communication must take the form of instruction. Instruction could range from explaining clerical routines to a new employee to having the technician teaching the staff members how to operate new video equipment.

Far more important than any of these other tasks of instruction is that of instructing *students* in how to use the media center. This instruction ranges from the simple task of orienting students to the locations of the varieties of materials in the center to the more complex tasks of locating specific subject matter and evaluating the content and the format in which it is presented. More explicitly, an example of a problem in locating information might be to describe the topography of Nigeria and to evaluate the effectiveness of the information as presented on a globe, relief map, or 8 mm film loop. A convincing argument presented by many noted professionals is that the only true life-long learning comes when a student learns where to locate information. Much of cognitive learning or the learning of facts becomes out-of-date very soon but a student who possesses the skill of knowing how to locate information and evaluate it possesses learning tools that serve for an entire lifetime. Another impressive aspect of inquiry is that authorities who specialize in predicting the future emphasize that most people will experience the need for life-long learning, since their job requirements will change a number of times during their life time. The skill of locating information is the one skill that will remain a constant throughout the learning process.

The above activities constitute the function of instruction as interpreted in this chapter.

GENERAL RESOURCES FOR ACQUIRING COMPETENCIES

Even though each of these competencies deals with different audiences and the implementation technique may differ, some of the basic concepts are the same. Basic to this function is the knowledge of communication skills and knowing how to deal with people. The fundamental educational background needed could be obtained through college courses in communications and interpersonal relations. More specialized courses in public relations and group dynamics would also be helpful. To teach skills in locating and evaluating information requires a high level of teaching ability, so courses in pedagogy offer another possibility for college preparation. This skill is also necessary for conducting in-service education for faculty and administration.

One of the most important factors in carrying out these functions is to develop an awareness of need. The media professional must be constantly alert to those messages that need to be communicated to these diverse groups and also be cognizant of the various channels of communication that can work effectively in a variety of situations.

Much of what is needed in the form of skills, abilities and perceptions must come through experience. This experience can be gained through working with a professional who has developed expertise in instruction.

Another component that must be mastered is the substantive knowledge required in some of these areas of instruction. For example, to be able to provide in-service training for teachers, it is essential for the media professional to have a thorough knowledge of the entire program, services, materials and equipment and how all of these can be of optimum use by teachers. Similar substantive knowledge is essential to be able to teach students how to locate and evaluate information. Sources that would be helpful in attaining these competencies will be discussed under each specific competency.

COMPETENCY 1   Plans and implements a public relations program.

It always has been important to keep parents informed about educational programs. With the current emphasis on community involvement and accountability it is imperative that the media center conduct a comprehensive public relations program. Such a program has a number of objectives. First, it should provide the public with general information about the program. An example would be to send a press release to the local newspaper to inform the public that a new assistant had been employed in the center, and to indicate the new employee's educational background and experience. Another example would be to develop a pamphlet to send to all parents with a brief description of the program and a listing of the hours the center is open. A display in a department store window could inform the public by showing the variety of new formats in which information is stored, such as 8mm films, microforms, videotape, and audio cassettes. A second objective is to provide specific information about special programs in which parents or other community members might wish to participate. An example of this type of communication might be spot announcements on the radio station to inform the public about the times at which book reviews are going to be given or the time films are scheduled to be shown in the center. If the media center has adequate materials and equipment it might be possible to allow materials such as films, videotapes, and filmstrips to be circulated to the community. In this case a good public relations vehicle would be to prepare a regular column for the local paper which gives brief reviews of materials available to the public and to give reviews of films to which the public is invited.

One of the Knapp demonstration project libraries, Roosevelt Library in Portland, Oregon, implemented a program in which the senior high school students held story hours for preschool children. This program was extremely popular, beneficial for both the young children and the high school students, and served to build excellent public relations.

These are examples of traditional approaches to public relations. Changes are taking place that focus attention on public relations and make this an area that could provide unprecedented opportunity and challenge. One obvious change is the increased interest of parents and the public in the program and activities that are taking place in schools. This interest ranges from concern for providing optimum learning opportunities for the students to monitoring the expenditure of the school budget. In any case, there is a real desire by the public to be more thoroughly and more accurately informed. Another factor that is currently influencing the area of public relations is the development of technology and mass media. A few years ago the means of disseminating information was comparatively limited and unsophisticated. Traditionally, information might be disseminated through news releases in the newspapers, newsletters or brochures, window displays, bulletin boards, radio announcements and announcements at meetings such as PTA's or mothers' clubs. The development of new media makes it feasible to create innovative public relations programs. For example, the programs of the media center can be described through slide tape presentations, through 8mm film clips, through filmstrips, and through films. All of these media can be used effectively by students. This involvement of students in using media for public relations purposes often accomplishes beneficial side effects, since the students often become more enthusiastic users and supporters of the media center when they become involved in producing programs using media or TV channels which have been made available to them. When programs developed by the media center are cabled into thousands of homes, the public relations program has a potential for great impact—positively or negatively. In any case, the use of media and technology for public relations will demand creativity and ingenuity, but if it is used effectively it will result in real payoffs in public support.

Cora Paul Bowmar stresses the responsibilities a media center has for communicating in two major elements, reporting and public relations. Under her discussion of reports, she includes financial and administrative reports of existing or projected program activities to users, a selective dissemination of information for users, and recommends a survey of user interests and needs. Under public relations she delineates a variety of techniques to be used with different audiences.[1]

---

[1] Cora Paul Bowmar, *Guide to the Development of Educational Media Selection Centers* (Chicago, Illinois: American Library Association, 1973), pp. 43-45.

RESOURCES: PLANNING PUBLIC RELATIONS PROGRAMS

For persons who are interested in developing special expertise in this area it would probably be advisable to take college courses in public relations, journalism, and advertising. Courses in television production would be of particular relevance. Experience in working with persons knowledgeable in these areas would be valuable in developing expertise in public relations.

Carleton W. H. Erickson's *Administering Instructional Media Programs* is a book in the media field that presents a thorough discussion of activities related to developing a public relations program while Cora Paul Bowmar's work provides a less extensive, yet pragmatic discussion. Both of these works are listed in the bibliography.

MASTERY ITEM: PLANNING PUBLIC RELATIONS PROGRAMS

List five examples of specific activities which could be advertised as part of a public relations program and select the medium that could be used.

Response: Planning Public Relations Programs

1. A Book and Film Fair to be held all day on Saturday could be advertised in spot announcements on television or as a television news item.
2. Film showings during noon hours could be advertised in the school newspaper.
3. An announcement inviting visitors to an author's tea could be made in the daily newspaper.
4. Story hours and announcements about story hours could be made on the radio station.
5. A filmmaking contest could be announced through the newsletters of sponsors, or such civic organizations as the Lions Club and Rotary Club.

COMPETENCY 2   Conducts in-service media training for teachers.

Working with teachers to assist them in making optimum use of the materials and equipment in the media center is one of the top priorities of the media professional. Working with teachers can be extremely rewarding, since they influence other teachers and numbers of students. As teachers become more informed, self-sufficient, and enthusiastic about using media, they not only enhance their teaching skills but they also transmit this knowledge to students. In-service training for teachers should be individualized as much as possible, since some teachers are well informed and sophisticated and others are lacking in some of the skills and knowledge about using media. In-service training includes the following range of information: An orientation as to the location of all materials, training sessions (or auto-tutorial sessions) on equipment operation; and information regarding services of the center (such as how to borrow equipment and how to check out materials). It is also important for teachers to understand all of the services and programs the media center personnel can provide. These services include locating and acquiring all types of materials, compiling bibliographies (or, as some persons call them—"mediagraphies"), and the production of teaching and learning materials such as transparencies, audiotapes, and videotapes.

Teachers also need to learn the more intricate skills of locating specific materials through using the card catalog and indexes of all kinds.

Another in-service aspect of instruction is to teach production activities so that teachers can make their own instructional materials. When they produce their own materials they will feel self-confident enough to encourage students to produce materials.

A special expertise which teachers should be assisted in acquiring is that of selecting and evaluating materials. These skills can very appropriately be taught through in-service training.

Probably the most complex exercise for in-service training is that of developing teaching modules or units. This procedure demands the coordination of many of the previously identified skills. A thorough knowledge of the subject matter and the ability to select the appropriate teaching strategies is necessary. Appropriate types of media must be identified and the best titles must be selected from the media available or new materials must be locally produced. All of these elements must be orchestrated to meet the individual needs of the students.

The media center staff must be sensitive to the needs of the teachers and organize in-service sessions so they will be stimulating and relevant. It is necessary to work cooperatively with the administration to arrange scheduling and other details such as compensation through released time or extra salary. It is also important for the administration to make a commitment to support the teachers with resources at the culmination of the in-service program.

RESOURCES: CONDUCTING IN-SERVICE TRAINING

To organize and manage in-service training for teachers, media personnel need a background in teaching. For substantive knowledge about locating materials and using bibligraphic tools, courses in librarianship are helpful.

Sources of information about production techniques can be found in Chapter 12, while sources of information dealing with selection and evaluation are found in Chapter 14.

Relatively little has been written about conducting in-service training for teachers by media professionals; however, this need is attracting increasing attention. One good example of this interest is the Instructional Development Institute.

The Instructional Development Institute (IDI), developed and operated by the University Consortium for Instructional Development and Technology (Indiana University, Michigan State University, Syracuse University, U. S. International University, and the University of Southern California) is a forty hour in-service program for teachers, administrators, board members, and specialists (including media professionals). At the completion of the institute each person has acquired skills in designing instruction in a systematic fashion using a wide range of media. Evaluations of the program have shown a high degree of success in achieving the objective of the institute with the audiences for which is was designed.[2]

Currently, in-service programs are being considered under the larger scope of continuing education. It seems that many professions are realizing the increasing need for extensive continuing education programs. Cora Paul Bowmar states: "Continuing education experiences both for staff members and for users of educational media selection centers are essential elements in developing a program of service in these centers."[3]

In Bowmar's work with the Educational Media Selection Centers Program Phase I report, respondents to an inquiry identified the following as the most frequently used in-service approaches; workshops, programs conducted at meetings, orientation programs, displays and exhibits, demonstrations and conferences. Other methods identified were extension courses, sessions for previewing materials, field trips, materials production activities, media review groups and seminars. The following are examples of continuing education strategies used in educational media selection centers which have been established under this program.

1. Self-instruction laboratories are used to provide ongoing opportunities for individualized instruction in the operation of media equipment. Permanent stations are outfitted with essential equipment and a manual of step-by-step instructions for equipment use. The self-instruction programs are revised as needed to make each step clearer to the learner and to reflect changes in equipment.

2. Educational television is being used to disseminate information about

[2] For further information about the Instructional Development Institute contact the IDI National Coordinator, Syracuse University, 130 Huntington Hall, Syracuse, New York 13210.

[3] Cora Paul Bowmar, *Guide to the Development of Educational Media Selection Centers* (Chicago, Illinois: American Library Association, 1973), p. 34.

media in a workshop offered for credit to school personnel by a state department of education. It is also used for previewing new films available from local school system centers.

3. One state department of education is using a mobile unit to extend the services of its educational media selection center. This unit carries collections of materials to areas beyond convenient access to the center, for use in workshops on selection and use of media conducted by professional staff members from the center. Collections in the mobile unit are changed to meet specific interests, e.g., foreign languages, African studies, state geography, history, and government. Following the workshop presentations, the mobile unit remains in the local school system for one or two weeks, where its use by local school personnel is guided by a school system coordinator.

4. A large suburban school system reports that the in-service activities most sought by teachers, principals, and librarians are workshops in the production of materials, equipment use, and effective utilization of media, including television. These workshops, conducted during the school year in fifteen sessions each, offer a combination of demonstration and first-hand experiences. Participants (twenty-five per workshop) receive salary increment credit and/or credit towards the renewal of their state certificate.[4]

Books by Bowmar and by Davies, listed in the bibliography, give general background in this competency.

By comparison, the publication *Media Programs: District and School* stresses the importance of public information more than any standards previously published. Guidelines for a public information program are delineated as follows:

> Public information is the communications process by which the media staff provides and transmits information about media program objectives and functions to develop public awareness and support.

Guiding Principles

1. Goals for the public information program are established through the planning process and reflect understanding of the various audiences to be reached.
2. Satisfaction of user needs is the most essential component of effective public relations.
3. Public information and public relations are considered in all areas of media program operations and are provided on a continuing basis.
4. The public information program provides for coordinated exchange of information with other agencies at district, regional, state, and national levels.
5. Provisions for collection and analysis of data on the media program are

[4] Ibid., pp. 37-38.

based on the utility of the data for program evaluation and public information purposes.
6. Public information is recognized as an effective tool in assuring intellectual freedom for users.

Teachers and students should know the ways in which the media program can help them achieve learning objectives. Administrators need to know how the media program functions in relation to other components of the educational system and they require supporting data for budget and planning purposes. Parents should understand the relationships among media, instructional design, and the curriculum. The board of education reflects and influences community attitudes through its priorities, explanations, and budgets. The general public is concerned with both the effectiveness and the efficiency of the educational program.

A well-planned program of public relations interprets the role of the media program and extends public expectations. Satisfied users of a media program are a crucial link in the public information system. Staff development programs offer significant opportunities to extend teachers' knowledge of and competence in using media. Consultative work with administrators and consultants in using media for public information purposes, plus production of materials for such presentations, promotes broader recognition of the role of media in the total educational program.

Public information programs have a responsibility for protecting intellectual freedom in the media program. Sharing goals and objectives with the community and soliciting input in return provide a rational basis for decision-making and reasonable interchange in times of philosophic disagreement.

The director of the district media program has general responsibility for planning the public information program, working with district and school media staff members and with the school district public information officer. A process for the exchange of views and ideas insures continuous participation by individual schools.

Data collection by the district media program and individual school programs is closely related to public information needs. The district media program director determines the types of information needed in terms of potential use and sets forth the means to be used in collecting, storing, and analyzing data (see Table 13-1). The heads of school media programs are oriented in and given the means to fulfill their part of the program. State and national guidelines are followed in collection and reporting of statistical information.[5]

---

[5] *Media Programs: District and School,* (Chicago: American Library Association, and Washington, D.C.: Association for Educational Communications and Technology, 1974), pp. 55-56, 58.

TABLE 13-1 Recommendations for an Effective Public Information Program

Audience	Types of Information Needed	Means for Providing Information
Students	Media center resources and program functions Ways of using media in reaching educational objectives Contributions of media to personal interests and goals	Displays, posters, news releases Media production Media presentations Personal contact Classroom visits Indirect contact through teachers Bibliographies Media packages
School Staff (faculty and administrators)	Media program goals and functions Ways of using media to achieve educational objectives Role of media in the total educational program Use of media to reach personal and professional goals	Memoranda, handbooks, information sheets Personal contacts and conferences Staff meetings Staff development programs on media utilization News releases Media production Media presentations Bibliographies Annual reports
Parents, Citizens, Board of Education, Other Public Officials	Media program goals and functions and their role in the achievement of overall educational goals Media program operations in relationship to the total educational program	News releases, radio and television coverage Media presentations Personal contacts Open house programs, public exhibits Budget justifications Annual reports
Media and Education Agencies and Associations	Media program goals and functions Program plans and activities as they relate to other agencies	News releases Annual reports Information sheets and handbooks Personal contact Participation in association activities Contribution to professional publications

Media Programs: District and School (Chicago: American Library Association and Washington: Association for Educational Communications and Technology, 1974). p. 57.

MASTERY ITEM: CONDUCTING IN-SERVICE TRAINING

Prepare an outline for a one day teacher in-service training session on teaching production skills, including content and time allocations. The in-service training session would be held in the production laboratory and thirty teachers would be invited to attend.

Response: Conducting In-Service Training

8:30- 9:00	Introduction by the Media Center Director. The services of the center and the equipment and materials available are described.
9:00- 9:30	Demonstration of making both diazo and thermal transparencies.
9:30-10:30	Group divides to practice making transparencies.
10:30-10:45	Break.
10:45-11:00	Demonstration of use of Instamatic camera and copy stand.
11:00-12:00	Group makes slides using copy stand.
1:00- 2:00	Demonstration of video camera and playback equipment.
2:00- 4:00	Group divides into teams to write a brief script, make props, back drops, and videotape a brief sequence.
4:00- 4:30	Show and tell time for viewing products developed—with description of how they are to be used in the classroom.

COMPETENCY 3   Provides information about media program to administrators and school board.

Much of the success in performing this competency comes through acute perception. The media professional must have a keen sense of awareness about what the administrators and school board need to know. He or she also needs to be knowledgeable about the media center goals, its programs and problems of management, so that all important information can be communicated. All appropriate modes of communication should be explored to reach these audiences. Differing situations and personalities require different strategies. In some cases it would be appropriate to invite administrators and school board members to visit the center, in other cases the media center personnel may be invited to visit school board meetings to describe various aspects of the program. It is very important to confer with the building principal to assess which modes of communication are appropriate and acceptable.

Even though this competency is difficult to prescribe precisely, it is of inestimable value if performed effectively. Administrators and school board members must be thoroughly informed about all aspects of the media center. They need this information partly to enable them to do their jobs better, since the media center is a vitally important part of the total educational program. The other reason is that they must be informed so that they can allocate adequate financial support for the center.

RESOURCES: INFORMING ADMINISTRATORS AND SCHOOL BOARD

The dynamics of human personality are so variable in this communication situation that it is difficult to recommend ways in which the competency can be gained. One good procedure for acquiring the competency would be to observe several successful models, analyze their reasons for success, and be able to combine those facets that seem most appropriate to the situation. It is not wise to suggest that if at first you don't succeed, try, try again, because the caution here is that you need to be certain of success at every attempt. Communication is so important that it demands the most careful thought and attention. Any suggestions for public relations or communication modes that are judged as appropriate should be added to a catalog of approaches. These ideas could come from books, professional journals, conferences, or coworkers. All of these would be sources for gaining competencies.

MASTERY ITEM: INFORMING ADMINISTRATORS AND SCHOOL BOARD

Write an outline for a thirty minute informational program about the media center which would be appropriate to present to the Board of Education.

Response: Informing Administrators and School Board

The presentation would be in the form of a panel or symposium made up of the Director of the Media Center, a student and a teacher. Each would give about a ten minute presentation.

A. The Media Center director would speak first and present the following points:

1. The objective of the center is to serve the user.
2. Give brief information concerning personnel, facilities, collections, equipment, and services.

This portion of the presentation would be illustrated by slides.

B. The teacher would speak next and present the following points:

1. The services of the center are organized to assist teaching/learning activities.
2. Identify ways in which the center supports instruction.

This portion of the presentation would be illustrated by examples of multi-media kits, or realia, or models.

C. The student would speak next and present the following points:

1. The services of the center are organized to support instruction.
2. Identify ways in which the center supports individualized instruction through creative inquiry.

This portion of the presentation could be illustrated by a short film made by students.

D. If there is time available encourage the School Board members to ask questions of any of the speakers.

COMPETENCY 4   Develops learning programs to assist individuals in using media center materials and equipment.

Learning programs to assist individuals in using media center materials and equipment include a vast range of skills and knowledge of every degree of complexity. The user must first know the general lay-out of the facilities of the center. For example, the user must know where to locate periodicals, microfilms, books, filmstrips, audio-cassettes and every other type of information format. Many media centers have followed a plan of total integration, in that they arrange all of the various formats together on the shelves. In other words, if a user wishes to locate all the materials the center has on Shakespeare, whether in print form or audiovisual format, these materials would be located together on the shelf. Other centers, generally for space reasons, prefer to keep all similar formats together. For example, all filmstrips are stored together, all audiotapes are stored together and all records are located in one place. This latter arrangement requires that the user be more knowledgeable about the physical location of materials. Another factor that contributes to the ease of location of materials is whether the card catalog is totally integrated. The most efficient locating device for users is usually provided by having all materials classified and cataloged with the catalog cards all filed together in one catalog. Some media centers start by placing all catalog cards for audio and visual materials in a separate file. This necessitates looking in two files to locate all materials on a subject, so therefore it is not as efficient.

In addition to knowing general locations of materials, users must be able to locate the necessary equipment. Equipment may be available in electronic carrels, such as recorders for playing audio cassettes, record players for discs, and television sets and videotape recorders for showing videotapes. Some centers schedule these audio and visual programs so that arranging for the use of equipment is minimal. Other centers make equipment available only through a special request scheduling arrangement.

After the user knows the general location of materials and equipment then the retrieval systems for locating specific materials must be known. For example, the card catalog may indicate the location of subjects by classification codes, or by accession members. Indexes will help locate journal articles, short stories, essays, or plays within publications. Thesauri will help locate vertical file materials. In addition, each encyclopedia will have a different locating device, either an index, a *Propaedia,* or alphabetized entries. This is true for each kind of reference book, so all of these locating skills need to be learned. Schools use different storage plans for storing films and videotapes, so special locating skills may need to be learned for locating these materials. As locating tasks become more specific, different tools are needed, such as cross references, descriptors, and in some cases, on-line computer search techniques are used.

To become proficient in locating specific subject matter in an explicit format is an exceedingly complex task, but one that stands users in good stead throughout a lifetime. Learning to locate information has been described as being analogous to the Chinese proverb that says "Give a man a fish and you've fed him for a day, but teach a man to fish and you've fed him for a lifetime." The rationale for stressing the skills in learning to locate information is that facts can change quickly in this time of rapidly advancing knowledge. However, if a student learns to locate information, this skill can last a lifetime.

Many fine books have been written to serve as guides to learning these location skills. It is important to build up a collection of these books. Review them to ascertain which sections are most appropriate for teaching location skills in your school, and then make the necessary adaptations. There are fine teaching materials developed commercially in audio and visual format which can be used effectively to teach location skills. Several resource guides list specific titles and sources of materials for teaching about the use of the library media center and three excellent resources are listed in the bibliography.

Even though learning to use the library/media center is of utmost importance to users, relatively little has been written on the methods of teaching these skills. The materials that are related to this competency within the function of instruction are mainly those developed to be used by the students. These are in the form of guide books, programmed texts, slide-tape presentations, filmstrips, or transparencies dealing with the content to be learned by the students. Much of the material was developed a number of years ago and has not been superseded by more current materials. The following list are materials recommended by the American Association of School Librarians with a limited number of new items added.

AIDS FOR TEACHING THE USE OF MEDIA

Printed Materials

BECK, MARGARET V., and VERA M. PACE. *Guidebooks for Teaching Library Skills.* Minneapolis: T. S. Denison, 1966. (Three books to be used in the 4th, 5th, and 6th grades).

BOYD, JESSIE EDNA. *Books, Libraries, and You.* New York: Scribner, 1965. (For use in the junior and senior high school.)

CLEARY, FLORENCE DAMON. *Discovering Books and Libraries; a Handbook for the Upper Elementary and Junior High School Grades.* New York: Wilson, 1966.

GULLETTE, IRENE et al. *National Test of Library Skills.* American Testing Company, 6301 S.W. Fifth Street, Ft. Lauderdale, Florida 33314.

MLI Associates. *How to Use the Library.* Boston: Allyn and Bacon, 1966. (Programmed text for junior and senior high schools).

MOTT, CAROLYN, and LEO BAISDEN. *Children's Book on How to Use Books and Libraries.* New York: Scribner, 1961. (For use in elementary and junior high schools).

ROSOFF, MARTIN. *Using Your High School Library.* New York: Wilson, 1964.

School Library Association of California (Northern Section). *Library Skills: Teaching Library Use Through Games and Devices.* Fearon, 1958. (2165 Park Boulevard, Palo Alto, California).

TAYLOR, MARGARET, and KATHRYN LIEBOLD. *Libraries Are for Children.* New York: Fordham Publishing. 2377 Hoffman Street, Bronx, 1965. ("Participation sheets" can be reproduced on spirit duplicating machines).

Wisconsin Department of Public Instruction. *Learning to Use Media.* Bulletin #197. Division for Library Services. Bernard Franckowiak, School Library Supervisor. Editor, Jane Billings. Madison, 1970. Single copies: $.50 each.

Audiovisual Materials

Beginning Library Skills. John W. Gunter, Inc. 1027 South Claremont Street, San Mateo, California, 26 charts, 17″ x 22″, spiral binder. Coronet Films, Coronet Building, 65 East South Water Street, Chicago, Illinois 60601. Each of the following is a 16mm film, available in either black and white or color.

Book Is to Care For.

Know Your Library.

You'll Find it in the Library.

Your Study Skills: Using Reference Materials.

DANES, MARGARET F., and ELIZABETH W. KOENIG. *Library Learning Laboratory Series.* New York: Fordham Publishing Company, 1972.

Libraries Are For Children. Program includes manual, transparencies, set of book spines, spirit duplication manual, posters, and book marks for grades 4 through 6.

Stepping Stones. A guide and duplicating manual for teaching grades kindergarten through 3rd grade.

Seeking and Finding. Program includes transparencies, posters, charts, sound filmstrip, film, slides, and record.

(Address: Fordham Equipment Company, 2377 Hoffman Street, Bronx, New York 10458.

Getting to Know the Library. 1 cassette tape, grades K-3. Troll Associates, 320 Rt. 17, Mahwah, New Jersey 07430.

Looking up Facts and Information. 1 filmstrip, grades 3-6.

Taking a Trip with a Book. 1 filmstrip, grades 1-5.

Using Reference Materials. 1 filmstrip, grades 2-6.

Visit to the Library. 1 filmstrip, grades K-2.

How Materials are Classified. Nifty Division, St. Regis Paper Company, Instructional Materials Consultants, Birmingham, Alabama or Houston, Texas. 12 charts, each 24″ x 36″, grades K-4.

How to Find a Book in a Library. Dewey Decimal System, #1 and #2. Wollensak Teaching Tapes, Mincom Division 3M Company, 3M Center, St. Paul, Minnesota 55101. Cassette tapes.

Introduction to the Library. Warren Schloat Productions, Inc., Pleasantville, New York 10570. 4 filmstrips, 4 recordings, primary grades.

Library Instruction. Tecnifax Education Division, Holyoke, Massachusetts 01040. 26 transparencies.

Library Reference Skills and Advanced Reference Skills. Flipatron Book; 5-section program in 40 transparencies each. Encyclopaedia Britannica Educational Corporation, 425 North Michigan Avenue, Chicago, Illinois 60611.

Library Research Tools. 10 filmstrips. Eye Gate House, Inc., 146-01 Archer Avenue, Jamaica, New York 11435.

Library Services. 4 filmstrips.
Using the Library. 10 transparencies.

Library Science Projecto-Aid Transparencies. General Aniline and Film Corporation; distributed by Western Publishing Educational Services, 1220 Mound Avenue, Racine, Wisconsin 53404. 41 transparencies.

Library Skills. Ideal School Supply Company, 11000 South Lavergne Avenue, Oak Lawn, Illinois 60453. Worksheet masters, plus 18 charts and 18 transparencies.

Library Skills. Tapes Unlimited, 13113 Puritan Avenue, Detroit, Michigan 48227. 10 light-hearted tapes.

Library Tools Series. 6 filmstrips. McGraw-Hill Films, a Division of McGraw-Hill Book Company, 327 West 41st Street, New York, New York 10036.

School Library Series. 6 filmstrips.

Look-It-Up Skills with a Dictionary. Field Enterprises Educational Corporation, Merchandise Mart Plaza, Chicago, Illinois 60654. 12 transparencies and 3 booklets.

Look-It-Up Skills with an Encyclopedia.

Media Center. 6 sound filmstrips. Educational Services, Inc., P.O. Drawer 3130, Hueytown, Alabama 35020.

Media for Moppets. 6 sound filmstrips.

Use Your Library: for Better Grades and Fun Too! American Library Association, 50 East Huron, Chicago, Illinois 60611, 1959. 1 filmstrip, for junior and senior high schools.

Using the Elementary School Library. Society for Visual Education, Inc. 134 Diversey Parkway, Chicago, Illinois 60614. Six sets of filmstrips and recordings.

Using the Library. Colonial Films, Inc., 752 Spring Street, N.W., Atlanta, Georgia 30308. Four sets of transparencies.

Using the Library. DCA Educational Products, Inc., 4865 Stenton Avenue, Philadelphia, Pennsylvania 19144. 10 transparencies.

Using the Library. Encyclopaedia Britannica Educational Corporation, 425 North Michigan Avenue, Chicago, Illinois 60611. 6 filmstrips.

Using Your Library. Instructor Publications, Inc., Instructor Park, Dansville, New York 14437. 32 posters, elementary grades.

Media personnel responsible for this area of instruction should be constantly alert for new materials which are being developed for use with students to be sure they are using the most contemporary and effective materials available. Many persons become so interested in this field of instruction that they work to develop their own creative teaching materials (see Chapter 12). These self-produced materials have the added advantage of relating most specifically to the situation, to the materials and facilities available locally and to the user's needs.

The scheduling of these learning programs must be flexible and adapted to the users' needs. Foremost in consideration is that no matter what the instructional level, these skills must be taught when the learner has specific need for using them. Insofar as possible they should be taught when the student has a pressing need for specific information and learns the skills as a means of locating that which he needs. Experience and research support the fact that location skills learned under these conditions are retained much longer than those learned without being related to specific needs.

One major advantage of using audio and visual teaching materials is that in many instances they can be developed as a self-instructional unit or package, so that students can use them when most appropriate for their needs, can use them at their own pace, and can repeat the instruction at any time.

Locating materials is a term that can be interpreted at many different levels of sophistication. Up to this point the focus of attention has been on locating diverse types of formats, such as books, films, filmstrips, audiotapes, etc. Other plans for organizing collections are described as classification schemes such as Dewey Decimal Classification Schedules, the Library of Congress classification code, and simply, accession number. To understand the complexities and intricacies of these systems requires both study and experience in locating materials. In addition, there are numerous other locating devices such as indexes, guides to periodicals, abstracts, and digests, that need to be learned if the user expects to locate information with any degree of specificity.

Another approach to locating information is through the subject content. The user needs to learn to use a thesaurus, the card catalog and subject headings, such as those used in vertical files. With the increased use of the computer for accessing data bases, it is reasonable to expect that in the foreseeable future, students may need to develop competency in the use of the computer for the purpose of retrieving information. For information related to the organization of materials for retrieval purposes see Chapter 10.

RESOURCES: INSTRUCTING INDIVIDUALS IN USE OF MEDIA

Paradoxically, this competency deals with developing learning programs to teach students the locating skills, however the competency is in actuality based on how well the media center personnel know these skills themselves. Having a thorough background in locating information gives the person who is providing the instruction a breadth of knowledge to develop teaching materials and to develop innovative teaching approaches, all based on his or her own knowledge and the use of these locating skills. Part of this knowledge will be gained through course work, particularly courses in librarianship such as Organization of Knowledge, Information Retrieval, and Media Center Administration. Another part of the knowledge must be acquired through continuous personal use of these locating skills. Another avenue for developing the competency is to work closely with other persons in your own school or other schools who have developed effective learning programs. Carefully following the development of commercially produced learning materials is also helpful, as they indicate new trends and innovative approaches to teaching these skills.

MASTERY ITEM: INSTRUCTING INDIVIDUALS IN USE OF MEDIA

Make an outline for teaching a seventh grade class how to use the media center. The class would be held in the Media Center and be team taught by the teacher and the Director of the Media Center. It would be scheduled for one hour each week.

Response: Instructing Individuals in Use of Media

Weeks 1 and 2   An orientation to the general location of areas (such as the circulation desk), materials and equipment. A discussion of procedures.

Weeks 3 and 4   Demonstration of how to use equipment such as slide projectors, tape recorders and film projectors.

Weeks 5 and 6   Individual practice operating equipment.

Weeks 7 and 8   Demonstration of production techniques such as how to make transparencies with individual practice.

COMPETENCY 5   Communicates with producers and publishers regarding materials and equipment.

In a forecasting study instrument which was distributed from the University of Texas at Austin, several of the checklist items read as follows:

Indicate the date on which you expect the following activity will be accepted and operational:

Commercially prepared prepackaged materials are validated and purchasers are supplied with full validation information.

On-demand publishing produces textbooks which teachers design for individual pupils. These may be in the form of pamphlets, single chapters, microforms, audiotapes, loose leaf pages, etc.

The content of the data base from which on-demand publishing is done is determined by curriculum specialists and teachers rather than by publishers.

Teachers use on-line data bases to identify optimum combinations of materials and methods suited to particular pupil's needs.

Cost-effectiveness data are supplied for all commercially prepared learning materials.

Pupil learning measured in quantifiable terms provides the data used in determining the efficiency and cost effectiveness of a given instructional program.[6]

Even though this is a forecasting survey based on opinion it does give evidence that educators are thinking in terms of accountability and of closer

---

[6] Billie Grace Herring, "Questionnaire on Factors Affecting Media Related Competencies for Teachers" (Austin, Texas: The University of Texas at Austin, May, 1974).

association between publishers, producers, and school personnel. Visionary educators are obviously thinking about cost effectiveness and identifying alternatives whereby the communication and cooperation with publishers and producers can be enhanced to produce improved learning materials.

To get back to current reality, everyone is aware that publishers and producers are in business for a profit. Most educators would probably agree that publishers and producers do have conscientious concern for quality education, and have the best interests of students in mind. For them to design and publish materials that are of the finest quality they must, for the most part, depend on input from teachers and media center personnel. They must know how students respond to the materials, whether the language is appropriate, whether illustrations are clear, whether the materials are substantial in their physical attributes and can withstand wear. Likewise manufacturers of equipment need to be informed about performance aspects of the equipment; parts that are not substantial, difficulty in replacing parts (such as, projector bulbs), if the equipment damages the software (such as filmstrips); the convenience of use; and the ease of transporting it (if appropriate). All of these aspects are important as producers, publishers, and manufacturers work cooperatively with educators to develop learning materials and equipment most effective in reaching educational goals.

The question arises as to how these communication channels can be kept open. The most obvious answer is to become acquainted with the sales representatives of the various companies. They are usually extremely well-informed about all aspects of their publications or products and are also aware of the new developments and trends. In addition, they are usually receptive to listening to the reactions and feedback they receive from students, teachers, and media personnel.

The Educational Products Information Exchange (EPIE) serves as a consumer's organization for educators. They routinely report on the good and the bad aspects of educational products and offer, through a feedback form in each monthly newsletter, an opportunity for users to express their observations and problems which, in turn, are relayed to the appropriate producer or manufacturer.

It is also recommended that ideas of real importance be conveyed to officials of a company. For example, ideas for new films might well be communicated to a vice-president of a film company.

As noted in the forecasting survey, visionary educators are at least thinking in terms of materials designed to meet individual student characteristics and needs, and this goal cannot possibly come about without close communication among all parties involved. This also relates very closely to the role which students play in evaluation as discussed in Chapter 14.

One final comment is essential in this section—and that is to justify the inclusion of this competency under the function "Instruction." The justification is that the producers, publishers, and manufacturers really need to be informed about the strengths and weakness of their products. This becomes vitally important when they begin to modify the product in response to the needs of the user.

RESOURCES: COMMUNICATING WITH PRODUCERS AND PUBLISHERS

Experience combined with practice is of great importance here. Some approaches that would be helpful are: build up a resource file of catalogs of publishers, producers, and manufacturers so that you will be familiar with their names and products; build up a resource file of names, addresses and phone numbers of sales representatives and company officials so that they can be contacted readily; build up a resource file of commentary and notes so that when requests are made for this type of information, it is available.

Part of the difficulty in identifying the means for gaining this competency is that, in the past, communication with producers and manufacturers has been done so informally and (one might also add) haphazardly that it is difficult to be more specific at this time. This responsibility must be looked on as one which is beginning to take on increasing importance and one area that new media personnel will have to develop and improve.

There are certain established unbiased assessments of equipment which give very pragmatic feedback to producers. One of these is (EPIE) the Educational Products Information Exchange and another is *Previews*. It is imperative that media personnel read the evaluations in the publications on a continuing basis to keep up-to date and to learn the criteria on which these evaluations are made.

MASTERY ITEM: COMMUNICATING WITH PRODUCERS AND PUBLISHERS

In order to communicate with producers and publishers you must be able to locate their addresses. List five sources from which you could locate producers, publishers, or their representatives.

Response: Communicating with Producers and Publishers

1. Look in the yellow pages of the telephone directory of the largest city close to you under the following headings:

   Audiovisual equipment and supplies

Book dealers

Motion Picture—Consultants, Equipment, Film Distributors and Exchange, Film Editing, Film Producers

Photo Finishers

Slides and Filmstrips

2. *Books In Print* (New York: Bowker, 1948-).
3. *Audio-Visual Equipment Directory: A Guide to Current Models of Audio-Visual Equipment* (Fairfax, Virginia: National Audio-Visual Association, 1953-   )
4. *Audio-Visual Marketplace: A Multimedia Guide.* (New York, Bowker, 1969-   )
5. James W. Brown, ed. *Educational Media Yearbook,* 1973. (New York: Bowker, 1973-   ).

COMPETENCY 6   Establishes regular communication channels between media center personnel and users.

This competency is one of the most important, but one of the most difficult to describe and prescribe in detail. Much of a person's success in this competency depends on his or her ability to communicate using a multitude of informal communication channels in addition to formal ones. For optimum effectiveness in running a program and in the utilization of staff, communications must be clear and continuous. Media center personnel must be carefully and thoroughly informed about their job responsibilities, about daily schedules or changes, committee responsibilities, special seasonal programs, new material and equipment, school routines and all other information necessary to keep the center functioning effectively. Many alternatives are available for establishing these communications channels. The style of the person communicating, the means which prove successful, and the situation, determine the mode or means. Some of the more common procedures that have worked are preparing a handbook or manual of procedures, supplementing this with frequent memoranda, newsletters, bulletin board notices, individual conferences, staff meeting, and daily announcements on the intercom. All of these are acceptable and have been used in various combinations. Media professionals who know their staff and are sensitive to their preferences will most likely be able to use these methods but also will be able to develop creative and innovative approaches.

To communicate with the users of the center poses similar problems and calls for similar solutions. However, the complexities of communicating with all users is even more demanding. All of the previously mentioned modes of communication should be used and additional ones are needed.

The users of the media center are mainly students, teachers and administrators; however, greater efforts are being made to serve clients in the community. Each client group has special interests and by necessity has to be reached through different communications channels. The users within the school can be contacted through in-school newspapers, memos, newsletters, and intercom announcements.

Media center personnel must familiarize themselves with the means of communication used in the community, such as newspapers, advertising circulars, radio broadcasts, neighborhood action group newsletters, P.T.A. newsletters, service club newsletters, community bulletin boards, television announcements and cable television opportunities. All of these modes of communication need to be explored to find the best combination to convey information to users and potential users of the center.

RESOURCES: ESTABLISHING COMMUNICATION CHANNELS

Educational background in communications and journalism would be helpful. In addition, knowledge of the community is extremely important. Determination of what means of communication are most effective usually comes about through trying several approaches and constantly striving to improve all communication. Some centers find that holding book fairs, open houses, demonstrations, teas, or other social events serve to attract users. Special displays also serve this purpose. All approaches would not work equally well in each community, so careful planning and careful assessment of effectiveness are necessary.

MASTERY ITEM: ESTABLISHING COMMUNICATION CHANNELS

List persons you could contact in most any community whom you could work with to develop a communications network to disseminate information about the media center.

Response: Establishing Communication Channels

1. The principal of your school to coordinate announcements on the school intercom and news bulletin to teachers and students.
2. The editor of the school newspaper.
3. The editor or appropriate department manager of the daily newspaper.
4. The manager or director of the television stations.
5. The manager or director of the radio stations.

6. The editors of all civic group newsletters such as Optimists, Rotary, Lions Club.
7. Be aware of professional journals that accept articles about innovative practices you have implemented.

REFERENCES

Competency 1   Plans and implements a public relations program.

BOMAR, CORA PAUL. *Guide to the Development of Educational Media Selection Centers,* pp. 43-45. Chicago, Illinois: American Library Association, 1973.
ERICKSON, CARLETON W. H. *Administering Instructional Media Programs,* pp. 584-97. New York: Macmillan, 1968.

Competency 2   Conducts in-service media training for teachers.

BOMAR, CORA PAUL. *Guide to the Development of Educational Media Selection Centers,* pp. 34-39. Chicago, Illinois: American Library Association, 1973.
DAVIES, RUTH ANN. *The School Library Media Center; A Force For Educational Excellence* (2nd ed.) pp. 33-43. New York: R. R. Bowker and Co., 1974.
Media Programs: District and School, pp. 137-141. Chicago, Illinois: American Library Association and Washington, D.C.: Association for Educational Communications and Technology, 1974.

Competency 3   Provides information about media program to administrators and school board.

Competency 4   Develops learning programs to assist individuals in using media center materials and equipment.

BRADSHAW, CHARLES. *Using the Library: The Card Catalog.* Provo, Utah: Brigham Young University Press, 1971.
Booklist. "Library Media Center Skills." Chicago: American Library Association, May 15, 1972. (Available by ordering through American Library Association.)
HOPKINSON, SHIRLEY L., *Instructional Materials for Teaching the Use of the Library.* San Jose, California: Claremont House, 1971.

Competency 5   Communicates with producers and publishers regarding materials and equipment.

Competency 6   Establishes regular communication channels between media center personnel and users.

14 The Evaluation Function

To be of optimum value, the collection in a media center must be matched as closely as possible to the needs of the users. Evaluation is one way of achieving this objective. This chapter explores the many facets of evaluation and the competencies needed to develop evaluation skills. The increasing focus on evaluation as related to accountability is emphasized.

During the early stages in the development of school libraries, books were extremely limited so libraries accepted and added books of any kind to their collections. This was done without regard to their relationship to the needs of the users. As books became relatively less expensive, as paperbacks became popular, and as attention was focused on the abilities and interests of students, increasing care began to be paid to the selection and evaluation of materials. Individualization of instruction is becoming a dominant approach in education and a corollary to this approach is that appropriate materials are needed to match each student's specific needs. Because media personnel have primary responsibility for acquiring and supplying materials, it becomes an appropriate task for them to select and evaluate a variety of materials.

The major emphasis in this chapter will be on the function called *evaluation;* however, evaluation will be interpreted to include selection. The definition of evaluation used here is "to examine and judge the worth, quality, and significance of specific media and programs of instruction." To select means "to choose."

It could be said that, traditionally, librarians have focused much attention on the selection of materials and on the development of selection tools. Audiovisual specialists have stressed the values of previewing materials. These

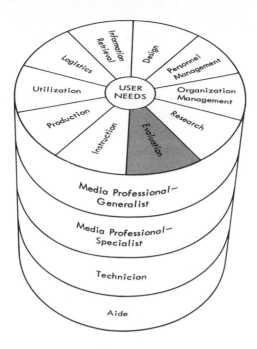

Information Retrieval
Design
Logistics
Personnel Management
Utilization
USER NEEDS
Organization Management
Production
Research
Instruction
Evaluation

Media Professional—Generalist

Media Professional—Specialist

Technician

Aide

COMPETENCY 1   Analyzes present and future curriculum require-ments to identify material and equipment needs.

COMPETENCY 2   Writes and applies criteria and guidelines for the selection, use and evaluation of materials.

COMPETENCY 3   Synthesizes teacher and student requests and rec-ommendations for acquiring materials.

COMPETENCY 4   Collects and uses review and evaluation tools to aid in selection.

---

traditional approaches each have value and have made a contribution. But in the contemporary educational scene, these approaches are not enough. Evaluation is comprised of many steps and can be interpreted as occuring along a continuum. (See Figure 14-1.)

First, materials must be identified according to criteria which have been developed for that purpose. Those materials must be appropriate to the geographic area, the community, the culture, the economic demands, the school, and the interests, needs, and abilities of the students. This identification leads to the *selection* process.

EVALUATION PROCESS

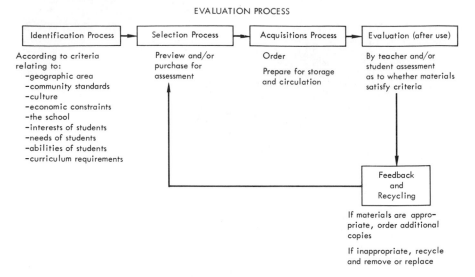

Figure 14-1   **The Evaluation Continuum**

After the materials have been selected, ordered, and have become a part of the collection of a media center, a next step in the process takes place when each teacher makes an assessment of the materials to determine which would be most appropriate for use in the teaching/learning process for a specific unit, and for a particular learning task within that unit. In most cases, assessment of special materials for use by individual students requires even more stringent evaluation.

To complete the process, a further step in evaluation is required after the materials have been used. It is at this time that a most critical *assessment* must be made to determine what impact these materials have had on learning. There should be an assessment as to the appropriateness of the media format, the match of the material to the student's interest, needs, and ability, and the effect the material had in motivating the student.

The total process includes cooperative interaction among teachers, students and the media center personnel. Many school districts and commercial firms have developed evaluation forms which can be used at different stages in the evaluation process. Examples of these evaluation forms can be found in Appendix A.

Persons serving as media center personnel are expected to be particularly able in the areas of selection and evaluation. They are responsible for acquiring, storing, and retrieving all varieties of materials. In performing these tasks they must use references, indexes and lists that aid them in performing efficiently. An important facet of their professional role is the handling of materials. Another facet is to know the users and what their information needs are. To bring these two together—the users and the materials needed—is a major objective of the program. Selection and evaluation are important components of achieving this goal effectively.

Many readers might expect to find *the evaluation of the overall media program* as a part of this chapter. The assessment of how adequately the entire program is meeting the stated objectives is a task that falls into the organization management function, and is considered in Chapter 7.

Selection and evaluation are fundamentally important to the success of the entire media program. Each of the competencies comprising this function is very closely related to the other competencies. In addition, they are all closely tied to understanding people and being perceptive about fulfilling needs. For these reasons, this introductory section will present a general coverage of means for gaining evaluation competencies which serve for all competencies in this chapter.

Selection and evaluation involve matching materials to people. To do this, obviously one has to know both the materials and the people. Let's consider the people "component" first. How can media personnel develop the skill of understanding the user well enough to fulfill his or her information needs? This is a complex and probably lifelong task. As preparation, college courses would certainly be essential. It would be expected that the media professional would understand the user from a great many viewpoints. For example, it would be important to understand the user psychologically, emotionally, physiologically and sociologically. To provide background for these understandings it would be helpful to have taken courses such as child psychology, adolescent psychology, physiology, human growth and development, educational psychology, communications, group dynamics, and human relationships. Another facet necessary for understanding the needs of the user is to have a thorough knowledge of curriculum, curriculum development, learning theory, and teaching methodology. College courses in these areas form the foundation for developing such understanding, but continuous work in curriculum development is essential. It would probably be correct to state that one never completes his or her learning in the area of understanding the user, primarily because each user is an individual and is somewhat different from every other user. Even though the general characteristics of students are constantly changing, a similar statement could be made with respect to curriculum. It is virtually impossible for a media professional to be totally familiar with all details of each subject area. However, it is possible to gain a broad overview of scope and sequence of each subject area through college course work in curriculum. Further knowledge can be readily gained on the job by working closely with teachers, by cooperating in developing units, by visiting classrooms, and by working continuously with students as they progress through each unit of study during the school year. What are some of the things that it might be helpful to know about the student as a user of the materials? Student profiles which contain information listed below, could be developed. While it might be difficult to obtain this extensive information, it would be of value in matching users and appropriate materials.

Age

Sex

I. Q.

Reading ability

Test scores

Assessment of creativity

Health: Hearing, vision, physical disabilities

Special interests

Hobbies

Language fluency

Socioeconomic information

Home conditions: rural or urban

Progress in discrete subject areas

Mental health

Physical coordination

Optimum mode of learning: Kinesthetic, Aural, Visual

Style of learning: Rapid, deliberate, structured or flexible, guided or self-initiated

Vocational interests

Visual literacy

What would be important to know about the teacher as the user of materials?

Courses taught

Teaching methods used: Lecture, discussion, role playing

Assignments given

Class schedules of field trips

Examinations: Type, schedule

Materials requested to put on reserve

Objectives of courses

Kinds of materials preferred for class use

Kinds of materials preferred for individual student use

Physical facilities in which class is to be taught: How well these facilities accommodate the use of audio and visual equipment and materials

Openness to consider the use of new media

Selection and evaluation require a complex mix of skill, attitudes, and knowledge. Of primary importance is an attitude of helpfulness to the teacher and learner. The media professional must convey a willingness to be of help or the process of selection and evaluation cannot function. Rapport with the teacher and/or the student must be established to supply effectively and accurately the materials and services which will be of optimum use to them.

Next, there has to be a "perceptiveness." The person who is doing the selecting must be alert to pick up all varieties of clues which will assist in this process. Most persons expect that requests for materials and order information related to such requests will be clearly stated in verbal transactions, or through written memoranda. This is not necessarily the case. In many instances the teacher and/or students do not know exactly what it is they want and it is up to the media professional to be perceptive enough to decipher all possible clues that will indicate these needs. This information may have to be acquired through informal conversations, through observations of the teacher's and students' activities in the classroom and in special projects.

In addition, the media professional needs to be imaginative in thinking of innovative approaches to the teaching/learning process and in identifying materials which will facilitate these strategies. Several professional journals give help in developing such ideas. One example is *Learning Resources* published by the Association for Educational Communication and Technology, a publication devoted to helping the teacher develop and utilize media.

Underlying all evaluation efforts must be an attitude of flexibility. Both students and teachers will inevitably change or modify their objectives as a unit of learning proceeds and the media professional will have to be able to adapt to these changes in direction and be of some help in facilitating such changes.

The attitudes of helpfulness and flexibility must permeate all relationships. For some persons, these attitudes are already well developed; however, others will have to work diligently to nourish them. How? First of all, these attitudes can be developed by being constantly aware of their importance and by practicing these attitudes continuously. A further step is working with others who possess these skills, observing their behavior, and attempting to emulate their successful relationships with others. Third, it is possible that progress could be made through personal involvement in sensitivity training sessions, and group therapy sessions. Course work in group dynamics, human relations, and communications would be helpful. There is the need to understand the user and to have a thorough knowledge of the curriculum. In addition, it is necessary to know resources, such as references, indexes and lists which provide the bibliographic information that is needed for locating and ordering materials. Another aspect is to be familiar with evaluation techniques and evaluation forms to perform the assessment role.

One means of acquiring these competencies is to take courses in librarianship and in educational technology which might be entitled "Material Selection," "Selection and Evaluation," "Selection of Print and Non-Print Materials," "Film Evaluation," "Instructional Materials," or other courses similar in title and content.

Another means of acquiring the competency would be to work closely with a media professional who is skilled in performing these selection and evaluation tasks. Examples of places to acquire these competencies would be in large city or county systems where selection and evaluation processes have been carefully developed. Specific examples of such school systems would be the Montgomery County school system in Maryland and the Los Angeles County school system in California.

Whether the competencies are acquired through course work or on-the-job training it is vitally important to keep up-to-date on the developments in the area of selection and evaluation through the reading of current books and articles in professional journals.

An example of a publication representing the concern of educators for media selection and evaluation was developed by the National Association of Secondary School Principals. This brief publication offers suggestions for establishing the selection committees, establishing criteria, reviewing the process, case studies, and bibliographies. The Executive Secretary of NASSP states, "Instructional materials are an educator's tools. . . . Selecting instructional materials, always an important task, has become increasingly difficult as more and more materials have become available. *Sharper Tools for Better Learning* acknowledges this difficulty and provides valuable information to the administrator searching for ways to improve the selection process.[1]

COMPETENCY 1   Analyzes present and future curriculum requirements to identify material and equipment needs.

Historically, certain factors have had an influence on the selection process. Some of these important factors have been the laws relating to educational responsibility, the changing curriculum, the change in the teaching/learning process, the role of the textbook, the development of audio and visual materials and the influence of the publication and production industry.

It is essential to understand the legal aspects of the selection of materials, as decisions about the purchase of materials oftentimes fall under legal regulations because they involve expenditure of public funds. Under the U. S. Con-

---

[1] *Sharper Tools for Better Learning* (Reston, Virginia: National Association of Secondary School Principals, 1973) p. v.

stitution, states have the right to regulate education within their borders and state legislatures have delegated their responsibilities to state and local boards of education. In most states legal procedures established by boards of education at both the state and district level have distinguished between textbooks and supplementary materials. In other words, many states have established regulations for the adoption of textbooks at the state and district level. They may also provide guidelines for the purchase of supplementary material, however these regulations are usually not nearly so stringent. For example, state departments of education may develop lists of recommended supplementary materials, but will not usually prohibit the purchase of other materials. The media professional will not normally be expected to take the initiative in the selection of textbooks in geographic areas where there is a legally established textbooks adoption procedure. However, it is important to be informed about this process, as the media professional may play an important role on the selection committee. To acquire information about state selection policies, hold discussions with the district supervisor of media services, the assistant superintendent of instruction, curriculum supervisor or contact the state department of education.

Historically, it has been common practice to select one textbook for a course and this decision essentially determined the content of the course, the methodology, the objectives, and the examinations. Supplementary materials, even as limited as other textbooks, were seldom used. Unfortunately, some schools still function according to this pattern today.

In most school systems there have been either evolutionary or revolutionary changes in the curriculum and in the teaching-learning process. There is a definite movement away from self-contained classrooms which are teacher dominated. The focus of attention is moving more and more toward the individual student and his needs, and away from the subject-centered curriculum.

Concomitant with these changes has been the development of a tremendous diversity of audio and visual materials. It seems fortuitous that just at the time when attention is focused on the needs of the individual student, there should be the developments which facilitate this individualization. Such examples as single concept films, computer-assisted instruction and the entire range of audiovisual materials can be geared to individual learning styles and interests. It is in this area of materials, both print and audiovisual, which are used in addition to, or in lieu of the traditional textbook that the demanding selection-evaluation process takes place.

A factor which cannot be overlooked is the role that is played by industry—the publication and production companies. While these companies must be knowledgeable and up-to-date on developments in curriculum, they also develop products which are financially rewarding. Much of their resources are spent on advertising. Sometimes promotion of certain products can be very misleading. Persons involved in selection and evaluation must be aware that advertising information can be valuable at times but misleading at other times. Alertness and experience are necessary to be able to interpret the advertising and not make erroneous decisions.

RESOURCES: IDENTIFYING MATERIAL AND EQUIPMENT NEEDS

This competency involves many activities. Some of these activities may have been established in the school system in which you are employed or you may have to initiate others. These activities may include the following:

(1) Requesting an overview of all courses taught. This information could be acquired through requesting a course outline, syllabus or project description from the central office for each course or unit taught. If these are not on file you may have to request them from individual teachers.

(2) Serving on curriculum development committees. Oftentimes all teachers in a department in a high school, or a team of teachers in elementary schools form committees to plan an entire curriculum, or a unit within the curriculum. A media professional can be of most assistance if he or she is involved in the initial planning, helps in determining teacher and student objectives, and identifies preliminary types of materials that are available and appropriate.

(3) Developing forms and procedures for requesting materials. This provides a mechanism for teachers and students to easily request materials which they wish to use.

(4) Informing all users that materials may be acquired through a diversity of ways, by rental, purchase, interlibrary loan, as gifts, exchanges, or free. Users should be encouraged to consider all alternatives in their planning.

The text by Brown, Norberg, and Srygley, listed in the bibliography, will provide background information for this competency. This work includes a comprehensive overview of textbook selection and evaluation. It presents a historical perspective in the section on trends in use and development, delineates textbook selection policies, describes selection at the state and local level, and gives textbook evaluation criteria. This is important background reading that is not readily available elsewhere.

MASTERY ITEM: IDENTIFYING MATERIAL AND EQUIPMENT NEEDS

List five activities you could engage in that would help you to determine curriculum requirements for new materials.

Response: *Identifying Material and Equipment Needs*

1. Serve as a member of the curriculum development team.
2. Ask the teacher's permission to visit classes to determine if there are ways the media center could provide appropriate materials to help the teacher.
3. Request outlines of units to be taught and then analyze these to determine materials which would be appropriate.
4. Develop a team of student aides who could take appropriate materials and equipment into class rooms.
5. Have both formally scheduled and informal discussion with teachers to assess their needs.

COMPETENCY 2   Writes and applies criteria and guidelines for the selection, use and evaluation of materials.

All aspects of the selection/evaluation process are so closely integrated that it is difficult to separate one from the other. It is a circular or feedback process. Criteria for selection are established, the material is then used by teachers and students in the teaching/learning process. The evaluation process pervades the entire period of use from assessing the appropriateness of selection through the consideration of the alternatives which might accomplish the same objectives more effectively or at less cost.

Evaluation is one of the major responsibilities and one of the most important tasks performed by media professionals. Evaluation determines the quality of materials selected and this in turn determines the adequacy of the materials made available to the users. Media professionals must actually participate in the evaluation process and must also take responsibility for establishing an ongoing evaluation program.

Evaluation must be based on the criteria established for selection. If these criteria are not appropriate or sufficiently inclusive, then the selection criteria should be adapted, expanded or changed.

Some of the criteria generally used for evaluation are the following:

Authority and competence of author or producer
Clarity and accuracy of presentation
Scope of the presentation
Accuracy, objectivity and up-to-dateness
Organization and presentation of contents
Quality of format
Value commensurate with cost and/or need
Potential usefulness

Additional criteria that may be used for leisure materials are:

Originality
Coherence
Sustained interest
Sympathy and conviction
Consistency of characterization

The evaluation process can take place in a number of ways, but the media professional should work closely with the students, faculty, and administration to establish a consistent and comprehensive system of evaluation. Evaluation can be done by individuals, both students and faculty, by informal groups who have used certain materials, and by more formally established evaluation committees. These committees should be comprised of both faculty and students.

A practice that works with reasonable success in many school districts is to develop evaluation forms. Some schools use one form which is adaptable to all kinds of materials, while other schools use different evaluation forms for different types of media. Examples of such evaluation forms will be found in Appendix A.

A basic requirement in the selection process is to develop a written selection policy. The media professional will need to assume the responsibility for leadership in the development of this policy statement, but representatives of students, parents, faculty, and administration should serve as members of the committee which works to develop the policy. A materials selection policy must be clearly and succinctly stated to provide readily understood guidelines for selection. It must be consistent with the official policies of the school system and the individual school. The purpose for having such a policy is to provide an efficient means of selecting and acquiring materials which will assist the school to adequately reach its teaching/learning goals. A related purpose is to provide viable and defensible guidelines for reassessing materials which have been challenged as being inappropriate. Some materials have been questioned on grounds of political, religious, and sexual connotations.

The publication, *Media Programs: District and School* places great emphasis on the selection. The following guiding principles are stated:

1. Every school, regardless of size, has its own collection of materials and equipment. This collection, which is organized and ready for use when the school opens, is developed and expanded on a planned basis.

2. The district provides collections of materials and equipment such as 16mm films, professional materials, and examination collections of new materials, to supplement collections in the individual schools.

3. Selection of collections is guided by a selection policy formulated by media staff, administrators, consultants, teachers, students, and representative citizens, and adopted by the board of education. The district policy is supplemented by selection and acquisitions guidelines formulated by individual schools within the district.

4. Selection of materials is a cooperative process involving the media staff, curriculum consultants, teachers, students, and community representatives, and is coordinated by the director of the district media program and the head of the school media program respectively.

5. Materials and equipment are evaluated prior to purchase by use of reliable evaluative selection tools and by firsthand examination, wherever possible.

6. Collections are reevaluated continuously to insure that they remain current and responsive to user needs.

7. Organization and arrangement make the collection easily accessible to users.

8. Materials in print, visual, auditory, and tactile formats, with associated equipment constitute the collection.

9. Collections include textbooks and related instructional materials and systems.

10. Current professional materials for faculty and staff use are a part of the collection.[2]

It is important to note that all of these processes and procedures are developed to achieve one goal which is to develop a collection of materials that will be adequate enough to guarantee satisfaction of user needs. Media professionals must be concerned with developing collections at the school level, at the district level, at the multi-district level and developing professional collections for administrators, faculty, and other media staff.

Media Programs: District and School presents comprehensive and contemporary guidelines as a resource with which you can check as you develop your collection.[3] This publication describes both basic collections in the school and extended provisions. Collections are described both qualitatively and quantitatively by the following categories: print materials; books, periodicals, newspapers, pamphlets and microforms; visual materials; still images, visual materials, moving images; auditory formats; tactile formats; and instructional systems including textbooks. Helpful guidelines are also given for acquiring adequate equipment required for using the audio and visual materials.

---

[2] *Media Programs: District and School* (Chicago: American Library Association and Washington, D.C.: Association for Educational Communication and Technology, 1974), pp. 62-63.

[3] Ibid., pp. 66-86.

Formulation of a district media selection policy which guides the selection of materials and equipment is coordinated by the director of the district media program. This policy, developed cooperatively with representatives of media staff, administrators, consultants, teachers, students, and other community members, is adopted by the board of education as official district policy.

The media selection policy reflects basic factors influencing the nature and scope of collections, such as curriculum trends, innovations in instruction, research in learning, availability of materials and equipment, the increased sophistication of youth, and the rising expectations of teachers and students. It establishes the objectives of media selection, identifies personnel participating in selection and their roles; enumerates types of materials and equipment to be considered with criteria for their evaluation, as well as criteria for evaluating materials in specific subject areas; and defines procedures followed in selecting materials, including initial selection, reexamination of titles in existing collections, and handling challenged titles.

The selection policy reflects and supports principles of intellectual freedom described in the *Library Bill of Rights,*[4] the *School Library Bill of Rights for School Library Media Center Programs,*[5] *The Students' Right to Read,*[6] and other professional statements on intellectual freedom. Procedures for handling questioned materials follow established guidelines and are clearly defined.[7]

The district selection policy is supplemented by selection and acquisitions guidelines formulated by each school which provides more detailed and specific guidance for decision making in the ongoing selection process as it is applied to building and maintaining its collections.

The process of examining and evaluating materials and equipment being considered for purchase must be continuous and systematic. The district media program supports the selection process by providing examination collections of materials and equipment, arranging for released time for preview and examination of materials, and conducting an active evaluation program involving media personnel, teachers, other staff, and students. Published evaluations, including those in reviews, recommended lists, and standard bibliographic tools are used in selection. Materials and equipment within existing collections are monitored and examined continuously in order to replace worn items and to withdraw out-of-date and inappropriate items.

Examples of materials selection policies can be acquired by writing to

---

[4] *The Library Bill of Rights* was adopted by the Council of the American Library Association in 1948 and revised in 1967.

[5] The *School Library Bill of Rights for School Library Media Center Programs* was approved by the American Association of School Librarians in 1969.

[6] National Council of Teachers of English, *The Students' Right to Read* (Urbana, Ill.: National Council of Teachers of English, 1972).

[7] "Intellectual Freedom and School Libraries: An In-Depth Case Study," *School Media Quarterly,* I (Winter, 1973): 111-35.

most large city or county school systems. It is important to note that each policy statement should be developed to meet the needs of a specific school, that it should be formulated and endorsed by the school administration, the media professional, the faculty, and adopted by the school board.

In addition, it is necessary to formulate selection criteria. In some cases, the statement of criteria may be incorporated into the selection policy statement. In other cases, the selection criteria may be more closely related to other documents, such as, the statement of educational goals. Under any circumstances, there are certain general criteria which apply to all types of instructional materials which can serve as general guidelines. These include: appropriateness, authenticity, and interest.

In many cases it is not possible to purchase commercial audio and visual materials that precisely fit the needs of a teacher and/or student for a specific purpose. Another factor is time. Frequently the audio or visual materials are needed very quickly, and there is not time to locate and order appropriate materials. When materials are produced locally it is as important to evaluate them as it is to evaluate commercial materials. The authors believe that locally produced materials should be tested and evaluated according to the same criteria that are applied to commercially produced materials.

Paradoxically, there are no "along-the-way" opportunities for assessment of the success of the selection activity. The only true evaluation takes place when students and teachers use the materials selected in the teaching-learning process.

RESOURCES: APPLYING CRITERIA FOR SELECTION, USE, AND EVALUATION

How can this competency be learned? Certainly, continuous involvement in the activity is most helpful; working with selection committees, conferring with teachers and students about their interests and needs, keeping careful records of student profiles, and working with persons skilled in selection techniques are all developmental activities.

Readings that provide information and background are those listed in the bibliography by Erickson; Hicks and Tillin; and Davies. Chapter 9 in Brown, Norberg, and Srygley is succinct yet comprehensive in providing sound guidelines for developing selection policies and procedures. A variety of approaches for developing criteria is presented.

MASTERY ITEM: APPLYING CRITERIA FOR SELECTION, USE, AND EVALUATION

Write a selection policy for textbooks and other instructional materials that would be appropriate for use in your school.

Response: Applying Criteria for Selection, Use, and Evaluation

Materials selection policies must be written with great care, as they serve an extremely important function. To be comprehensive and to serve the diverse purposes for which they are intended, policies should contain these major parts: (1) A statement of the intellectual framework on which decisions are made. This section usually includes the following:

> Library Bill of Rights (Adopted June 18, 1946, and amended February 1, 1961, by the ALA Council)
> Statement on Labeling (Adopted July 13, 1951, by the ALA Council)
> School Library Bill of Rights (Adopted July 8, 1955, by the ALA Council)
> Freedom to Read Statement (Prepared by the Westchester Conference of ALA and the American Book Publishers Council, May 2-3, 1953)
> Policies and Procedures for Selection of School Library Materials (Approved by the AASL, February 3, 1961)

Copies of each of these can be obtained by writing the ALA, 50 East Huron Street, Chicago, Illinois.
(2) A definition of the role of those who share the responsibility for the selection of materials, including those who must assume legal responsibility for selection and those to whom selection has been delegated; (3) Criteria for selection and evaluation of materials; (4) An outline of the process to be used for applying the criteria; (5) A statement on the handling of problem materials including gifts and controversial subjects; (6) A means of communicating to the community the philosophy and procedures used in selecting and evaluating materials; (7) Provision of a procedure of reconsideration of materials if there are objections to the use of particular materials.

The following is a model of a materials selection policy and Figure 14-2 is a guide for developing a form to serve as a citizen's request for reconsideration of instructional material.

A MATERIALS SELECTION POLICY (MODEL)

Introduction and Statement of Purpose

In the education of children, to help them meet their optimum potential, a great diversity of print and audiovisual materials are essential if individual interests, needs, and abilities are to be met. All formats of information are the resources which are the basic tools needed for effective teaching and learning.

The purposes of this materials selection policy is:

1. To provide a statement of philosophy and objectives for the guidance of those involved in the procedures for selection.
2. To define the role of those who share in the responsibility for the selection of instructional materials.
3. To set forth criteria for selection and evaluation of materials.
4. To outline the techniques for the application of the criteria.
5. To clarify for the community the philosophy and procedures used in evaluating and selecting instructional materials.
6. To provide a procedure for the consideration of objections to the use of particular materials in the educational program.

Philosophy and Guidelines

It is the policy of this school district to establish procedures for selection and evaluation of materials that will:

1. Support and enrich all subjects of the curriculum, taking into consideration the varied interests, abilities, and maturity levels of the pupils served.
2. Present the many racial, ethnic, religious, and cultural groups and portray the role of their contribution in the development of America.
3. Give an extensive background of information and factual knowledge which will enable pupils to make intelligent judgments in their daily lives.
4. Support and be consistent with the objectives and goals of specific courses of study approved by the Board of Education.
5. Stimulate growth in knowledge, literary appreciation, aesthetic values, and ethical standards.
6. Present all aspects of social, economic, and political systems and issues so that students have practice, under guidance, in the processes of critical reading, thinking and evaluating—processes that undergird an informed citizen's part in the preservation of American institutions and ideals.
7. Offer the student an opportunity to develop an awareness of a social order which values freedom and allows for the fullest development of the individual.
8. Develop the lifelong habit of wide reading which fosters freedom in the exchange of ideas, a basic principle in the operation of democracy.

The selection of materials shall be guided by the philosophy and principles set forth in the following documents:

Library Bill of Rights (Adopted June 18, 1948, and amended February 1, 1961, by the ALA Council)

Statement on Labeling (Adopted July 13, 1951, by the ALA Council)

School Library Bill of Rights (Adopted July 8, 1955, by the ALA Council)

Freedom to Read Statement (Prepared by the Westchester Conference of ALA and the American Book Publishers Council, May 2-3, 1953)

Policies and Procedures for Selection of School Library Materials (Approved by the AASL, February 3, 1961)

(See last pages of the policy for copies of these documents.)

Responsibility

The responsibility for the acquisition of materials is legally vested in the Board of Education. The Board of Education delegates to the Media Center staff the responsibility to make final recommendations for purchase. It is expected that the librarian will work closely with the school staff, administrative personnel and students in the selection and evaluation of materials.

Procedure

Materials are to be ordered through the district Supervisor of Media's office. Purchases within an individual school should be distributed in such a way that balance in selection is maintained. The budget should allow for flexibility in purchasing print and/or nonprint materials.

Whenever possible both print and nonprint media are to be examined or previewed through exhibits, fairs, materials displays, or through selection meetings held in coordination with other districts, public libraries, or media centers.

If materials cannot be physically examined, selection should be based on reviews from recognized aids (such as those listed in the next section).

Criteria for Materials Selection

GENERAL CRITERIA

1. Needs of the individual school based on the knowledge of the curriculum, and the requests from staff and students.
2. Needs of the individual students based on a knowledge of children and youth and the requests of parents, teachers and students.
3. Provision of a wide range of materials on all levels of difficulty with a diversity of appeal and the presentation of different points of view.
4. Provision of materials of a high artistic and literary quality.

SPECIFIC CRITERIA FOR SELECTING MATERIALS

1. Authority and competence of author or producer
2. Clarity and accuracy of presentation
3. Scope of the presentation
4. Accuracy, objectivity and up-to-dateness
5. Organization and presentation of contents
6. Quality format
7. Value commensurate with cost and/or need
8. Potential usefulness

SPECIFIC CRITERIA FOR SELECTING LEISURE MATERIALS

1. Originality
2. Coherence
3. Sustained interest
4. Sympathy and conviction
5. Consistency of characterization

Basic Publications

Many aids are available to assist in the selection of materials. The following publication lists and describes such aids.

Aids to Media Selection for Students and Teachers. Washington, D.C.: U.S. Department of Health, Education, and Welfare, Office of Education, 1971.

In addition, each state may have guidelines and lists of selection tools recommended for use within the state.

The following are recommended in addition to those listed in the above publication:

Good Reading, rev. ed., by J. S. Weber, National Council of Teachers of English (NCTE), 1971.

I read, you read, we read . . . (culturally disadvantaged reader) American Library Association, 1971.

Index to black history studies, National Information Center for Educational Media (NICEM), 1971.

Index to ecology, NICEM, 1971.

Index to Educational Audio Tapes, NICEM, 1971.

Index to Educational Records, NICEM, 1971.

Index to Educational Video Tapes, NICEM, 1971.

Kane, Michard, *Minorities in textbooks:* a study of their treatment in Social Studies, Quadrangle, 1971.

Media and culturally different learner, National Education Association, 1971.

Resources for learning, core media collection for elementary schools. Bowker, 1971.

Sensitive Areas

1. In any pluralistic society, materials in a given media collection may be questioned or criticized by individuals or groups.
2. Some areas that may be questioned are: politics, religion, sex, profanity, and sex education. The previous selection criteria should be used in selecting materials for these sensitive areas.

Questioned Materials

If materials in a given school collection are questioned, they should be reviewed in an objective manner.

Because individual schools within the district may have different wants for their schools, any reviewing of questioned material should be handled on the local level. This will enable parents and teachers to choose what is best for their school. To achieve this, the following procedure is to be followed.

1. Questioner is invited to fill out the Request for Reconsideration of Materials Form which is given him by principal. (See Figure 14-2.) Forms can be obtained from Supervisor of Media Services.
2. Questioner returns completed form to principal.
3. Upon receipt of written request, the principal
   a. Discusses request with the director of the Media Center
   b. Selects an "ad hoc" reviewing committee, to be composed of the following persons: 3 parents, 2 teachers, school Media Center Director (Chairman), Supervisor of Media Services.
   c. In the meantime he/she has copies made of the request and sends one to the Associate Superintendent of Instruction and the Supervisor of Media Services. Additional copies would be made for distribution to members of the reviewing committee.
4. Media Center director temporarily removes item from circulation.
5. Within 30 days after the establishment of the review committee, it will submit its written review and recommendations regarding the material involved to the principal.
6. Within 10 days, the principal will prepare in writing the recommendation of the committee, and his subsequent action regarding the material. He will send copies of this to the Associate Superintendent of Instruction, the Supervisor of Media Services, and other members of the committee, and to the questioner.
7. Following the principal's decision about the handling of the material, the Media Center will either remove the material from circulation, put restrictions on its use, or put it back in circulation.
8. If the questioner is dissatisfied with the decision of the principal, he may appeal by writing to the Associate Superintendent of Instruction.

(Sections of this materials selection policy were adapted from policies of the Port Angeles, Washington; Jackson, New Jersey; Oakland, California and Arlington, Virginia selection policies.)

COMPETENCY 3   Synthesizes teacher and student requests and recommendations for acquiring materials.

Analogies are always less than precise, but several seem appropriate here. In the selection process, the media professional serves in some ways like a radar screen, picking up signals from every possible source. There has to be

Figure 14-2

CITIZEN'S REQUEST FOR RECONSIDERATION
OF INSTRUCTIONAL MATERIAL

Title _____

Author _____

Publisher (if known) _____

Request initiated by _____

Telephone _____ Address _____

_____
City   Zip

Complainant represents:

Himself _____ Name _____

Organization _____

Other (identify) _____

1. To what in the material do you object? (Please be specific; cite pages)
_____
_____

2. What do you feel might be the result of reading or viewing this material?
_____
_____

3. For what age group would you recommend this material? _____

4. Is there anything good about the material? _____

5. Did you read or view the entire item? _____ What parts? _____

6. Are you aware of the judgment of this material by literary critics? _____
_____

7. What do you believe is the theme of this material? _____
_____

8. What would you like your school to do about this material?

_____ do not assign it to my child.

_____ withdraw it from all students as well as from my child.

_____ send it back to the appropriate department for re-evaluation.

9. In its place, what material of equal literary quality would you recommend that would convey as valuable a picture and perspective of our civilization?
_____

Signature of Complainant

contact with formalized curriculum development committees as they plan courses and units, with formally structured materials selection committees, scheduled interviews with teachers and with students, and informal discussions about interests and needs related to materials. In addition, the antennae must always be alert to pick up clues in faculty meetings and in informal discussions in the faculty lounge or lunch room. Still another source of input are the new releases from publishers and producers.

A simple form should be developed, possibly on a 3″ by 5″ card, for a student or faculty member to use in submitting a request for materials. This card size is suggested, as it can be filed in catalog drawers. Careful records must be kept of all these requests. To be of greatest help in developing a final purchase, the cards should be filed in an organized way, possibly by subject or by the course in which they would be used, and cross-listed.

After these records are developed and the amount of the budget is known then it is necessary to synthesize all requests, assess them as to relative value to the users, and spend the available money in the wisest way. These decisions are not easy to make and require careful attention and sound judgment; they require many compromises and the weighing of many factors. Some questions to be asked are: How much material should be purchased for the slow learner? How many filmstrips should be purchased if they are more expensive than printed material containing similar information? How many duplicate copies of materials are needed? Should requests for highly sophisticated materials to be used by a small number of able students be honored? Budget is usually never adequate, so what priority shall be given to each request? There are no easy answers to any of these questions, but the questions are inevitably found in every media center, so they have to be faced each time selection of materials takes place. One important aspect of this step of the process is to be able to specify the factors on which the final decisions are based. This step is to assist the media professional so that decisions are not made quixotically, but with sound rationale.

RESOURCES: SYNTHESIZING REQUESTS FOR MATERIALS

Working with a knowledgeable person in the selection process is a helpful experience. A limited amount of guidance can be found in books providing general background, such as the text by Brown, Norberg, and Srygley that is listed in the bibliography. Relatively little, however, has been written on this aspect of selection. The one factor that must always be kept in mind is that selection skills must constantly be developed and continuously evaluated in light of the users' needs.

MASTERY ITEM: SYNTHESIZING REQUESTS FOR MATERIALS

Develop a form appropriate for students and faculty members to use to request materials.

Response: Synthesizing Requests for Materials

Author _____

Title _____

Format:	Check	Book _____	Transparency _____	Game _____
		Filmstrip _____	Kit _____	Slides _____
		Film _____	Videotape _____	Other _____

Publishing Company or Producer _____

To be used in what class? _____

To be used primarily with: Groups _____   Individuals _____

An Evaluative Review was found in _____

Date needed _____

Signature of person making request _____

Figure 14-3   A Sample Request Form

COMPETENCY 4   Collects and uses review and evaluation tools to aid in selection.

Ideally, the most effective review process would be for each teacher or the media professional who is going to use materials to read, view, or listen to the materials personally. Practical considerations of time, the unprecedented rise in numbers of materials produced, and the difficulty in acquiring materials for preview make this suggestion exceedingly difficult to implement. For these reasons, it is necessary for persons responsible for selection to turn to secondary sources for evaluation to help make selection judgments.

There are several steps in the selection process for which special information is required. First, the product must be identified correctly. Second, the order information must be complete; (title, producer or author, company which produced the material, address of company, price, identifying features such as sound, color, number of frames, etc.). Third, there should be evaluative reviews available, so that selection can be guided by the perceptions of skilled reviewers and critics.

RESOURCES: USING REVIEW AND EVALUATION TOOLS

The book field has over a long period of time developed relatively effective tools for assisting with all of these steps. It is necessary to have selection information that is current, as well as having information that is retrospective. Publications that provide current information are *American Book Publishing Record* and *Publishers' Weekly*. Others are retrospective in that they are published monthly or quarterly and then cumulated annually. (e.g. the *Cumulative Book Index*). Many publications publish evaluative book reviews. *Book Review Digest* is one publication which serves as a guide to evaluative reviews, by publishing compilations of the reviews and listing the sources of the original reviews. Up to the present time the selection tools have tended to separate book materials from audio and visual materials, though selection tools are being developed which deal with the entire range of media.

The problem has been that the audiovisual field is emerging so rapidly that the tools for locating and evaluating these materials is in an amorphous developmental state. Even though there are ongoing attempts to publish tools to identify the entire range of audiovisual materials, particularly materials being produced currently, the tools have not yet given complete nor retrospective coverage. To give retrospective mediagraphic coverage is an overwhelming problem. The most difficult area in which to make progress seems to be in the area of evaluation. There are still persons who work in the audiovisual field, who have steadfastly previewed all materials before purchase. School systems which are small, or have a large staff in the media center might find that this procedure is possible, but most schools or school districts must depend, at least in part, on evaluative reviews done by others. Everyone appears to agree that audiovisual materials do pose complex problems related to evaluation, partly because they combine so many variables of sight, sound, color and also that they can be used with such a diverse range of listeners and viewers.

Several guides have been developed that will be of help in identifying selection-evaluation tools. The works listed in the bibliography by Chisholm; Carter; and Carter et al. will be helpful. The work by Rawnsley indicates which sources serve different purposes and whether or not they provide evaluative information.

In response to the pressing need for a central catalog of media information, C. Edward Wall has served as editor to develop a sequence of publications to respond to these needs. In chronological order, *Multi-Media Reviews Index* was published first.

Multi-Media Reviews Index is an annual mediagraphy of reviews of educational and feature films, filmstrips, records and tapes, and other nonbook media forms. The initial volume covers 70 journals published in 1970 and includes more than 10,000 reviews and cross references; the second volume, covering 1971, increased these figures to 130 periodicals and 20,000 reviews and cross references; and the third volume to 214 and 30,000 respectively.[8] Citations are listed which contain review ratings that indicate the general nature of the evaluations given by the reviews. In addition to the annual reviews, monthly installments are published in the periodical *Audiovisual Instruction,* which are limited in inclusiveness due to space limitation.

The *Media Review Digest* was developed as a successor to *Multi-Media Reviews Index* annuals, and was first published in 1974. The title change reflects the change in content, as this publication includes brief descriptions of the educational materials reviewed and excerpts from the reviews. Special sections include: Film and Record Awards and Prizes, a list of mediagraphies in the literature, and an address list of producers and distributors. The format includes an alphabetical subject index and a classified subject index to all materials and covers approximately 40,000 citations and cross-references. A part of this publication is titled *Media In Print* and provides full mediagraphic data on new and available audiovisual materials whether or not they have been reviewed. These entries are interfiled alphabetically in appropriate sections of the *Media Review Digest.* Supplements to the annual volumes are issued three times a year to provide continuous up-dated information.[9]

One of the first obligations of a media professional is to acquire an adequate collection of selection tools since they are essential if the task is to be performed effectively. This collection should be kept as comprehensive as is needed and as current as possible. The following are some important basic tools which could be used as a beginning collection.

Books containing order information:

Books in Print: An Author—Title Index to the Publishers' Trade List Annual. (New York: Bowker, 1948-   ) Annual.
Children's Books in Print. (New York: Bowker, 1969-   ) Annual.
El-Hi Textbooks in Print. New York: Bowker, 1956-   ) Annual.
Paperbound Books in Print. (New York: Bowker, 1955-   ) Monthly. With two cumulative volumes a year.

[8] C. Edward Wall, ed. *Multi-Media Reviews Index.* Vol. I, 1970; Vol. II, 1971; Vol. III, 1972 (Ann Arbor, Mich.: Pieron Press).
[9] C. Edward Wall, et al., eds. *Media Review Digest* 1973/74 (Ann Arbor, Mich.: Pieron Press, 1974).

Index to Instructional Media Catalogs. (New York: Bowker, 1974)

Learning Directory. (New York: Westinghouse Learning Corporation, 1970-71) Supplement 1972.

Index to 16 mm Educational Films (3rd vol.) 5th ed. (Los Angeles, Calif. National Information Center for Educational Media, University of Southern Calif., 1974).

Index to 35 mm Filmstrips (2nd Vol.) 5th ed. (Los Angeles, Calif. National Information Center for Educational Media, University of Southern Calif., 1974).

Index to Educational Videotapes, 3rd ed. (Los Angeles, Calif. National Informational Center for Educational Media., University of Southern Calif., 1974).

Index to 8 mm Motion Cartridge, 4th ed. (Los Angeles, Calif. National Information Center for Educational Media, University of Southern Calif., 1974).

Index to Educational Records, 3rd ed. (Los Angeles, Calif. National Information Center for Educational Media, University of Southern Calif., 1974).

Index to Educational Audio Tapes, 3rd ed. (Los Angeles, Calif. National Information Center for Educational Media, University of Southern Calif., 1974).

Index to Educational Overhead Transparencies. (2 vol.) 4th ed. (Los Angeles, Calif. National Information Center for Educational Media, University of Southern Calif., 1974).

Index to Educational Slides. 2nd ed. (Los Angeles, Calif. National Information Center for Educational Media, University of Southern Calif., 1974).

Index to Producers and Distributors. 3rd ed. (Los Angeles, Calif. National Information Center for Educational Media, University of Southern Calif., 1974).

National Center for Audio Tapes Catalog 1970-72. (Boulder, Colo. National Center for Audio Tapes, 1971).

The Dobler World Directory of Youth Periodicals. Lavinia Dobler and Murill Fuller, eds. (New York: Citation Press, 1970).

Books containing evaluative reviews which are retrospective:

Children's Catalog 12th ed. Estelle A. Fidell, ed. (New York: Wilson Company, 1971).

Resources for Learning: A Core Media Collection for Elementary Schools. Roderick McDaniel, ed. (New York: Bowker, 1971).

Junior High School Library Catalog 2nd ed. Estelle A. Fidell and Gary L. Bogard, eds. (New York: Wilson, 1970).

Senior High School Library Catalog 10th ed. Estelle A. Fidell and Toby M. Berger, eds. (New York: Wilson Company, 1972).

Periodicals that contain reviews which are current:

The Booklist. (Chicago: American Library Association). Semimonthly but only one issue in August.

Bulletin of the Center for Children's Books. Zena Sutherland, ed. (Chicago: University of Chicago Press.) Monthly except August.

Library Journal. (New York: Bowker). Semimonthly, monthly in July and August.

School Library Journal is reprinted as part of the mid-month issue of *Library Journal*

EFLA Evaluations. (New York, Educational Film Library Association, 1948-) monthly.

Landers Film Reviews. (Los Angeles, Calif.: Landers Associates, 1956-   ) monthly except July and August.

Library Journal/School Library Journal Previews: News and Reviews of Non-Print Media. Phyllis Levy, ed. (New York: Bowker, 1972-   ) Monthly September through May.

Guides to evaluative reviews:

Media Indexes and Review Sources, Margaret E. Chisholm. (College Park, Maryland: School of Library and Information Services, 1972).

Media Review Digest, C. Edward Wall and others. (Ann Arbor, Michigan, Pieron Press, 1974-   ) Annual.

The current supplement is published monthly in *Audiovisual Instruction.*

Directories:

Audio-Visual Equipment Directory: A Guide to *Current Models of Audio-Visual Equipment.* (Fairfax, Va.: National Audio-Visual Associates, 1953-) Annual.

Audiovisual Market Place: A Multimedia Guide. (New York: Bowker, 1969) Biennial.

For a more complete description of contents and format and for additional tools, both basic and selective refer to:

CHRISTINE L. WYNAR. *Guide to Reference Books for School Media Centers.* (Littleton, Colo.: Libraries Unlimited, Inc., 1973).

It is important to examine each of these tools and assess the strengths and weaknesses of each to understand how they can be used best.

In addition, it is essential to set up files of ephemeral materials such as catalogs and brochures, which will aid in the identification and evaluation process. Another step is to set up and maintain a file of evaluations which relate to materials which have been ordered, or are under consideration for purchase. Other ways to keep up-to-date with evaluation tools is to keep in touch with commercial representatives who are aware of the most current materials. Attending conferences, workshops, and demonstrations helps to obtain up-to-date information about the latest materials.

A concomitant responsibility for a media professional, is not only to be able to make the best use of selection tools, but also to conduct training sessions to inform faculty and students as to how these tools can be of assistance.

This competency is of such importance that probably the best way to develop the competency initially is to take college courses entitled "Instructional Materials," "Materials Selection," "Evaluation," or materials courses which include components in selection and evaluation.

To develop competence in the use of selection tools demands continuous use of the tools and on-going assessment of how they can be used most effectively. Some sources for obtaining information are the works listed in the bibliography by Brown, Norberg, and Srygley; Chisholm; Hicks and Tillin; and Davies.

It is important to be constantly reminded of the goal of the selection/evaluation process, which is to facilitate learning. It is easy to become so caught up in the selection and evaluation of materials that this process appears to be an end in itself. The materials, their selection and evaluation are only a means to that end. They are an important means, but the effective education of the individual is the goal on which all selection/evaluation processes should be focused.

MASTERY ITEM: USING REVIEW AND SELECTION TOOLS

Describe the following selection tools by filling in the columns with appropriate descriptions:

TABLE 14-1

Tool	Current or Retrospective?	Book or Periodical	Descriptive or Evaluative?
1. Book List			
2. Previews			
3. Books in Print			
4. Learning Directory			
5. NICEM Media Indexes			
6. School Library Journal			
7. Children's Catalog			

Response: Using Review and Selection Tools

TABLE 14-2

Tool	Current or Restrospective?	Book or Periodical?	Descriptive or Evaluative?
1. Book List	Current	Periodical	Evaluative
2. Previews	Current	Periodical	Evaluative
3. Books in Print	Retrospective	Book	Descriptive
4. Learning Directory	Retrospective	Book	Descriptive
5. Nicem Indexes	Retrospective	Book	Descriptive
6. School Library Journal	Current	Periodical	Evaluative
7. Childrens' Catalog	Retrospective	Book	Evaluative

REFERENCES

Competency 1   Analyzes present and future curriculum requirements to identify material and equipment needs.

BROWN, JAMES W., KENNETH D. NORBERT, and SARA K. SRYGLEY. *Administering Educational Media.* (2nd ed.), pp. 205-22. New York: McGraw-Hill, 1972.

Sharper Tools for Better Learning. Reston, Virginia: National Association of Secondary School Principals, 1973.

Competency 2   Writes and applies criteria and guidelines for the selection, use, and evaluation of materials.

BROWN, JAMES W., KENNETH D. NORBERG, and SARA K. SRYGLEY. *Administering Educational Media.* (2nd ed.), pp. 165-202. New York: McGraw-Hill, 1972.

DAVIES, RUTH ANN. *The School Library Media Center; A Force for Educational Excellence* (2nd ed.), pp. 71-76. New York: R. R. Bowker and Co., 1974.

ERICKSON, CARLETON W. H. *Administering Instructional Media Programs,* pp. 65-76. New York: The Macmillan Company, 1968.

HICKS, WARREN B. and ALMA M. TILLIN. *Developing Multi-Media Libraries,* pp. 13-27. New York: R. R. Bowker and Co., 1970.

"Intellectual Freedom and School Libraries; An In-Depth Case Study," *School Media Quarterly* I (Winter, 1973):111-35.

Media Programs: District and School, pp. 59-76. Chicago: American Library Association and Washington, D.C.: Association for Educational Communication and Technology, 1975.

Competency 3   Synthesizes teacher and student requests and recommendations for acquiring materials.

BROWN, JAMES W., KENNETH D. NORBERG and SARA K. SRYGLEY. *Administering Educational Media.* (2nd ed.), pp. 171-75. New York: McGraw-Hill, 1972.

Competency 4   Collects and uses review and evaluation tools to aid in selection.

BROWN, JAMES W., KENNETH D. NORBERG and SARA K. SRYGLEY. *Administering Educational Media.* (2nd ed.), pp. 171-77. New York: McGraw-Hill, 1972.

CARTER, YVONNE et al. *Aids to Media Selection for Students and Teachers.* Washington, D.C.: U.S. Government Printing Office, 1971.

CARTER, YVONNE. *Supplement to Aids to Media Selection for Students and Teachers.* Washington, D.C.: U.S. Government Printing Office, n.d.

CHISHOLM, MARGARET E. *Media Indexes and Review Sources.* pp. 1-70. University of Maryland: College of Library and Information Services, 1972.

DAVIES, RUTH ANN. *The School Library Media Center: A Force for Educational Excellence* (2nd ed.), pp. 77-88. New York: R. R. Bowker and Co., 1974.

HICKS, WARREN B. and ALMA M. TILLIN. *Developing Multi-Media Libraries.* pp. 29-39. New York: R. R. Bowker and Co., 1970.

RAWNSLEY, DAVID E. *A Comparison of Guides to Nonprint Media.* Stanford, California: Education Resources Information Center (ERIC), Clearinghouse on Information Resources, 1973.

WALL, C. EDWARD, ed. *Multi-Media Reviews Index,* Vol. I, 1970; Vol. II, 1971; Vol. III, 1972. Ann Arbor, Michigan: Pieron Press.

WALL, C. EDWARD, ed. *Media Review Digest, 1973/74.* Ann Arbor, Michigan: Pieron Press, 1974.

15 The Research Function

Research exists on several levels, from very simple exploration of a topic to answer a user's question to a rather complex experimental study to determine the learning effectiveness of a new media curriculum. Media professionals are both producers and consumers of research. The research competencies described in this chapter are applicable regardless of the degree of sophistication and whether or not media personnel are doing research or using the results of existing research.

Research usually begins with a problem to be resolved or a question which requires an answer. In the broadest sense, research can be interpreted as any inquiry into a problem or question for the purpose of resolution. More specifically, Good defines research as "careful, critical, disciplined inquiry, varying in technique and method according to the nature and conditions of the problem identified, directed toward the clarification or resolution (or both) of a problem." [1] Thus research can be conceived along a continuum from very simple question-raising through sophisticated and disciplined inquiry.

The media professional confronts daily a number of questions which require research into existing literature and, in some cases, the organization and conducting of research. It might be argued that a large portion of the media professional's time is spent in research-like activities given the nature of the library tradition in which clients are constantly seeking answers to questions through the help of professional librarians. But rather than to emphasize the

[1] Carter V. Good (ed.), *Dictionary of Education* (3rd ed.), New York: McGraw-Hill, 1973, p. 494.

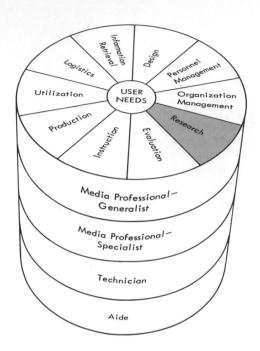

COMPETENCY 1   *Defines research needs.*
COMPETENCY 2   *Reviews the literature.*
COMPETENCY 3   *Develops research design.*
COMPETENCY 4   *Collects, processes, and analyzes data.*
COMPETENCY 5   *Assesses results of research.*
COMPETENCY 6   *Disseminates information about research.*

research that is done for users of the media center, let us consider the nature of the research tasks which assist in job performance. Let's consider a typical day.

The first teacher who arrives in the morning wants to know whether it is better to use a film or a filmstrip in her fifth grade social studies class. (A quick scanning of *What Research Says to the Teacher: Educational Media* [2]

[2] Gerald M. Torkelson, *What Research Says to the Teacher; No. 14: Educational Media* (Washington, D.C.: National Education Association, 1972).

and the *Review of Educational Research,* Vol. 38, No. 2 April, 1968 [3] indicates that the film may be more interesting but students would learn as much cognitive information from either medium if the content is identical.) The next request is from the principal who wants to know how much the media program costs per pupil so that he can justify an increase in the budget request. (This requires some fast footwork if a continuing budget analysis is not available. It also leads to further questions such as: Are salaries included in determining per pupil costs? Is equipment included or amortized over a period of years? All of this is a type of research.) And before the day is over the media professional has to decide on purchasing new additions to the media collections. On what basis can these decisions be made? What are the information needs of the teachers and students in that school? To what extent does existing curriculum dictate certain additions to the collection? Etc., Etc., Etc.

These question, and others, constitute daily research requirements. They lead to literature searches, some quantitative analysis, and some fundamental research. They point up the research needs which must be faced by media professionals within an individual school building.

COMPETENCY 1   Defines research needs.

How can research needs be defined? Very simply, you could look at each of the chapters in this book which discuss the various functions and ask: "What do I need to know about _____?" (Fill in the blank with design, evaluation, logistics, management, information retrieval, production, instruction or utilization.) For *you,* that is an information need and you then may proceed to a variety of sources to find the information you require. If it does not exist anywhere, and you have formulated your question specifically, you have defined a research need. For example, you are concerned that social studies materials are not being used as frequently as other materials. You then proceed to design your strategy to discover the answer to that question. This is research at at a simple level.

A little more sophisticated approach might be illustrated by the teacher who is using multi-image presentations (e.g., slides on three screens simultaneously with taped audio music and narration) and wants to know whether or not there is any research to justify this teaching procedure. The teacher is wondering whether or not it is worth the investment of time and money in terms of payoff in learning. The media professional is asked to help. An ERIC

---

[3] *Review of Educational Research, Instructional Materials: Educational Media and Technology,* Vol. 38, No. 2, April, 1968 (Washington, D.C.: American Educational Research Association).

search may be initiated. Research monographs such as *AV Communication Review, Library Literature,* and *The Review of Educational Research* could be scanned. A telephone call to a knowledgeable source might be made. If no answers or clues to answers emerge from such a search, it would then be reasonable to prepare a researchable question: "Do learners who are exposed to a multi-image audiovisual presentation perform better on written examination after the presentation than a comparable group of learners who take the same examination after seeing a single screen audiovisual presentation?" Research begins with curiosity and questions.

RESOURCES: DEFINING RESEARCH NEEDS

Look around. What are you curious about? Are there answers or even indicators which might lead to answers? What about the day-to-day operation of the media center? Are there questions which are not being answered? Are there practices in teaching and learning that you wonder about? To define research needs a media professional has to be "stumped."

A basic research course can often help a person to observe how others have raised researchable questions. However, it may tell you more than you want to know.

Look through several research-oriented journals such as *AV Communication Review,* the *Journal of Communication,* the *Educational Broadcasting Review,* and the *Review of Educational Research.* As you scan the titles or abstracts of each article, ask yourself: "What question was *this* researcher trying to answer?"

Take a look at a delightful book, *The Art of Asking Questions.*[4] It will help you to get started.

MASTERY ITEM: DEFINING RESEARCH NEEDS

Formulate a research need question from each situation.

1. The jacks on the headsets used with the record player are usually broken within one week's use.
2. A film is available in black and white or color. The rental price for the color film is almost twice that of the black and white film. Which one should be ordered?
3. The media center seems to be used most frequently by the highest achieving students.

[4] Stanley L. Payne, *The Art of Asking Questions* (Princeton: Princeton University Press, 1951).

Response: Defining Research Needs

1. a. Is the breakage resulting from misuse of the headsets? What is the nature of the misuse?
   b. Is the breakage resulting from poor construction of the headsets? Can this be corrected?
   c. Is the breakage caused by a combination of misuse and construction?
2. a. Is color necessary to communicate the concepts of this film?
   b. Is there any evidence to indicate that more learning is elicited from a color film than a black and white film if color is not essential to the content?
3. a. Why do other students not use the media center?

COMPETENCY 2   *Reviews the literature*

A product of research is a body of recorded and documented knowledge. To locate this knowledge the media professional has to comb the literature of the field and related areas. Confirmation of the media professional's own work and fruitful insights are obtained through such searches. The adroit researcher can sometimes see a commonality between two separate lines of research and exploit that commonality. Or he/she can identify an anomaly and disprove a line of reasoning or research. The researcher should read the literature and, considering his/her own experience, draw both synthesizing and question-raising conclusions. Insight comes from many sources and in unexpected ways. A skillful reading of the literature can be an important contribution to this somewhat mysterious process of perception.

The *Behavioral Requirements Analysis Checklist* provides several tasks related to this competency. The media professional should:

Locate existing research for application to specified research needs of the media program.[5]

Maintain a collection of bibliographic research tools to locate research findings.

Identify people and sources of information to assist in meeting specified research needs.

Utilize communications networks to locate and retrieve research.[6]

[5] *Behavioral Requirements Analysis Checklist* (Chicago: American Library Association), p. 48.

[6] Ibid., p. 50.

RESOURCES: REVIEWING THE LITERATURE

A review of the research literature is like a bibliographic search with a fairly narrow scope. The basic courses in library science will help an individual to gain this general skill. Search strategies leading to research information about media are somewhat specialized and may not require a formal course.

Some comprehensive books and literature reviews that you will find helpful are the works by Lumsdaine; Chu and Schramm; Hoban and Van Ormer; Reid and MacLennan; Twyford; and the *Review of Educational Research*. All of these works are listed in the bibliography for this competency. Some periodicals that you will find particularly helpful are:

AV Communication Review. (Quarterly) Association for Educational Communications and Technology, 1201 Sixteenth St. NW, Washington, D.C. 20036

Educational Broadcasting Review. (Bi-weekly) National Association of Educational Broadcasters, 1346 Connecticut Ave., Washington, D.C. 20036

British Journal of Educational Technology. (Quarterly) National Council for Educational Technology, 10 Queen Anne St., London, WIM 9LD, England

Library Literature. (Annual) H. W. Wilson Co., 950 University Ave., Bronx, N.Y. 10452

It is often necessary to go beyond the literature directly related to the media field to insure a comprehensive literature review. A good overview of this literature is found in Lorraine Mathies' *Information Sources and Services in Education*.[7] This useful booklet includes "Search Strategies for Automated Files," "National and Regional Information Systems," "Selected Reference Works and Periodicals," and "ERIC Clearinghouses: Brief Scope Notes."

Media professionals should know about the ERIC Clearinghouse on Information Resources (Stanford Center for Research and Development in Teaching, Stanford, Calif. 94305) which combines the former Clearinghouse for Educational Media and Technology and the Clearinghouse for Library and Information Science. This is probably the most comprehensive source of current research information regarding media in the world. This Clearinghouse is one of a nationwide network of eighteen information centers in education. A monthly publication, *Research in Education,* describes all the new reports and studies added to the system. Copies of the original documents are available in microfiche and hard copy from a central source—the ERIC Document Reproduction Service. (Currently located at Computer Microfilm Inter-

---

[7] Lorraine Mathies, *Information Sources and Services in Education* (Bloomington, Indiana: Phi Delta Kappa Foundation, 1973).

national Corp., P.O. Box 190, Arlington, Va. 22210.) An additional tool is the monthly *Current Index to Journals in Education* which indexes articles from more than six hundred journals. *Dissertation Abstracts* reports research completed by doctoral students in major universities.

The Stanford Clearinghouse publishes a regular newsletter (which is available without charge), current awareness research summaries pertaining to specialized aspects of the media field, monographs and research abstracts. The current list of publications is a useful guide to the newest developments in the field.

The process of literature review is a kind of treasure hunt. One reference often leads to another. The best way to learn how to review research literature is to do it. Select the topics and descriptors from the basic question; scan the general references; check the periodicals; request an ERIC search; and then seek out specific titles from those that appear to be most promising. A bonus is usually found in the bibliography that follows each research article or report since most of the citations will be related to the topic you are pursuing.

MASTERY ITEM: REVIEWING THE LITERATURE

Using the general books and literature reviews given in this chapter, list the pages in each reference which refer to the studies concerned with comparing black and white and color visual materials.

Response: Reviewing the Literature

1. Lumsdaine, "Instruments and Media of Instruction," *Handbook of Research on Teaching*, pp. 635-636.
2. *Review of Educational Research*, Vol. 38, No. 2, April, 1968. (No references)
3. Chu and Schramm, *Learning From Television: What the Research Says*, pp. 24-25.
4. Hoban and Van Ormer, *Instructional Film Research 1918–1950*, pp. 8-25; 8-26.
5. Reid and MacLennan, *Research in Instructional Television*. (No references)
6. Twyford, "Educational Communications Media," *Encyclopedia of Educational Research*, p. 371.

COMPETENCY 3   Develops research designs

The design of a research study usually follows the statement of the problem and a systematic review of the related literature. In this instance, design is the organization and approach to finding solutions to stated problems. It sometimes starts with hypotheses to be tested. From this point on, the following steps are followed in many research studies:

1. Define target population
2. Specify methods and tools to be used
3. Establish timelines for completion of activities
4. Develop data collection instruments and strategies
5. Design data analysis procedures
6. Design or locate appropriate computer program for analysis
7. Develop criteria for judgment

Some research designs may be relatively simple involving interviews with several people or a brief questionnaire sent to the faculty. Others may be more sophisticated and require classical experimental designs requiring various kinds of statistical analysis. The basic requirement for any research design is that it will yield an answer (or strong indicators) to the question or hypothesis being considered. If it does not have the potential of achieving this end, it is wise to recycle and begin again.

Types of research designs include: historical, status-survey, experimental, case studies, and others.

RESOURCES: DEVELOPING RESEARCH DESIGNS

Research design competency is probably best learned through the tutelage of a good instructor. Beginning courses in research are offered in colleges of education and library science. These courses usually offer sufficient content to develop general skills for the first level of research competency.

For a general orientation to research design at an elementary level, consult "Simplified Designs for School Research" by James W. Popham in *Instructional Product Resources,* Robert L. Baker and Richard E. Schutz (eds.) (New York: American Book Co., 1972).

For more advanced skills in research, use the following references as starters:

1. For *historical* research: W. Gray. *Historian's Handbook* (2nd ed.) New York: Houghton Mifflin, 1956.
2. For *status-survey research:* Paul L. Erdos. *Professional Mail Surveys.* New York: McGraw-Hill, 1970.
3. For *experimental* research: D. T. Campbell and J. C. Stanley. *Experimental and Quasi-Experimental Designs for Research.* Chicago: Rand McNally, 1963.

Some people who are just beginning to do research find it helpful to design and conduct pilot studies. Pilot studies are exploratory or "try-out" ventures using small populations in order to discover rough spots in the research design.

MASTERY ITEM: DEVELOPING RESEARCH DESIGNS

1. What type of research is required for each of the following cases?
    a. You want to compare the effectiveness of a captioned filmstrip with a noncaptioned filmstrip of the same title having a tape recorded narration of the captions.

    b. You want to determine how the current classification system used in your media center evolved.

    c. You want to determine the information needs of students in regard to career selection.

2. What research design would you recommend to determine which media form students prefer in rank order?

Response: Developing Research Designs

1. a. Experimental
   b. Historical
   c. Status-survey
2. a. To answer this question you would have to assume equivalent information being available in the same topic in a variety of media. If this were the case you could record preferences as students check out the media.
   b. You might devise a questionnaire which elicits preference responses.

COMPETENCY 4   Collects, processes, and analyzes data

To collect, process, and analyze data is to carry out the design of the research. Data are usually in the form of verbal responses to questions raised in an interview, written responses to a questionnaire (response card, test, etc.), or written notes of an observer. Once the data have been collected they should be organized to correspond to the question being considered. This process can simply be a collection of all responses into tables, or if there is a considerable amount of data, keypunching of data processing cards may be required. Computer programs are sometimes used if data are extensive and complex statistical procedures are required for analysis. It should be pointed out that data processing equipment and computers are tools to help get the job done. They cannot be considered as short cuts around statistical analysis. The researcher must know what statistics, if any, will be used to analyze the data and why those statistics are being used. An important element of this competency is the ability to analyze data so that it is in proper order for interpretation. This interpretation can only be as good as the original data and the way in which it is organized.

Data collection, processing, and analysis does not have to be sophisticated. It can be as simple as collecting quantitative information on needs, trends, and use of media and equipment. It can be a survey to determine the adequacy of facilities, materials, equipment, and services of the media center. Regardless of how simple or complex, the steps of collection, processing, and analysis must be accomplished.

RESOURCES: COLLECTING, PROCESSING, AND ANALYZING DATA

This is one of those competencies that requires active participation in order to accomplish it. Therefore, the individual who wants to achieve this competency should seek out opportunities to serve as an interviewer for a research study. College campuses are breeding grounds for studies which require interviewers. Individuals are usually trained before actually conducting interviews. Structured questions or questionnaires are usually used. Interviewers learn how to probe in order to get at the information which is being sought. This type of experience is helpful for future research endeavors.

Researchers on college and university campuses and in research organizations (such as city government, public opinion, and consumer agencies) are constantly gathering data. Opportunities often exist to work on the not so very elegant job of tabulating responses from questionnaires, key punching data processing cards, and organizing data for later analysis. Knowing how data is prepared for later interpretation is a useful skill. Patterns used in presenting data can be found in doctoral dissertations, research reports, and government statistical documents. The important questions here are: "How does it get that way?" and "Can I do it?"

Almost anyone who does research beyond the most elementary survey needs to know how to use data processing and computer programs. It may be that the media professional will never prepare and run programs but he/she must be able to plan for the use of these tools. It is often necessary to tell someone what you want to have done, but first, you need to know that it is possible. Learning what is possible requires on-the-job training with an experienced person or familiarization with the hardware and software through brief orientation courses which are usually offered to students and faculty by the computer center in most colleges and universities. Short courses are often given by manufacturers of the equipment. Local high schools and community colleges often offer adult education courses in the evening where data processing and computer skills may be acquired. There are many opportunities. The media professional should gain these competencies.

If an individual has worked with computer-based information systems, competencies gained in information handling are often transferable to the domain of research.

MASTERY ITEM: COLLECTING, PROCESSING, AND ANALYZING DATA

1. You want to determine which films in the media center require additional copies because of extensive use. You have the booking card for each film in the collection and a tally of refusals. How would you organize the data to permit decision making?

2. You are trying to build the record collection in the media center based on the interests and needs of the faculty and students. You have designed an instrument to collect data, you have responses to that instrument which indicate needs in ten specified areas and interests in fifteen other areas plus an open-ended response for additional interests not specified. How would you organize these data to help achieve your objective?

Response: Collecting, Processing, and Analyzing Data

1. You would first have to set a reasonable cut-off point for inclusion in your list of films that may require additional copies. Let's say that five or more refusals would determine eligibility for inclusion. You would then go through the booking cards and list each title which is eligible for consideration, noting the number of bookings and the number of refusals. You would then rank order the titles from largest number of bookings and refusals to lowest number. You would then be able to determine those which would be considered as highest priority according to demand.

2. A frequency count tally of the "needs" list and the "interests" list would be an indicator of priority areas. In this case "needs" means a higher priority than "interests." You should check the open-end responses to see if they fit the needs or interests categories and, if they do, add them to the tally. The product of your effort would be a rank ordered list of needs and a similar list of interests. From these data you could move on to the next step of selection and evaluation using the high demand areas as your starting point.

COMPETENCY 5   Assesses results of research

This competency has to do with the ability to read, interpret and understand research whether it has been done by the media professional or another person. An individual ought to be able to review the data which has been collected, processed, and analyzed and interpret its findings in light of questions and interests of the media professional. In its simplest form, this is the "So What?" question. The major reason the results of research are reviewed is to discover answers to questions for which no immediate recall is possible. In most cases, however, direct answers are not found; rather, information related to the question is usually found and must be interpreted for use in a specific context.

This competency implies an understanding of basic statistical techniques: derivation of mean, mode, standard deviation, correlations, and analysis of variance. It also demands a type of insight which is not easily learned except through observation of a perceptive interrogator. This technique may be observed in a press conference with a government official just after a significant report has been released such as unemployment figures, gross national product estimates, or a rise or fall in the consumer price index. Getting at significance—an interpretation of the degree of confidence we can have in a quantitative report—is at the heart of this competency. A second basic element is drawing a relationship between the research result and the immediate question which needs resolution. The closer an individual is to the design, data collection, and analysis of a research study, the more likely the results will be relevant to the concern at hand.

RESOURCES: ASSESSING RESEARCH RESULTS

Pick up a research study on a topic in which you have an interest. Read it through to the presentation and analysis of data. Write the conclusions you would draw from the data presented. Compare your conclusions with the findings of the study. If your conclusions are consistent with those of the researcher, you have probably made a valid conclusion (unless, of course, you both are wrong!). If your conclusions vary from those of the researcher, try to determine where you differ and the reasons why your interpretation varies from that of the author. You might try to do this with several studies to see how well you are able to assess research findings. If you feel that you are missing the interpretation, seek out help from a teacher or friend who you feel can provide sympathetic tutorial assistance.

There are several publications which offer some initial help in the interpretation of data. Chapter 17, "How to Evaluate Research in Educational Psychology" in John P. DeCecco, *The Psychology of Learning and Instruction: Educational Psychology* [8] offers an excellent summary of the nature of educational research. Evaluation of research is something that utimately depends upon dialogue with a knowledgeable person—someone who can confirm your interpretation or help to modify your misperceptions.

Another useful guide is *Understanding Research: Some Thoughts On Evaluating Completed Educational Projects* by Karlene H. Roberts, prepared as an Occasional Paper for ERIC at Stanford. It is available from that source.

MASTERY ITEM: ASSESSING RESEARCH RESULTS

A researcher hypothesized that if a group of students were given training in listening skills, they would perform better on examinations. He divided his freshman English class into a control and an experimental group and gave half of each group a session in listening training. He used College Entrance Examination Board scores to insure comparability of groups. How would you evaluate the result of his research based on the following data:

TABLE 15-1

		No.	CEEB Mean Verbal Score	Mean Examination Score
Control	P_2	28	442.07	48.13
Experimental	P_1	33	439.93	53.87

P_1 - listening training P_2 - no listening training

Response: Assessing Research Results

The results show that the groups which had listening training performed better than the groups which did not. The relatively small difference does not seem to indicate that listening training helped much with this examination.

COMPETENCY 6   Disseminates information about research

---

[8] John P. DeCecco, *The Psychology of Learning and Instruction: Educational Psychology* (2nd ed.) (Englewood Cliffs, N.J.: Prentice-Hall, Inc., 1974), pp. 520-57.

A never-ending concern of agencies who provide money for educational research is that the results of research are not communicated to persons who can use them. Even if attempts to disseminate this information are made, the presentation is often not understandable to those who need the information. Most lamentable of all is the fact that results of research are seldom put into practice.

The media professional fulfills two purposes in this competency. One purpose is to disseminate information about research to users who request such information. This aspect of the competency requires that media professionals know the most promising sources of research information. This would include the ERIC system, educational research journals, abstract services, and compilations of research from the various fields which impinge upon the instructional programs of the school or school system.

The second dimension of this competency is the dissemination of research information in response to specific questions about media to the faculty and students. There may be still another and more personal purpose—to use research reference sources to answer questions about the media program itself. The internal dissemination aspect of this competency is just as important as external dissemination since it keeps the media professional up-to-date and provides the rationale to support the activities within the program.

The *Behavioral Requirements Analysis Checklist* [9] (BRAC) lists the tasks which make up this competency.

1. Maintain a collection of bibliographic research tools to locate research findings.
2. Identify people and sources of information to assist in meeting specified research needs.
3. Utilize communication networks to locate and retrieve research.
4. Demonstrate the ability to analyze and apply the findings of a variety of research studies.
5. Abstract and report specified research findings upon request.
6. Communicate educational research findings to appropriate members of the educational team.
7. Assist users to interpret a variety of research studies.

RESOURCES: DISSEMINATING RESEARCH INFORMATION

How does one learn how to disseminate information? Probably the observation of a good dissemination program is one of the best approaches. General dissemination would include such techniques as newsletters to all

[9] *Behavioral Requirements Analysis Checklist*, p. 50.

faculty, demonstrations for faculty in-service programs, and bulletin board displays in the media center and teachers' lounge. More specific dissemination would include such procedures as sending abstracts of research to persons who have raised questions about the use of media in their classes.

This competency requires an ability to clarify a problem or question, review the appropriate sources, summarize the relevant information and prepare it in a form that is readable and informative. There is no one course or book which can help the media professional to learn all the techniques of dissemination.

Perhaps one of the best ways to approach this competency is to ask what information you would like to receive and in what format it would be most helpful. Chances are that your specifications would be like those of your colleagues. Consider this procedure as a beginning.

MASTERY ITEMS: DISSEMINATING RESEARCH INFORMATION

1. A teacher has asked if there is any research evidence to indicate that students are more likely to read paperback books than regular books. What approach would you use to disseminate this information if you discovered a study which showed that high school age people checked out more paperback than hard bound books?

2. You receive several monthly newsletters and journals which routinely report recent findings in media research. How could you use such resources for your dissemination program?

Response: Disseminating Research Information

1. After reporting directly to the teacher who asked the question, you could summarize the research and include it in a newsletter which is sent regularly to all teachers. You might ask teachers if they would consider having a small recreational reading depository of paperback books in their room for distribution to students.

2. You might use abstracts of research in a newsletter to all teachers if the research results have general applicability. You should probably highlight the implications of the research for teaching. If the research is specific to a certain field or a certain mode of teaching, you could identify those teachers who would be most interested in the studies and send them a copy of the pertinent article—a selective dissemination of information. Finally, you should probably keep a file of the research reports for future reference.

REFERENCES

Competency 1   Defines research needs.

PAYNE, STANLEY L. *The Art of Asking Questions*. Princeton, New Jersey: Princeton University Press, 1951.

Competency 2   Reviews the literature.

CHU, G. C. and WILBUR SCHRAMM. *Learning From Television: What the Research Says*. Stanford, Calif.: Institute for Communication Research, 1967.

HOBAN, CHARLES F., JR. and EDWARD B. VAN ORMER. *Instructional Film Research 1918–1950*. Technical Report No. SDL 269-7-19. Port Washington, N.Y.: U.S. Naval Training Devices Center, 1950.

LEEDY, PAUL D. *Practical Research: Planning and Design,* pp. 58-63. New York: Macmillan, 1974.

LUMSDAINE, A. A. "Instruments of Media and Instruction," pp. 583-682 in N. L. Gage, ed., *Handbook of Research on Teaching*. Chicago: Rand McNally, 1963.

REID, J. C. and D. W. MACLENNAN. *Research in Instructional Television and Film*. Washington, D.C.: U.S. Government Printing Office, 1967.

Review of Educational Research. "Instructional Materials: Educational Media and Technology," Vol. 38, No. 2, April, 1968. Washington, D.C.: American Educational Research Association.

TORKELSON, GERALD M. *What Research Says to the Teacher, No. 14: Educational Media*. Washington, D.C.: National Education Association, 1972.

TWYFORD, LORAN C., JR. "Educational Communications Media," *Encyclopedia of Educational Research*. New York: Macmillan, 1969.

Competency 3   Develops research design.

CAMPBELL, DONALD T. and J. C. STANLEY. *Experimental and Quasi-Experimental Designs for Research*. Chicago: Rand McNally, 1963.

ERDOS, PAUL L. *Professional Mail Surveys*. New York: McGraw-Hill, 1970.

GRAY, W. *Historian's Handbook* (2nd ed.). New York: Houghton Mifflin, 1956.

LEEDY, PAUL D. *Practical Research: Planning and Design,* pp. 71-157. New York: Macmillan, 1974.

POPHAM, W. JAMES. "Simplified Designs for School Research," in Robert L. Baker and Richard E. Schutz, eds., *Instructional Product Resources,* pp. 139-59. New York: Van Nostrand Reinhold, 1972.

RESTA, PAUL E. and ROBERT L. BAKER. "Components of the Educational Research Proposal" in Robert L. Baker and Richard E. Schutz, eds., *Instructional Product Research,* pp. 89-131. New York: Van Nostrand Reinhold, 1972.

Competency 4   Collects, processes and analyzes data.

LEEDY, PAUL D. *Practical Research: Planning and Design,* pp. 64-68. New York: Macmillan, 1974.

WOLF, RICHARD M. "The Use of Library Computer Programs for Statistical Analysis," in Robert L. Baker and Richard E. Schutz, eds., *Instructional Product Research,* pp. 193-227. New York: Van Nostrand Reinhold, 1972.

Competency 5   Assesses results of research.

DECECCO, JOHN P. *The Psychology of Learning and Instruction* (2nd ed.), pp. 520-57. Englewood Cliffs, N.J.: Prentice-Hall, Inc., 1974.

ROBERTS, KARLENE H. *Understanding Research: Some Thoughts On Evaluating Completed Research Projects.* Stanford, Calif.: ERIC Clearinghouse on Information Resources, 1969.

SULLIVAN, HOWARD J. "Classifying and Interpreting Educational Research Studies," in Robert L. Baker and Richard E. Schutz, eds., *Instructional Product Research,* pp. 2-30. New York: Van Nostrand Reinhold, 1972.

Competency 6   Disseminates information about research.

Educational Media. 35mm filmstrip, sound (record), color, 16 min., Washington, D. C.: National Education Association, 1969.

LEEDY, PAUL D. *Practical Research: Planning and Design,* pp. 161-78. New York: Macmillan, 1974.

RESTA, PAUL. "The Research Report" in Robert L. Baker and Richard E. Schutz (eds.), *Instructional Product Research,* pp. 233-91. New York: Van Nostrand Reinhold, 1972.

16 Utilization— the Synthesis

The primary purpose in performing all the functions and competencies mentioned in the previous chapters is to permit optimum use of the resources by teachers and learners. Utilization is the engagement of resources and learners to achieve objectives. Media professionals assist in making utilization work as they consult with users.

Utilization is a unique function. It is the culminating function since it deals with the actual interaction between the user and the medium. Utilization is the engagement of the student with ideas and with the medium of communication. In this case, the teacher is considered to be one medium of communication. It is during utilization that learning is most likely to occur.

This function is unusual in that it is perhaps the most critical and vital function, yet the competencies comprising it are dispersed throughout the other functions. The competencies within the functions of logistics, research, design, and management all focus on one goal—the engagement of the student with ideas and materials for the purpose of learning. The competencies involved in utilization are actually those of the teacher. The only time the utilization competencies refer to the media professional is when he/she is serving as a teacher as described in the instruction function. The media professional's major contribution up to the time of actual use is in the preparation for use.

The media professional insures that materials, equipment and facilities are ready for use. This statement is not a utilization competency, but refers to an *activity* which is derived from the logistics and management functions. The purpose is to establish a favorable learning environment including both the psychological climate and the physical setting. Just as we hear educators speak of reading readiness, so there is a "learning readiness." There are endless numbers of ways in which media center personnel are able to assist teachers and students by working with them to insure that all materials, equipment, and facilities are ready for use. Media center personnel must be familiar with the teaching methodology that is being used and must also be informed about the learners and their learning styles. All of these elements converge during utilization. In every teaching/learning situation, there could be an infinite number of possible combinations of materials, equipment, and facilities. It is the task of the media professional to work with the teacher and the learner to determine which of these options would be most effective and appropriate. The next step is to insure that the materials, equipment, and facilities are available and ready for use. These competencies are discussed in Chapter 11, The Logistics Function.

The media professional assists teachers and learners to effectively interact with media to achieve learning outcomes. Brown, Lewis and Harcleroad identify four major phases in implementing instruction: (1) the introductory phase—the motivational or exploratory activities which precede (2) the development phase—the presentation of objectives and activities in which content is outlined; (3) the organizational phase—when ideas are pooled and generalizations are drawn; and (4) the summarizing phase—in which all collected information is "fed back" to the teacher and to other learners.[1]

Just as reading skills can be developed, so listening and viewing skills can be developed and enhanced. It is the responsibility of the media professional to assume the responsibility of working with teachers and students, or any users of the media center to develop and enhance these skills. There are many approaches for acquiring these skills. One way is through demonstration. Media professionals can present demonstrations in which media is used effectively. The same objective can be achieved by showing videotapes of the effective use of media. Another approach would be conducting tutorial sessions in which media professionals work with individuals to assist in enhancing utilization skills.

The development of the visual literacy movement is probably one of the most clearly identifiable thrusts in this area of developing effective utilization of media. "The term *visual literacy* originally referred to the group of skills that enable an individual to understand and to use visuals for the purposes of intentionally communicating his own messages or interpreting and understanding the intentional visual communications of others." [2] One of the most useful handbooks in this area is *Visual Literacy: A Way to Learn— A Way to Teach.*[3] This booklet discusses visual language and provides exam-

---

[1] James W. Brown, Richard B. Lewis and Fred F. Harcleroad, *AV Instruction: Media and Methods* (3rd ed.) (New York: McGraw-Hill, 1969), pp. 35-38.

[2] *The Elephants of Visual Literacy* (A supplement to *Visuals are a Language*) (Rochester, N.Y.: Eastman Kodak Co., 1971).

[3] *Visual Literacy: A Way to Learn—A Way to Teach* (Washington, D.C.: Association for Educational Communications and Technology, 1972).

Visual literacy can be taught.

ples of successful visual literacy programs in the schools. This primer summarizes much that is known about visual literacy and offers an extensive list of resources in all media formats.

The concept of visual literacy means to develop the learner's viewing ability. Elements that can be developed are increased attention, perceptiveness, detail, general relationships, use of color, sensitivity to magnification or reduction from real life size, and contrasts. These elements and others can be taught as visual literacy concepts.

The teaching of listening has been developed as a highly specialized skill. Modules and listening units have been developed by experts in this field.[4] Some of these units can be used for group instruction and some for self-instruction. The media professional will need to assess the special needs of the teachers and students in the school and determine which approaches would be effective in assisting to develop listening and viewing skills.

The media professional evaluates and modifies the use of media in teach-

[4] Ella A. Erway, *Listening: A Programmed Approach* (New York: McGraw-Hill, 1969).

ing and learning. Teaching is a never-ending cycle or loop in which the teaching/learning activity occurs and is then evaluated. This evaluation in turn is used to change or adapt parts of the process so that the entire process becomes more effective. The evaluation can take many forms. Pretests and posttests taken by students can indicate the effectiveness of teaching and learning. Students can also give an assessment of the methods used and the appropriateness of the media. In a team teaching situation, team members can work cooperatively to evaluate the process and outcomes. In computer-assisted instruction, the evaluation of cognitive learning takes place continuously and is transmitted to the learner. Evaluation is a complex process. The important aspect of evaluation is that when the teaching/learning processes are evaluated the findings and recommendations be recycled, so that improved procedures involving students, physical settings, and media options can be instituted.

The process of modifying the use of media may be seen in the following example. In a sewing class a teacher showed a 16mm film on how to lay out a pattern for cutting out a dress. After the class a number of students asked questions that could have been answered by seeing the film again. Based on this feedback, the next time the skill was taught, the film should probably be an 8mm loop film which could be used over and over again by those individuals who need specific assistance or need to watch the process again.

Although the activities mentioned in this chapter are discussed in more detail in other chapters, the authors felt that it was important that they be emphasized here since utilization is the focal point of teaching and learning—a true synthesis of all the other functions.

REFERENCES

Brown, James W., Richard B. Lewis and Fred F. Harcleroad. *AV Instruction: Media and Methods* (3rd ed.), pp. 35-38. New York: McGraw-Hill.

Donis, Donis A. *A Primer of Visual Literacy.* Cambridge, Mass.: The MIT Press, 1973.

Hey, Look at Me! 16mm, motion picture, sound, color, 12½ min., Washington, D.C.: Association for Educational Communications and Technology, 1970.

How Does a Picture Mean? 35mm filmstrip, black & white, Washington, D.C.: Association for Educational Communications and Technology, 1968.

Making Sense Visually. 35mm filmstrip, color, Washington, D.C.: Association for Educational Communications and Technology, 1968.

Putting New Excitement into School Pictures. 35mm filmstrip, sound (record), color, Washington, D.C.: Association for Educational Communications and Technology, 1967.

Rhetoric of the Movie. 6-8mm, motion picture, color, Association for Educational Communications and Technology, Washington, D.C.: AECT, 1967.

Selecting and Using Ready-Made Materials. 16mm motion picture, sound, color, 17 min., New York: McGraw-Hill, 1963.

Using Motion Film in the Classroom. 16mm motion picture, sound, color, 11 min., Austin, Texas: Educational Media Labs, 1968.

A Visual Fable. 35mm filmstrip, sound (record), color, Washington, D.C.: Association for Educational Communications and Technology, 1968.

Visual Literacy: A Way to Learn—A Way to Teach. Washington, D.C.: Association for Educational Communications and Technology, 1972.

Worth How Many Words? 16mm motion picture, sound, color, 8 min., Rochester, N.Y.: Kodak, 1969.

17 Education in the Future

One way of looking at the future is to prepare scenarios describing what the world might be like several decades hence. Scenarios in this chapter set in 1990 predict alternative educational styles as they might emerge in an advanced technological society. The purpose of this chapter is to serve as a stimulus for further individual projections regarding the role of the media professional in the future.

A SAN DIEGO SCENARIO

The time is 1990. Peter, born in 1975 is fifteen now. He lives with his parents (or foster-parents of his choosing, for periods of up to a month) in a suburb of San Diego. Like most children, he is healthy and well-built, the result of a good climate and an intelligent diet which has laid increasing stress on natural foods (following the series of poisoning scandals in the early 1980s). His father works a four-day week in a local electronics company. His mother is a mobility counseler—one of a team who advise anyone moving into (or out of) the area on problems of housing, employment, welfare benefits, social life, etc.

Since the age of twelve, Peter has been a working-man, in a manner of speaking. Not the old newsboy stuff, though. Through his local tutor, he has been able to find a number of jobs, which occupy no more than the regulation two days a week, and pay no less than three dollars an hour. First, Peter set up in business with two other boys, making toys and selling them to local chain stores. This worked satisfactorily for a few months, but then one of his partners got tired, quit, and the deliveries got behind. Despite penalties for this, Peter and his friend managed to save $200 which they proceeded to blow in one week of endless partying, trips to the mountains and so on. Next Peter worked successfully as an electrician's helper, a waiter in a local hotel, and a gas station attendant. After about a year of this, he got tired of these diverse activities, and decided to go back to full-time study of electronics, going through the necessary chore of learning basic physics and electricity.

Apart from his work, he spends a good deal of time at the local learning center, either in small groups with other teenagers, in mixed groups with adults, or alone with the Information Resource System (IRS) which gives him good access to a wide range of materials and equipment—cassettes, both audio and video, books, slides, and models. Part of this system is an up-to-the-minute worldwide video information system which gives him the most recent and in-depth coverage of news both national and international. Peter seldom watches the "news" any more, as he finds it too shallow in its coverage and irrational in its selection. The small groups he has joined do a variety of things—dance, meditation, political analysis, acting, producing a newspaper, Mexico (not just the language, but total immersion in the country and culture, including stays there). Peter tends to have fits of energy and enthusiasm, when he is active in five different groups at the same time, and then days, even weeks, of lassitude and uninterest, when he sits around at home playing his guitar, or motorcycling in an aimless fashion round the neighborhood. Once, in one of these periods, he got into drugs but through the action of his friends in the meditation group, was influenced to go for a cure before he really got addicted.

Peter's one day of compulsory instruction per week (Tuesday for him) consists of some work in math (differential equations and statistics), language (constructing and deciphering codes), information search strategies, problem-solving, and law. There are also some sessions on divergent thinking, U.S. history and anthropology, but these are not tested, although they are mandatory. Peter's "credentials" at this point are a curious mixture of documents— grades for a few specific core tasks, certificates of activity for other work, recommendations from a number of people he has worked for, and some of his own "reports" on subjects that interest him.

Apart from the six or so "teachers" who teach Peter his core subjects, he has two "tutors" who combine advice and information in varying mixes. They base their advice on his past record, a number of formal tests, and talks with his parents, foster-parents, friends and others. They have quick access to a wide variety of information such as data banks of available validated learning materials, learning networks, employment opportunities, skill-tests, opportunities for work and living elsewhere, and courses offered anywhere in the region. But often as not, they find Peter has his own contacts, his own information networks, and doesn't bother with the formal system, except to come in and chat periodically about this, that, or the other.

Since they know his family, one of these tutors may also be chosen as tutor to Peter's youngest sister, Eileen, aged four. There in another sister, Barbara, aged nine. (For this family, Zero Population Growth has not worked.) Ever since her birth, Eileen's parents have been able to call for advice and resources from the Early Development Agency (EDA). This has a varied staff, consisting of doctors, nurses, nutritionists, psychologists, reading and numeracy experts, materials advisors, supervisors of play groups, etc. EDA assures first of all that the child has the basics for physical health—proper food, comfort, clothing, etc. (EDA is a free state service available to all.) As usual, it is somewhat better in the suburbs than in the cities. Country people do not use it as extensively, as they regard it as something for city people. EDA also helps parents to join or form nursery groups, which takes care of day-nurseries and baby-sitting at night, trains parents in visual/audio symbolic stimulus techniques, so that the child has a stimulating environment. Where necessary they offer counseling on emotional and marital problems. Despite this, the number of divorces has risen steadily, though neighborhood organizations have become increasingly active in looking after children of broken marriages. EDA also provides a range of stimulus materials of which Sesame Street was an early, if crude, example. One thing EDA has done, in collaboration with ecology groups, is to set off natural areas where children can live and play in a natural, but not too hostile environment. These tend to be up in the hills or by the water, and parents usually take their children there at least once a year for a week or so.

Peter's father, who tends in his old-fashioned way to regard learning as something he did at school, also had occasion to use another agency, this time the city-run Adult Learning Information Centre (ALIC). His company, in connection with a contract with the Brazilian government, decided to send him to Brazil for three months to supervise installation of a laser communications system in Sao Paulo. They gave him three weeks to prepare for this—linguistically, culturally, and physically. Language was the least of the problem. Most Brazilians know some English, but it would be useful for Peter's father to know some Portuguese to be able to order a cup of coffee, and to know the names of basic components of the laser equipment. His other information needs are related to climate, diet, and culture.

First he went to the company personnel department for advice, but their recommendations were unimaginative. So, somewhat against his will, but prodded by his wife, he called up ALIC and made an appointment. ALIC questioned him about his needs, tested him, supplied him with learning materials and got him into a cultural adaptation course at the local university, all in two hours. He was suitably amazed. However, he didn't enjoy this actual course since it placed him with a number of Fantasists (descendents of the Hippies) whom he didn't understand at all. In any case he said he would have done better to spend two weeks in Brazil, preparing on the spot. Peter said it wasn't ALIC's fault, but his father said he never did believe in adult education. He agreed, however, that ALIC made a valuable contribution in retraining people for jobs—everything from skilled manual jobs, to high-grade professional work, like medicine and management.

San Diego, being one of the most progressive cities on the west coast, had set up a highly controversial system for its own administration called PIF (Planned Innovation and Feedback). Back in 1976, the City Council had decided that the current system of city government (which had been rocked alternately by scandal and sabotage) needed to be replaced. Hence, they received funds from the Fiasco Foundation to set up an alternative system, which would run side by side with the existing system for a trial period of three years (1978-81) and then replace it entirely.

Basically the new system was divided into two loops, maintenance and evolution. The maintenance loop was concerned with attaining the goals set for that year (or two years), a kind of housekeeping function. The evolutionary loop was concerned with managing change in the city. It collected information through surveys, polls, data analysis, constructed simulations of proposed changes, and then presented the options to the citizens in the form of mediated presentations or simulated environments. The information-gathering was the least interesting and most controversial part of the loop. It was sabotaged by the Beach Communities which had in any case almost become cities within cities with a semitribal structure and a new Declaration of Independence (1976). Many old-style liberals resisted the information gathering system as an invasion of privacy and an affront to democracy.

The simulations based on these data were mainly human ones, using interactive sociodrama and futurist groups to explore the ramifications of each change. (Futures study had moved almost entirely out of the business of prediction, and into the business of simulation.) Computers were used for the more difficult simulations.

Finally, the total scenario of the change was presented at scheduled performances in the city center, either in mediated form, followed by discussion or option-response readouts, or as a simulated environment where people could experience a new type of housing, or shops, or streets or weather control. The Planned Innovation and Feedback System also selected parts of the city as guinea-pig areas for extended simulations such as banning automobiles, abolishing nudity laws, and implementing communal dining.

All in all, the experiment was interesting, rather than successful. It could be argued that the main result was to raise the consciousness of the citizens about their city to a remarkable degree. The results of actual change were more debatable. But it was America's first attempt at a "city which learns." A great deal had been learned in turn from the Danish experiments.

Another unique aspect about the city was its radio and television stations. Many of these had been discontinued in the late seventies because of protest groups who were, for different reasons, appalled at the hedonistic emphasis of American advertising. Faced with these protests, the radio and television stations did an about-turn, and instead of broadcasting advertisements, set up information services which would give any consumer who called, details of products which were relevant to him (and which were produced by companies which sponsored that station.) As a result, most companies sponsored all stations to some degree, and the stations in turn acted as public relations and marketing agents for the companies. Of course, this would hardly have been possible without the arrival of "talk-back" capacity on both cable and broadcast channels.

San Diego in the 1980s was a stimulating pleasant place to live. Pleasant, because the city had managed to cope with tensions which destroyed, morally if not physically, other cities. This was not because of any particular foresight on the part of its inhabitants, but because it was a late starter. When obsolescence was already setting in elsewhere, San Diego had just began to plan. Unfortunately, one obsolescent aspect of the city was its giant, cumbersome freeway system sprawled across the landscape like a stranded octopus which had come up out of the ocean one night and promptly collapsed on land. But as one businessman who lived two hundred miles away said, "Why should I commute when I can communicate?"

Since it was a city with a good climate and mild winters, it attracted a large population of retired people. These people tended to live in large mobile-home parks in the hills and desert behind the city. Many of these little communities had a vigorous life of their own, with leisure activities and neighborhood welfare schemes. This was due mainly to the people themselves, since the city (in common with the rest of the nation) had largely ignored the problem of the old, especially with the newly imposed age limitation on voting for those over 75. If these was any real sense of community, paradoxically it was here among the very old or among the very young, both drop-outs in different ways from the main socio-technical system: the old by necessity, the young by choice. There were some who said that for all the work of enlightened planners—that the truest community existed in precisely those subgroups which were least amenable to, or the concern of, planning.

As is usually the case, there are two sides of the coin; the advanced industrial society brought mobility and opportunity, but at the same time brought problems of personal anxiety, loneliness and rootlessness.

In order to cope with the inherent problems and the information needs of the advanced industrial society alternative educational opportunities have been established.

A NEW YORK CITY SCENARIO

Johnny Brooks, eight years old, is a student in New York Public Education Total Tutorial Center. To his parents' consternation, Johnny's "classes" at Total Tutorial Center apparently consist only of him.

. The pupils frequently do gather in groups, for seminar-like discussions: for visits to museums, to the zoo, the symphony, the supermarket, the monorail station; for physical education; for public speaking; for meetings of the Junior Astronauts Club which Johnny belongs to; and for a variety of other activities. And rehearsals of his choral group seem to be conducted in much the same way as the school classrooms his grandmother described to him from her girlhood.

But for the most part, the children meet with their teachers individually. In addition to the "regular" teachers, there are some rather unusual people such as a violinist and a furniture designer, and his favorite this year is a retired sea captain. Johnny knows where Brazil is and what Sao Paulo looks like because he signaled his learning console to project films that would show him, but it was his conversations with the sea captain that moved Johnny to ask the console about Brazil in the first place.

The learning console at which Johnny spends much of his time in Concenter 417 appears to be an enclosed desk with a television set and a typewriter built into it. He starts his lesson by inserting his aluminum identification plate into the console demand-slot. Within a few seconds, the screen projects a problem in mathematics. Johnny recognizes it; he had the same problem at the end of yesterday's lesson. He picks up his electronic stylus and writes the answer on his response slate; this resembles an old-fashioned square of blackboard except that is has several hundred thousand tiny pores that receive impulses from the stylus and translate handwriting into machine language.

A voice from the speaker in the console congratulates Johnny on getting the right answer, then urges "Now try this one" as the screen projects a new problem. If he gets a wrong answer, the screen projects the same kind of problem a different way; if Johnny gets three wrong in a row, a soft tone rings in Betty Raschke's lapel alarm and brings her into his console.

Dr. Raschke, the Concenter monitor, isn't the only person keeping track of Johnny's progress. His console and Concenter—like all the other Concenters around the New York metropolitan area, more numerous than neighborhood heliports—are connected to the Educational Resource Center downtown. There, the record of Johnny's progress that has been tabulated by computers is combed by a team of psychologists, programmers, expert teachers of everything from arithmetic to zoology, remedial specialists, and guidance counselors.

Neither Johnny nor anyone else knows what grade he's in. As quickly as he masters one "learning unit," his programmed courses offer more difficult material. He proceeds at his own pace, neither holding back other students on subjects he finds difficult nor being slowed down by them on subjects in which he excels.

Johnny rides to Total Tutorial Center each morning with his sister,

Fran, who is 19 and hopes to be a surgeon. She takes her course work in the morning, on a console one floor above Johnny's, but goes to a medical center in the afternoon for laboratory work.

The Brooks family has two learning consoles at home. Fran uses hers in the evening to ask the Educational Resource Center for help on her calculus or literature research papers. When her father is in an ambitious mood, he picks up the program guide and dials either Elementary Japanese Conversation or Advanced Econometrics. He hasn't yet decided whether to accept a promotion that would require moving to his firm's Kyoto branch, but if he does, he'll be ready. Mrs. Brooks has *decided,* and three afternoons a week she dials Oriental Cuisine and watches it on her kitchen extension screen.

In Johnny's world, education never stops; learning is a year-round life-long process.

Woven within these scenarios is the obvious fact that information will play an increasingly central role in many facets of living; particularly in all aspects of formal and informal education. Implicit in these assumptions is the message for all media professionals that their responsibilities will become more pervasive and demanding. As alternative formats for education develop it seems probable that they will depend increasingly on individual access to a wide range of information sources.

REFERENCES

ALLEN, WILLIAM H. *Trends in Instructional Technology.* Stanford: ERIC Clearinghouse on Media and Technology, 1970.

BELL, DANIEL, ed. *Toward the Year 2000: Work in Progress.* Boston: Houghton Mifflin, 1968.

Child of the Future. 16mm motion picture, sound, color, 58 min., New York: McGraw-Hill, 1965.

DOYLE, FRANK J. and DANIEL Z. GOODWILL. *An Exploration of the Future in Educational Technology.* Montreal: Bell Canada, 1971.

The Future as Metaphor. Syracuse: Educational Policy Research Center, Vol. 2, No. 2, Spring, 1971.

HAMREUS, DALE. *Media Guidelines: Development and Validation of Criteria for Evaluating Media Training.* Monmouth, Oregon: Teaching Research, 1970.

KAHN, HERMAN and ANTHONY J. WEINER. *The Year 2000: A Framework For Speculation on the Next Thirty-Three Years.* New York: Macmillan, 1967.

MORPHET, EDGAR and DAVID JESSER (eds.). *Designing Education for the Fu-*

ture, No. 6: Planning for Effective Utilization of Techonology in Education. New York: Citation Press, 1969.

No More Teachers, No More Books. 16 mm motion picture, sound, color, 24 min., Toronto, Ontario: Document, 1971.

ROGERS, CARL. "Interpersonal Relationships: U.S.A. 2000," *The Journal of Applied Behavioral Science,* 4, no. 3 (1968).

TOFFLER, ALVIN. *Future Shock.* New York: Random House, 1970.

TOFFLER, ALVIN (ed.). *The Futurists.* New York: Random House, 1970.

TOFFLER, ALVIN (ed.). *Learning for Tomorrow: The Role of the Future in Education.* New York: Random House, 1974.

WORTH, WALTER. *A Choice of Futures.* Edmonton: Queen's Printer for the Province of Alberta, 1972.

Appendix A:
Evaluation Forms

In the process of evaluating specific media products, it is helpful to have a form which assists in gathering and recording evaluative information. The four forms which follow provide examples of evaluation instruments. They are included because they represent four different approaches to evaluation. You will probably want to develop your own form, which meets the unique requirements of your media program.

The form of the Educational Film Library Association (EFLA) has been used for over 20 years to evaluate films. Compilations of the evaluation eventually appear on EFLA cards—a subscription service.

The form for the Lincoln County (Oregon) School District offers a comprehensive checklist of items pertaining to any medium being evaluated. It is designed specifically for one school district, to meet its needs. It was developed by William Beaston.

The Sample Media Evaluation Form is a composite of several forms which provide for descriptive information, evaluation of potential use, content assessment and technical evaluation. It can be used for any medium.

The Evaluation of Instructional Materials K-12 Summary Card combines descriptive and evaluative information. It also serves as a system for organizing and managing evaluative information for use in later purchasing and cataloging. The accompanying "List of Criteria for Selection of Instructional Materials" is used by the evaluators when making their judgments. The criteria selected by the evaluator as relevant are entered on the Summary Card. The last item in this system is the "Record of Evaluation for Instructional Materials" which provides a permanent record of the evaluation, purchase and recommended use information.

EFLA EVALUATION

Film Title:

Subject-Matter Field:

Producer Source:

So.____Si.____B&W____Color____Sale Price____Rental____Free____

Evaluation Institution:

Names and Titles of Evaluators:

Synopsis: (about 75-100 words, as detailed as possible. Do not use producer's
summary)

I. List the possible audiences, and the purposes for which the film would
be used. Rate probable value for each purpose.

	Audience	Purpose	Value Low				High
1.			1	2	3	4	5
2.			1	2	3	4	5

II. Recommended age level: Primary____, Intermediate____,
Jr.High____, Sr.High____,
College____, Adult____.

III. Structure: (organization, editing, continuity)

        1 2 3 4 5

Picture quality: (clarity, framing,
color, etc.)   1 2 3 4 5

Sound quality: (audibility, voice
fidelity, music
effects   1 2 3 4 5

IV. Comment and General impression: (Note here any special points
as to authenticity, creativity or attitude; also a brief statement
of how the film affects you. Use back of sheet if necessary).

V. Your estimate of the value of the film: Poor____Fair____
Average____Good____Very Good____
Excellent____.

LINCOLN COUNTY SCHOOL DISTRICT
EVALUATION REPORT—INSTRUCTIONAL MATERIALS

Name of Evaluator_____ Date_____

Title (of item)_____

Series title _____ Copyright_____ Cost_____

Type of material_____ Distributor_____ Producer_____

A. Does it meet the objectives specified on request form? Yes_____ No_____

Does it meet any other objectives? Yes_____ No_____

What are they?_____

_____

B. Principal uses:

_____ Provides factual information   _____ Raises questions
_____ Introduces topic or problem   _____ Attitudes
_____ Culminates activity   _____ Appreciation
_____ Individual study   _____ Multiple concept
_____ Skill builder   _____ Single concept

Other _____

C. Appropriate grade level(s) K 1 2 3 4 5 6 7 8 9 10 11 12

D. Characteristics of material meet the requirements of #4 on preview request

form? Yes_____ No_____ Specify if other_____

E. Will this material be dated in the near future? (5 years) Yes_____ No_____

F. Potential for pupil interest: 1 2 3 4 5

                                      Low   High

G. Content organization: 1   2   3   4   5

                                 Low   High

H. Preparation for use time:_____
Is the amount of time to use this item justified by the content?
                                        Yes_____   No_____

I. What skills are necessary to properly use this item?_____

J. Is this the best medium; does the item justify its cost given the objective(s)?
                                        Yes_____   No_____

K. Is the subject of the item an area of weakness in the District?
                                        Yes_____   No_____

If the item duplicates content in materials already owned by the District, then is it sufficiently superior to warrant supplanting the older items?
                                        Yes_____   No_____

L. Are the vocabulary and/or phrases appropriate?   Yes_____   No_____

M. Are instructions, teachers guide and/or stated objective(s) included? (Circle) Others:

SAMPLE MEDIA EVALUATION FORM

(Circle) Book, Chart, Film, Filmstrip, Recording, Map, Model, Sound Filmstrip, Videotape, Other_____

TITLE_____ Reviewed by_____ Date_____

    Description: Color_____ Time_____ Pages_____ Size_____ Date_____

    Purchase Price_____ Purchase Source_____

USE DATA: Recommended Grade Level_____ Unit of Study_____

    Is the content valid, correct, and truthful? Yes_____ No_____

    (Does this material provide additional desirable information which is above and beyond what you can now provide with materials currently used in this context?)

    Yes_____ No_____ If "Yes", what?

EVALUATION

    Objectives: Explicit and Stated_____ Implicit; not stated_____ Not evident_____

    Content: Superficial_____ Too Detailed_____ Well Balanced_____

    Authenticity: Acceptable_____ Not acceptable_____

    Vocabulary: Excellent_____ Good_____ Poor_____

    Organization and Continuity: Excellent_____ Good_____ Poor_____

    Photography or format: Excellent_____ Good_____ Poor

    Sound: Excellent_____ Good_____ Poor _____

    Teachers Guide or Manual: Excellent_____ Good_____ Poor_____

GENERAL RATING: Excellent_____ Good_____ Poor_____

RECOMMENDED FOR FUTURE USE? Yes_____ No_____ Reason:_____

_____

CONTENT: (Brief description of the material):

Prince George's County Public Schools
Department of Educational Communications
Instructional Services Center

Evaluation of Instructional Materials K-12
Summary Card

Copy 1 Taped to Material (WHITE)
Copy 2 To Supervisor (YELLOW)
Copy 3 To Vendor/Publisher (PINK)
Copy 4 To Director (BUFF)

A. Requested by: 1 ☐ 2 ☐ 3 ☐ 4 ☐

B. Date Evaluation Completed

C. Disposition of Materials 1 ☐ 2 ☐
   Da.   Mo.   Yr.

D. Approved ☐   Rejected ☐   Referred to ☐
   Committee

E. Justification for Acceptance/Rejection

F. Comments (Optional)

G. Textbooks Only: Basal ☐   Sup. ☐   T. E. ☐   Ref. ☐

H. Media Materials Only: (print or nonprint) Class No.

I. Kind of Material: TB ☐   MP. ☐   NP ☐   P ☐   F ☐   NF ☐

J. Identification of Nonprint Materials: ☐

K. Instructional Level K ☐ 1 ☐ 2 ☐ 3 ☐ 4 ☐ 5 ☐ 6 ☐
   7 ☐ 8 ☐ 9 ☐ 10 ☐ 11 ☐ 12 ☐ A ☐

USE BALL POINT PEN — PRESS HARD
EASIM FORM 1

L. Subject Area

M. Full Title

N. Author   O. Price

P. Publisher
                    Name

                    Address

Q. Copyright Date

R. Signature of Reviewers and Evaluators Approving Materials.

1. Classroom Teacher

2. Classroom Teacher

3. Specialist/Administrator

4. Lay Person

5. Others — Optional

6. Date Approved by Board of Education

PRINCE GEORGE'S COUNTY PUBLIC SCHOOLS
DEPARTMENT OF EDUCATIONAL COMMUNICATIONS
INSTRUCTIONAL SERVICES CENTER

A LIST OF CRITERIA FOR SELECTION OF
INSTRUCTIONAL MATERIALS

POINTS OF QUALITY	POINTS OF INFERIORITY
Accept	Reject

AUTHENTICITY

1. Accurate facts	4. Inaccurate facts
2. Facts impartially presented	5. Facts distorted by bias
3. Up-to-date information	5S Stereotypes by sex
	5R Stereotypes by race
	6. Fake revised version; date only changed.

APPROPRIATENESS

7. Vocabulary at user's level	11. Vocabulary too easy, difficult or objectionable
8. Concepts at user's level	12. Concepts too easy or difficult
9. Narration, dialogue, sound effects related to subject	13. Narration, dialogue, sound effects unrelated
10. Individual and/or group use suitability	14. Limited individual and/or group use suitability

SCOPE

15. Full coverage as indicated	18. Gaps in coverage
16. Superior concept development by this means	19. Better concept development by other means
17. Content to satisfy demands for current subjects	20. Irrelevance to current topics

INTEREST

21. Relationship to user's experience	26. No relationship to user's cultural environment
22. Intellectual challenge	27. No intellectual challenge
23. Imagination appeal	28. Prosaic presentation
24. Human appeal	29. Negative human values
25. Sensory appeal	30. No stimulation
31. Logical development	34. Confused development
32. Pertinence of all sequences	35. Unrelated sequences
33. Balance in use of narration and dialogue, music and sound effects	36. Ineffective or overpowering use of the same elements

TECHNICAL ASPECTS

37. Clarity
38. Intelligibility
39. True size relationships
40. Unified composition
41. Effective color use

42. Extraneous sounds, visuals too detailed
43. Difficulty in following image and/or sound
44. Unreal size relationships
45. Confused composition
46. Color is less effective than black and white

SPECIAL FEATURES: FORMAT

47. Descriptive notes, teacher's and/or user's guide
48. Print size legible
49. Well-designed layout
50. Illustrations, photos and prints creative
51. Charts and maps clear
52. Plot interesting, clear
53. Characterization well-defined
54. Style creative
55. Detailed index or bibliography
56. Information fair and impartial

57. Absence of useful notes, guides
58. Print crowded on page
59. Print not balanced with illustrations
60. Illustrations, photos and prints trite.
61. Charts and maps cluttered
62. Plot skimpy and confusing
63. Vague characterization
64. Style forced, artificial, dull
65. Lacks index or bibliography
66. Information of inflammatory or sensitive nature

PHYSICAL CHARACTERISTICS

67. Minimum instruction for individual use
68. Attractive packaging
69. Durability
70. Ease of repair

71. Special training requirements for use
72. Unattractive packaging
73. Flimsy construction
74. Difficulty in repairing damage

COST

75. Conformity to budget
76. No less expense for satisfactory substitutes
77. Inexpensive or already purchased equipment
78. Average supplemental costs

79. Too costly for budget
80. Satisfactory substitutes
81. Expensive equipment needed
82. Too expensive to replace, repair, process for use

RECORD OF EVALUATION FOR INSTRUCTIONAL MATERIALS MCPS FORM 365-25

REQUESTED BY SCHOOL NUMBER_____		SIGNATURES
STAFF MEMBER (S)	DATE ORDERED	1. _____
		2. _____
REC'D BY E & S	SENT TO SCHOOL	3. _____
		4. _____
DATE	DATE	5. _____
RETURNED FROM SCHOOL	RETURN TO PUB.	* SUPERVISOR
DATE	DATE	* COMMITTEE
☐ APPROVED	INSURANCE NO.	
☐ DISAPPROVED		DATE

COMMENT

RETURN THIS FORM TO DEPARTMENT OF EDUCATIONAL MEDIA AND TECHNOLOGY EVALUATION AND SELECTION DIVISION	* FOR FILMS AND TEXTBOOKS ONLY

FULL TITLE

AUTHOR	COPYRIGHT DATE
VENDOR OR PUBLISHER	VENDOR CATALOG NUMBER

KIND OF MATERIAL	IDENTIFY INSTRUCTIONAL MATERIAL		FILM LENGTH
☐ ☐ ☐ ☐ TB LB F IM			B/W ☐ COLOR ☐
SCHOOL LEVEL	SUBJECT AREA	SUBJECT CODE	GRADE LEVEL
CIRCLE E J S			
LEARNING GROUP	READING LEVEL	UNIT	COST
DISABILITY GROUPING	TEXTBOOKS ONLY ＞ CIRCLE TYPE	B - BASIC S - SUPPLEMENT	T - TEACHER ED. R - REFERENCE

DISTRIBUTION: ORIGINAL/E&S permanent file WHITE/vendor PINK/E&S circulation file
BLUE/E&S subject file YELLOW/E&S temporary file GOLD/staff file

Appendix B:
Producers' Code

Throughout this book various audiovisual media are cited as resources for gaining competency. Each citation indicates the place and date (when available) of production and identifies the producer. The producer's complete name is not given because of rather lengthy company names.

The producers' code which follows gives the complete name and address of each producer mentioned in the book.

AECT
Association for Educational
Communications and Technology
1201 16th Street, N.W.
Washington, D.C. 20036

ALA
American Library Association
50 E. Huron St.
Chicago, Ill. 60611

AMCIN
American Cinema Editors
6776 Hollywood Blvd.
Hollywood, Calif. 90028

BATTELLE
Battelle Memorial Institute
Information Research Center
505 King Ave.
Columbus, Ohio 43201

BFA
BFA Educational Media
11559 Santa Monica Blvd.
Los Angeles, Calif. 90025

BNA
BNA Communications Inc.
5615 Fishers Lane
Rockville, Md. 20852

BOWKER
R. R. Bowker Co.
1180 Avenue of the Americas
New York, N.Y. 10036

CAROUSEL
Carousel Films, Inc.
1501 Broadway (Suite 1503)
New York, N.Y. 10036

CORONET
Coronet Instructional Films
65 East South Water Street
Chicago, Illinois 60601

DOCUMENT
Document Associates
573 Church St.
Toronto 285, Ontario

DUART
Du Art Film Labs, Inc.
U.S. Government Film Ser.
245 West 55th Street
New York, N.Y. 10019

EBE
Encyclopaedia Britannica
Educational Corp.
425 N. Michigan Ave.
Chicago, Ill. 60611

EMI
Educational Media, Inc.
106 West 4th Ave.
Ellensburg, Wash. 98926

EML
Educational Media Labs
4101 South Congress Ave.
Austin, Texas 78745

GPIT
Great Plains National
Instructional TV Library
University of Nebraska
Lincoln, Neb. 68508

GPT
General Programmed Teaching
Quail Hill
San Rafael, Calif. 94903

HESTER
Hester and Associates
11422 Harry Hines Blvd.
Suite 212
Dallas, Texas 75229

IDEA
Institute for Development
of Educational Activity
P.O. Box 628
Far Hills Branch
Dayton, Ohio 45419

INSGROUP
Insgroup, Inc.
One City Boulevard West
Suite 935
Orange, Calif. 92668

IOWA
University of Iowa
Extension Division
Bureau of AV Instruction
Iowa City, Iowa 52240

IU
Indiana University
Audio-Visual Center
Bloomington, Indiana 47401

KODAK
Eastman Kodak Company
Audio-Visual Service
343 State St.
Rochester, N.Y. 14650

LFC
Library Filmstrip Center
3033 Alomo
Wichita, Kansas 67211

MAGER ASSOCIATES
Mager Associates
13245 Rhoda Drive
Los Altos Hills, Calif. 94022

McG-H
McGraw-Hill Book Company
Text Films Dept.
330 West 42nd St.
New York, N.Y. 10036

MSU
Instructional Media Center
Michigan State University
East Lansing, Mich. 48824

NAVA
National Audio-Visual Assoc.
1201 Spring Street
Fairfax, Virginia 22030

NEA
National Education Assoc.
Dept. of Audio-Visual Instruction
1201 16th St., N.W.
Washington, D.C. 20036

NMAC
National Medical Audiovisual
Center (Annex)
Station X
Atlanta, Ga. 30324

PENN STATE DEPT
Pennsylvania Dept. of
Public Instruction
Harrisburg, Penna. 17101

PHOTO LAB
Photo Laboratory, Inc.
3825 Georgia Ave., N.W.
Washington, D.C. 20011

ROUNDTABLE
Roundtable Productions
275 South Beverly Dr.
Beverly Hills, Calif. 90212

SYRU
Syracuse University
Educational Film Library
1455 East Colvin Street
Syracuse, N.Y. 13210

TNG SERV
Training Services
8885 West F St.
Kalamazoo, Mich. 49009

UCCEMS
University of California
Chemical Education Materials Study
Lawrence Hall of Sciences
Berkeley, Calif. 94720

UCLA
University of California
University Extension
Educational Film Sales Department
Los Angeles, Calif. 90024

USAV
U.S. National Audiovisual Center
National Archives and Record Service
Washington, D.C. 20409

VanNR
Van Nostrand Reinhold Co.
450 West 33rd St.
New York, N.Y. 10001

VIMCET
Vimcet Associates Inc.
P.O. Box 24714
Los Angeles, Calif. 90024

Index